ALL I WANT TO DO IS KILL

At the base of the stairs, Brenna observed the elderly white female lying on her back, spread eagle on the light green carpet. She was wearing blue Hawaiian shorts and a matching top, now discolored and stained with blood. Her feet were covered in white socks, the left sock and foot completely soaked in blood. The front of her shirt had been ripped open and the right interior sections of her chest cavity were clearly visible through the wide, bloody openings.

On the other side of her body, the damage was just as great, where a pair of deep and wide gashes stretched from her chest across her stomach. Her left arm had literally been sliced open to the bone.

The dead woman's gray hair was matted and saturated with red blood. Her glasses were still perched on the bridge of her nose, the frames twisted and bent and the lenses splattered and partially covered in red. Her eyes were fixed and there was an ugly grimace on her face. Her mouth was gaped open and her hands were frozen by her side.

Like the body upstairs, the female was also surrounded by a puddle of congealed blood. Ironically, there were half a dozen blue Wal-mart bags lying near her, all filled with merchandise, and with the large yellow smiley faces still turned upward.

ALL I WANT TO DO IS KILL

DALE HUDSON

PINNACLE BOOKS
Kensington Publishing Corp.
http://www.kensingtonbooks.com

PINNACLE BOOKS are published by

Kensington Publishing Corp.
850 Third Avenue
New York, NY 10022

All Kensington Titles, Imprints, and Distributed Lines are available at special quantity discounts for bulk purchases for sales promotions, premiums, fund-raising, and educational or institutional use. Special book excerpts or customized printings can also be created to fit specific needs. For details, write or phone the office of the Kensington special sales manager: Kensington Publishing Corp., 850 Third Avenue, New York, NY 10022, attn: Special Sales Department, Phone: 1-800-221-2647.

Pinnacle and the P logo Reg. U.S. Pat. & TM Off.

ISBN-13: 978-0-7860-1861-1
ISBN-10: 0-7860-1861-5

First Printing: November 2007

10 9 8 7 6 5 4 3 2 1

Printed in the United States of America

In memory of Edward W. Hudson, my father, my mentor, and my friend. Not a day has passed in the last four years without my talking to him.

Author's Notes

Information for this book was provided by those who personally observed what people said, thought, or did. Without the cooperation of the names contained in these pages, this book would not have been possible.

First of all, I am deeply indebted to the Fayette County Sheriff's Office (FCSO). Lieutenant Colonel Bruce Jordan, and especially Ethon Harper, provided large amounts of information, photos, and encouragement. As a general rule, most police departments are cooperative and helpful, but the officers at FCSO were very generous and eager to assist in every way.

A special word of thanks also goes to the department heads of the Fayette and Spalding County dispatchers, Peggy Glaze and Trudy McDivitt, respectively. Their assistance was invaluable.

Of course, as with all true crime stories, I could never have accomplished this without the help of those closest to the victims and the convicted teenagers. Each of these persons provided photos and tons of information: Tim and Beth Ketchum, Kevin Collier, Anita Beckom, Carol Morgan, and Carla Harvey.

I am also indebted to Sandy Ketchum for her prompt response to all my letters. She answered all my questions honestly and sincerely, and never once wavered in her account of the Colliers' murders. I believe she is truly remorseful and would do anything to take it all back.

In addition, I would also like to thank District Attorney Scott Ballard, Robyn Cobb, Judy Chidester, and Lloyd Walker for their warm receptions and contributions to the book.

My gratitude also goes to three special people, Jo Clayton, Dale Dobson, and George Dargus, who freely took of their time to read the earlier drafts and offer valuable suggestions. They helped shape and polish the rough drafts into a readable manuscript.

Also, my appreciation is extended to colleague Kevin F.

McMurray, whose book *If You Really Loved Me* is an excellent rendering of this case.

And to my newfound friends and family at New Directions Community services, I offer a thousand thanks. Because they are so dedicated to the business and were willing to cover for me while I finished this manuscript, this book was brought in on deadline. Your attaboys and pats on the back helped me make it through those many sleepless nights.

Finally my appreciation to Peter Miller, my agent, and Michaela Hamilton at Kensington Publishing Corporation for believing in this project. Their foresight and encouragement motivated me to write this book.

On a personal note, I am always grateful for three people in my life who have kept me afloat for the past twenty-plus years in business: my lawyer, Ralph Stroman, my banker, Richard Causey, and my accountant, Morgan Lewis. Without their continual guidance and expertise, my ship would have surely run aground.

To my mother, Katherine Hudson, I am forever grateful. I can honestly say she has never failed me as mother and her unending love has been a special gift from above. This year I am proud to announce the addition of Billy Byrd to our family. He has stepped in and filled some mighty big shoes, and for that, he has my fondest appreciation.

And to the persons who always make the greatest sacrifice of all, my wife, Deborah, and children, DJ and Deegan. For your patience and understanding, I owe you a lot of downtime and several supersized vacations. And I will deliver on that promise just as soon as I finish my next book. (Just kidding!)

Part I

DOUBLE HOMICIDE

Chapter 1

"Spalding County 911 Emergency."

The dispatcher at the Spalding County Sheriff's Office (SCSO) logged the call in at 6:14 P.M. on Monday, August 2, 2004. The caller identified herself as Jamie Donaldson, the mother of fifteen-year-old Sara Polk. There was pure fright in her voice.

"Yes, sir, there were two girls over at my house who just claimed to have killed their grandparents," Donaldson said, not quite steadily. She took a quick, deep breath, then blurted out, "They had blood all over them . . . knives and everything."

The dispatcher had difficulty hearing everything Donaldson was saying. A young girl, with a voice shrill and breaking, was wailing in the background. "Where did they say the girls—" the soft-spoken dispatcher asked before the girl's wailing drowned out his words.

"Huh?" Donaldson asked dryly.

The dispatcher raised his voice. "Where did they say they were at?"

"Where did the girls say they were at?"

"Yes," the dispatcher acknowledged colorlessly.

"Well, my daughter knows more about it, but she's got to stop screaming to be able to tell you."

The dispatcher correctly assumed the woman's daughter was the one wailing. "Then get her to calm down, okay?" he suggested politely.

"That's who they called," Donaldson clarified, referring to her daughter. "They had blood on them and stole their truck and everything."

"Where are they at now?"

"They're in a blue model-Chevrolet truck," Donaldson replied. "A pickup truck." She then put her distraught daughter on the phone.

Speaking through her tears, Sara Polk, the daughter, began, "This girl named Holly Harvey, who lives in Riverdale, she came over to my house with my friend Sandy . . . Sandy Ketchum."

She breathed in little gasps. Panic spurred her on.

"It's Holly Harvey and Sandy Ketchum. And they came to my house in a big blue pickup truck. King Cab. They had presents in the back and a big butcher knife in the car with blood all over it and they were covered in blood from head to toe. Everywhere. First she told me she got mugged and I asked her why and she didn't tell me. I gave her a towel to dry off and then she told me she wasn't [mugged], that she killed her grandparents."

"Okay, do you know—"

Sara cut the dispatcher off in midsentence. As if reading his mind, she replied anxiously, "I don't know where their house is, but it is in Riverdale."

"Where are they at? Where is Holly and Sandy at now?"

"They just left my driveway."

"Which direction would they be headed in?"

Sara sounded dazed. "I don't know which direction they would be headed in, but they just left my house." She gave the dispatcher her home address.

"Okay, and you're at that address right now?"

"Yes, sir," Sara acknowledged, repeating her street address.

"Okay, and your name."

"Sara Polk." Panic still spurred her on. "And Sandy lives at . . ." She paused, consulted with her mother, who gave her the correct address, then repeated it back to the dispatcher. "[It's on] Chandler Street in Griffin."

"Did you say her name was Sandy Ketchum?"

"Sandy Ketchum and Holly Harvey."

"Now, what's your name again?" The dispatcher was working to get both Sara and the situation under control. "Calm down and give me your name again."

"Sara Polk."

The dispatcher asked her to repeat her name a second time and she complied. "All right, Sara, and both of these are white females?"

"They are both young white females. One is fifteen . . . both are fifteen . . . ," Sara said, hardly daring to breathe.

"Okay," the dispatcher said in a calm voice.

"And Sandy is on probation and the other one is too. If you'll look them up on the record, you'll find them both, I know you will." She described both teenagers, then added, "Sandy has short brown hair, looks like a boy, and the other one is really girly."

"And you say Sandy lives in East Griffin at the address you provided earlier?"

"Yes, I can show you where she lives, but I don't know the name of it."

"It's okay, we've got the address. An officer is on his way there now."

Sara felt her heart swell with fear until she was sure it would burst. With an expression of gratitude, she assured the dispatcher she and her family would be on the lookout for the officer, then hung up the phone.

Dead and bloated bodies. Bloodstained butcher knives. Killer friends.

Those thoughts flittered in and out of Sara's mind in one

long, hard deafening sound. Her face, a twisted mask of emotion, was puffed and streaked with tears. She felt like her stomach was full of leaping frogs and her head was being worked on with a jackhammer.

Afraid her nerves might crack, Sara didn't like the way she was feeling.

Not at all!

Chapter 2

Police communications are essential, and to facilitate communication, codes have been devised in which one or two words tell the whole story. Inside the SCSO dispatch cubicle, the radio crackled with lots of codes. "We have a 10-25 (made contact) with a Sara Polk."

Silence.

Then the dispatcher provided Polk's address before completing his urgent message: "A 10-37 activity and a 10-43, already occurred in Riverdale. Sara Polk complained about her friends who had just left that location and complainant advises that they had already committed a 10-43 in Riverdale. These two white females by the name of Holly Harvey and Sandy Ketchum, they left that location in a blue Chevrolet King Cab. One of the suspects lives on the east side of Griffin; complainant not able to provide exact location."

The dispatcher's tone was neutral, but everyone knew what he meant. A deadly assault using a knife as a weapon had taken place.

Another officer broke in. He asked for dispatch confirmation of suspects and the vehicle. His eyes were locked on a Chevrolet King Cab truck making a "ueey" in the middle of the highway.

"Yes, two white females in a Chevrolet King Cab truck, one with short brown hair. They would be covered in blood and had a 10-32 knife in the truck with them."

"Do you know what direction they're traveling?"

The dispatcher said he couldn't advise.

A few minutes later, another of the patrol officers came back with, "Are you pretty sure the truck is blue?"

"Ten-four. It's a blue King Cab."

The patrol officer had spotted a blue-and-silver Chevrolet truck headed south on Highway 362. It was occupied by two white females. They were trying to turn around in the middle of the highway.

The radio crackled, followed by: "We are in pursuit of a blue-and-silver Chevrolet truck."

The dispatcher straightened up in his chair. Sirens could be heard in the background. He held his breath, waiting for the officer to respond. Every second seemed like an eternity. He was relieved when the officer came back on and the sirens could be heard blaring again. He and another officer were both in pursuit of the truck headed south on Highway 362.

"We have apprehended the truck in question," the officer finally announced after a few long seconds. "It has a silver stripe. But it's not blue on blue. The driver of the car is dark-headed, but there's a child in the car. It doesn't check out."

The dispatcher let his pent-up breath escape in a low, slow sigh. "Ten-four," he shot back.

A few minutes later, the radio crackled again. This time, Spalding County deputy D. W. Gibson acknowledged he was familiar with Sara Polk's address. The dispatcher informed him that Sara Polk would probably be upset when he arrived at her Griffin home. As expected, Gibson found Sara still in a grip of fear and anxiety.

"Both girls were covered in blood," Sara volunteered to the deputy. Tears blurred her eyes, and she agonized over her friends' troubles, the way a mother would agonize over her own daughter's troubles. "They had a butcher knife with blood on it, too."

Gibson talked softly and soothingly to Sara, quieting her bit by bit. "Okay, start from the beginning and tell me what happened."

Sara's pulse thudded steadily and deeply in her throat. "Sandy and Holly called me and said they needed to come see me. I said, 'Okay.' They came over and pulled in by the house."

Familiar thoughts of Sandy Ketchum suddenly passed through Gibson's memory. She was well-known to him and other deputies in the Spalding County Sheriff's Office. He took notes while Sara described what happened.

For a moment, Sara fixed on the shocking memory and her mind seemed to jump backward, replaying all the details all at once.

"At first they told me they got into a fight, but they had no wounds at all. I got them a wet towel; then they told me they had killed Holly's grandparents from Riverdale and left the bodies in the house. They were covered in blood, mostly their arms and pants. When they took off their shoes, their socks had blood on them. Even their underwear had blood on them."

On the verge of tears, Sara stopped talking and looked away. She was bent over and wheezing like an old man with an ache in his belly. She was trying so hard not to cry, trying so hard to be mature. Whatever that means for a fifteen-year-old girl.

"Are you okay?" Gibson asked sympathetically.

Sara shook her head slowly, as if she were trying to dismiss the memory, then nodded she was okay. Looking up at the wide-eyed deputy standing across from her, she told him the last thing she remembered was seeing the bloody knife in their truck.

"They had about a seven-inch butcher knife on the floor-board. It had blood all over it. That's when I told them to leave and not come back. I was talking to my boyfriend on the phone and hung up with him. I laid my phone on the dash in their truck they were driving. When they were pulling out, I ran down the driveway and got my phone. I then lit a cigarette and threw the lighter in the woods. I got my phone and walked back to the house."

"What can you tell me about the truck?" Gibson asked.

"The truck belongs to Holly Harvey's grandparents," Sara said in a low voice. "Their names are Sarah and Carl Collier, I think. The truck was dark blue. Two-door. An extended cab. It was clean and looked almost new."

"Did you see which way they went when they left?"

Vague thoughts of which direction they were headed passed through her mind, but something else about what had happened was beginning to nibble more strongly at her. She thought about what might happen to her friends, then let it pass. Through her tears, she said, "No, sir, I'm not sure which way they went when they left."

The jackhammer in Sara's head had returned. She sat at a table across from Deputy Gibson, thinking about her friends and wiping the tears from her eyes. She showed him a picture of Sandy Ketchum, and for a moment, she fixed on the memory of her friend. Then her thoughts again panned back to all that had happened during the previous hours.

Holly Harvey! she suddenly thought, searching for an answer why all this had happened. *It must have all been for Holly. Why else would Sandy have done this?*

Chapter 3

Deputy Gibson had been through this routine hundreds of times. Although he was confident Sara Polk was telling the truth, there was a possibility her two friends, for whatever reason, had made up the whole story. Gibson was aware that small pieces of information needed to connect someone to a crime often came to the police a little at a time, and sometimes that information revealed a person has fabricated the story. So it didn't surprise him when he relayed all the information garnered from Polk to the SCSO, only to learn from the dispatcher they could not locate anyone by the names of Carl and Sarah Collier residing in their jurisdiction.

Maybe this was some kind of sick practical joke? Just maybe they were trying to frighten this poor girl to death?

Over the years, Gibson had learned to expect the unexpected. There was only one way to find out for sure. He turned to Sara and asked if she had Sandy's cell phone number.

Sara was silent for a moment. Then a thought shot through her head like a meteorite, too bright and too quick to hold, but she caught the tail end of it. "I don't know her cell number, but I can punch star 69 on the phone and the number she called from will pop up."

"Would you mind calling Sandy and ask her for the names and addresses of the grandparents?"

Sara shrugged, her eyes sliding away. The deputy was asking her to call her friend and rat her out. That was a bitter pill to swallow.

"All I need is for you to tell her you want to make sure these are the deaths of the grandparents when they are reported on the TV news," Gibson added. He suspected Sara was reluctant to make the phone call.

With the approval of Sara's parents and Deputy Gibson, Sara walked to her bedroom, punched in *69, and waited for the number of her last incoming call to appear. The number to Sarah Collier's cell phone suddenly appeared on the small screen.

The call to Sandy Ketchum was not answered.

Sara stood nervously by the phone, suddenly aware that the room had grown deathly silent. A minute passed, then two, and by the third minute, her heart was whamming frightfully against her chest. She guessed this was going to be like some kind of surreal game of hide-and-seek, but felt she had to do something to help. Sara hit *69 again, but this time Sandy did answer.

"Sandy, there are reports all over the news about a double homicide," Sara said huskily, repeating exactly what Gibson had told her to say. Her mouth felt as if it had been stripped of its moisture; her words were dry and bare. "I just want to know if the people you said you killed were Holly's grandparents? Can you tell me what their names were?"

"Sarah and Carl Collier," Sandy answered in a flat and emotionless voice. "And they live on Plantation Drive in Riverdale up in Fayette County."

Tears blurred Sara's eyes. "Listen, Sandy, you better get out of town." When her friend didn't respond, she quickly asked in a whisper, "Which way are y'all headed?"

The phone suddenly went dead.

Somehow, Sara believed, Sandy must have caught on that

she was working with the police. Sara redialed the number several times, but Sandy never answered.

Still dazed, Sara walked into the living room. Staring wildly at Deputy Gibson, she surrendered the information Sandy had given her, saying she recognized it as the names and the address of Holly's grandparents.

"A couple of weeks ago, Holly ran away from her home in Riverdale to be with Sandy in Griffin. I was there, that particular day, visiting Sandy at her mother's home. We finally convinced Holly she should call her grandmother and have her pick her up at Wal-Mart in Griffin, before she got in any further trouble. We waited with Holly in the Wal-Mart parking lot until Sarah Collier had arrived."

Sara paused for a moment and lowered her head to regain her composure. She then looked up, put her hand over her mouth, and said in a small, tearful voice, "I still remember what her grandmother looked like."

Deputy Gibson scribbled the Colliers' names and address on a piece of paper. He walked out to his patrol car and immediately contacted SCSO headquarters. At first the Riverdale Police Department (RPD) and the Clayton County Police Department (CCPD) had been contacted in an attempt to locate the Colliers' address. After they learned the residence was in Fayette County, the Spalding County 911 dispatcher alerted Fayette County 911, which, in turn, relayed the same information on to the Fayette County Sheriff's Office (FCSO).

The FCSO received the call in official police jargon at approximately 7:32 P.M. In layman's terms, the message was loud and clear: "We need a welfare check on two of your elderly residents. There's a possibility they have been stabbed to death."

Chapter 4

The town of Griffin, Georgia, is just off the beaten path, thirty-two miles south of downtown Atlanta. Since its inception in 1840, this railroad boomtown had grown from a little dot on the state road map into a thriving metro Atlanta suburb of twenty-two thousand people. Located in Spalding County, Griffin is some twenty miles south of Fayetteville.

In 1823, the town of Fayetteville was incorporated and made the county seat of neighboring Fayette County. Both the town and the county were named in honor of the Marquis De Lafayette, a French nobleman who sailed across the Atlantic Ocean to fight with George Washington against England in the American Revolution. Built in 1825, Fayetteville's courthouse is the oldest in the state of Georgia.

Fayette County has a long and glorious history, especially during the Civil War and the famous Battle of Atlanta. The burning and looting of this Southern city by Union general William Tecumseh Sherman helped bring the war to an end, and the event was later dramatized in Margaret Mitchell's blockbuster novel and film, *Gone with the Wind*. Mitchell's great-grandfather was a landowner in Fayette County in the 1830s and he and his family probably were the models for Scarlett O'Hara's family that resided in the antebellum mansion Tara.

The county so rich in history is also one of the most affluent counties in Georgia. In 1925, the construction of the Hartsfield-Jackson Atlanta International Airport (HJAIA) helped spawn Fayette County's rapid development and growth and energize a vibrant economy. Even though the county is the smallest in the state, its close proximity to Atlanta, low taxation, and unbridled growth made it one of the most attractive communities for families when the airport expanded in the 1950s. By the 1980s, with its astonishing growth rate, Fayette was viewed by most of the state as a county with safe neighborhoods, superior schools, and a clean, conservative, and affluent atmosphere. *Progressive Farmer* magazine ranked Fayetteville eleventh on its list of best places to live in the Southeast, and *City Business Journal* had named it the eighteenth best county in the nation for corporate and family relocation.

Carl and Sarah Collier lived in Fayetteville, a town where the Delta airline employees had built custom homes in the early 1970s. For a couple of decades, life in Fayetteville moved at a slower pace. Everyone was happy to be away from the rat race in metropolitan Atlanta, and in those days, that was a special way of life.

The Colliers lived in a modest gray-and-white split-level brick home, in the northern section of Fayetteville, just off Highway 314 and a paved road in the community of Riverdale. The flower beds along the front of the Colliers' house were weedless and received daily attention, and between them and the road was a long and wide lawn, thick and well cut. Their driveway was cemented and led into a double carport, where Carl kept his blue Chevrolet King Cab Silverado and his S-10 pickup truck. It was a pleasant little home, only a stone's throw from their nearest neighbor. The Colliers enjoyed living there, where everyone knew them by name and treated them like family. Even though the south side of Fayetteville was rapidly developing into a thriving and emerging metropolis on its own, the Fayetteville population in 2004 was still a comfortable number at 13,912.

Both of these towns, Griffin and Fayetteville, have their share of colorful tales, personalities, unique places, and unforgettable events, but on the evening of August 2, they became the hotbed of a crime so brutal that people still have a hard time believing it really happened.

At 7:35 P.M., the Spalding County dispatcher relayed the message to the Fayette County Sheriff's Office emergency dispatcher about the possible double homicide at the home of Carl and Sarah Collier. They also needed assistance.

"Okay, what's the problem?" the FCSO dispatcher asked.

"Earlier today, the Colliers' granddaughter came to a friend's house in Spalding County and vowed she had killed her grandparents. When we did a little backtracking, we found out the Colliers' names and that they lived somewhere on Plantation Drive. But we don't know the exact address of their home."

"Did she give you a number for the location? That would then tell me which Plantation Drive in Fayetteville it would be."

"Yes," the SCSO dispatcher responded. He repeated the Colliers' home phone number as it had been given to him by Deputy Gibson. "We don't have contact with the granddaughter. Supposedly, she is still somewhere down in the county, riding around."

"How old is she?"

"She is fifteen years of age." In a sorrowful addendum, the SCSO dispatcher added, "Her name is Holly Harvey. And she advised her friends that she had killed her grandparents."

"Did she say how she had killed them?" the FCSO dispatcher asked gravely.

"Stabbed them." The voice on the other line came back curiously flat. "And she was also covered with blood."

The FCSO dispatcher lost her breath and words at the same time. "Covered with blood?" she clucked.

"Uh-hum."

"What's her friend's name?"

The SCSO dispatcher heard the stagger in his voice, but was unable to control it. "Her friend's name is Sara Polk and we've got a unit with her out at her residence."

The radio crackled. "Twenty-one–fifty-one, copy to 117," another dispatcher called in.

"Twenty-one–fifty-one, go ahead."

"Plantation Drive crosses Travis Street and Plantation Circle, then meets in Plantation Subdivision. We have it listed as the residence of Carl and Sarah Collier. Stand by for further."

At 7:37 P.M., the FCSO dispatcher contacted Deputy Dave Martin and requested he complete a welfare check at the Colliers' residence in the Riverdale community, at the north end of the county. Martin was told, "We're receiving information from Spalding County that they got a call from a female advising that the granddaughter of those two people may have 10-43'd her grandparents by stabbing. Female is also advising Spalding County that the girl was also covered in blood."

Martin had to think for a moment. *Riverdale Drive? Oh, yes. Riverdale Drive. Just off Highway 314. Nice neighborhood. Not far from here on the north end of town.* He switched on his emergency lights, then responded, "Ten-four." It took him approximately five minutes to drive the quarter-mile distance from his present location to Riverdale Drive. Watching for the home address on the mailboxes, he then spotted what looked like a split-level white-brick ranch house.

Martin turned off his squad car's lights as he pulled halfway into the driveway leading into a two-car carport. A light blue S-10 pickup truck, spotted with paint specks and loaded with paint buckets, was parked on the far side. He radioed his arrival to the dispatcher, then got out of his vehicle and walked to the carport area of the home. The neighborhood was quiet, filled with tidy houses bearing neatly trimmed and manicured front yards. It was getting dark. The light outside the home had already begun to fade appreciably, but through the carport and past the glass portion of the carport door, he could see the warm glow of light coming from inside the house.

Martin walked to his left, past the carport, and looked around the corner and to the back of the home. He quickly surveyed the backyard for anything leery, but found no lurking perpetrators or any suspicious signs of foul play.

Deputy Sheriff Mike James had been patrolling north of Georgia's I-85, when he received a call from dispatch that he was needed to back up Deputy Martin. Arriving only seconds after Martin, he saw Martin's patrol car parked in the driveway and Martin standing at the garage. James parked his vehicle on the street and met with Martin at the entrance of the garage.

The two deputies had been on dozens of calls like this. Nothing new to them. Usually, it was adult children concerned over their parents when they wouldn't pick up their phone, only to discover their parents had taken an unannounced trip. Or even less disturbing, the parents were found outside their home, enjoying themselves and grilling out with the next-door neighbors. Only occasionally did police find something even approaching a problem.

Since there was nothing suspicious outside the Colliers' home, Martin and James decided to try and rouse someone inside. The two well-trained officers cautiously stepped through the carport and approached the door located at the rear. A glass storm door protected the wooden door and the wooden door supported a glass window, covered only by partially opened blinds. The opened blinds allowed for clear visibility into a kitchen area.

As the deputies peered through the carport door window and into the kitchen, they spotted the body of an elderly white male lying facedown on the floor. The man was wearing blue jeans and a white undrershirt. His face was turned away from them, but his head and upper body were centered in a pool of blood. A white telephone receiver lay to the right of his bloodied body, only inches away from his right hand.

Deputy Martin took a step backward and away from the door. He involuntarily sucked in his breath, then breathed into his radio, "Twenty-one–five-one."

"Go head," the dispatcher shot back, immediately recognizing Martin's call number.

"I've got a subject laying here in cold blood." Martin cleared his throat, shedding the slight quaver in his voice.

There was a quick flurry of activity over the police radio. A few seconds later, Lieutenant Tom Brenna advised dispatch he was en route to assist Martin.

Martin shook the storm door. It was unlocked. He opened the storm door and tested the wooden door. It was also unlocked. At least he would not have to force entry, risking damage of potential evidence or contaminating the crime scene.

Pushing the door open and stepping into the kitchen, Martin focused his attention on the body lying on the kitchen floor. The man's head and upper body were completely surrounded by a pool of blood. The blood had already started to coagulate. It looked as if water, colored with red dye, had been mixed with Karo syrup and the two had already separated. The victim had lost so much blood, there was no reason to check his pulse. He was dead.

Martin was a seasoned officer, but nothing had prepared him for anything as macabre as this. Blood was strewn throughout the kitchen around the cabinets and on the floor. The victim had urinated on himself. "Let's go this way," he suggested, leading Deputy James to the left of the body.

Careful to avoid disturbing any evidence, the two deputies walked gingerly through the kitchen and around the body. They cautiously walked into the living room, looking around for any other victims and/or perpetrators.

A female dispatcher's voice suddenly blared out over Martin's radio. "Do you know if the person is breathing?"

"I'm in the house now, checking everything out," Martin responded in hushed tones. From the doorway in the living room, he could see another door, which led to a carpeted staircase. A dog was barking downstairs. "I can hear a dog yapping in the background."

"But do you know if the person is breathing?" the dispatcher repeated. She was eager to start emergency medical services and, if needed, as soon as possible.

Martin turned and looked closer at the victim. Still no movement of the man's body; he was not breathing. His blood had not only coagulated, but there were several spots of blood that had already dried on the floor around him. The left side of his face was a scarf of blood. Surely, he had been dead for some time.

Martin had to find his voice before he finally answered in a matter-of-fact tone, "I doubt it at this point." He stared at the white phone lying only inches away from the dead man's hand.

Had the victim attempted to make a call for help before he was killed?

How chilling it was that Martin was now making that phone call at almost the same identical spot. A shiver ran down his spine like a cold, boney finger.

Martin and James continued clearing the upper level, room by room, but found no one else on the top floor. As they made their way back to their start point in the living room, Martin observed a white male walking up the driveway. He watched as the male subject walked into the carport area and up to the kitchen door, and peered in through the kitchen window at the body lying on the floor. Martin sensed from the furrowed look on the visitor's brow that he was probably a concerned neighbor, and waved him back.

The visitor, who would later identify himself as Del Hargrove, was a friend of the Collier family. He and his wife, Lisa, had been in the neighborhood, checking out one of their houses, which was just across the street from the Colliers.

They saw the patrol cars in the driveway and became concerned. The couple knew the Colliers were having trouble with their granddaughter and wondered if that was what all the fuss was about.

"Somebody's in trouble up there," Del had said to his wife, with a befuddled tone in his voice. He thought there probably had been some argument between the Colliers and their granddaughter, but he was totally blown away when he stepped into the carport and peered into the kitchen door window, only to see Carl's bloody body lying on the floor and growing stiff in his own blood.

Jesus Christ. Del's face fell, a common symptom of an "Oh, shit" look.

After the deputy waved him back from the garage door, Del cautiously retreated to where Lisa stood and told her what he'd seen.

"You gotta phone Kevin," he said in a panic. "Quick!"

Lisa reached for her cell phone and called Kevin's cell phone number. She secretly wished she didn't have to call him, that this was all part of a bad dream. When he didn't answer, she left a message on his voice mail that said, "Kevin, there's been some kind of trouble at your parents' house." Her voice was strained. "Kevin, I need for you to come home as soon as you can!"

While Martin kept the Hargroves at bay, James continued his search, proceeding slowly down the basement stairs. At the top of the stairs, he felt his breath catch in his throat. About ten feet down the stairwell, he saw a form lying in the shadows. He stepped down another two steps, where the light from downstairs made it possible for him to see it was an elderly female. She was lying at the bottom of the stairs, faceup, with her knees partially pulled up and spread apart. Her face and chest were a bloody fright.

James called out to Martin, saying that he had located another victim in the basement. He turned and met Martin at the top of the basement stairs, then stepped onto the landing. This time it was Deputy James who had to find his voice. From the top of the stairs, he radioed into headquarters, "Twenty-two–forty-two, we got a second one down in the basement."

"You advise another one found in the basement?" the dispatcher responded.

"Ten-four," James affirmed.

Martin stepped around James. He walked halfway down the stairs until he spotted the body of an elderly white female. Even more horrible than the body upstairs, she was lying faceup in an even larger pool of coagulated blood. He winced. She had several large wounds to her chest and her arms. Her mouth was gaped open and she had a horrified look on her face, as if she had been attacked by some rabid animal.

The room where the victim lay was a small room with clothes hung and merchandise packed on some shelves. It appeared to be a storage room of some sort. This room led into a living room strewn with magazines, bags, and several other shopping items. There were trails, spatters, smears, and droplets of blood strewn throughout this room. Several of the shopping items had droplets of blood on them that looked to have been cast off from the items used to cut the victims or from the victims' movements throughout this room. It was a god-awful mess.

Deputy James rejoined Martin halfway down the stairs. Every step they took presented them with a full-frontal view of the woman's wounds. Every step they took brought them closer to the woman's body, even more repelling and repulsive than the one upstairs. The victim had defecated on herself and every step they took toward her redefined their definition of the word "horror."

Finally able to unlock his eyes from the bloodied corpse, Martin suggested, "Maybe we need to pull back and wait outside for EMS."

Martin and his partner were both feeling a little queasy, but they still had enough wits about them to know they needed to preserve the crime scene. Leaving the home in reverse order and touching nothing, they exited through the carport door.

Once outside, Martin caught his breath, before notifying FCSO headquarters and contacting his supervisors. "Are we still in contact with the county and the suspect's friend?" he curiously asked the dispatcher.

"No, they are out at the girlfriend's residence," the dispatcher replied. "We no longer have them on land line."

"Well, contact them and tell them if they've got that friend, then they need to hold on to her."

"Ten-four. We'll try to reach Spalding County and get a location."

When the FCSO dispatcher called the SCSO dispatcher for information, she was informed they still had not made contact with Holly Harvey, only her friend Sara Polk. "If, by any chance, y'all do have contact with Holly Harvey, then keep her where she is at," she advised. "Because it's real."

"You mean to say they've found the grandparents?"

"Yes, I don't know if they're actually dead or not, but we have found two people down with multiple stab wounds."

"Thanks for the information," the SCSO dispatcher acknowledged. "We'll go ahead and confirm them."

Chapter 5

Law enforcement agents have an advantage in their official status. They compel a certain level of cooperation and are able to establish instant rapport with total strangers. People give them information—and give it to them quickly—and information is the agent's stock-in-trade.

Outside the Colliers' home, Del and Lisa Hargrove stood at the driveway and waited patiently until the deputies emerged. The look on the deputies' faces spoke volumes to the Hargroves.

"So, the persons who *lived* here were Carl and Sarah Collier?" Deputy Martin asked.

"Yes, Carl and Sarah Collier," Del repeated.

The Hargroves were speaking with lawmen and fully aware that all lawmen feel the need to be evasive at times. They already knew Carl was dead, but they wanted to know had Sarah been found dead also. Still dazed and mildly confused, they were too afraid to ask straight out, "Is Sarah dead?" So, they tactfully mentioned to the detectives that if they had found an elderly woman dead in the house, too, then it was probably Carl's wife, Sarah.

"Thank you," Martin said politely.

The Hargroves exchanged glances, confirming what they already suspected.

"Their fifteen-year-old granddaughter also lives with them," Lisa volunteered. "Her name is Holly Harvey, and in all likelihood, if she is not in the house, then she is the person you will probably need to look for."

A minute before 7:44 P.M., FCSO deputies Clark Vickery and Thomas Mindar arrived at the Colliers' home. They pulled their squad cars up in front of the house, parked on the grass, then hustled over to the carport. Deputies Martin and James were standing inside, talking with the Hargroves.

"It's probably not a good idea to enter the house," Martin said as the two men came around the corner and into the carport. He thumbed toward the carport/kitchen door, inviting them to look at the elderly male lying on the kitchen floor. "We also found an elderly female, dead, in the basement. Since both victims are deceased, I think we should try and protect the crime scene."

The deputies agreed.

Deputy Mindar suggested he go back out front and tape off the yard. Just as he approached his car and attempted to locate some crime scene tape, FCSO lieutenant Tom Brenna pulled in the driveway. "Do you have any tape in your car?" he asked.

"Sure," Brenna said, tossing him a roll from the front seat.

Mindar started taping off the Colliers' front yard, beginning at the telephone pole on the left of the driveway to a tree on the right side of the house. When another deputy pulled up, he asked him to finish the job and rope off what he had missed.

Deputies Martin and James met Lieutenant Brenna at the end of the carport and advised him they had two deceased persons inside the house.

"Any signs of life in either subject?" Brenna asked.

"None," Martin advised, believing the Colliers had been dead for some time. "But you're welcome to look for yourself."

Martin led Brenna through the carport door and into the kitchen area, where he saw the male's body lying facedown in a large pool of blood. He noticed immediately the man was not breathing and had lost an incredible amount of blood.

For Martin, it was his second look at the crime scene. During his first look, he had given it only a cursory glance. Now, during this more thorough survey, it was more horrifying than he remembered. There was blood spread all around the center-island cabinet in the kitchen from the sink area all the way to the back door, splattered over a twelve-pack of Coca-Cola and pooled around gallon bottles of purified water.

The dead man was lying facedown on the tiled white floor, embossed in green-and-gold squares. He had fallen between the island and the kitchen cabinets, the top of his head resting but a few inches away from a large bag of Mighty Dog on the opposite wall. A detached white phone and cord rested to the left of his body and the dog food.

The man was barefoot—the bottoms of his feet were caked in blood—and his body was clothed in blue jeans and a white undershirt. Both the front and the shoulders of his undershirt were saturated with blood. What looked like crusted blood covered his face and nose, and dark and puffy bruises appeared on his neck just below his chin. His body was as stiff as egg white.

Martin then led Brenna toward the back of the residence, through the living room, and to a stairwell that led to the basement. At the base of the stairs, Brenna observed the elderly white female lying on her back, spread-eagle on the light green carpet. She was wearing blue Hawaiian shorts and a matching top, now discolored and stained with blood. Her feet were covered in white socks, the left sock and foot completely soaked in blood. The front of her shirt had been ripped open and the right interior sections of her chest cavity were clearly visible through the wide, bloody openings.

On the other side of her body, the damage was just as great, where a pair of deep and wide gashes stretched from her chest across her stomach. Her left arm had literally been sliced open to the bone.

The dead woman's gray hair was matted and saturated with blood. Her glasses were still perched on the bridge of her nose, the frames twisted and bent, and the lenses splattered and partially covered in red. Her eyes were fixed and there was an ugly grimace on her face. Her mouth was gaped open and her hands were frozen by her side.

Like the body upstairs, the female was also surrounded by a puddle of congealed blood. Ironically, there were a half-dozen blue Wal-Mart bags lying near her, all filled with merchandise, and with the large smiley faces still turned upward.

Even with sidelong glances, the two police officers had to swallow hard when they looked at the dead woman. Staring at the large amounts of blood spread around her and throughout the basement, it looked as if someone had bathed in blood, then got out of the tub and staggered down the hall like a wino after his last drink. Blood was everywhere, on the walls and on the carpet, and appeared to have started in a bedroom on the far end of the house and went all the way to the opposite end, where the elderly female was located.

Standing at the bottom of the stairs, looking over the still-wet, dark puddles of blood encircling the body, these men had no question as to what they had seen. These were the pitiful bodies of a husband and wife who had suffered a horrifying and unimaginable death. This had to be the handiwork of someone with a diabolical and twisted mind.

Of course, the FCSO deputies were intensely curious as to what had happened. As expected, they had a deep, abiding desire to know and understand everything about this crime. They continued looking around downstairs. In the back bedroom, where it appeared the attack on the female had started, they observed a sandwich sitting on a dresser. The sandwich had been cut in half, and one bite taken out of it.

Obviously, someone hadn't taken the time to finish their sandwich.

After Brenna and Martin had surveyed the crime scene, they left the Colliers' residence through the staircase and exited the same carport/kitchen door they had entered, touching nothing. Just as the two men walked outside, FCSO headquarters notified Brenna that via the computer-aided dispatch (CAD) system, fifteen-year-old Holly Harvey was also listed as a resident at Plantation Drive. Even though the SCSO assumed she and her friend were driving around somewhere in their neighborhood, there was still the possibility they could have sneaked back into the home and were hiding somewhere inside.

Brenna shuddered at the thought of scenes he remembered from the movie *Psycho*. He imagined something reminiscent of Norman Bates: two teenagers hiding behind a shower curtain in the downstairs bathroom and yielding a bloody butcher knife. He thought about the butchered bodies in relation to his present responsibility, then asked Deputy Martin, "What areas of the house have you cleared?"

"Just the upstairs," Martin said sheepishly. "We didn't want to disturb the crime scene, so we only completed a limited search of the house."

It occurred to Brenna there were still large parts of the house that had not been searched, including the entire basement. After conferring with the four deputies, he decided the crime scene protocol called for them to reenter the house and search for other residents or suspects. The ground level—the upstairs of the house—was empty, but they needed to go downstairs and search the basement. He suggested the three deputies clear the basement, while he and Deputy James secured the outside.

After Brenna and James walked around the carport and to the backyard, they observed a sliding glass door that led into the Colliers' basement. From this location, they could see Sarah's body at the bottom of the stairs. They could also prevent any unauthorized person from going in or coming out of the basement.

When Deputies Martin, Mindar, and Vickery were given the signal to proceed downstairs, they entered through the carport/kitchen door, walked around to the left of the dead body, then followed the carpeted stairs to the basement area. Halfway down the stairs, they heard what sounded like a small dog barking and running around inside the basement. They opened a door to a utility area and found a tan-and-white collie. So as to keep the animal from corrupting the crime scene, Mindar opened the sliding glass door and let him out into the backyard.

The deputies continued checking the basement carefully. They walked toward the stairs and, once again, gazed at the body of Sarah Collier, lying near the stairs on her back. As with most people who die unexpectedly, the cops are the first faces their staring open eyes can't see. Her body was covered in blood, as if someone had poured a bucket of red paint on her. They cautiously stepped around the body and followed a blood trail, which led from her body, down the hall, and into the back bedroom. Large smears of blood—some deeper and wider than others—were found on the painted white Sheetrock walls in the halls and on the walls in the bedroom. Someone had been stabbed and had fallen against the walls. They finished clearing the basement, checking all the bathrooms and closets, then exited along the same path they had come in.

Police officers are good at solving puzzles. That's the nature of their work—trying to figure out just what in the hell happened in a particular situation. By closely examining a crime scene, the smarter ones can often obtain a fairly accurate idea of what took place. They can take bits of information that appear unconnected and somehow fit them together into a progression of the crime as easily as a preschooler draws a picture by connecting the dots.

The FCSO deputies believed the trouble at Plantation Drive

most likely started in a bedroom on the far end of the house in the downstairs basement. It appeared both Carl and Sarah Collier were stabbed in that room and fought with their assailants down the hall and all the way to opposite ends of the stairs. While Sarah lay at the foot of the stairs, the melee must have continued up the stairs and into the kitchen, where Carl received a fatal wound and collapsed on the kitchen floor.

Although the deputies found a large amount of blood spread throughout the home in their initial examination of the crime scene, they did not locate anyone else in the home, dead or alive. If Holly Harvey and Sandy Ketchum had committed this crime, then they had enough street sense not to return to the scene. The deputies secured the scene and waited for the Criminal Investigation Division (CID) to arrive. They remained on the scene, keeping the front yard clear of neighbors and rubberneckers, and waited until they were instructed to go back into service.

Police work is inherently stressful. Law enforcement officers can't help but feel affected when they get involved with people who are in trouble, when lives are falling apart. They may act as if they aren't affected, but it is only a mask to help them remain calm in a sea of crisis. One major source of stress in police work is ambiguity. Real-life situations don't always make good sense and police are often involved in situations they don't fully understand, and over which they have absolutely no control.

Chris Nations, with the FCSO, contacted the department's headquarters. "How old did you say the granddaughter is?" he asked, intensely curious.

"Fifteen," the female dispatcher replied.

If that was true, Chris thought, then they may never really know what took place. "She's fifteen?" he asked incredulously. "God almighty."

"Yes, I know," she said softly, pushing that ugly fact away long enough to do the job.

"Do you have any description on her?" Chris asked, pretending he, too, was impervious to the ugliness.

"We're getting reports now from her friend, Sara Polk, that she changed clothes, so I am trying to get a description on her now. Let me give you the number for the deputy on the scene and he can give you all the information. His name is Deputy Gibson."

"Does the fifteen-year-old suspect also live at the Griffin location?"

"Negative."

"Do we have further contact with her?"

"Negative. Spalding County never made contact with the suspect. But we're trying to get a description from them."

"So we have no further contact with the female suspect?"

"No, Spalding County never made contact with the Harvey subject. But we still have contact with the friend, I believe."

"Okay."

"Are the grandparents coming in DOA?"

"Yes, this is one horrific crime."

The dispatcher's tone was sympathetic. "Oh, my. Oh, my," she kept saying over and over.

The dispatchers weren't the only ones who were at a loss for words. Police work is emotionally tough. It's always difficult for those who earn their livings off the suffering of other people to face that level of pain and suffering on a daily basis. They all have their ways of coping, but the ugliness never goes away. It is even more frustrating when police are involved in situations they don't fully understand and don't have answers to questions people are already asking.

Who committed this murder? Who wanted the Colliers dead? What kind of people commit such an unlawful act? What do you call it?

The questions were meant to be rhetorical, but the answer was obvious to the police.

Some kind of whack-'em-up, homicidal Lizzie Borden maniacs.

Chapter 6

At 7:47 P.M., Fayette County Crime Scene Unit (FCCSU) investigator Ethon Harper arrived at the crime scene. At six feet four inches and 265 pounds, the twenty-nine-year-old blond-haired Harper had been a detective for a little more than a year. He had started working in the jail at the sheriff's office when he was nineteen, decided to go to the police academy, and graduated there in 1996. Harper had been a corporal in charge of a patrol shift and a member of the SWAT team before moving over to join the CID and about thirty other well-trained investigators in April 2003. That night he had been working the evening shift at the FCSO and was on call the rest of the night.

While the deputies finished checking the basements for suspects and other victims, Harper exited his vehicle and braced himself for a tour of the crime scene. It wasn't that he was bracing himself for what he knew he would find inside the Colliers' home. Make no mistake about it, he felt no revulsion at the sight of bright red blood and bloodied bodies that looked like displays from a Halloween wax museum. Age marks everyone differently, and Harper, at twenty-nine, was much too young to have seen it all, but in situations like these, he had only boundless sympathy for the victims and their families.

However, crime scenes are very fragile and fraught with danger. A crime scene begins to deteriorate the moment a person enters it. The more people who enter it, the more damage is done, and the greater the potential for an irrevocable error. And if an investigator makes a mistake at the crime scene, that mistake could come back to haunt him in a criminal trial. The more mistakes an investigator makes, the more likely a defendant could walk.

Needless to say, crime scene investigators have huge responsibilities.

The deputies directed Harper to the carport door, where he could clearly see Carl Collier's body lying facedown on the kitchen floor. There was blood on the floor and all around the unresponsive male, including the walls and kitchen cabinets. Harper then walked outside the carport and was escorted around the back of the home and into the backyard.

Harper remembered the yard out front was clean and attractive, but the backyard appeared neglected and thrown into disarray. What was once a nice-sized Olympic swimming pool had faltered under the collapse and strain of a black liner filled with several seasons of rain, leaves, and debris. The diving board was missing from its frame, pool chairs were strewn about on the lawn and in trees, and a lawn couch was overturned and rusting. The outdoor barbeque grill was faded and in poor condition.

At one time, the Colliers' backyard may have been the hub of family and recreational activity, but not any longer. Harper did observe a well-maintained Mallard model camper trailer parked at the back of the lot. He innocently assumed the Colliers were spending more time on the road these days than they were in their backyard.

Standing at the sliding glass door opening and looking into the basement, Harper could see the white female lying on her back at the bottom of the stairs with blood all around her. He also observed what appeared to be blood on the white walls in the interior of the basement.

The FCSO deputies informed Harper they had exited the residence through the sliding glass door and verified that the male and female inside were already deceased when they arrived. Mindar confirmed the sliding glass door was locked from the inside when they initially entered the basement and he had to unlock the door to open it.

Harper made certain the crime scene had been secured, and, with all that said and done, there wasn't much left for him to talk about. It was time for the forensic CSU to go to work. He contacted the other on-call investigator, Gwen Imberg, and their on-call investigative supervisor, Sergeant Tracey Carroll. Both on-call people made notifications up the ladder. Imberg contacted Lieutenant Tray Powell and Carroll contacted Lieutenant Colonel Bruce Jordan.

At approximately 7:55 P.M., Chris Nations phoned Deputy Gibson, who brought him up to speed on the unfolding case.

"I know y'all just got word of all this," Gibson conceded. "But what happened is that we have 2 fifteen-year-old juveniles that supposedly went to a friend's house. And we are told now that you-all have two subjects down in your county. That is a 10-43 probably?"

"Yes, the EMS is still waiting on the sergeant to give them some kind of confirmation."

"Well, according to the information I'm getting here, they're going to be DOA." Gibson seemed chafed at the thought.

"Yes, according to the DSO, they're pretty much DRT," Chris confirmed. "But we haven't officially called it yet."

"If y'all can get a tag number, they are in the grandfather's truck. Now, when they committed this said act, I got IDs on them. I got the whole story. They came to this girl's house, where I am at now. I still have her and I already have her writing a statement for y'all now. I've got her detained right now."

Chris's heartbeat ratcheted up a notch. He grasped at the receiver, hanging onto every word of what he had just been told.

"My point is are you going to want to come to our sheriff's office and wait for y'all or what?" Gibson asked in his deep Southern drawl. "Basically, this girl, Sara Polk, pretty much knows the whole story. They had called back here to this residence since I've been here. She got a little nervous and disconnected the call. They are somewhere still in this area. Now, as to who they are and what they got on . . ." He stopped in midsentence, then offered unconvincingly, "They're trying to burn the clothes and the knife now."

Chris snickered. "They're trying to burn the knife, that's pretty funny."

"Yes, they're just teenagaers," Gibson forced himself to say. "One of them is a problem child in our county anyway."

"Yeah, I know one girl, every time her mother brings her up here, she runs away. The Ketchum girl, we're familiar with her, too."

"Okay, whenever you find out what you want. If you'd rather me go to the SO, so Sara Polk's parents can help her get ready for this, then I will. She's sixteen, but she's been told the whole story and she witnessed them being covered in blood. She even witnessed the knife they used."

Chris Nations refocused their conversation on the Griffin address he had heard about, and told Gibson the girls hung out with somebody at that address.

"Yes, that's the girl," Gibson exclaimed. "That's the home address of the girl with Holly Harvey. I've already secured that and there's no one at home."

Chris paused, then advised, "I'm going to give Lieutenant Brenna or one of our CID guys your cell phone number. Is that kosher with you?"

Gibson agreed he would speak directly with those in charge.

A few minutes later, the SCSO dispatcher phoned the Fayette-ville office and asked if the Colliers were dead or injured.

"Possibly dead," the FCSO dispatcher informed.

"Well, my sergeant wanted to know if they wanted to talk with the witness," the frustrated voice on the other line responded.

"Well, we already have someone talking to your deputy Gibson on the other line now."

The SCSO dispatcher was apologetic. Her supervisor had told her Gibson was apparently not moving fast enough, and had asked her to get the information.

It was 7:58 P.M., and the pot of details from Sara Polk's testi-mony was still brewing. In a conversation with Detective Ethon Harper, Deputy Gibson said Polk described the teenagers' get-away vehicle as a 1990s blue Chevrolet truck and was very spe-cific about the girls being covered in blood and admitting to stabbing Holly's grandparents.

"Sara described the large knife the two girls showed her and it had blood on it," Gibson recalled. "She said she thought it was a prank at first, but then, when the girls began telling her more details about what had happened, she took it for the truth."

Harper was fishing for information. He tossed out, "Did Sara say why they would have wanted to kill Holly's grand-parents?"

"Only something about Holly not liking the rules at her grandparents' house. The girls apparently got scared when Sara's mother pulled up to the house, and then they took off. She also said the two girls stopped at the end of her drive-way and changed clothes. And that they planned to burn their clothes and destroy the knife."

Harper was aware Sara Polk had made cell phone contact with the two runaway teenagers. For Polk's own safety, he asked Gibson to transport her to the SCSO and hold her there until someone from FCSO arrived.

Harper then phoned FCSO detective Bo Turner on his cell

phone. Turner shared the duties of juvenile investigations with Detective Phil McElwaney.

"Hey, Bo, sorry to bother you, but I'm investigating a double homicide," Harper casually asked. "Does the address [Colliers' address on] Plantation Drive ring a bell for you?"

"It sounds familiar," Turner responded. "But I can't place it."

"Well, what we have here is the bodies of an elderly couple, who supposedly have been stabbed by two teenagers. One of them is their granddaughter and the other is the granddaughter's friend. It is a pretty brutal murder, probably the worst I've seen yet."

"And the teenagers?"

"Fled the scene," Harper informed. "At this point, we believe she might still be somewhere in Fayette County. Apparently, after they committed the murders, they drove over to one of their friend's house in Griffin. The girl there in Griffin said they were covered in blood from head to toe and that they had admitted to killing their grandparents. She refused to let them take a bath, then called 911 after they left and reported the crime."

Turner had already put in his eight hours at work. He was off-duty, with his wife and kids, looking at a house they were considering buying. However, he didn't hesitate. "I'll be right over," he said immediately.

Minutes later, as Turner approached the Riverdale Plantation subdivision from Route 314 and climbed the hill onto Plantation Drive, a name suddenly registered in his memory bank.

Holly Harvey.

Turner first recalled the name and then the details:

Two or three weeks ago, this cute little girl, about fifteen years of age, ran away with her girlfriend, Sandy Ketchum. She was the one with shiny dark hair, freshly cut. Found them at Sandy's mother's home in Griffin. Grandparents were very upset.

Turner advised Harper he would locate the Griffin address

and have the SCSO check it out. He then phoned the dispatcher in Spalding County and provided a physical description of the murder suspects.

"Her last name is Harvey," Turner confirmed. "Her first name is Holly. Middle is Ann. White female. She is five-four, one hundred ten pounds. Brown shoulder-length hair, blue eyes. And I believe the friend she is talking about is . . . If this is the same friend I am thinking of, it is a Sandy Ketchum. She is a sixteen-year-old white female."

The SCSO dispatcher was familiar with Sandy Ketchum.

"Yes, they run away together all the time, actually. Miss Ketchum's mom has called me once before, like freaking out."

"Miss Ketchum lives on Chandler Street in Griffin," Turner informed her. "That might be a good spot to check also."

The dispatcher assured Turner she would pass on the information. She didn't know Deputy Gibson had already called for a security check at Sandra Ketchum's home.

Between the police finding the Colliers' bodies and the revelation they had been murdered by their granddaughter, the horror was growing. When the Fayette County EMS vehicles arrived at the Colliers' home, Lieutenant Brenna met them at the top of the driveway.

"You guys might as well turn around and go back," he said frantically, the images of the butchered bodies still fresh in his mind. "There's nothing you can do for those folks inside."

The ambulance took its time turning around in the driveway. The EMS paramedics went away empty-handed, thus they were in no hurry to leave.

Chapter 7

Crime scene evidence is the critical point on which trials are weighed in the balance. The more evidence pointing toward a defendant's guilt, the more likely there is to be a conviction. The FCSO crime scene unit was present for many reasons. They were a well-trained and equipped unit that used the cutting-edge technology and sound investigative practices to inspect every crime scene. Not only would their evidence help lead to the arrest of the persons responsible for this crime, but it would help police understand what had actually happened at the crime scene and why the crime had occurred in the first place. If crime scenes are truly the residue of criminal behavior, then it is that behavior that reflects the criminal's state of mind at the time the crime was committed.

At approximately 8:30 P.M., a special squad of highly experienced investigators and police detectives entered the Plantation Drive residence. The forensic squad consisted of Lieutenant Colonel Bruce Jordan, Lieutenant Tray Powell, Sergeant Tracey Carroll, Investigator Gwen Graham, and Investigator Ethon Harper.

The director of FCSO investigations, Lieutenant Colonel Jordan, was officially in command of this investigation. Forty-year-old Jordan began his career with the sheriff's department when he was just nineteen. He was a nighttime operator and then, six months later, signed on as a patrol officer. It took him three years to earn his stripes as a patrolman before being promoted to sergeant. For five years, he worked as detective sergeant until 1998, when he was promoted to division commander of detectives. In 2004, Jordan had forty detectives under his tutorage. In addition to the supervision, he was responsible for all criminal investigations, the K-9 corps, and the tactical division of FCSO's 250-man department.

Those who had served with or under Bruce Jordan appreciated the fact that his job always came first in his life. They respected Jordan not because of what he told them, but what he showed them. He had boundless energy, as if he lived in and breathed from a well of adrenaline. A curious certainty grew inside Jordan, and although his cockiness was often misunderstood, he had a keen insight for investigation and was amazingly accurate in his predictions. He was firm and relentless in his investigative techniques, personally working every homicide and never giving up on any of them until there was a conviction. When it came to solving homicides, Bruce Jordan walked the walk and talked the talk.

Wearing gloves and protective booties so as not to contaminate the crime scene, the five-member forensic team stepped inside the Colliers' home for the first time. Their first look was at Carl Collier, lying facedown on the kitchen floor, surrounded by a large amount of blood. There were also a voluminous amount of blood splatter on the cabinets, countertops, appliances, and island area of the kitchen, which led them to believe a violent struggle had taken place in the kitchen area. A white AT&T trim-line phone was on the floor beside him. The cord had been torn out of the wall connection. Across from the body was a desk area covered with miscellaneous checkbooks, credit cards, bill statements, car insurance, passports, and papers.

Ethon Harper's eyes traveled across the kitchen floor and his nostrils flared a little. Once the smell hit him, it was too clear to dismiss. The smell of death. The scent was unmistakable, like the stink of rotting meat left out during long days of a Georgia summer, with its unbearable heat and humidity. He looked down at Carl Collier's body and a soft sigh, too quiet to be a groan, escaped from his lips. His stomach took a queasy little lurch, more in sympathy than anything else.

After passing through the kitchen, the forensic team checked each room on the first floor. All appeared undisturbed. There did not appear to be any signs of forced entry into the residence.

Upon entering the living area just off the kitchen, Lieutenant Colonel Jordan observed a bloody footprint on the carpet. The small footprint appeared to be pointed in the same direction, as if the person had exited the kitchen near Carl Collier's head and walked toward the basement on the light green carpeted stairways. Investigator Graham photographed the stairway and the small amounts of blood on the handrail.

As the team of investigators moved to the basement stairway, they could see the body of Sarah Collier at the foot of the stairs. She was lying on her back, surrounded by a large amount of blood, and immobile as a sculpture. Seeing her in this position would have pained and saddened those who knew her.

Spines stiffened as the foursome descended the staircase and stood at the lifeless body of Sarah Collier. Someone in the rear murmured, "Good God almighty!" They could see she had been stabbed repeatedly, as her shirt had been sliced open and the upper right side near her heart literally hung open. Her left arm had suffered an open wound and the flesh was literally carved from the bone. It was as yellow and runny as the yolk from an egg.

Another soft sigh escaped from Harper's lips. He noticed great red flecks of dried blood on the walls in the hall. *My God, what in the name of Christ happened here?*

At the bottom of the stairs, the investigators entered into an open living/storage area, with outside access through the sliding glass door. On the wall next to the sliding glass door, they observed an area of blood, and it appeared as though a struggle had taken place near the sliding glass door. But as they checked the door, they found it to be locked. Deputy Mindar later confirmed the sliding glass door was locked from the inside when they arrived, and that was the same door he had to unlock to put the Collier's dog outside.

The forensic team also observed a wall phone next to the sliding glass door that had its phone cord cut. They also observed blood on items that were being stored along the wall, as well as on the floor in this open basement area. The blood on the floor seemed to lead from the back bedroom in the basement, up the hallway, to the sliding glass door, on to Sarah Collier's body.

At the entrance to the hallway, investigators followed the walls splashed and matted with blood. Horror crept softly into their brains and into their veins as they began the short walk down the hall, knowing more death images were waiting for them in the back bedroom. They turned and looked inside the rose-colored carpeted bedroom with matching curtains fixed in the windows.

The room obviously belonged to the granddaughter, Holly Harvey. Decorative pieces of expensive wicker furniture—a dresser, a mirror, two nightstands, and a headboard—accented the room, while a white overhead ceiling fan and light completed the ensemble. The room, however, was a pigsty. Empty Coke cans and Deer Park water bottles littered the dresser and were stacked on top of an already overflowing wastebasket. Clothes, pictures of Holly and her friends, beach scenes, and several large stuffed animals were strewn about in the room. Food and drinks were piled high on top of a stereo system and spilled over onto the floor. A half-eaten sandwich still rested on top of the dresser. The bedspread and covers to Holly Harvey's bed were bunched together and pushed to the front of the bed. Dried areas of blood were not only found on the carpet and bedsheets, but were splattered against the wall and the door.

Lieutenant Colonel Jordan's eyes looked toward the bloodied sight and a harsh grunt escaped him. This was not just some rowdy horseplay that suddenly got out of hand. He stepped inside the bedroom and the pungent smell of marijuana blasted against his nostrils, causing him to wince as if he'd been slapped in the face.

"Jesus," Jordan said quietly. He was looking as if all the muscles in his body had suddenly tightened like piano wire.

On the floor and near the bed, Jordan spotted a broken, bloodstained pair of eyeglasses, which no doubt belonged to Carl Collier. The remains of what looked like a seashell lamp were spread out across the bed. It appeared someone had disassembled the lamp and let the seashells tumble out across the bed.

Upon further inspection of the bed, there were several mysterious knife cuts in the bedsheet and mattress, but no bloodstains were found around them.

Perhaps someone had taken a swing with the knife and missed their intended target, the detectives tossed around.

But upon further observation, an oil painting of a litter of puppies was found hanging on the wall with similar cuts through it and without any damage to the wall behind the picture. It appeared to the investigators that the picture was placed on the bed and stabbed—for whatever reason—causing the cuts to the picture and the sheet, and then placed back on the wall.

But why? Who knew?

The forensic team checked the remaining areas of the basement, but there were no signs of a struggle. Only the bedroom, hall, and living areas appeared to be disturbed. Since there were no signs of forced entry into the residence through the basement, they agreed the assailants were already inside the home.

In all his years of police work, Jordan had never seen anything this horrific, and he had seen plenty. He could only shake his head. It was incomprehensible to him that such a vicious attack could be launched on an elderly pair—especially by a family member, which, from what he'd been told by the early arriving deputies, was likely the case. His locked vocal cords finally opened, and at approximately 9:00 P.M., he asked Detective Harper to notify the coroner.

It appeared to Harper that Lieutenant Colonel Jordan was seemingly unaffected by all this horror. Jordan was one of the best, and it never ceased to amaze Harper how quickly he could take command of a seemingly chaotic situation and exert control and order over it. Jordan's mind was working in dozens of directions and he began instructing his deputies accordingly. His manner was firm and direct, and in an instant, the investigation took on the ambiance of a military operation. Bo Turner and Phil McElwaney were instructed to drive down to the SCSO in Griffin and talk with Sara Polk. Crime scene investigators Manny Rojas and Josh Shelton had joined Investigator Graham and were documenting the crime scene and powdering for latent fingerprints. Jordan had also alerted the U.S. Marshals' Southeast Regional Fugitive Task Force (SERFTF). Formed in 1983, the SERFTF's sole purpose was to track down and arrest people for whom felony warrants had been issued. The Fayette County Sheriff's Office had an attached member to their regional task force and this special deputy was empowered by the authority of the U.S. Marshals to travel anywhere in the United States to track down and apprehend wanted fugitives from Fayette County.

Jordan phoned the district attorney (DA) Bill McBroom and advised him of the viciousness of the double homicide and the age of the suspects.

"This is horrible," McBroom barked in protest. "We'll

charge them both as adults. I'll send my assistant over to your office and he'll help draft the warrants."

Jordan pulled Detective Harper over to the side and told him he was going to be the lead detective on this case and would be meeting later with Assistant District Attorney (ADA) Dan Hiatt to help draft arrest warrants for the suspects.

It was now Harper's turn to experience a lot of the stress that went along with the job of leadman. As he began photographing the prone body of Carl Collier, he felt the pressure settling in the back of his throat. It was as if Collier were staring straight at the camera. His body had turned very pale, almost gray, and his lips were drawn back from his teeth in a frozen death grimace.

When Harper photographed Sarah Collier, it was as if she had sat up for a moment, stared at him, then had fallen back down in the pool of blood. Her face was ashy pale and her shocked eyes were set.

Harper winced. He could not imagine what the Colliers' last moments had been like, but he knew before the night was over he would have to do just that. He saw the horror in the Colliers' faces, and he involuntarily backed up at times to step away from the bodies, to catch his breath, and to think about what he was doing. Photographing these two drawn bodies, frozen in position, gave him a weird, unreal feeling, as if something outside himself had propelled him into this dream. Like any normal person, a cop has dreams that can turn into nightmares, too. Just ask any cop's wife and she will tell you about those dreams.

Chapter 8

Thirty-nine-year-old Kevin Collier had worked the second shift at the Hartsfield-Jackson Atlanta International Airport. The airport bears the proud distinction of being the "world's busiest passenger airport." HJAIA has long been known as the major connecting hub serving numerous destinations around the world. Because air travelers always start or finish their journeys in the Southeast region of the United States at HJAIA, the standing joke is that all persons must first check in at the Atlanta airport before flying on to heaven.

Kevin was a University of Georgia graduate and had a good job with Delta at the HJAIA. He had gotten off early so he could attend orchestra practice at the First Baptist Church in the northern Atlanta suburb of Dunwoody. The rehearsal was for a summer theater dinner, where they would be performing *The Sound of Music*. Kevin was one of their trombonists.

Around 8:30 P.M., Kevin retrieved a voice message from Lisa Hargrove. Lisa and her husband, Del, were lifelong friends with his parents. During a break, he dialed the cell number Lisa had provided. She answered the phone and told him there had been some problems at his parents' house and he needed to come home.

Lisa's voice was breaking. She didn't sound like herself.

"Is this an emergency?" he asked. "Can it wait until rehearsal is over?"

Lisa was caught in a moment of surprised silence on the other end of the line. She held her breath. *No, I'm not going to tell him his parents are dead. At least not over the phone.* In a voice as thin as an old man's hair, she finally insisted, "Please just come now."

"Okay, I am all the way north in Dunwoody, so it's going to take me at least an hour to get there."

Kevin joined the traffic on Interstate 85. He was feeling the irregular thumps of a headache begin at his temples. Such checks on his parents had become ritual. Kevin owned a comfortable home just outside of Fayetteville. Once or twice a week, he would stop in on them, just to satisfy himself that everything was going well with them and Holly.

With one hand on the steering wheel and the other hand on his cell phone, Kevin navigated in and out of traffic. On the drive south toward Highway 314, Kevin Collier called Lisa on her cell phone again.

"I'm concerned about what is going on with my parents," he admitted. "Are you sure nothing has happened to them?"

"All I can tell you now is that things don't look good for them at this point."

Kevin persisted. He needed to know if they were hurt in any way.

"Your dad's been hurt, Kevin. But there's no need to rush."

No need to rush? Kevin thought that was an odd thing to say. He stepped on the gas pedal. The night was growing dark and so full of shadows. From all he had heard in Lisa Hargrove's voice, he braced himself for whatever might be there—knowing he better expect the worst. By the time he reached the turn into West Fayetteville Road, he had worked himself into a juicy thumper of a headache.

When Kevin turned onto Plantation Drive, he saw cops

everywhere. His parents' front yard was packed with sheriff's deputies and crowded with what looked like anybody who had access to a uniform and a police scanner. Since police cars made it impossible to get close to their house, he had to park near a couple of houses up the street.

Kevin got out of his vehicle and saw that the cops had already cordoned off the house and the front yard. A group of neighbors were huddled across the street, at the corner, and in a neighbor's yard. He had seen enough cop shows to know when there is a crime scene, police cars materialize like moths to a flame. And here they swarmed.

This isn't good, Kevin thought, his anguish barely under control. As he surveyed the unfamiliar scene—neighbors gawking, flashing police car lights and uniformed cops entering and exiting the house that he had grown up in—his head dropped and he let out a groan. He put his hands to his head and followed the asphalt street leading toward the driveway. He could see lights, white and mute, coming from the back of the house.

The fluorescents from inside the kitchen, he quickly surmised.

Staring at his parents' house, Kevin saw a group of official-looking people moving around inside and taking pictures. Each time the camera flashed, the house—mostly dark, except for the faint glow in the kitchen—took on a creepy, distorted, and dreamlike quality. He half-expected Rod Serling to step out from somewhere in the dark and announce: "You have entered another dimension. . . . You have entered the twilight zone."

Kevin's fear deepened. He knew there was something wrong, but he just couldn't put his finger on exactly what it was yet.

Fayette County sheriff Randall Johnson was standing on the other side of the yellow crime-scene tape draped around the house. Now pushing seventy years of age, Johnson had been the Fayette County sheriff for twenty-seven years, ever since Kevin was a boy. He had known Kevin's parents a long time and considered them great friends. To the sheriff, Kevin was still a kid, who only needed to shave twice a week.

Immediately, when the sheriff saw Kevin hurrying toward the driveway, he walked away from the crowd of deputies and moved toward him. "Hello, son," he whispered, softly clamping him on the shoulder, as if they were old buddies. His grasp was very strong.

Maybe it was the vacant look in the sheriff's eyes that told Kevin what he already knew. Or maybe it was the fact that after seeing all those police cars in his parents' yard, he had already figured it out for himself. But either way, Kevin knew in his heart of hearts that his parents were dead.

"You need to remember how you saw your parents last," the sheriff said with great sorrow.

Still cringing involuntarily at the sight before him, Kevin was nodding even before the sheriff had finished. He had always been impressed with the sheriff. He was tall and trim, and had a thick crown of white hair. He called everyone "Mr.," and said, "sir" and "ma'am." He spoke in a slow, rich drawl that was very Southern, and he closely resembled James Dickey's portrayal of the sheriff in *Deliverance,* only without the round belly characteristic of most Southern sheriffs.

The sheriff kept Kevin at bay and behind the yellow tape. He stood there with him, giving him his usual smile, as if to say these encounters happened all the time. Kevin looked around and saw his father's blue Silverado was missing. He silently cursed and bit his bottom lip, then blurted out to no one in particular, "Holly must have done this."

By now, Detective Harper had emerged from inside the house and was standing outside the carport, talking with several other policemen. When he heard someone say in a low voice, "There's the Colliers' son talking with the sheriff," he looked up and saw Kevin standing at the end of the driveway with an expression of doom on his face. Instead of going back to his car and getting a legal pad, he grabbed one of Detective Mindar's small wire-bound notepads and walked toward Kevin.

Harper stepped under the yellow tape, pulled Kevin aside, and introduced himself. Kevin looked back at him like a man who had just been told a story that was too horrible to believe.

"Do you see anything missing?" Harper asked, breaking the vacant look shading Kevin's face.

"Yeah, my father's Chevrolet Silverado."

Harper opened the notebook and jotted down a memo, making a note to later secure the license plate number of Carl Collier's truck. He remembered the connection between Kevin and Holly and inquired, "Can you tell me a little about your niece?"

Kevin paused, staring at nothing for a moment, then recounted, "Carla Harvey is my sister. She is Holly's mother, but she is in jail at the moment. My mom and dad were taking care of Holly, but were having a difficult time of it."

It was still an open question. Kevin paused again, thinking back. Some families could keep secrets and some families couldn't. Obviously, his family could, and had, but this was no time for secrets.

"My niece and her girlfriend, Sandy Ketchum, had been running off together." Coals of resentment began forming around Kevin's heart. Still in a state of shock, he answered as best he could, continually muttering that "Holly must have done this." His head was thudding crazily and he could feel the dry rasp in the cradle of his throat. "They were both on drugs," he said weakly.

Harper remained focused, despite all that was going on around them. He was patient, waiting for Kevin to continue. Kevin admitted his niece was having a romantic relationship with Ketchum, one that his conservative Baptist parents discouraged.

"My parents had been really struggling to discipline her while she had been living with them," Kevin said, feeling the harsh breath in his throat finally slowing. "I was working with my father just last week and he told me that Holly had threatened to kill him."

"In what way?" Harper asked. "Do you recall anything she might have said?"

Kevin's pulse thudded steadily and deeply in his throat. "Holly had threatened to kill them a couple of times this summer. They weren't sure what she was capable of, but I think they were a little concerned at that point."

Harper understood Kevin to say that because Holly had threatened his parents before, Carl Collier was only vaguely disturbed by that. Mentally he had written it off as nothing more than a teenager mouthing off. It wasn't until the next day after he had slept on it, that he had good reason to question what had happened and wonder if there was a more sinister threat than he previously had imagined.

While Harper was interviewing Kevin, Investigator Tracey Carroll approached them with a stack of photos found in Holly's bedroom. Nearly all of the photos had been taken with what appeared to be family and friends, but someone had snapped a lot of candid shots of Holly and her friends at the beach. As if they were fashion models, two girls were seen amusing themselves in the surf, posing like beach bunnies and enjoying the sun and sand. Harper asked Carroll to hand Kevin the photos and he began thumbing through the pictures, identifying his niece in each of them.

"I do recall Holly asking my parents if she and Sandy could drive to Florida," Kevin said glumly. "But my parents told her there was only a week or so before school started and refused to let her go."

All the while Kevin thumbed through the photos, he upbraided himself, *Why couldn't I see this coming?* As he pointed out his niece in the photos, his mind kept asking that question and played on that thought over and over, like an old 45-record caught in the grooves.

Why didn't we take her threats seriously?

Kevin's guilt deepened. He had not believed it was possible, but his parents' death was a hundred times worse, knowing he had been forewarned by his father, but knowing he had done nothing to stop it.

Harper did not think Kevin should see his parents in their last moment. At least not like this.

Chapter 9

The official all-points bulletin (APB) blasted out across the police radio at approximately 8:30 P.M. *Alert, all units be on the lookout for Holly Ann Harvey and Sandy Ketchum. Two white female juveniles occupying a blue Chevy Silverado Cab. Subjects needed for questioning in reference to a 10-43.*

When Sara Polk heard the APB come through Deputy Gibson's radio, something inside her head snapped. For a few moments, she was aware of it in a muffled, muted way, as if she were merely observing what had transpired earlier through a cloudy wrapping of gauze. Then the full consciousness came back, and the horror and pain came with it. As her friend's sensational story began to sink in, she imagined her first glimpse of tomorrow's newspaper headlines. No doubt the boldest one the Georgia newspapers had run in years, it would probably read: TEENAGE GIRL TURNS FRIENDS INTO COPS.

Sara was having mixed feelings about helping the police. On the one hand, if Sandy had killed those people, she believed she should be arrested. She knew turning Sandy into the police was the right thing to do. But, on the other hand, Sandy was still her friend and she didn't want to see her arrested until she at least had time to think about what she had done and turn herself in.

On the night of August 1, Sandy had called Sara on the phone. She had been staying in Griffin with her mom, but had hitchhiked to Fayetteville to be with Holly. "I just want to chill and talk," she said.

Sara had her first day in the eleventh grade the next morning and just wanted to go to bed. Unable to grasp what Sandy really wanted to say, she kept the conversation short. All that night, her chest and back ached so much that she tossed and turned and had trouble sleeping. For some weird reason, she had a premonition that something bad was going to happen and it involved Sandy Ketchum.

Sara was having a hard time believing Sandy could actually kill anyone. She had known her since childhood. She wouldn't put it past Holly, but Sandy? Never. Sandy didn't have a mean bone in her body.

But, by now, the police were convinced there was less of a mystery about who had murdered Carl and Sarah Collier than Sara Polk wanted to believe. Lieutenant Colonel Jordan had already directed Detective Harper to meet with Fayette County's assistant district attorney Dan Hiatt at the sheriff's office for the purpose of drafting arrest warrants for Sandy Ketchum and Holly Harvey.

Upon Harper's arrival at the sheriff's office, he was met by members of the SERFTF. He provided Lieutenant Mahon McDonald with all of the information on the two teenagers, including the make and license tag number of the Silverado truck.

Harper also had a surprise visit with Scott Moore, of Fayetteville. Holly and her mother had lived with Moore before Carla went to prison and he wanted to provide information to aid in the investigation.

"Holly recently cut her hair short so she would look more like Sandy Ketchum," Moore advised, providing Harper with Holly's cell phone number. "She's also taking the prescription drug Adderall."

Just before midnight, Detective Harper met with Chief Magistrate Charles Floyd, who issued warrants for the arrest of Sandy Ketchum and Holly Harvey. But the burning question on everyone's minds still remained the same: "Why would two teenagers want to murder Carl and Sarah Collier?"

Part II

TWO TEENAGERS

SANDY KETCHUM

Chapter 10

March 2004

Beep, beep, beep.

Sandy Ketchum hated that dreadful sound. Stretching out across the bed, she looked over her shoulder and extended her right arm directly over the digital clock on the nightstand, then came down, hard and quick, hammering the snooze button with her balled fist.

The annoyance ceased immediately.

Five more minutes of sleep, she promised herself, *then I'll get up.*

Beep, beep, beep.

Again that same dreadful, droning noise.

Beep, beep, beep.

The red digital numbers inside the clock blinked in unison like some red-eyed monster trapped inside a black box.

Sandy had it timed perfectly. *Just five more minutes. I'll skip breakfast. I can still make it on time.*

When Sandy was younger, her waking up at 7:00 A.M. and getting ready for school was a fun thing. In those days, she got excited about going to school and seeing her friends, but those days had passed her quicker than a New York minute.

The excitement and freshness of going to school was long gone, and nowadays Sandy's school days moved painfully slow.

After attending school eight hours a day, five days a week—and with all that extra homework—there was barely enough time to do the things Sandy enjoyed doing, and she saw her weekends passing soon after they had gotten started. There was nothing more Sandy enjoyed than partying on the week-ends, hanging out with friends and doing drugs, but, when Mondays rolled around and the alarm clock fired off, she just couldn't seem to get back in the flow of things.

What the hell, Sandy presumed. *The only reason anybody would ever want to get up at 7:00* A.M. *on a weekday was because that's when the best cartoons were on.*

Beep, beep, beep.

Before Sandy could hammer the snooze button again, she heard her newest stepmother, Beth, holler from the next room. "You better get your ass out of bed or you're going to cause me to be late again. We can't afford for me to lose another job on account of you not wanting to get up in the morning," she yelled, trying to keep her voice pleasant.

Sandy rolled out of her warm cocoon of a bed, swallowing the rest of what she heard with a grimace, and sat up on the side. She sat there, silent for a moment in the cool, unwel-coming air of the morning, as if in a daze, then turned back, looked at the clock, and murmured under her breath, "So what if I'm late? Who the fuck cares?"

Sandy Ketchum was feeling the vagabond blues. It had not been a banner year. In fact, there had been very few banner years in her life. She had never been one to sparkle, admittedly so, but why was her life always in turmoil? Since the age of thirteen, she had changed addresses seven different times. Since starting kindergarten, she had enrolled in ten different schools. Although that might have had a lot to do with trailing her father's girlfriends and wives all around the state of Geor-gia, she still didn't like it.

As with any teenager, the ebb and flow had been especially devastating for her. She didn't like leaving her friends behind, then having to make friends all over again. Very possibly muddled by the consequences of self-doubt and self-fears, she'd grown tired of having the sudden sensation that her new classmates would be watching her with contempt, staring at her, and laughing behind their hands. She could almost hear them whispering, "Hey, don't pay attention to *her*. She's just the new kid at our school," like she was some kind of circus freak. And worst of all, she hated it when the teacher asked— and they always did—something like, *Would anyone volunteer to show our new student around?*, only to look up and see that no one had raised a hand. Not one person!

Sensing the onslaught of an early-morning vise gripper of a headache, Sandy massaged her right temple with her thumb and forefingers. She fell spread-eagle on her back, closed her eyes, and let the thought turn over and over again in her mind: *So why am I having to go through all of this again? Just as soon as I get comfortable in this school, I know we're going to move again.*

Finally the pain eased above her eyes and, with the dexterity of the Scarecrow from *The Wizard of Oz,* she slid out of bed, wobbled into the bathroom, and switched on the overhead light. She rinsed her face, then stood and gazed at her reflection in the mirror. Breathing in and out, she stared in the mirror and waited for the flood of old memories. Suddenly images of her friend Holly Harvey flashed through her mind.

Sandy had met Holly in the eighth grade at the Fayetteville Middle School. She remembered it was a sunny day and she was standing in her bus line when someone called out her name. Sandy turned around and saw this beautiful girl walking toward her.

"Hey, Sandy! I'm Holly Harvey." The young girl's smile was contagious. She had bright blue eyes and a model's face, wrapped in honey brown hair and falling against a shirt covering her summer tan. "Your cousin told me all about you, and when I saw you, I had to come and speak to you."

The name suddenly clicked with Sandy. Her cousin had gone steady with a girl named Holly and he had said nice things about her. "Everyone thinks she's great," he had bragged. "And it's that smile of hers that wins you over. You'll see what I'm talking about when you meet her."

Sandy's cousin was right. When Holly smiled, her whole face lit up.

"Oh, yeah," Sandy said shyly, looking all pie-eyed. "I remember him talking about you."

"Of course, he talks about me." Holly laughed innocently. "Let's get together with him sometime and have a party."

Sandy felt the fire burning in her heart for the very first time. Holly smiled at her again and something started happening to the lower half of her body. Her legs were beginning to feel like salt water taffy on a hot summer day. At that moment, a single thought overcame her: *My God, she's so beautiful. I hope she's gay.*

A lot of the decisions in Sandy's life had been based on emotion and feelings, rather than common sense. She had often leapt without thinking, and that had brought her much heartache. But she was very careful about what girls she got romantically involved with, and when it came to relationships, she didn't get involved with just anybody. Many of her friends changed partners as often as they changed clothes, but not Sandy. She was interested in only those people she knew she could trust and those people who, she believed, would love her. And for some reason, Sandy felt she stood a good chance with Holly.

It was hard for Sandy to describe what it was that attracted her to Holly—and Holly to her—as they were two very different people. She was very quiet and reserved and didn't communicate very much or talk a lot, while Holly chattered like a magpie and never seemed at a loss for words. Sandy dressed like a rapper; Holly dressed like a Barbie doll. They had, by most measures, almost nothing in common; yet, in many ways, they were a lot alike. Because of their rough upbringings, both their behaviors were, more than anything, natural styles of street smarts. And whatever they wanted—be it cigarettes, drugs, or beer—they went after it with a vengeance.

Although Sandy and Holly were an unlikely pair, they did create some kind of magic. Their quirky relationship clearly existed on its own terms of endearment. On the surface, they were as complementary as thunder is to lightning. Sandy had been involved in gay relationships before, but she wasn't so sure about Holly. She questioned Holly's sexual preference, especially when she chatted up sweethearts and admirers.

Sandy and Holly started out at first as friends. They went out together a few times, socialized with their friends, then started flirting with one another. But when their flirting got their love juices flowing, their relationship deepened and they eventually turned into lovers. In a matter of months, Sandy was beginning to realize it was Holly that she wanted, and vice versa.

"I think it took six months to a year for us to develop a deep romantic relationship," Sandy confided. She said she didn't realize Holly already had an eye for her, until Holly spoke to her flirtatiously using her hot, little-country-girl voice.

"I have known I was gay ever since I was a child. I knew something was different about me because I always hung around more boys than girls. I also didn't look at boys the way other females do. I found myself looking at females the way females look at males. When Holly came along, I thought she was, and always would be, the greatest love of my life.

"I was always more faithful to Holly than she was to me. I never even thought twice about looking at another female or male when we were together, but for her, it was the other way around."

Sandy had been in serious relationships with other girls, but none ever excited her like this one. For reasons Sandy could not begin to articulate then, or now, she had grown passionately and absolutely in love with Holly Harvey. But while there was a prettiness Sandy loved about Holly's pouty lips, cherub face, and dimpled cheeks, which would make any girl go mushy on matters of the heart, Holly was a spirited, hot-tempered fighter, who always wanted to keep something going.

Shortly after their friendship turned intimate, Holly wrote Sandy a letter and expressed her affection, in an odd sort of way:

Last night I walked in and Gina (pseudonym) was on top of Mike (pseudonym). I wuz like "do what you do Gina. I'm jus gonna sit over here and smoke my Newport." She put a hickey on my neck—over the one u put. She hurt me! Please don't be mad at me. . . . I told her that u brought [up] how we went out, but u don't believe we didn't do nothing, so she wuz like let's give Sandy a reason to say we did sumthin, or sum shit like that. I wuz on this waterbed and I kissed her, well she kissed me. Whatever! We kissed. Then, when I come in and she wuz on top of Mike. He wanted us to kiss so we did again. I got a lap dance from Gina. It should have been u tho. Why won't I kiss u? I don't kno. Just kiss me if u want to. I won't do you like I did Mary (pseudonym). That bitch forced her tongue in my mouf. She can't kiss, but u can. I just hope we don't get stuck together. LOL! "Click click!" Let me feel ur tongue ring.

Parroting the advice of so many of her friends, Sandy told Holly in no uncertain terms she needed not only to decide which lifestyle she preferred, but which girlfriend. She then reassured Holly they had weathered so many storms together, she was confident this one, too, would pass. Even though they were now living in separate towns, some sixty miles apart, they would be together again.

Sandy grabbed her toothbrush and a flattened tube of Colgate from above the sink, and squeezed it out onto her tooth-brush. She then hung farther over the sink, working the tooth-paste in and around her teeth and gums, thinking only of Holly. She was convinced her and Holly's love for each other was one of the only certainties about life.

"When you smile, you have my undivided attention," Sandy murmured in a low voice. "When you laugh I want to laugh with you. When you cry, I want to reach out and hold you. And when you said you loved me, then you had my heart forever."

Sandy spat out the gob of toothpaste into the sink and watched it slowly swirl into the drain. She rinsed her tooth-brush and laid it back on the shelf above the sink. Cutting off the bathroom light, she walked back to her bedroom, removed her nightclothes, and began dressing for school. Pulling on an oversized pair of jeans, she again considered how much she missed Holly and her old friends back in Fayetteville.

Why is it so hard for my parents to understand that I just want to be with my friends? she mused, guiding a pair of dark blue socks over her feet before slipping into her black Reebok tennis shoes. *Why does everything have to be so damn com-plicated?*

Sandy grabbed a white and wrinkled undershirt from her dresser drawer, pulling it over her head and down across her chest to her waist.

Wife beater, yeah, that's what they call these, baby.

She pinched the bottom of the cotton shirt between her thumb and forefinger, looked in the mirror, and laughed at the image of her wearing such a shirt.

Me wearing a wife beater! Ain't that a bitch!

It was still a little nippy outside; Sandy could see outside looking through her bedroom window. She was pleased, though, for the cool Georgia spring air; it allowed her to get away with wearing long sleeves. Choosing a larger long-sleeved light blue shirt from her closet, she wrestled it off the hanger and wrapped it around her shoulders. Hopefully, she had a reprieve for, at least, a few more weeks.

Yeah, that's good. The corner of Sandy's mouth turned upward as she stretched her arms through the large shirt. *No one will notice my arms and wrists as long as I keep my sleeves pulled down.*

Sandy was a pro when it came to hiding the tapestry of scars on her arms and legs. She had long ago lost count of the scars on her body. Careful not to let them show, she dressed in such a way, always wearing baggy pants and oversized shirts—the hip-hop look her friends called it—that no one really paid much attention to the scars on her body. She was relieved at having avoided all those nonsensical questions— like the one a former classmate had asked.

"So, tell me," the girl had said snobbishly, pointing at Sandy's wrists, "why did you go and do something stupid like that?" Sandy played dumb, but vowed afterward that she had way too much guilt in her life already without having to face any more brutal interrogations, especially from this prom queen bitch.

Sandy had learned life was so much easier to face when she avoided talking about her past. *Out of sight, out of mind,* she remembered her stepmother saying—although she couldn't remember which one had actually said it. In the future, she'd just keep her mouth shut, and if anyone at her new school did notice her little "secret," she could always cover by saying something like, *Oh, you're talking about those things? Yeah, that's where my dog, Poowaa, scratched me.* That would work for her. Hell, she could even claim she'd been scratched by her bird, Tweetie. *Who the fuck would ever know? Or care, for that matter?*

Chapter 11

The cutting.

Sandy knew it was weird and that people who had never experienced this type of behavior probably wouldn't—no, couldn't—understand, but the act of cutting her body was kind of like self-medication with a drug—kind of like when people try drowning their sorrows after work by taking drugs or drinking 2 six-packs of Budweiser. She had never told anyone, even her therapist she had started seeing several years ago, but to her, cutting had become a ritual, an act of pleasure that almost always produced some kind of release.

"I don't know, it just makes me feel better," she would say to her friends when they asked her about it.

Even though Sandy couldn't say why it made her feel better—just that it did—cutting was something she began looking forward to. Somehow, she found it helped release the feelings of guilt over the things she couldn't cope with. Maybe not long-term, but at least for that moment anyway.

Sandy never did this type of thing in the view of others. She made sure it was always in the privacy of her own room. She didn't do it with a razor; she did it with a knife so that her injuries would be sort of superficial. It was a kind of delicate cutting, a nicking that barely broke the skin's surface. Harmless, at first, much like picking at her skin with a plastic fork.

But as Sandy's cutting became more of an obsession, and when the need for release of tension became greater, her cuts went deeper into her skin. Careful to avoid the "whoops cut," Sandy learned in time not only where to cut and how to cut, but especially to look and see who was around, just in case she really did hurt herself and needed help.

Sandy was actually very skillful at staying alive. Once in 2002, at the age of fourteen, she had actually tried to commit suicide. She said she hadn't meant to do it, that it was an "accident." Well, at least, that's what she called it. That was almost two years ago to the date, and she was very young then and very confused. She was depressed and had a low self-image. *You know, the usual problems teenagers encounter when they're bored with life and start thinking of how easy it would be to check out.* She would later tell this to her therapist.

"But it *was* an accident!" Sandy hissed. She had taken a lot of pills that day. It was pills she had gotten from the neighborhood kids. She didn't even know what they were. But she had swallowed them, every last one of them. One by one, just like some medicine a doctor had given her for the cold or flu, she had downed those puppies until they were all gone. But, for the life of her, she couldn't remember why. *There must have been something that caused me to take all those pills?* She thought maybe she had blocked it all out.

Sandy never quite figured out why she had wanted to die that day. Her therapist had told her, in what she perceived as some kind of psychological mumbo jumbo. "It's very possible that your actions were muddled over by the consequences of self-doubt, by self-fears, and by feelings of love and responsibility," or something to that effect. She never understood any of that, but just knew there were moments in her life when she wished she had died that night.

Not too long after her suicide attempt, Sandy remembered, was when all the cutting behavior started. Keenly aware that her parents were concerned about her strange behavior, she kept the cutting hidden from them. They were completely in the dark about it until the therapist pointed it out.

"I had wanted to stop, hoped it would stop, before my parents ever found out about it," Sandy would later confess. "One of my greatest fears was that one day, I would go too far. That in a moment of deep depression, I would press harder on the knife than normal, slicing deeper in my wrist until it severed a vein. I could see myself lying in the room and the blood flowing so quickly from my severed vein that I would pass out before I could alert anyone. And there I'd be, helpless, watching myself bleed to death on my bed, finally losing consciousness until all of life oozed out of me."

Although Sandy saw a therapist once a week, she was non-compliant and refused to talk about her problems. During counseling sessions, she would curl up in her seat in a fetal position and ignore all attempts from her therapist at getting her to open up. Fortunately, Sandy's stepmother was there to guide her through the process.

"It's called self-injury, or cutting," Sandy's therapist had revealed to Beth Ketchum after one of Sandy's sessions. "It's all part of a growing problem in our nation. Almost every teenage girl knows about it."

Beth nodded, then moved in closer. She didn't want to miss anything.

"Why, I've seen many kids who seem perfectly normal, but are so psychologically distressed that they hurt themselves to cope," the therapist continued in a singsong fashion. "Some of the girls I've heard about go as far to burn themselves with cigarette lighters and literally scorch the flesh, but cutting is the most common behavior I've seen and worked with."

Beth winced at the thought of little girls mutilating themselves with knives and cigarette lighters. She asked curiously, "Why would someone want to do something as horrible as that? Why do they want to hurt themselves?"

The therapist lifted her glasses from her face, rubbed her tired eyes, then shifted in her seat. In the past two years, the number of kids she had seen hurting themselves had doubled. It was quickly becoming the fastest growing symptom of mental-health disorders among teenagers in America.

"Cutting is only the tip of the iceberg," she explained in layman's terms. "These teenagers are suffering from depression, bipolar disorder, and borderline personality disorder. These are all severe mental illnesses and characterized by pervasive mood swings."

Beth didn't understand all the psychological jargon, either, but knew that Sandy had problems similar in nature to those the therapist was describing. She had recognized Sandy's problems were a lot more serious than her skipping class from time to time.

"They hurt themselves for various reasons," the therapist explained. She paused, looked up for a moment, as if she were in deep thought, then added a postscript. "I believe that teenagers like Sandy are cutting themselves so as to bring feeling into a body that is otherwise numb and hurting. Life today is very fast-paced and teenagers have so much thrown at them that they are having difficulty focusing. Their thoughts about life, school, companionship, sex, drugs, and all these other issues are being whirled at them so fast they can't control themselves."

"Yes, I can understand that," Beth acknowledged. "Times have changed a lot since we were young. Life was a lot slower when—"

"And times are a lot more complicated," the therapist interrupted before Beth finished her sentence. "And with this cutting, they are attempting to communicate—even though the behavior is inappropriate—some kind of an outward sign of their inner pain. It's their way of coping with demanding social and academic expectations they, as teenagers, find impossible to meet."

"Sandy is a straight-A student," Beth protested. "But I don't know how she does it. God only knows that child never studies or brings a book home from school. But she must have some smarts to get the grades she's gotten."

"Oh, don't let that fool you, Mrs. Ketchum. Most of the teenagers I see are good students. Many of them are popular kids in school, some of the brightest and best kids in school. You know, we see them every day and never think a thing about it. Who would ever believe that among the high-school cheerleaders and basketball players, why even the president of the math club, there would be a cutter? Or two?"

Beth looked confused. This cutting behavior had to have started from somewhere? It wasn't like it was contagious. Like smallpox or something? She wanted to know.

"Oh, yes, there is the contagion effect," the therapist clarified. "There are a lot of kids out there whose needs are not being met at home. The thoughts of cutting are planted when one student sees a friend doing it and she then thinks it is an acceptable way of handling troubling emotions. She tries it, starts cutting sporadically, then becomes as addicted to that behavior as a smoker is to nicotine. The behavior quickly increases to the point where it becomes more than a habit, it becomes an obsession."

After the conversation with the therapist, Beth Ketchum was insistent about Sandy getting the psychological counseling she needed, and made certain she never missed an appointment. Sandy received a combination of individual therapy and medication therapy. After assessing how psychologically distressed Sandy was, her therapist referred her to a psychiatrist and he prescribed three medications: Risperdal for her sleeping difficulties, Depakote for her bipolar disorder, and Paxil for depression.

Sandy's therapist had hoped Sandy, in time, would discover the real enemy she had battled for most of her young life—the pain she had been trying so hard to carve out of her skin—was not made of flesh and blood. The enemy she fought to cope with, as well as the reason for her deliberate attempt to scratch and cut herself until she bled, was her emotional pain inside. Little by little, Sandy began to offer a glimpse of that pain.

"I don't remember my birth mother," she had told her therapist in a soft and sorrowful voice. She looked as if she had wanted to let it all out. Slowly she said in tears, "My real mother deserted me when I was just a baby. I always thought my first stepmom was my real mother. She was the best thing in my life until she had to have surgery to remove two brain tumors."

Sandy told the therapist she and her stepmother had a good relationship until the first neurological surgery altered her stepmother's behavior significantly. "After the first surgery, she became aggressive and hostile, while a second one literally turned her into a vegetable." Sandy said her stepmom and her father had agreed that if either person ever became incapacitated to the point of being a burden on one another, then they would split up. And when that happened to her stepmother, she and Sandy's father divorced amicably. Sandy was ten years old when they divorced.

"How about your father?" the therapist probed. "How is your relationship with him?"

A sweet smile surfaced across Sandy's face for a moment.

"Oh, I've always had a good relationship with my father." She sat up straight in her chair, seemingly purring like a cat that had suddenly found a bowl of tuna. "His name is Tim Ketchum. We're like best friends, in that I can always talk to him about anything. He's been my shoulder when I needed to cry and basically my support system."

Sandy recalled that she and her father were alone together for three years after Tim's second marriage had ended. For a while, they had lived with Tim's mother, and it was her grandmother who had helped to look after her and take care of her. When her father remarried a third time, he told her he had high hopes that he had found another stepmother for her who would also love her and shower her with affection. But that never materialized.

"You're nothing but a bitch," Sandy especially remembered

her second stepmother screaming at her. "For no reason at all, she would glare at me and scream, 'Don't mess with me, Sandy, or I'll knock your fucking teeth down your throat.'"

Sandy's smile faded. She shifted uncomfortably in her chair, as if it no longer fit her body frame. She said she had been terrified and sought protection from her father.

"At first my father thought I was making it all up," she told her therapist, "that maybe I was jealous of my new stepmom. She had a daughter of her own, and she and my father had a two-year-old girl together. She seemed to be the perfect mom with those two children; so why would she want to pick on me like that? He didn't understand it."

"So how did you finally convince him?" the therapist asked, pleased that Sandy was finally communicating.

"Well, I just finally blurted it all out. 'I'm telling you, Daddy,' I said to him in tears, 'this woman is as mean as the devil. She purely hates me for no reason at all. And she has beat me the whole time y'all have been together.'"

Sandy said that she finally couldn't take it anymore. She said she became so insistent her stepmother had been physically abusing her that she personally called the Department of Family and Children Services (DEFACS) and reported her. The next day, a social worker visited the Ketchums in their home, took pictures of Sandy's bruises, then presented the photographs to Tim Ketchum.

"And did your father believe you then?"

Sandy lowered her head. She let out the breath she had been holding, then shook her head slowly from side to side. "No, he still didn't believe me."

"So what about the bruises? Didn't your father see those?"

Sandy nodded, then said barely above a whisper, "She lied. She said to my father, 'Oh, those bruises?' like it was no big deal. 'All that happened at school, when Sandy was playing on the playground.' That was what *she* told him."

The therapist cleared her throat, and then asked in a sympathetic tone, "But in reality, they were a result of the beatings she had administered. Is that what I hear you saying?"

Sandy nodded again. Suddenly sensing how good it felt to speak to someone about her childhood pain, she continued, "So I told my daddy, I said to him, 'You know, I hate it when you don't believe me about the beatings. She's messed up my life and I hate her for it. I can never do anything right in her eyes.'"

Now, two years after the event, Sandy found herself sitting in a counseling session and confessing to her therapist that she still suffered from nightmares and thoughts of her stepmother's abuse.

Ain't life a bitch sometimes?

When asked how she felt this had affected her, Sandy, however, was surprisingly insightful.

"I think all this has something to do with me losing my temper easily when people aggravate me," Sandy concluded, as if she had discovered by her own revelation one of the many missing pieces to her life's puzzle. "I've been so mad before that I even crushed my knuckles on a cement wall once."

Sandy revealed how easily frustrated she could become, especially when she couldn't do the things she wanted to do. She wasn't particularly fond of being told what she had to do. Sandy was sixteen years old, old enough to think and act on her own, and she especially resented people on the outside, like her new stepmother, Beth, trying to tell her how to live her life.

Sandy's therapist was pleased that she had chosen to finally discuss her feelings. Maybe, now, they could develop ways to help her cope that didn't involve hurting herself. Sandy needed to take control of her life, and she was encouraged to find a way to focus her attention on something besides cutting. The therapist suggested she spend some quality time with an old friend.

A friend? Suddenly a thought formed in Sandy's mind and the words "Holly Harvey" formed across her lips.

Chapter 12

In 1987, Timothy Wade Ketchum met a beautiful, dark-haired French girl by the name of Sandra Faye Ross. Tim was twenty-four, and Sandra was nineteen. She had already been married, given birth to two children, and divorced, but Tim liked the way her legs moved graciously under a short skirt and started dating her. A short time later, Sandra revealed she was pregnant and carrying his child. No surprise to Tim, and on April 19, 1988, she gave birth to a healthy girl they named Sandy.

Tim was reluctant at first to marry Sandra, but finally gave in and did what he thought was right. His own father, who had once had a promising career as a steel guitarist at the Grand Old Opry, was an alcoholic and had deserted Tim, his older sister, and his mother when Tim was just a child. His mother had worked in a clothing store to support her children.

Every child deserves a father and mother, Tim reasoned. At least that was his two cents' worth of knowledge on the subject of marriage and parenthood.

Tim was working with Fayetteville Plumbing and knew it would be difficult to support a wife and three kids on his meager salary of $9 an hour. But he was determined to be the kind of husband and father he needed to be. He rented a little home in nearby Griffin and moved his ready-made family into it, thinking that would do the trick and they'd live the rest of their lives like the television family he grew up with, the Cleavers. The only problem was, while he didn't mind playing Ward Cleaver and bringing home the bacon, Sandra, sure as hell, wasn't interested in being June Cleaver. Instead, she preferred living like the Ozzy Osbourne family—staying out late, partying, and sleeping until noon the next day.

While Tim worked, Sandra did little to make a home for Sandy and her other two children. She lay around the house all day, ate, slept, and fashioned herself into a genuine couch potato, leaving the children to fend for themselves. Rarely did she prepare a meal or change a diaper, and when Tim arrived home from work at the end of his long day, he was greeted by hungry and crying children, still wearing a wet or soiled diaper.

Spalding County's Family and Child Protective Services (CPS) had already received an anonymous call about Sandra Ketchum's lack of attentiveness to her other two children and decided they might need to check on her new baby as well. During an unannounced home visit, the social worker noticed Sandy had a dirty diaper and asked Sandra several times to change the child's diaper, then finally insisted she change her. When Sandra reluctantly agreed, the social worker observed that Sandy had a severe case of diaper rash and she threatened to take the baby away from Sandra.

Even after being told she was at risk of losing her children, Sandra still did not mend her ways. She and Tim argued daily about her lack of attentiveness toward her children and he threatened to divorce her. Several weeks later, Tim found out one of the reasons she had been neglecting her children was because she was having an affair. Feeling like a wooden stake had been driven through his heart, he gave her her walking papers and kicked her out of his house. She packed her possessions in cardboard boxes and left, taking her two kids and Sandy with her.

That night Tim drove to a bar, and after a few long pulls on a few short bottles of beer, he felt much better. Later, he'd get a well-deserved good night's sleep and think about everything tomorrow.

Tim Ketchum had never claimed any type of mastery in the game of love. He'd be the first to admit that all his life experiences came via the hotel of heartbreak and the school of hard knocks. But his mother had raised him and his sister to be decent, loyal, and honest folk. He was proud of that and he'd just be damned if he would live with anyone who could not be true and faithful to him. He'd miss Sandy, but he had a suspicious feeling he'd see her again, soon.

Just as Tim predicted, Sandra grew tired of caring for their fifteen-month-old child. In the middle of the day, when she knew Tim would still be at work, Sandra slipped inside his house and left a handwritten note on the kitchen table.

Dear Tim, she had written in big, bold letters, *Come get your daughter.* A name and address were penciled in at the bottom of the letter.

Later that day, Tim found the note and rushed over immediately to the mobile-home park where his estranged wife and children were staying. Sandra's best friend, Barbara Nelson (pseudonym), met him at the door with Sandy.

"Where's Sandra?" Tim said curtly.

Barbara stepped in front of the door and extended her left arm across the doorway. In her right arm, she held on to Sandy as if she were a bargaining chip. She thumbed over her left shoulder and toward the room at the back of the mobile home. "Sandra's in the back bedroom, but she doesn't want to come out. Says she doesn't want any trouble."

Tim drew back his hands, palms facing upward in surrender. "Oh, I don't want any trouble, either. I just want my baby girl and her things," he said flatly, pointing at Sandy. "I promise I'll leave then."

Barbara turned and nodded toward the couch. All of Sandy's clothing, bottles, diapers, and stuffed animals were packed in two cardboard boxes and stacked on the couch. She looked over her shoulder, then turned and motioned to Tim. He walked sheepishly over and picked up the boxes.

Barbara followed Tim to the door, holding Sandy against her hip like a sack of dried potatoes. "We like you, Tim, and don't want to see you hurt any more than you already have been. I don't know why Sandra is like she is. Hell, I even found out she has been screwing my husband, too."

Tim shook his head, feeling his face flush. Nothing about Sandra's permissiveness surprised him anymore. He did wonder though how he could have been so blind as not to realize what had been going on behind his back.

"Can you believe that?" Barbara rattled on, cursing Sandra for everything she had done. "My best friend . . . screwing my husband . . . in my damn house. . . . Now, that's a friend for you, huh?"

After listening to Barbara rant for another five minutes or so, Tim asked for his daughter, grabbed the last of her things, and then left without ever seeing Sandra. The next day, he took Sandy over to his mother's house. Doris Ketchum had agreed to watch Sandy while he worked, and until other arrangements were made.

A couple of days later, a pusillanimous Sandra came to see Tim, acting like a whipped puppy. He suddenly realized that her long hours glued in front of a television, watching one soap opera after another, had been good for something. She had learned to play the role of drama queen so very well, choosing just the right amount of sorrowful facial expressions and tears, which turned off and on like a faucet. There were rehearsed apologies that would shame even Susan Lucci (the actress best known as Erica Kane from *All My Children*) as she begged Tim for forgiveness. What she basically said was all she'd ever wanted to be was a mother and a wife, and now she knew where she'd gone wrong. If only Tim could forgive her and let her come home, she would prove it.

Partly because of Sandy and partly because he had a soft spot in his heart for tearful women, Tim agreed. Even after all she had done, he let her return home and move back in with her children, knowing the odds favored him winning the Georgia lottery more so than Sandra straightening up and being a real wife and mother. He should have called his bookie.

"I'm pregnant," Sandra confessed openly a few weeks later. "I'm going to have another baby."

"Pregnant?" Tim echoed. He felt himself break out in a cold sweat and was soon nodding along with her.

Sandra took on a sour look.

Tim cut his eyes at Sandra, then turned away in disgust. "Oh, really?" he responded, acting as if he were surprised, but not before dinging her with, "Well, whose baby is this one?"

Sandra shook her head, slowly, from side to side. "I don't know," she answered truthfully. Taking a step backward, she murmured something under her breath that resembled an apology.

Tim reminded her of her previous indiscretions and pressed her for more details. After he got the full helping, he told Sandra he had learned a lot about marriage from her. As a result of their relationship, he had learned that it's damn near impossible for someone to take back something hurtful they've said or done. And every time something hurtful was said or done, a little bit of a person's love dies along with it. He'd also learned from their marriage that apologies don't make everything right, and they sure as hell don't make everything better. Sandra had hurt him once; then she did it again and again, until, finally, after a while, there was nothing left in their relationship. Since Sandra confessed running around this time, he thought the right thing to do was to tell her he had had enough.

"I learned that life is way too short to continue in a relationship that can never be fixed," Tim said to Sandra after they separated. "If the other person isn't trustworthy, tell me, why should I want to continue the relationship? I just hate that Sandy is hopelessly caught in the middle of all this."

Tim wasted no time in filing for a divorce and petitioning the courts for full custody of Sandy. Sandra never contested the court's decision and was ordered to pay Tim $35 a month in child support. Tim admitted he really did not want to be tied to his ex for the rest of his life, especially for that paltry amount of money. Divorce without a child would have been less painful and much less expensive, but given the situation, he felt paying $35 per month was the least Sandra could do for the daughter she had birthed.

After their divorce was final, Tim never forgot about Sandra's child support, but eventually he gave up trying to collect it. The problem was, she never lived in one place long enough for the sheriff's office to serve legal papers on her. From time to time, one of Tim's friends would mention he had seen Sandra and how she was living the life of a gypsy pauper, taking up residency with any Tom, Dick, or Harry she knew. Tim never talked bad about Sandra, other than to say he was sorry he had gotten involved with her and spent the last eighteen months of his life in a failed marriage.

But right then it meant nothing to Tim that a couple of six-packs couldn't resolve. He was still young and had vowed not to date anyone he didn't think he could stand being married to. And for the next two years, he worked hard at making himself the kind of person someone besides Sandra would want to marry.

One weekend night, at a little club in Griffin called Country Rock, he met Mary Barker (pseudonym), an attractive girl with a gentle sense of humor. He and Mary danced several dances, then sat and chatted. Mary was also divorced and had a son about the same age as Sandy.

Mary was just the opposite of Tim's first wife, Sandra. She was a good Christian girl, worked very hard at her job at the textile mill, and took a genuine interest in Tim and Sandy's welfare. Tim liked her most of all for her kind heart and especially appreciated her loyalty and trustworthiness. Their courtship was brief, and for the first time, Tim was in love. He considered himself very fortunate to have been smitten by a woman so willing to devote the rest of her life to being *his* wife, and a mother to Sandy. Seemingly happy they had wasted little time on romance, their relationship got better and better.

Unbeknownst to either Tim or Mary, there was a ticking time bomb inside her body. For some time, a fluid-filled sac had lodged in the wall of an artery to Mary's heart, until it ultimately erupted and gave way to a debilitating aneurysm of the brain. There was health and disability insurance, and, of course, family, friends, and church members were always there to help lighten the burden. Tim's mother also pitched in and did all she could to help out, but Tim was the only one working after her surgery and his take-home salary of less than $300 a week barely kept them afloat. And when Mary started having daily multiple seizures, her costs for medicine, doctor's visits, and hospitalization skyrocketed. Her illness continued for two additional years without any improvement, until finally she suffered two back-to-back aneurysms.

Mary and Tim had a candid, heart-to-heart conversation, admitting to one another that Mary's life and their future, as they had once hoped for, was over. Drastic changes were coming as quickly as the rain, and Mary was well on her way to becoming an invalid. Knowing that Mary's chances for recovery and living a normal life were less than zero, the hopeless couple made the painful decision to part ways. Mary and her son would move in with her mother, while Tim and Sandy got on with the business of living a normal life, as if life without Mary would ever resemble *normal* again.

Tim didn't like the idea of separating from Mary, and swore, somehow, they could make it through all this. But Mary's mind was made up, pointing out the devastating effects her illness was already having on Sandy. She assured Tim she would always love him, that true love burns the brightest—and sometimes the brightest flames can't help but leave the deepest scars.

Both Tim and Sandy were crushed and grieved for months on end. For three years, Tim remained single, hoping against hope Mary would get better. His mother helped out with Sandy and he watched with great pride as she grew into a lovely little girl. It was hard to believe his little girl—daddy's little girl— had just turned ten. She was a smart girl, made all A's in school, helped out around the house, and watched after her daddy. But what she needed most of all, Tim thought, was a role model.

What Sandy Ketchum really needed was a mother.

Chapter 13

Although Tim Ketchum considered himself about as unlucky in love as an alcoholic living in a dry county, he soon discovered a lonely man rarely stops and asks how compatible a person might be, or what her flaws are, before plunging ahead and letting the animal instincts inside him drive him to look for the love of a beautiful woman.

Tim would boast years later he had known and loved Mary Barker, but it wasn't love that had driven him to marry Tracey Beckhowell (pseudonym). It was convenience.

"Honestly," he would hold up his right hand and swear like a Boy Scout reciting the Scout's Oath. "I was looking for a meal ticket. I wanted somebody to support me for a while, and Tracey filled that bill."

Tracey lived in nearby Macon with her daughter from a previous marriage. Although still grieving for Mary, Tim enjoyed going out to bars and dancing with his friends. He met Tracey at the Whiskey River Club in Warner Robins. What attracted Tim the most to her was that she worked with the U.S. Postal Service, made a very good salary, and had excellent insurance and benefits. She appeared to be ambitious and had him thinking, at first, that she would be good for Sandy. While they were dating, he particularly noticed how she doted on Sandy, just like she was her own child. It was the small things, like letting Sandy sit on her lap and pretend she was driving the car, that gave him the impression she genuinely cared for his daughter.

Approaching forty years old, Tim now believed that compatibility in relationships was largely a "luck of the draw," like playing poker, when you make the best of what hand you are dealt. It wasn't that he was looking for a wildly romantic relationship or hungry to get that last hormonal rush again before he was over-the-hill. Far from it! It was just that he had grown up, faced life as it was, and had gotten smarter. Life was way too short for this bucking cowboy, and as he got older, he began to see the years start flying by faster and faster. Both for him and for Sandy.

Tim thought he knew Tracey about as well as he had known any of his other ex-wives. To be honest, just how well did he *really* know anyone? But he didn't see any flaws in Tracey that he couldn't live with. And he had to admit, it did feel good seeking the thrill of a new love.

Tracey had been married before, but who was Tim to judge? When it came to matrimony, he had a lousy batting average. Remembering his youthful days playing baseball, he chuckled at the idea of being married a third time.

Okay, buddy, remember now, three strikes and you are out. This is your last chance to hit a home run, so you best make it good.

Tim and Tracey dated for a couple of months, then began living together. In 1999, all seemed well in the Ketchum home. They got married, bought a house and two brand-new cars. Then Tracey got pregnant, and months later, the Ketchums welcomed into the world a baby girl and named her Payton.

Tim was thrilled at having another daughter, but gradually he saw some changes taking place in his wife. For some reason, their relationship was constantly off-balance, and she acted as if she hated Sandy. Tracey became moody, angry, and was impossible to please. It seemed as if all of her efforts were now directed toward getting Sandy into trouble so Tim would send her away to live with her grandmother or move her in with one of her friends.

"Maybe this is what they call the 'baby blues,'" Tim had stated after Tracey jumped him about Sandy. He'd watched enough episodes of *Oprah, Dr. Phil,* and *The Montel Williams Show* to know this was some sort of woman's thing. And this was some serious shit. Hell, he'd even heard of some women being driven to murder by what they called "postpartum depression." He understood it to be some type of affliction when women were trying to adjust to new motherhood, but were just too whacked-out to cope.

Now that Tim thought about it, it all made sense. A woman was used to sleeping eight to ten hours every night, and after the baby was born, she'd be lucky to get five hours on a good night. It also had a lot to do with a woman's self-image. Pregnancy is never kind to the female body, and suddenly a woman finds herself going from a size 7 to a size 18. Not to mention that a woman's boobies, those milk-manufacturing machines, grow to about three sizes bigger than their normal size. It was understandable why for a few months after a baby was born, a mother's self-esteem would take a serious plunge and she wouldn't want anyone looking at her because of how fat she had gotten.

But all of this didn't matter to Tim. He did not think Tracey was any less of a woman for it. It was true, she had put on a lot of weight since he had met her, but he didn't care how fat she had gotten. He just loved her more for giving birth to his baby daughter, Peyton. All he wanted was for her to love him and Sandy in return and treat them with respect.

Was that too much to ask?

Tim guessed Tracey was experiencing so much stress with the new baby that that was why she had started taking it all out on him and Sandy. He noticed she was always screaming and yelling at Sandy. For no apparent reason, Sandy was always in the doghouse, being constantly disciplined and sent to her room for hours upon end. Tracey was always playing the heavy hand and even went so far as to remove Sandy's bedroom door—she took it off the damn hinges—to keep her from slamming it after they had a disagreement.

So, here was a teenage girl, who needed her privacy, suddenly with no bedroom door. Concerning the incident with the bedroom door, Sandy expressed her own displeasure, saying to her father, "I don't like living with her, Daddy. She's always on my case. I can't do anything to please her. Every time I do something, she hollers at me. I hate living here."

Tim found himself between a rock and a hard place. Sandy was his life—and there was nothing he wouldn't do for her. He had talked with Tracey about her lack of respect for Sandy's feelings. Pointing out a particular incident on Christmas Day relating to the quality and quantity of Sandy's gifts under the tree, it was obvious Tracey favored her own daughters more than Sandy.

"Sandy's beginning to feel unloved. She feels you are treating her like a redheaded stepchild and it's having a bad effect on her," Tim admonished.

Tracey denied mistreating Sandy and showing favoritism to her other children. Sandy was just imagining things, she wanted him to know, but if his daughter was going to live in their house, there would be certain rules she would have to abide by.

"Sandy's problem is Sandy," Tracey said flatly. "I can't help it if she doesn't want to take orders from anyone. But she is a child and that means she has to learn to do what she is told to do." It was as simple as that.

Tim understood all that and maybe he was a little too lenient on his daughter, but he pleaded with Tracey to cut Sandy a little slack.

For a while, things got better, until Tracey started up again and her relationship with Sandy went from bad to worse. For four years, Tim kept the home fires burning, believing Tracey would have a change of heart and his marriage would get better.

He had seemingly done everything he could to ensure they would have a happy future, but it looked as if it just wasn't going to happen.

What concerned Tim most was the fact that Sandy was afraid of Tracey. She had been for a long time. He had suspected Tracey was physically abusing Sandy, but he never had actually caught her. But if for one moment, he wanted her to know, she thought all was fair in love and war, then she was woefully mistaken.

Tim arrived home early from work one day and heard Sandy screaming from her bedroom. As suspected, he rushed in and found Tracey in bed and straddled over his daughter. She had pinned Sandy to the bed with her knees and was beating her in the head with fists flailing like a mechanical pinwheel.

"What's wrong with you?" Tim screamed at Tracey as he pulled her off Sandy and threw her against the wall. "Have you gone fucking crazy?"

Tracey caught herself at the last moment, her face blushing crimson. She had to swallow a few times before she could apologize.

Tim was clenching his jaw so tight, he was afraid his teeth would shatter.

Sandy crawled away like a wounded animal and curled up in the corner of the wall. Frightened and crying, she kept repeating over and over, "Don't let her hurt me, Daddy. Please don't let her hurt me again."

Tracey cleared her throat again, feeling like her tongue had swollen twice its size. She apologized, saying, "Sandy started it," and hoped Tim would leave it at that. But he didn't.

Tim took care of Sandy, then came back into the living room with his jaws still locked. His voice was as dire as his mood. "Tracey," he began slowly.

Tracey avoided Tim's gaze, mumbling, "It was her fault . . . all her fault."

Tim winced as he thought about what had just happened.

His hands were clenched tightly. He was furious at Tracey, but he was more angry with himself for not believing his daughter. He had closed his ears to things he had not wanted to hear, but he'd be damned if he'd close his heart to the things he had just felt and seen with his own eyes. His daughter's life was in jeopardy and he had to get her out of this situation, far away from his abusive wife.

"You keep your goddamned hands off my child," Tim screamed. He walked over to Sandy, still curled up in the corner. He put his hands on her back. She was shaking and he could feel her heaving up and down. He took a deep breath and hissed between his teeth, "It's over between us!"

Tracey felt the heat of Tim's stare boring down into her like a laser, but she knew better than to challenge him. She raised a disapproving eyebrow, but with so many things she had done lately, he didn't give a shit and let it pass.

Right then and there, Tim made a decision to leave his wife and take Sandy with him. That night he slept in the living room and thought about what he needed to do. But before he could even act on his plans, a friend who was visiting Tracey called him on his cell phone at work a few days later with shocking news. "I don't want to get into your business, Tim, but you might want to come home and check on your daughter." All this was said in a low, quiet voice. It sounded as if his friend was cupping her cell phone with her hand so as not to be heard by anyone but him. "I hate to tell you this, but I just saw Tracey beating Sandy on the head with her fists."

Tim's face got red as a plum and the veins popped out in his neck like spaghetti. He told his boss he had an emergency at home and he needed to leave immediately. As soon as his boss gave him the okay, Tim hopped in his truck and raced home at breakneck speed. He didn't even take the time to kill the engine, but opened his door, jumped out, and ran inside his home, where he found Tracey in her bedroom. He marched over to the bed and got right into her face, and then confronted her: "What the hell have you been doing to my daughter?"

"I don't know what you're talking about," Tracey said. "I haven't been near your daughter all day."

Tim wanted so much to believe it hadn't happened, but he knew his friend had no reason to lie. And, later, when he pulled Sandy aside and asked her for the truth, she confirmed it.

"Yes, she hit me in the head again, Daddy. She called me names and told me I was white trash, just like my mama. Said I'd end up just like her one day. A whore and a drug addict. I didn't do nothing and she just started hitting me again."

The veins popped out in Tim's forehead. Growling through a throat tight with rage, he was consumed with anger. Tracey had never seen Tim that out of control. He turned toward Tracey and swore if she ever laid another hand on his daughter, she would never again see the light of day.

Externally, Tim felt like he had blown a pressure valve. Internally, something had changed. As his fury slowly dissipated, he began to believe the real truth about his wife and their sham marriage. He'd have to make some decisions if he was going to protect his daughter. One day he'd have his revenge, but for right now, Sandy was his biggest concern.

While Tim stewed and argued with Tracey, Sandy devised a simple plan of escape from her abusive stepmother. Several days later, she hopped on another bus with a classmate and rode across town to her friend's house. When Tim got home and was told Sandy had not come home after school, he knew what had happened. Making a few phone calls to her friends, he found out where she was, then drove across town and picked her up at her friend's house.

"Sandy, why would you do that?" Tim angrily asked when they got in the car, and rightly so. "Why would you scare the hell out of me like that?"

Sandy lowered her head. "I wasn't trying to scare you," she mumbled, looking at an imaginary spot somewhere between her legs. "I just didn't want to go home anymore."

Tim didn't have to ask *why* she hadn't wanted to go home. He knew Sandy had taken all the abuse she could stand. The next day, he picked his daughter up from school and announced he was leaving Tracey for good.

Sandy was elated. She broke out in a big grin, then shouted, "Oh, thank God, Daddy. We are free at last! Free at last!"

Tim and Sandy rode back to the Forsyth home, where they had lived with Tracey and her two girls for the past four years. No one was home. Sandy then helped her father load their things out of the home and into his 2001 blue Ford Ranger.

"I'm so sorry, baby, for putting you through this," Tim apologized after they had finished loading the truck and were on their way to Griffin. "Please forgive me."

Sandy nodded. Her eyes welled up in tears. All water under the bridge, she assured him.

Tim reached out and placed a comforting arm around his daughter's shoulders. He rolled down his window, extended his left arm outside, and formed with his third finger one of the most recognizable gestures of humanity. "Bye, bye, bitch. Good riddance!" he shouted, laughing all the time.

Sandy tried to hold her solemn face, but couldn't. She was on the verge of tears again, but broke out in a wide grin. Tim could see she was relieved, it was there, plain as day, in her face. She suddenly raised both hands and clenched them above her head. She laughed along with her father, shouting, "Yaho-o-o-o! Yaho-o-o-o!" almost the entire trip to Griffin. Finally, she believed, her nightmare was over.

It was a moment—an epiphany, if you will—that, up until then, Tim had only read about. He looked over at his daughter sitting next to him and saw how much she had changed. She looked much older and was wiser than any thirteen-year-old he had known. He was satisfied he had done the right thing and prayed to God that it hadn't been too late, that Tracey hadn't done more damage to his daughter than he could undo.

But no matter. His daughter was finally safe. Tim clenched his own hands into fists, then raised them beside his face. He looked at his daughter and hissed, *"Yess-sss."*

In February 2001, Tim paid dearly for abandoning his wife.

Finding himself seated in a courtroom on the opposite side of Tracey, he was being sued for divorce and legal custody of his daughter Payton. When the gavel fell, Tim heard the judge grant an uncontested divorce, then ordered him to pay child support for Payton. That wasn't a problem for Tim. He would gladly pay. Payton was his child and he believed it was his responsibility to help support her. But shortly after the court appearance, he fell ill, was diagnosed with a hernia, and then had to undergo surgery. He'd been a plumber all his life, and had missed very few days of work. But now his health problems had kept him out of work for over three months and he had fallen behind in his child support payments. He was hoping Tracey would understand his situation and be a little forgiving. He had said nothing in the courtroom about her abusing Sandy, and thought she would have taken that into consideration. No dice! Before it was over, Tracey's lawyer nailed his ass to the wall and left him hanging out to dry. The legal papers they served on Tim spelled it out in plain English: "No child support; no visitation rights."

Tim was broke, and Tracey knew that. She also knew that he couldn't afford a lawyer, and to avoid spending time in jail, he would be forced to sign an agreement freeing him of child support. The catch was that Tim would also give up all rights and privileges to see his daughter Payton. He had no other choice but sign. His heart was broken, but what else could he do?

Tim sat in his old bedroom at his mother's house. Smoking a cigarette and looking out the window into the dark of night, he suddenly remembered what his second wife, Mary, had said to him in their most difficult situation: *the love that burns the brightest flames sometimes leaves the deepest scars.* He was out of work, nearly bankrupt, and back home living with his mother again. His third marriage had just ended in divorce and he would probably never get to see his youngest daughter.

Just how much lower could a man fall than that?

Chapter 14

In 2001, when Beth Ozley met Tim Ketchum, she, too, was beginning to feel that love had passed her by. Beth grew up in Forest Park, Georgia, graduated from Forest Park High School in 1978, then enrolled in the city's School of Cosmetology. A year later, she graduated at the top of her class with honors and set out to find her place in the world of shampoos, perms, cuts, and curls.

Like Tim, Beth had been burned in the war of love too many times. At forty-two, she still longed for a man who would truly love her. If only at a subconscious level, she was waiting for her prince to come along and rescue her. Lord knows, she had kissed enough frogs in her life to think that it wasn't likely to happen, but she never gave up hope. Every night she wondered if this night might turn out to be her lucky night.

What Beth really wanted was a man to be faithful. Somebody, willing and able, to be by her side through both thick and thin. She wasn't asking for much, just a tender touch now and then, and just to be happy.

Beth loved to dance and had heard about some respectable dance clubs. Out on the dance floor, she could laugh, have a good time, and forget her troubles. There had been too many sad times in her life. Too many failed dreams. A young lady of moderate habits, she would occasionally have a drink or two at a club, but that was about it. She enjoyed the dancing and the flirting, looking at all the eye candy, but she always came home—and came home alone—at a reasonable hour.

On a sultry Saturday night in May, Beth was invited to accompany a friend to a dance at the VFW club. They had visited another club on a Friday night with the promise that Beth would go wherever her friend wanted to go on Saturday night. Her friend chose the VFW Club in Griffin.

"I'm not too happy about going there," Beth protested. And she kept saying she wasn't going, up until the very last minute. On the drive over to the club, she reiterated several times, "I'm telling you, I still don't want to go to no VFW club. There ain't nothing but a crowd of fifty-and-sixty-year-olds who go there. And who wants to go sit around and watch a bunch of old farts putting around the dance floor?"

Even though the crowd at the VFW wasn't her cup of tea, Beth finally relented. After she and her friend had been there for several hours, she grumbled she had seen nothing worth writing home to her mama about and nagged her friend about leaving. However, about an hour before closing time, she looked toward the bar and noticed this good-looking guy. He was tall, trim, and decked out in Western attire, standing by himself at the bar. He was dressed in black jeans, a black shirt, black boots, and a black cowboy hat. She sat there stunned for a moment and silently watched him as he leaned against the bar and finished a beer. Finally she got up from her seat and walked past him to get a better look. Pretending to go to the bathroom, she walked past him a second time and got another good look, then returned to her seat.

The smartest half of Beth's brain appreciated being single and treasured her independence. The other half of her brain still believed in fate and falling in love at first sight. When the band played a few boot-scooting-boogie songs, she kept her eyes pinned on the cowboy in black, hoping he was interested enough in her to invite her for a spin on the dance floor, but he didn't mosey over to her side of the room. Then the band played a slow song, a real tearjerker written by country legend George Jones, and before the first two bars were complete, he came over to where she was sitting. He sat down behind her as close as he could get and tugged on the back of her chair. Holding out his hand, he told her his name was Tim Ketchum, then whispered softly, "Come on, baby, let's dance."

As quick as a quarter falls in a jukebox, Beth and Tim were out on the dance floor. Just like the characters from *Urban Cowboy,* she, the hairdresser, and he, the cowboy, were dancing hand in hand. Bodies close together. Close enough to taste each other's mouthwash.

"George Jones is my favorite singer," Tim said, breaking the ice. "And this is one of my favorite songs."

Beth smiled and nodded. She kept her mind focused on not stepping on Tim's toes and coming off as a real klutz. She counted out the steps. *First the right foot in, then back, left foot in, then back. . . .* "I like your outfit," she shouted into his ear over the roar of the music, still trying to follow Tim's lead.

"Why, thank you." Tim smiled and tipped his hat. "This is what I call my Johnny Cash look." He paused and waited for a smile from Beth. He could tell she was attracted to him. Making light conversation, he confessed, "I saw you at the table with your girlfriend when I first came in. I waited until I had a few beers to get up enough courage before I came over and asked you to dance."

Beth blushed, then finally surrendered the smile he was looking for. "What did you do that for?" she said, pushing away and looking up into his face.

Tim had dreamy blue eyes, the kind a girl could easily get lost in.

And she did.

Beth and Tim danced the next dance and the next dance, then the dance after that one, and kept on dancing the rest of the night. In a short hour, they had gone from being face to face, then cheek to cheek, and, finally, body to body. After the club bartender announced his customary *last call for alcohol,* that the bar and the club would be closing for the night, Tim walked her to her table and waited for her to gather her things.

As Tim and Beth walked out of the VFW and into the parking lot, he slid his arm around her waist. He already liked her a lot, and in his mind's eye, he could see them one day waking up as lovers. They exchanged phone numbers before saying their good-byes and made promises like so many others had, that they would call again. Maybe it would be just to say hello, and they'd chat awhile on the phone. Maybe past midnight or more. Or if they were really set on each other, they'd go out to dinner or see a movie.

Beth wasn't sure what would happen next, but she was sure she wanted Tim Ketchum in her life.

Tim was a bit more optimistic. He joked that he was sure they would see each other again. He was as sure of that as he was that Wile E. Coyote would never catch the Road Runner, or that Paris Hilton would never go home alone.

When Tim got home, the first thing he did was raid the refrigerator. He didn't know what it was about drinking and dancing that always made him as hungry as a bear, but it did. He had just pulled some ham out of the refrigerator, and had slapped a few slices between two pieces of bread, when the phone rang. He thought, *Now who can that be at this time of the night?* Then he did what nearly everyone does when they receive a phone call after midnight, he froze, took a deep breath, then picked up the phone.

"Hello," he breathed into the phone, praying that a family member hadn't gotten into a serious wreck, been injured and was rushed to the nearby hospital. He breathed much easier when the caller identified herself. And he knew his luck was changing when he heard, "Hi, this is Beth. Remember me?"

Beth said she was calling to see if Tim had given her a real number. If it was his home number, then she wanted to see if there were any strings attached to it. It wasn't unlike a man to pass out a number and, when she called, some female would answer the phone. If that was the case with Tim, she wanted to know right now. "I just called you to see if you gave me the right number," she admitted.

"Well, looks like you found out I told the truth then," Tim countered. He took a bite from his sandwich and waited for her to respond.

"Yeah, I guess I did," she said, with an obvious glee in her voice. He had passed the first test. Now, on to the second part. "By the way, did you see what was on the back of the card I gave you?"

Tim finished chewing his bite of sandwich and swallowed. "No," he answered nonchalantly. "I got it in my wallet, but I haven't had a chance to look at it yet."

"Why don't you take it out and look at it." She said it clear enough so he knew it was a challenge and not a command. "Look at what is on the back."

"Okay," Tim said, pushing his sandwich to the middle of the table, "I'll do it." He stood up, removed his wallet, and then spread the contents out on the table. Turning Beth's card over in his hand, he saw her address written across the back. "It's got your address. What'd you put that on the back of the card for?"

"Duh!" Beth mimicked in her best "dumb blonde" voice. "I put it there so you could come see me whenever you wanted to." She was sure he would catch her drift. Finally he got it.

"Oh, so you would like to see me again?" Tim teased, even though he already knew the answer to that question.

It was late, and Beth wasn't interested in playing cat and mouse. She wanted him to know that was the whole idea of writing her address on the back of the card in the first place, and told him so.

Tim took the bait—hook, line and sinker. "Well, how about

right now?" he offered. "I'll come see you right now, if you don't mind."

Beth thought about it, then invited him to come and see her. Giving a shrug, she said honestly, "I got nothing else planned for the night."

Tim grabbed his hat and keys, then drove over to the address Beth had given him. On the drive over, Tim remembered her telling him before they left the club that she was single, lived by herself, and had never had any children. There was a chance, he surmised, that a relationship might be possible for them. He knew he was certainly interested in her and hoped the feelings were mutual.

Beth and Tim sat together in her living room that night, watched television and talked, until the sun came up over the horizon. She told him she had been married twice. The marriage with her first husband had lasted for six months. She guessed it was probably as much her fault as his, but recognized shortly after they were married that it wasn't true love, just "puppy love." Her first husband just wasn't the right one for her, she explained to Tim.

"There was just nothing between us," she said. "He just wasn't the right one for me and I wasn't the right one for him. Nothing personal, but it just didn't work out."

Beth fell in love shortly after her divorce. She lived with this guy for five years; then they married and lived together for another three years. She thought everything was okay in this relationship until her husband acquired the "Casanova syndrome" and started chasing anything that wasn't wearing pants.

From 1989 until 2001, Beth remained single, just about giving up on men and marriage, that is until she met Tim. She felt blessed that God had brought him into her life.

"I'm not hung up on fairy tales," she told Tim. "And I'm not standing around tossing pennies and waiting for some dream at the bottom of a wishing well to come true. A broken heart is a high price to pay, but I'm willing to take the chance on you. Men like you seldom come along twice."

Of course, Tim admitted to her up front that he was no different than she. He had fared no better in love. In fact, he had a lot worse luck in marriage than she had. "The first time, I married out of youthfulness and stupidity. She was a no-good mother and couldn't stop whoring around, so I eventually kicked her out," he confided. He told Beth that night all about his first, his second, and his third marriages.

"The second time I married, now that was for love. Mary was the love of my life, until she got sick and we had to divorce. The third time, I just got married for convenience, but damn if that wasn't a mistake. It ended up costing me nearly everything I had."

Tim laughed, taking another gulp from his beer.

All the while, Beth was beginning to believe it was fate that had brought her and Tim together. Her friends had always warned her to be cautious. She'd be the first to admit she knew nothing about Tim, but the more time she spent with him, the more she liked him. He was the dearest, sweetest, and most romantic man she'd ever known. All he seemed to be interested in was her happiness, and she'd never met anyone quite like that before. If she had sat down and written exactly what she was looking for in a man, her list would have described Tim to a tee.

Inwardly, Beth marveled at that. She had always been the woman who didn't easily trust men. Yet, here was a man who made it so easy to trust. She decided, then and there, she and Tim—through thick and thin—would be together forever.

Chapter 15

Just as Beth and Tim had vowed, they were inseparable after their first night together. Beth had a good job working as a hairdresser, but was living in a tiny one-room apartment in Griffin. Tim was growing stronger both emotionally and physically, and two weeks later, he asked if Sandy could come and live with them. Even though the apartment was over-crowded, Beth consented. She loved Tim and wanted to make him happy. She knew how much he wanted his daughter living with him.

Although Tim was happy living with Beth and Sandy in Griffin, he believed they all deserved a fresh start. He had grown up in Fayetteville and knew a lot of people there. He was physically able to go back to work and believed he could find a better paying job in Fayetteville. He was also familiar with the school system there, and believed it was far superior to the ones in Griffin. He planned on enrolling Sandy in the Fayetteville schools. She, too, would get her own fresh start in school. This time, he prayed, it would be a lasting one.

After talking it over with Sandy, the newly formed couple located a rental home and decided to move to Fayetteville. Sandy was enrolled in Fayetteville Middle School and seemed to be enjoying the change. She had just turned thirteen and was at a very impressionable age. Unfortunately, she started hanging around with the wrong crowd; a few weeks later, she and her friends got heavily involved in drugs and they started skipping classes.

While Tim worked late hours at his new plumbing job, Beth worked a job and helped out with Sandy. But the experience was very trying, as she never knew from one day to the next whether Sandy was at school or not. Just as soon as she dropped Sandy off at the front door, she would sneak out the back door with some classmate. Although she was making the honor roll without cracking a book, her problems quickly escalated from minor mischievous offenses to more serious ones. In a two-month span, she had gotten caught with a bottle of amphetamines and suspended on three separate occasions for drug use.

"How's Sandy's behavior at home?" the school's vice-principal inquired during a special parent's conference.

"As inconsistent as her attendance at school," Beth Ketchum responded. "Some days she's fine, but on other days, she is as ornery and cantankerous as a rattlesnake."

The vice-principal arched his eyebrows. "In my opinion, your daughter has a serious drug problem and I am going to recommend that she be admitted to a drug rehabilitation center in nearby Macon."

Based on the school's recommendation, Sandy was admitted to the rehab center in Macon, but escaped and ran away the very next day. After a brief court hearing, the rebellious teenager was remanded to a juvenile detention center for a full year. At great expense of money and time, Tim and Beth visited Sandy every weekend. They had already informed her the day she was released, they would be packing up and moving away from Fayetteville.

It seemed like every time Sandy met up with the Fayetteville girls around the corner from the school, right away there were changes in her life. Part of her problems, they knew, was a teenager's natural hunger for personal style. They didn't mind so much her supershort haircut and dressing differently. Over-sized shirts and the hip-hop–styled, low-cut jeans were customary outfits for cool girls who hung out in Fayetteville. Nor did they mind the teenage posse with their heads turned upward in the clouds, thinking they had to answer to no one.

But Sandy was definitely bothered by something, and that something had caused her to rebel against school, her parents, and to take drugs 24/7. Most of the time, she walked around like a zombie. And the more drugs she took, the more rebellious and less ambitious she became. It was scary.

"We're going to move from Fayetteville when you get home," Beth dropped the bomb on Sandy the week before she was released from the detention center.

"Mo-o-ving?" Sandy asked, searching for words. "Moving to where?"

"We're moving to Newnan, about sixty miles from here," Beth informed her. "Your father has already got a job and we've rented a house."

"Oh, no, you can't do that to me," Sandy cried. "What about my friends?"

"So what about your friends, Sandy?" Tim said sarcastically.

"Well, what will I do without them?"

"I'm sure you will think of something," Tim deadpanned. "Besides, it's your friends who got you into this mess in the first place. And it's not like Newnan is halfway around the world."

Sandy was more than a little skeptical about her father's sudden plans for moving. He was working on his fourth marriage—said he had finally found the girl of his dreams—but she wanted her father's attention, too, and was not getting much of it lately. She wondered if he was going to guarantee this relationship wouldn't end up in the toilet, just like the others? Was he going to wake up one night and discover he had married Frankenstein's bride all over again?

What was he going to do when wife number four started hitting her?

Later that evening, while Beth was busy putting away the dishes and clearing the supper table, Tim looked out the front window and saw Sandy, sitting on the porch steps, alone. He walked outside, lit up a Doral cigarette, and sat down beside her on the steps.

"Pretty night, huh?" he said in a low voice.

Sandy turned her head slightly, pretending to be more interested in the stars than chitchatting with her father.

Tim took a long draw off his cigarette and blew a steady stream of smoke out in front of him, before trying again. "You know, our moving has got nothing to do with Beth. I know this don't make you feel any better, but we're doing this all for you."

She gave him one of her "Yeah, right" looks, then turned her head away again.

"Look, Sandy, I got my education in the school of hard knocks, and I want you to know it ain't easy out there. Ever since I been married, I been crawling under houses and fixing people's plumbing and shit, so my family will have something to eat, a bed to sleep in, and a roof over their head. It ain't easy having to work like a damn dog all your life and see yourself getting nowhere. I've made a lot of mistakes in my life, but one of the biggest was not getting enough education so I wouldn't have to work like that. The reason we're moving is so you will get away from these temptations you're facing and get you a good education. I don't want you to be like me and make the same mistakes I made."

Sandy dropped her head and waited for her father to finish. She bit on her bottom lip, waiting until the courage was there.

Tim stressed he and Sandy were blood. He knew that sounded corny, but it was true.

"Like anybody who has kids," he preached, "they want to see their young uns have it better than they did. Hell, you can become anything you want to be: a doctor, a lawyer, a teacher, a nurse. But you gotta stay in school to get there."

"But, Daddy, you don't understand," Sandy finally spoke up. "I don't care about all those things. I just want to be happy. I just want to be with my friends."

Tim slipped his arm around Sandy's shoulders and gave her a squeeze. "I know how much they mean to you, but you can't put them over your education. You gotta stop all this partying and start thinking about your future. I know I like to party sometimes, but did you ever stop to think that if I missed as many days on my job as you do in school, they would fire me? Then, where would we be?" Tim asked, and then answered his own question, "I'll tell you where we'd be. Flat broke! On the streets starving and sleeping in a cardboard box. That's where we'd be."

Sandy nodded. He was right, after all, and she knew that. But that still didn't change the fact that she hated school. She wanted to tell him the real reason why she didn't want to leave Fayetteville. She considered telling him about Holly, that she loved Holly in a special way, which he might not understand, but, at the last moment, she decided not to. Instead, she moved in another direction.

"Daddy, when you were going to school, did any of the kids ever pick on you?" She wanted to ask him this question while he was relaxed and his recollections were still relatively fresh.

Tim threw his head back and belted out a gut buster. "Oh, shit, yeah," he laughed, then took a quick draw on his cigarette. "I don't think I ever told you this, but the bigger kids at school . . . well, they used to beat me up all the time. They'd seek me out and find me on the playground or walking home after school; then the chase would begin. Mostly, me running and them chasing after me, shouting, 'There's Tim "Ketchup," let's go get him.' And then they'd shout as I ran like a frightened rabbit, 'You come back here, Ketchup.' I guess they called me that because of my red hair and my last name being Ketchum."

Sandy shot her father a sad, but amused, look. She'd gladly settle for something as simple as being called Ketchup any day. *It's a lot better than me being called "Lesbo," "Dyke," "Muff Diver," or "Rug Muncher,"* she wanted to say, but didn't. She chose, instead, "So what did you do when they caught you?"

"Well, I'd run like hell. They'd be nipping at my heels, closing in behind me like a pack of wild dogs, until, finally, I'd outrun them or they'd give up."

"And did they ever catch you?" Sandy asked with a whimsical grin.

"Oh, yeah, a few times. There was always an older and stronger kid in the bunch. He could run faster than me and he'd usually catch me, grab me by the shirt collar and hold me down on the ground."

"And what would they do then?" Sandy asked, although she was certain she already knew the answer.

What happened next? Tim mused. *Oh, boy, who could resist telling that?* "Well, they'd beat the hell out of me. That's what they'd do!"

Before Tim could finish, Sandy asked, "Didn't it ever stop?"

"Eventually. They beat on me until finally they got tired of me and started picking on someone else. But as I got older, I vowed I wouldn't let them beat on me or anybody else, for that matter. No, sir! They weren't going to use me as their whipping boy any longer. I learned to fight back."

Sandy gave her father a nonplussed look. "Fight back? How?"

Tim licked his lips. He leaned into Sandy, like he was a pirate telling her where a secret treasure had been buried, then said just above a whisper, "I learned that a baseball bat and a nice home run swing into the rib cage kind of makes us all the same size."

Tim's confession hung in the air between him and his daughter like a pair of dirty underwear on a clothesline.

"God, I can't believe you did that. You've always been so passive." Sandy sounded shocked. She tapped him lightly on the arm.

Tim shook his head slowly. He knew it was probably stupid advice he was giving his daughter, but he thought she would appreciate his honesty. "Well, when a person decides he or she has had enough, then they have had enough, right?" He turned to Sandy and kissed her on the forehead. "Am I right?"

"Yep, you're right, Daddy."

After Tim and Sandy's conversation drifted into the weather and small talk, Sandy stood up, kissed her father again, and went back inside. Tim lit up another cigarette and waited for Beth to join him. In a few minutes, she walked outside with an unlit cigarette in her hand and took the empty seat on the step.

"Did you talk to Sandy?" Beth asked as she reached across Tim for her cigarette lighter.

Tim waited for Beth to light her Ultra Light 100s. "Yeah, I talked with her, but I don't know if I got through or not."

"Then I don't know what else we can do," she said angrily. "She's blown nearly all her chances, here, in this town. Newnan High School is probably her last chance to stay in school. If she don't make it there, I guess she'll just have to stay in juvenile jail until she's eighteen."

"I don't know why she hates school," Tim mumbled. "It's not always been like that. She used to love school and couldn't wait to get there. I guess it's my fault somewhere down the line. With all the problems we've had, somehow I let her get off course."

Beth leaned into her husband and rested her head against his shoulder. "You can't take all the blame," she consoled. "Under the circumstances, you did the best you could with what you had. Sandy's never had a mother who gave a damn about her, that's all."

As Tim and Beth discussed Sandy's situation, they were not so naive to think that they, or anyone else, were perfect parents. All parents make irrational decisions that end up making their children worse. It's just a fact of life. But what they didn't understand was now that Sandy was with the two people who loved her the most, why did she *still* have so many psychological problems? Why did she show so little interest in school? Why all of a sudden was she doing drugs, and why had she become so rebellious toward authority figures?

The Ketchums knew that Sandy had the answers to all those questions, but, for reasons known only to her, that information had been locked so far away that even Houdini would have had trouble picking the lock.

Chapter 16

Sandy Ketchum was an attractive girl when she desired to be—which was not very often. Almost routinely, she'd camouflage her breasts underneath an undershirt and cover it with a bulky man's shirt, then further redesign her shapely figure with a pair of baggy pants. She wore little to no makeup, and kept her hair cut short and pulled back tight on her head under multicolored bandanas. Because she had little affinity for the sun, her skin had a pale, ghostly look.

One spring day in 2004, Sandy lumbered out the front door, crossed the lawn, and walked toward the car, where Beth was anxiously waiting. As she opened the door, Beth greeted her with a cheery "How are you feeling this morning?" Holding her breath and trying to gauge the mood, Beth waited until Sandy was seated and in the car for a response.

Silence.

Sandy's energy died in the seat as quickly as the last stir of autumn leaves.

Beth studied Sandy's face. She looked tired and drawn, as if she hadn't slept enough the night before. Sandy had been complaining for a year that she had trouble sleeping, and the Risperdal was not helping, so finally Beth told her if it made her feel that bad, then she should stop taking it. Now as she observed Sandy slumping in the front seat like a wet noodle, she began thinking maybe that hadn't been the right decision. Maybe she did need to call the doctor again.

"Sandy, why don't we make an appointment at the mental-health center," she suggested. "Let's ask them about your medication?"

Sandy rolled her eyes, then offered with a barb of sarcasm, "Please, I'm okay. You don't need to call anybody. A few more minutes of sleep and I would have been fine, that's all."

Beth shook her head in disgust.

Teenagers are so thoughtless sometimes.

Because the Ketchums had only one vehicle, Beth had to get up at 5:30 every morning and drive Tim to work, then come back home and get Sandy up and ready for school. After driving her to school, Beth came home a third time, then showered and dressed, before rushing out to her own job.

Come on, give me a break here, Sandy. I'm busting my ass enough as it is.

Slowly Beth's disgust gave way to anger, until she blurted out, "Look, Sandy, you're obviously not happy with our arrangement here. And I know it's a hassle, getting up so early, but I have to do the same thing. Maybe you might consider riding the bus again. If you'd ride the bus like everybody else, then it would be a lot easier on me, your dad, and—"

"No, I can't stand riding that bus," Sandy said, cutting Beth off in midsentence. "You know how all the kids laugh at me and make fun of me."

Beth bit down on her lower lip. This subject had always been a sore spot with Sandy. Carefully wading in, she suggested, "Well, have you ever considered it might be because of the way you dress?" She sighed, then tossed out, "I'm trying to help here, when I say instead of wearing those old baggy clothes, why don't you wear some tight jeans and a little girl's top. That would help change your appearance tremendously."

Sandy gave her a look of shock, normally reserved for

people who walk out of mad doctor's labs with two bolts protruding from their necks. "What are you trying to say?" she mumbled, her bottom lip already beginning to quiver. "That I dress like a bum or something?"

"No, no, no . . . I'm sorry you thought that was what I meant," Beth recovered, watching the blood drain from Sandy's face. "Your father and I love you. We're just trying to help you out, that's all. When you say people make fun of you and you don't fit in, then I just made some suggestions that I thought would help. Nothing more, nothing less."

Sandy turned away from Beth and stared out the car window. Over the years, she had learned to hear what people were saying, yet not listen to what they were saying. She guessed it was her way of coping, when she didn't like how things were going in her life. Her thoughts drifted and she tuned Beth out like a station on a radio.

Nothing ever changes with you people, Sandy had wanted to say to Beth. *Sure, it's all what's best for me and my interest. Yeah, you expect me to believe all that bullshit? That's what you all say. That was what my mother said when she left me. That's what Tracey said when she punched me around like a punching bag. And, now, it won't be long before it happens again. God, is there anybody in this world I can trust?*

Sandy had wanted to say all that, but knew she best not tread into forbidden territory.

Beth was never one to mince words. She figured that was why she and Sandy had gotten along as well as they had.

"Then I guess your daddy told you last night how important your staying in school is to our family," Beth reiterated as she weaved in and out of traffic. "We've got to get you started off on the right foot this time. It's important that you be in school and on time. Honestly, this is your last chance. You either got to shape up or they're going to ship your ass out, right back to juvenile hall."

Sandy felt her head beginning to pound. *God, a hit off a*

*joint sure would be nice—a kinda pick-me-up, you know. It
would sure help me relax.* She slid downward and rested her
head against the back of the seat.

Beth took a deep breath, then let it slip out between her teeth.
She knew Sandy silently blamed her for all her problems. That
was normal for teenagers, as they were always looking for
someone to blame. Looking for someone to push the responsibility off on. Looking to turn away from those who truly loved
and cared for them.

You wicked, wicked stepmother! That's what Beth thought
Sandy was probably saying behind her back. But she had no
goddamn right. Beth loved Sandy as much as any mother loved
her child. She had devoted the last two years of her life to her.
Beth wanted nothing but happiness for Sandy, and she consis-
tently dared to say no to her for her own good. Why would
Sandy now see her as some kind of "Wicked Witch of the
West" for doing so?

Beth was growing weary of her stepdaughter's ingratitude
and was impatient with her defiant behavior. She had seen it
with other children Sandy's age. All of a sudden when they
hit those teenage years, they started thinking and behaving
like the world owed them a goddamned living. Well, if Sandy
didn't straighten up and fly right, she'd find out soon enough
that the world didn't owe her a living, and the only people she
could ever count on was Beth and Tim.

Although Beth loved her stepdaughter, she could see that
Sandy's problems were exacerbating an already intense situation at home. She and Tim couldn't keep moving every time
Sandy got involved in drugs and started skipping school and
hanging out with the wrong crowd. She had some real problems she was dealing with, but Beth was no psychiatrist and
had done all she could do. She was at a loss of how to help her.

"It's one of these 'I hope she'll grow out of it,'" she later confided to Tim. "But if we don't do something, and quick, I can
see Sandy's problems leading to bigger ones down the road."

"Well, I'll try and talk with her again," Tim assured her, "but she just keeps saying nothing is wrong."

"That's the same damn thing she does when I take her to see her therapist," Beth explained. "She curls up in a corner and refuses to answer her when she asks her questions."

"What the hell does she do that for?" Tim asked.

"I don't know. The therapist says Sandy may feel like she has been rejected, now that I am with you."

Tim had a betrayed look on his face. "What do you mean, 'She feels like she has been rejected'?"

Beth couldn't answer that question. Her own life hadn't been a bed of roses, either, and she believed the term "rejection" meant different things to different people. Beth's father had abandoned her mother, who was a nursing student and six months pregnant with her at the time. Beth never saw her father again until after she was grown and married. All the time prior, she lived with her grandparents in a small town outside of Albany, Georgia, until she was four. When her mother married again, she and her older sister were carted off from Albany and moved to Atlanta. Beth knew what it meant to be rejected as a child, but she had learned to love and appreciate her stepfather. She didn't understand why Sandy couldn't do the same with her.

You just have to learn to get over it. Put it all behind you and move forward.

When Tim didn't understand, Beth tried to explain.

"She's got this feeling," Beth began. "I think I know why, and, for a lot of reasons, she's angry at the world."

"Well, I can understand she's angry at her mother and her stepmothers, but what's she mad at you for?" Tim asked, with a quizzical look. "You treat her like she's your own kid. In fact, you treat her better than her own mother has ever treated her."

"Yeah, I know. I can't understand it, either," Sandy said in frustration. "I guess she's been angry for a long time and it is just now catching up with her."

* * *

Sandy lay as limp as a dishrag in the front seat of Beth's car. Her head was tilted backward, resting against the car seat, and her eyes were closed. Suddenly she began to hear music in her head, the rhythms and beats of a song that she was vaguely familiar with. She groaned a little, then slipped back into her own little world.

In her mind's eye, Sandy saw a sixteen-year-old girl sitting in her classroom at school. The girl was surrounded by other pupils, and they watched as she rolled up her shirtsleeves. First the right one; then the left one.

The girl then took a pencil sharpener out of her book bag and removed the blade out of the pencil sharpener. Her wide-eyed classmates stared in horror as she steadied the blade in her right hand, between her thumb and forefinger, then drew it across her left wrist.

Gouging it back and forth, the girl continued until the blood started to flow. The girl stopped and cradled her injured arm, like it was a newborn. Slowly, as if her life supply was running on empty and was having a hard time resurfacing, her blood began to trickle from her open wound.

It oozed out of the cut the girl had made, then fell across her wrist until it filled up her palm, before finally dripping off her fingertips. In a calm—but persistent—manner, the girl, whose eyes looked washed over by now, did it again and again until . . . .

"Sandy, Sandy." Beth grabbed her stepdaughter's elbow and shook her hard. She felt Sandy's body grow tense. "Wake up."

Sandy raised up in her seat, then craned her neck and peered out over the dashboard. "What?" she said, wiping her mouth with the back of her hand and swallowing at the same time. "What is it? What's wrong?"

Beth calmed her. "Nothing's wrong. You have been dreaming again. Are you okay?"

"Yeah, I'm okay," Sandy offered without further elaboration. "Just a little sleepy, that's all." She let her head drop against the door and felt the cool of the glass window. It felt good, pressed against her feverish brow. She saw a School Crossing sign up ahead and realized they were only minutes away from the drop-off point at her new school.

Below the tumble of her chaotic thoughts, below the beat of her hammering heart, she could hear the soft sound of her own voice.

Oh, shit, I hate school. This is such a waste of time. It's stupid and boring. I'd rather be spending my time sleeping, watching television, listening to my stereo, or hanging out with my friends. Anytime, anyplace, anywhere . . . but school.

Chapter 17

Sandy was surprised to see the halls were abuzz at Newnan High School and wanted to know what all the fuss was about. By the end of the day, she had pieced together from hearing other kids talk that a portion of the Georgia interstate highway was being named in honor of some singer by the name of Alan Jackson. Jackson had supposedly graduated from Newnan High and he and his band were traveling from Nashville to perform a charity concert in the school gym at the end of the month.

"Jackson? Alan Jackson?" a girl wearing thick glasses sitting next to Sandy in study hall asked. "Is he by any chance related to Michael Jackson?"

Sandy gave the girl a "what planet did you just come from" look, rolled her eyes, then asked, "Don't you know who Alan Jackson is?"

When the girl admitted she didn't have the foggiest idea who he was, another of Sandy's classmates informed her that Jackson was one of America's biggest country singers and superstars.

"He was born right here in this county, Coweta County. My father told me that his father worked as a maintenance supervisor in the county for a long time. Alan not only attended and graduated from Newnan High School, but most of his family still lives here."

The girl said Alan Jackson's name like he lived two doors down from her.

"Didn't you read about it in all the papers or see it on TV?" she said, all dreamy-eyed and disbelieving. "He and his band are coming to our school."

The bespectacled girl shrugged. "No, I don't read the papers much or watch a lot of television. But I still wouldn't have known who he was." She paused and opened her English book. Pretending she was reading from her book, she causally dismissed the girl sitting beside her. "And I'm not a country music fan," she said in a low voice. "I'm more into rap and hip-hop."

Sandy nodded, then looked back at the girl. "Cool," she added, as if it were a footnote in their English book.

The study hall teacher, looking stern and condescending, got up from her seat and walked toward Sandy. She nodded in her direction, then announced, "Need I remind you two girls that you're supposed to be studying and not talking."

Sandy leaned forward and pressed her face into her English book. She maintained that posture until the teacher turned around and returned to her desk. When she picked up her pencil and started working in a large spiral notebook, Sandy closed her book, folded her arms, then rested her head on top of her arms. Still feeling a little sleepy, she closed her eyes and tried to catch a few z's.

As Sandy thought about her first day at Newnan High, she had already decided her stay here would, no doubt, be short-lived. Sooner or later, she could see herself bumping heads with somebody. It would probably be when one of her teachers started telling her what to do. Her problem had always been with authority. She didn't like the thought of people having the audacity to think they had power over her. She wanted to stand alone. Right now they were all nice to her because she was the new kid, but that would all change in a day or two. Things were the same in every school. Her teacher would tell her to do some kind of bullshit work they had assigned. Sandy didn't want to work, she wanted to socialize, so she'd end up refusing. An argument would ensue, she'd get pissed and tell the teacher to shove it, and then it's off to the principal's office with a pink slip. The principal would deliver a nice, long lecture on how important education was to her future, then issue a three-day in-school suspension for insubordination.

Sandy had read in *Seventeen* that some university had done a study and their research showed it was the most creative kids who were the most apt to drop out of school. She remembered that same research also showed that the longer young people stay in school, the less creative they tend to be.

"Every child is born with different thinking patterns, or learning-style strengths," the article in the magazine had concluded. Sandy had clipped this part and even showed it to her father, underlining in red the sentences she wanted him to read. It included: "Our learning style is the way our brain perceives and processes information. In other words, it's the way we see our world."

Maybe that is why I hate school so much? Sandy had thought after reading the article. It wasn't that the schoolwork was too hard or that she didn't feel as smart as the other kids. It was just the opposite. For some of the kids she knew, just the act of reading their textbooks was difficult for them—and at this level, they were expected to do a lot of it. She knew plenty of students who had gotten further and further behind, and it seemed like they would never catch up, but not her.

The way Sandy saw it, it was the same thing year after year. Maybe if school had been something other than going to class all day, sitting in cramped desks, and listening to teachers yap-yap-yap about stupid and boring subjects, then she would have enjoyed learning. But spending her youth memorizing useless, out-of-date information wasn't her idea of fun.

Because of all Sandy was going through at home, she guessed she had lost interest in school sometime during the sixth grade. That was when she started skipping school a lot and got heavily involved in the drug scene. She didn't remember everything about grade school, but she did remember she was depressed and in a stupor from the fourth grade until the seventh grade.

"My doing drugs wasn't just something to do," Sandy would recall later. "I had a purpose. . . . I did drugs to escape the reality that I found myself living in. I did drugs to escape the vivid pain and emotional roller coasters, only to find myself facing reality again. So I continued using drugs and never intended to stop. Drugs were my comfort zone. My world away from home."

In spite of her drug use, Sandy stayed in school. There were some classes she enjoyed. She had always enjoyed drawing and art classes, and preferred writing poetry or writing in a journal or a diary. Self-expression was one of the ways Sandy had hoped would help her recover from drugs and stop injuring herself. Her therapist had told her the physical act of creating art was also cathartic and could release some of her tension, allowing for her feelings to surface and explode from her body, rather than coming out in blood. And that writing was a good release for someone like Sandy who lived in a world with very few outlets for expression of emotions, and for which most people have little understanding or patience. She was encouraged to take up the pen; then she could express and explore her feelings as often as she liked.

Although the schools Sandy attended did very little of the creative arts, she had found expressing the feelings in a literary manner was a great way to let out the emotions stuck inside her. It helped her sort things out.

As she sorted her life out, Sandy had come to the foregone conclusion that she lived in a different world; she was and would always be different than other girls her age. She had accepted the fact—and wished everyone else could—that she had never been interested in wearing dainty little tops and tight-fitting jeans. For her, it was big, baggy pants and oversized shirts. It didn't matter how other people saw her. If they thought she was a tomboy for dressing like that, then so be it. She just felt more comfortable in clothes she preferred to wear.

Once, when she was about ten, Sandy's father realized he'd be wasting his money on tap and ballet lessons and had tried to get her interested in sports. He had participated in sports when he was a child and knew the value of it, and was hoping that would help Sandy build her self-image. But she told him she wasn't interested in athletics, that all she really wanted to do was write poetry, listen to music, and hang out with her friends.

Earlier in her years, Sandy had shown an interest in boys, even dating and attending a military ball with one of her friends. But, as she got older, she could see she was not interested in guys, she was interested in girls. She was gay and didn't think it was weird to prefer girls over boys.

Sandy sat in study hall, half-asleep at her desk, thinking, looking bored, and waiting for that last bell to ring.

What am I doing here? she kept asking herself. *I'm never going to fit in.* And as if there truly were another person inside her head, echoing those same thoughts, she would hear a voice saying: "Yeah, *what are you trying to prove? Don't you know you'll never amount to anything? Didn't they tell you that you'd only end up just like your mother? Nothing but trash, that's what you are. White trailer-trash.*

Sandy had been told that so many times that she accepted it as fact. But it still hurt, especially when her parents said things like that to her. She'd get upset. Her chest would start to hurt and she'd get a terrible headache.

"Okay, students, let's get a move on," the short, rotund study hall teacher shouted at the sound of the bell. "Let's have no talking or shoving one another as we leave the room, please."

Sandy made her way out the door and into the hall. She

stopped by her locker near the chemistry lab, fought with the combination until the door opened, then tossed in her books. Walking down the hall, she thought about Holly and wondered if she'd be interested in coming to see her at the end of the month. They could have a housewarming party. At least it would be something to do and give them an excuse to get together.

Later that evening, when Sandy called Holly, she immediately sensed something was terribly wrong. Holly was crying and begging for Sandy to come see her. Sandy couldn't say for sure, but believed someone in her family had died.

"Oh, God," Holly cried out over the phone. "I don't know what I'm gonna do. I don't think I can handle this."

Sandy pressed the phone harder against her right ear and sat down on the bed. Holly was such a drama queen.

"Calm down, Holly," she said, bracing herself for the news. "Just tell me what has happened. Is it one of our friends? Did someone get killed, raped, or something?"

"It's my mama." Holly choked back her tears, then related, "She's going to prison. I don't know what I am gonna do. If she goes to prison, then I've got no place to live."

In April 2003, Carla Harvey had been busted for selling marijuana to an undercover cop. Since then, Carla had been housed at the county jail and was looking at a three-year stretch in the federal penitentiary. It took nearly a year for Carla's case to come to trial, and when it did, she had no choice but to plead guilty. This was not the first time Carla had been in trouble with the law, and she knew she was in for some jail time. The judge didn't disappoint her, sentencing her to those three years in jail.

"So what are you gonna do?" Sandy asked, already thinking maybe she could talk Tim and Beth into letting Holly move in with them. "I mean, who are you going to live with while she is in jail?"

"My mama has been talking with one of my friends from school and has asked her if I could stay with her. Her mom is pretty cool and I think I'd enjoy living there."

"Well, what about your grandparents? Have you thought about living there? I mean, after all, they are your grandparents. Why wouldn't they want to take you in?"

"Hell no," Holly said sharply. "I wouldn't want to stay there. My grandfather is fine. He and I get along great, but it is my grandmother that I would be worried about. We've already had a couple of knock-down-drag-outs with her already."

"What does she do that is so bad?"

Holly exploded into the phone.

"Bitch, bitch, bitch," she shot back. "Me and my mom tried living with her, but it didn't work out. They got in a fight one time and she called the cops on my mom."

"She actually called the cops on your mom?"

"Yeah, can you believe it?" Holly said with great disdain. "We had stayed with our grandmother one night and Mom came to pick us up. She got there a little late and Grandma said she wasn't going to wake us up. 'Oh, yes, you will,' Mama said, then went to get us up. It was then she and Grandma got into a fight."

"And the cops came and arrested your mom?"

"Yep, they put her in cuffs and everything, while we were standing there watching. Ain't that some kind of shit?"

"You damn straight," Sandy added with disgust. She paused, let Holly rattle a bit longer, before asking, "So, your mom got busted for selling marijuana?"

"Oh, hell no," Holly said. "That's just what she was charged with at first. The real story is that she and her boyfriend . . . you know the black guy she has been dating?"

"Yeah, I know who you're talking about," Sandy interjected.

"Well, it was actually his stuff," Holly continued. "Mama figures they had been watching her and this guy for a long time. Some undercover cop must have seen them smoking grass in the car and decided to pull them over. Mama says what the cop didn't know was that they had a bigger bag of marijuana in the trunk, and if they had known that, then she would have been in some real deep shit. They could have got her and her boyfriend for distribution of drugs, which carries about a ten-to-fifteen-year sentence."

"Your mom would have really been up shit creek then, huh?"

"You better believe it," Holly affirmed. "She also had her gun with her under the seat, and if the cop would've known that, he would have busted her for carrying a weapon without a permit as well. So, she thought the best thing to do was admit she had been smoking grass and hope they'd buy that charge."

Sandy always admired Holly's mother. Carla Harvey knew the law and she always had worked the police and the court systems like a finely tuned motor. Holly had told Sandy about some recent outlaw excursions, where she and her mom had fled the state of Georgia and lived like outlaws to avoid her mother being prosecuted.

"Why couldn't you stay with your father, Holly? What's his name, Gene?"

"Oh, he's worthless," Holly spit into the phone. "Did I ever tell you what he did to my mama?"

"I don't think so," Sandy said. "But if you did, tell me again."

"You remember when I told you he owed my mama all this money for back child support and she took him to court?"

"Yes." Sandy had remembered Holly telling her about that.

"He owed me about six thousand dollars in child support and Mama had sued him. But he claimed he wasn't making any money, that he was only drawing disability and couldn't afford to pay any child support. The stupid judge then believed him and said he only had to pay ten dollars a month. Can you believe that shit?"

"You have got to be kidding me? They let him off and all he pays is ten dollars a month?"

"If I am lying, then I'm dying," Holly said sarcastically. "And what made me so mad is that Mama said she was going to give me that money when she got it. I was looking forward to getting that money and maybe getting a car or something, but he cheated me out of it."

"That's awful that your father would do something to you like that." Hoping to cheer her up, she suggested, "When your mother goes to prison, Holly, maybe you can come live with me."

"Wow, you really think your dad and stepmom wouldn't mind me living with you for a while?"

"Oh, I don't think it would be a problem. You could even enroll in the same school I'm attending and we could go to class together."

"That would be great, Sandy. You know I would like nothing better than to be with you all the time."

"Yeah, that would be kind of neat," Sandy mulled over. "Living together and everything. And you'd like my school. The people are really nice and it's a cool place to be."

"Well, that would certainly be a change from my school, where I am going now. I just found out this week that I've already missed too many days of school and they're going to force me to repeat the ninth grade. Isn't that a bummer?"

Sandy agreed. "God, yes, I know you're going to hate that."

"It really sucks, Sandy, being stuck in the ninth grade for another year."

Happy she could give Holly something to look forward to, Sandy issued her an invitation to come and visit her.

HOLLY HARVEY

Chapter 18

Carl Collier wore the same honest face in 2004 as when he grew up the youngest of seven children in the small, rural northern Georgia town of Cartersville. It was Carl's honest face that finally convinced Sarah Jenkins, a pretty high-school basketball player and almost two years his junior, to go out with him. He was a handsome and rugged cheerleader and quite a catch for any girl in his high school. Their roles quickly defined their relationship, as Carl took a backseat to Sarah's activities and cheered her on from the sidelines. A steady relationship followed, and after Sarah graduated from high school, the amiable couple married.

Not long after Carl and Sarah wed, he decided it was a good idea to join the U.S. Army. Fortunately, his entire tour of duty was served stateside and not overseas. After Carl's discharge from the army, he landed a good job at a Ford automobile assembly plant in Atlanta, then one with the U.S. Army Corps of Engineers. But in 1955, during the advent of jet travel, and when Delta was undergoing phenomenal growth, he applied for and was hired in material services at the power plant. Carl was ambitious and a hard worker, and he eventually earned his college degree at night. When the position of supervisor of Delta's material planning became available, Carl applied for the job and was hired. He was in charge of a department that made sure the engine shop kept in stock and had all the necessary parts to overhaul the jet engines. He would work for Delta for thirty-six years, a position that paid handsomely, until his retirement in 1991.

With a good income and a desire to start a family, Carl and Sarah talked about having children. Because Sarah could not have children of her own, they adopted two children: a boy they named Kevin, in 1965, and a girl they named Carla, in 1967. Atlanta was not always the most convenient city in which to raise children, so the Colliers bought a home in Fayetteville and moved south of the Hartfield-Jackson Atlanta International Airport. Work was only twenty minutes away from Fayetteville, an ideal setting to rear a family. It was a solid middle-class neighborhood filled with hardworking, church-going Delta employees, like Carl.

The Colliers were very active in their community and their church, and very well-respected. Both Carl and Sarah attended Fayetteville Baptist Church and volunteered as county poll workers during elections. They had lots of friends and acquaintances. Carl had been elected to the Fayette County Board of Education and served admirably from 1973 to 1978. To everyone who knew them, they appeared to be the model parents who lived for their children. Sarah knew that kids appreciated honesty and candidness, so she and Carl never kept it a secret from their children that they were adopted. Supposedly, there was never an issue, until their daughter became a teenager.

In 1988, fifteen-year-old Carla Jean dropped out of school in the tenth grade and ran off with her boyfriend, Gene Harvey. Gene was ten years older than Carla, and introduced his young lover to a coast-to-coast gypsy jaunt that eventually led them from Atlanta to California. Before they left on their excursion, Gene had rifled through Kevin Collier's room and stolen his Social Security number. Because Gene and Kevin had similar physical characteristics, Gene believed he could get away with using Kevin's ID. During a long road trip to California, Gene was pulled over by a highway patrolman. Gene told the officer that he was "Kevin Collier" and had forgotten he was not in possession of his driver's license. When the officer called the license into headquarters, he suspected something was awry and arrested Gene on the spot. For "impersonating another," Gene was convicted and sentenced to a year in prison.

At the time, Kevin was attending the University of Georgia, and knew all about the struggle his parents were having with his younger sister. The Colliers did not approve of their daughter's friends, and she had begun challenging their authority. On visits home from school, Kevin watched in horror as his parents got into knock-down-and-drag-out fights with Carla. Most of the problems they had with Carla centered around the crowd of people she was hanging out with at school.

After Gene Harvey was released from a short-term prison stay, Carla moved in with him in a house thirty miles south of Fayetteville. By this time, she had lost contact almost completely with her mother, and her parents had resigned themselves to the fact that she was not only out of their lives, but was out of their control.

On March 23, 1989, Carla gave birth to a baby girl that she and Gene named Holly. Gene was listed on the birth certificate as the father, and Carla told her parents and brother that they were married. Although she and Holly had assumed the name of Harvey, the Colliers found out later that Carla and Gene had never married.

"It wasn't just that incident with Gene," Carla Harvey recalled. "My mother always hated me. When I was about four or five, she made it a point to tell me I was adopted. My brother, Kevin, was adopted, too, and she told him the same thing, but it never affected him the way it did me. I was hurt, and in my own childish way, I asked, 'Why doesn't my mother want me? Why can't I see my mother?' But I was told by Sarah

Collier, 'You can't ever see your mother because she is a slut and a whore, that's why. She doesn't love you.'

"What could I do? Absolutely nothing! Now, can you imagine someone telling a child this? But my mother had me convinced she was the only one that wanted me and loved me. And nobody else would ever love me like that.

"But in high school, I found out different. I discovered there were people out there who really cared for me. My friends and their families liked me just as good as my adopted mother. So I started spending more time with them than I did at home. That caused a lot of friction at home because my mama wanted to control everything I did. She wanted to know everybody I hung out with and wanted to correct everything I did. It seemed as if she never wanted me to be happy and was jealous of every relationship I had, including the one with my adoptive father."

Carla's earliest memories of her adoptive mother, Sarah, were not good ones. She remembered how her mother could act nice at times, but then, at other times, she was cold and downright mean. It was as if she said things to deliberately hurt Carla, and then her voice would turn cold and Carla's whole world would cave in.

Carla also remembered her mother was jealous over the relationship she had with her father. She did not want Carla sitting on her father's lap, and for some reason, she treated Carla like a seductive temptress.

"She was always telling my daddy, when he got home, 'Carla's been bad today,' or 'Carla didn't do what I told her. She needs to be spanked,'" Carla recalled. "But I'd look up in my father's eyes and ask, 'Daddy, after talking with Mama, do you think I've been that bad? That I've been so bad I need to be spanked?'"

Carla said her daddy couldn't refuse his daughter.

"'I don't think so,' he would say to me with a kiss. 'Let's just forget about that spanking today.'"

Carla and her father were very close.

"My daddy and I did a lot together. We swam in the pool, played games together, and planted a garden together. We had a great relationship."

Carla's adopted brother, Kevin, seemed to fare much better than his younger sister. He remembered his parents as good a set of parents as anyone could have ever hoped for.

"They never kept it a secret that Carla and I were adopted," Kevin said. "And it was never an issue for me. They were always involved in what we did. They never stood in our way and always let us do whatever we needed to pursue our dreams."

Kevin and Carla, however, grew up very differently. While Kevin excelled in school and developed a great gift for music, Carla struggled in school, and although bright and gifted as well, she showed no inclination to further her musical talents other than the mandatory piano lessons.

"I always believed my parents were concerned and diligent parents," Kevin opined. "They always made it their business to find out about our friends, and even learn about our friends' parents. They believed a child's background and upbringing determined character, and they didn't want their children led astray to problem peers.

"Church was very important to my parents and they tried to instill these values onto me and Carla. We were regular attendees at the Fayetteville Baptist Church, where we attended Sunday school and sang in the youth choir."

When Kevin demonstrated a great love for music, the Colliers suggested they attend the First Baptist Church in Atlanta. Even though it was an hour's drive from their home, the church had an outstanding musical-education program and was recognized throughout the South for its full-ensemble orchestra. Kevin excelled in their brass section, and his parents traveled all over the country and abroad to hear their son play. During high school, he garnered all-state honors for his musical ability and was offered a full boat to the University of Georgia in Athens.

Carla's development, on the other hand, was a bit more difficult. Like the incoming and outgoing tides, she was content on going with the flow in an ocean of people who always seemed to get her in trouble. Carla chose a lifestyle and surrounded herself with friends that always put her in direct conflict with her parents.

"When I went off to college, things got worse between my parents and Carla," Kevin said. "She and I had a normal relationship, like any other brother and sister, I assumed. You know, like loving one another one moment, then hating each other the next. She came and stayed with me a couple of times at college, but I knew she and my parents were not getting along. They were fighting like cats and dogs over her choice of friends at school. I don't know why Carla says she couldn't get along with our mother, I never had a problem."

It took Carla most of her life to try and figure out why Kevin got along with her mother, but she couldn't.

"I think Mama never saw Kevin as a threat," she surmised. "But she sure as hell did with me. I just got tired of her harassing me all the time, and the first chance I got, I jumped ship with Gene.

"And, yeah, we got in a little trouble. Kevin says I gave Gene his Social Security, but I didn't do that. Gene did that on his own. When he came to visit me at the house, he must have gone through Kevin's things and found his Social Security number. That's the only way I know he got it."

Carla would admit she made a lot of mistakes in her misguided youth, but what puzzled her the most was that her mother continually threw it up in her face. It wasn't enough for Carla's mother to leave her in the dust, Carla believed. It was an obsession for her to humiliate her and leave her helpless.

After Gene was released from prison, he and Carla tried to make a go of it. Carla had talked about reconciling with her parents, and on one particular Mother's Day, she purchased two dozen yellow roses for her mother and she and Gene drove over to her house and delivered them.

Carla remembered the event like it was yesterday.

"We parked the car at the top of the driveway. I had said to Gene, I told him, 'Now you stay here and I'll walk down to the house and give them to her. If everything is okay, then I'll come back and get you.'

"When I got down to the house, I said to Mama, 'Look, I brought you a Mother's Day gift.' But that didn't seem to faze her. I figured Kevin had already been to the house, because I seen where he had given her a dog for Mother's Day. She showed me the dog, then said to me, 'Look at this dog, isn't that wonderful?'

"Of course, I felt like shit, and I said to her, 'Yeah, I see the dog, Mama.' But I was so mad, I couldn't hold my anger any longer. I just blurted out, 'Fuck it, I've given up trying to give you anything as wonderful as Kevin gives you. But I do know you like yellow roses and here they are,' then slung them at her.

"We got in a big argument, and before long, Mama chased me out of her house. She was throwing those roses at me and yelling, 'You're nothing but a big whore and a slut. You're going to end up just like your mama.'"

Carla said Sarah was so mad that she chased her out of the garage and up to the top of the driveway, where Gene was waiting in the parked car.

"I thought Gene was going to have a heart attack when he saw my mama running after me throwing those yellow roses. I did make it inside the car. We thought she would go back to the house, but she didn't. She then started beating on the car and yelling, 'You son of a bitch, you bastards, get out of my yard. I'm not your mother and I don't want to ever hear you call me that again.'"

Gene was surprised to see that Carla was so calm. He was shaking all over.

"I guess I'm used to it," Carla said, lighting up a cigarette after they drove away. "She's treated me like that all of my life."

Gene shook his head. "I just hope she don't ever get mad at me."

"Oh, don't worry," Carla said, as if not giving it any thought. "She'll get over it. The next time she sees us, she'll act like it never happened."

As predicted, Carla and Gene drove into the drive-through at the bank where Sarah was employed. It was a few weeks after their ugly Mother's Day incident, but Sarah acted as if it had never occurred.

"Hello, Gene." Sarah smiled, then waved at him from the teller's window. "How have you been doing?"

Gene was a bit tongue-tied, but finally squeezed out, "I-I-I'm fine."

Carla poked Gene in the side and smiled. "See, I told you she would be like that," she teased. "In public, she tries to act like nothing has ever happened between us, like we're the perfect mother and daughter. But it is all for show. She just wants to give an outward appearance that everything is okay between us."

Gene drove away from the bank, his mouth gaped open. For several minutes, he stared at Carla, trying to make sense of it all. Finally he asked, "God almighty, what in the hell is wrong with your mother?"

"I don't know what's wrong with her," Carla snapped. "I can't figure it out. One day she loves me; the next day she hates me and blames me for all her problems. It's like she's got some kind of split personality or something."

"I'd say so," Gene agreed.

Chapter 19

Life often takes some serious turns.

Several months after Carla and Sarah's catfight on Mother's Day, their relationship was put to the ultimate test. Gene, Carla, and Holly, who was eighteen-months-old, were involved in a horrible head-on collision. Supposedly, Gene and Carla had been out drinking, and no one, including Holly, was wearing a seat belt. After all the dust had settled and the tires had stopped spinning, Gene found himself pinned against the steering wheel and between the steel frame of the car. It took the paramedics and firefighters almost two hours with the aid of the Jaws of Life to cut and remove him from the automobile. Carla was okay and had suffered only minor injuries, but Holly was thrown from the car. Because it was late at night and Holly was dressed in black, it also took the rescuers about the same amount of time they had spent freeing Gene before they finally located her hidden among the tall grass. Holly received a concussion, but eventually recovered. Gene, on the other hand, was left paralyzed and told he would never walk again.

Although Gene and Carla had attempted to save their marriage, it did not survive the strains of his handicap. Carla had cut off all ties with her parents, but she had no choice but to ask if she and Holly could move back into their home on Plantation Drive. The Colliers welcomed Carla back home, and seemed overjoyed to have their adorable granddaughter under the same roof with them.

But, according to the Colliers, Gene and Holly's near-death experiences had done little to set her on the straight-and-narrow pathway. Shortly after she moved in with them, she took a job as a stripper and started hanging out in clubs and bars, often not returning home until early in the morning—or not returning home at all.

Even in the darkness of the clubs, it was easy to see Carla Harvey was a beautiful woman. She had long, glossy brown hair and a sexy figure, which she kept taut by dancing. She had natural grace, and with a little bit of practice, it wasn't long before she was turning men's heads and getting admiring glances from other dancers in the club. The combination of the drugs, music, and social excitement seemed more than enough to satisfy her.

The Colliers suspected their daughter was taking drugs and was involved with a sinful crowd. They had heard stories about these strip clubs in Atlanta, and what went on after hours in these places was always a topic of conversation at parties, and the Colliers wanted no part of it.

As far as Holly was concerned, the Colliers loved their granddaughter, even doted on her, but they were retired and wanted to relax, travel, and enjoy the fruits of their labor. They were not interested in being surrogate parents to Holly, while Carla neglected her child and tried to recapture her lost youth. Battles over Carla's lack of responsibility and aberrant lifestyle ensued, until finally the Colliers informed Carla that she and Holly would have to move out.

To this day, Carla swore that wasn't how it happened.

"Yes, I was a stripper, but I was taking care of my business and coming home to my child. I was also visiting Gene at the hospital. When he moved back home, I took Holly over there and we tried to make a go of it. I wanted to make sure she knew her father. But Gene got into trouble again and went back to prison. Holly and I then had to go back a second time and live with my parents.

"Because Gene and I weren't legally married, and I needed financial help for Holly, I had to sue him for child support. The lawyers said our marriage was considered common-law marriage, and that it would hold up in court. Gene was sued and the papers served on him in prison. He tried to say Holly wasn't his daughter, but that was a lie. She was his, all right.

"When I got no help from Gene, I had to move back in with my parents. But I was still nothing to them. It was always 'Kevin this, and Kevin that.' I was always compared to Kevin. I couldn't do nothing right, but Kevin could do nothing wrong.

"One night my mama started screaming at me and we got in an argument. I was standing at the top of the stairs holding Holly in my arms when Mama pushed me and I went tumbling down the stairs. We were lucky no one was injured."

Carla believed at this time her mother's insecurities were unraveling, yielding to some bitter childhood history. In the 1940s, young Sarah Jenkins's parents both worked in a cotton mill and earned just enough money to feed themselves, Sarah, and her older brother. The roof over their heads was that of a two-room shanty and their lifestyle was barely above the poverty level. Carla was convinced the economical deprivation scarred Sarah emotionally and presented devastating problems in her adult life.

"As I look back on it now, my mother had serious issues. And I blame a lot of those on her lack of ability to manage her finances. My mother was a compulsive spender, and, though I didn't know it at the time, it was causing her some real problems at home."

Carla related that her father was not a profane man, and the only time she had ever heard him curse was when he found out Sarah had gotten them in severe financial debt.

"Daddy found out somehow that Mama had refinanced the house without telling him and had put a second mortgage on it that was way out of proportion with what they could afford. And when he found this out, he raised total hell. He demanded she bring all her credit cards and bills and lay them all out on the dining-room table. I saw the table strewn with all her cards and bills she owed. They nearly covered the entire table. When Dad added it all up, he was shocked to know they were hundreds of thousands of dollars in debt. Because Mama worked at the bank, she had been able to finance some of her spending habits—first with a credit card and then with a couple of second mortgages on their house. All of this was, of course, without my father's permission or his signature on the loans.

"It was like my mother had some kind of sickness. Every corner of the house was packed and every room filled with shopping bags of merchandise she had bought. It was like if she didn't buy something every day, she felt like she would literally die. She had to have this, had to have that, had to spend . . . spend, spend, spend. There were luxury trips to Hawaii she was taking with her friends, and on these trips, they were staying in the best hotels and sparing no expenses on anything. When she bought something, even if it was a souvenir, she had to have the best of everything.

"I had no idea this was going on until later in my life, but Mom and Dad were really in deep financial trouble. I can see now how me and Holly were just too much pressure for them."

After Carla was asked to leave her parents' home, she got an apartment in nearby Clayton County. But in a matter of days, she quickly saw she could not provide for her child on the meager salary she was now making as a waitress. Willing to do whatever she had to do, she returned to her gig as a stripper at the Gold Rush Club in Atlanta. Even though she made good money—a minimum of $1,200 each night, and as much as $6,000 on a good night—she still found being a single parent challenging—and all that went with it was over-whelming. When she was unable to locate someone to watch Holly while she worked, which was often, she had no choice but to drop Holly off at her parents' home. The Colliers never once refused Carla. After all, Holly was their granddaughter and they did love her.

In 1993, Carla reconciled with Kevin, and he invited her and Holly, who was four years old, to come live with him in his newly purchased home on the outskirts of Fayetteville. The Colliers were relieved when Kevin informed them of the decision. They had hoped, for Holly's sake, that she and her mother would find a stable environment, and had faith in Kevin that he could help provide that.

At first it looked as if things were going to work out between Kevin and Carla. Kevin was single, and he loved Holly and enjoyed having her around. But their arrangement also took a nosedive when his enviornment clashed with Carla's. Although Kevin was a bachleor, he saw the need for Holly to have some structure in her life and he didn't see Carla providing that.

"There was no discipline whatsoever with Holly," he noted. "It was like Holly was the parent telling my sister what to do. She even called Carla by her first name. That was one of the first signs that Holly had no respect for her mother. While they lived with me, Holly received no direction from her mom in her life. She had no designated time for bed, no time to wake up, no assigned chores, and no certain time to go to school. I could see then the only structure Holly had was when she stayed with my parents."

In the eight years Carla and Holly lived off and on with Kevin, he knew she had accumulated four DWIs. On the last of those charges, she was required to spend five months in jail, and Kevin was asked if he would look after Holly.

"That was actually one of our better times," Kevin said, referring to Carla's stay in jail. "Twelve-year-old Holly was old enough by then to be left alone at home, and I finally got the opportunity to restore some order in her life. Everything was fine, and Holly was becoming more responsible and making great strides in her life. That is until Carla got out of jail on probation and moved back in with us."

According to Kevin, one night in April 2001, after pulling into his garage after a day's work, he was met at the door by his twelve-year-old niece. Holly was in tears and told him that she and her mother had a spat and that Carla had hit her. Kevin was furious, and he and Carla went at each other's throats. The police were called to investigate and referee this domestic dispute. That night Kevin was arrested for domestic violence and carted off to jail.

Kevin was later acquitted for that charge when his lawyer got Holly to admit she was not telling the truth when the police officers talked with her. She admitted she was protecting her mother and that it was her mother who was actually choking her, and that Kevin was just trying to help her. But this incident was ultimately the proverbial straw that broke the camel's back. When Kevin returned home, he laid his own law down. Kicking both Carla and Holly out of the house, he let them know they were just too much of a disruptive force in his life, and he would no longer tolerate them.

Chapter 20

Anita Beckom remembered Carla Harvey, then known as Carla Collier, from high school. Carla had once dated Anita's brother and she was always so vivacious, full of life, and adventurous. Not long after Anita graduated from high school and was married, she bumped into Carla at a local shopping mall. Carla said she was divorced from her husband and that she had a little girl, Holly. Anita told her she also had a little girl, a few years older than Holly, and if she ever needed someone for her to play with, to give her a call. A friendship grew out of that conversation and soon Holly was spending a lot of time at Anita's home.

Anita knew about Carla's relationship with her parents. She was always bringing Holly to their home when she was a baby. They would live with the Colliers for a few months, they'd leave, and then they'd go back again. They moved in and out of Carl and Sarah's lives like the tide.

The Colliers were very cordial to Anita and her family, inviting them to join Carla and Holly for afternoon swims in the family pool. Anita also developed a platonic relationship with Carla's brother, Kevin Collier. She and Kevin had a lot in common and, in time, became as close as brother and sister.

Anita and her family fell in love with Holly. She was an

absolutely gorgeous child and grew up with lusciously plump lips and a dazzling smile, winning hearts everywhere she went. Anita used to joke that those wraparound smiles and cute little dimples were the kind that could melt snow-caps atop of Mount Everest at one thousand feet.

But where there was joy in Holly's face, there was also an underlying sadness. In her eyes, Anita could see some school-girl longing that cried out from deep within to be loved and to be held. Anita couldn't help but take Holly in and love her as if she were her own. The reason for Holly's insecurity, as far as Anita saw it, was the way she was being raised.

Carla Harvey was a single parent. Holly was her only daughter, but Carla was not willing to give up the single life to provide the kind of stability her child needed. Anita hated to admit it, but Holly, even at her young age, had seen and done things little girls her age should have never seen and should never have done.

Carla had quit high school and had no marketable skills of any kind. None. And she was on her own when it came to Holly. Anita tried to help Carla out by taking her in to her home and providing some of the normal everyday things for Holly. She bought Holly toys and clothes and invited her to join her family on their vacation outings at the beach and at Disney World. Anita paid for all her expenses, as if Holly were her own. At Christmas, Holly would come to stay with Anita and her family, and would be treated the very same as her other children. Whatever dollar amount she spent on her children at Christmas, she would do the same for Holly.

Because Carla had no marketable skills, her employment was limited to working in bars and nightclubs as a waitress or a stripper. She did, however, enjoy the perks. On many occasions, she took long, extended trips with friends from the strip club who would set her up in hotels and pay for all her expenses, while her daughter stayed with Anita. Anita often talked with Carla about her job, asking her if this was the kind of life and example she wanted for her young daughter.

"I don't see what the big deal is," Carla would argue. "I'm not doing anything wrong. I'm not a hooker. I'm not on welfare. After all, I am a single parent and I get no financial support from Holly's father of any kind. I'm just doing what I need to do to survive."

Anita understood the last part, but it was the nonstop drinking, drugs, and partying that concerned her the most. She made the usual excuses to Holly for her mother being gone a lot—the kind that adults make for each other—but Holly would hear none of it. She knew what her mother did and was proud that her mother was a stripper. She also knew what her mother's problems were and what her father's problems were, and didn't think anything different of it.

As Holly grew older, she began telling people at her school that Anita was her aunt and Anita's children were her cousins. Somehow, Carla had Anita named as Holly's "godmother." This caused some problems for Anita and her children. At her school, Holly would tell other students that Anita's children were her cousins. And around town, people would see Anita and tell her they saw her sister Carla—*at the strip club!*

Anita watched with caution as Carla's life got further and further out of control. She knew of at least a handful of serious skirmishes Carla had had with the Fayette County Police Department and court system. The most serious of those was when Carla had been granted bail and then had her sentence later reduced to probation. While Carla was still on probation and under a court order not to leave the state, she stopped checking in with her probation officer. She and Holly were living with a man Carla had met in the strip club and the decision was made for all three of them to suddenly move to Nebraska. That fiasco lasted about two days, before Carla and Holly hopped on a plane and flew back to Georgia. They arrived back in Georgia before the movers had time to ship their things to Nebraska.

Knowing she was in a lot of trouble, Carla loaded up her things again and she and Holly took off for Panama City. They stayed on the lam, hiding out in Florida for a couple of months, but were finally brazen enough to return home to Fayette County.

Among the first persons Carla and Holly visited when they arrived in Fayetteville were Anita and her family. Anita learned that both Carla and Holly had been doing some heavy partying in Panama City, which included drinking and smoking marijuana. She was shocked when she saw Holly, her eyes all bloodshot and her mind in a vacuum.

"I can't believe your daughter is stoned," Anita admonished Carla. She was angry at her for letting this happen.

"Why?" Carla half-shrugged. "What's the problem? I figure if she's going to smoke grass, she might as well do it around me."

"It's just not right," Anita pointed out. "If the police catch you violating your parole *and* taking drugs, they're going to send you straight to jail."

"Oh, they can't prove a thing on me," Carla sneered. "My paperwork for parole is already in, and by the time they get around to testing me for drugs, they can't do anything about it."

From that day onward, Anita could see a change in both Carla and Holly's behavior. Carla grew cold and bitter, and she and Holly started drifting apart. Anita would keep Holly with her most of the time and she tried to show Holly a better life than seeing her mom coming home drunk or drugged up and bringing different men home with her all the time. Carla wouldn't even come home at times because she knew Anita had Holly and she was being well taken care of.

Most of the time, Carla wouldn't even call to check on her daughter. But Holly got used to her mother's ways. She hardly asked to call her mom anymore, saying she knew what her job was and what she was doing.

When Holly turned thirteen, she was still staying with Anita and pleaded with her one day to spend the night at a classmate's house. Anita reluctantly agreed, but only after she had talked with the girl's parents and was assured their daughter and Holly would at no time be left unattended.

The next day, Anita learned Holly and her girlfriend had been left alone for half the night with the girl's older brother, at which time all three teenagers had smoked pot. She confronted Holly about this issue and she admitted she only tried the marijuana but threw the cigarette away when she decided it wasn't for her.

When Anita told Carla about the situation, Carla blamed her for the incident, saying Anita should have known better than to let Holly spend the night with her friends.

In time, the relationship between Anita and Carla greatly deteriorated. Anita believed if Carla would stay out of the strip clubs and stop her drinking and drugs, then she would be okay. But, as it was, she found her to be a manipulator and a liar, and she was doing a piss-poor job of raising her daughter.

In 2002, when Carla got into trouble again for the possession of narcotics, Anita took Holly in for about nine months. Anita's mother, Carol Morgan, had known Carla and her family since she was a child, and knew she was often getting into trouble. Carol felt that all Holly needed was someone to love and care for her and maybe she would avoid the same mistakes Carla had made.

"Holly's just like a granddaughter to me," Carol would tell her friends. "We've always made her part of our family since she was a small child."

However, Carol was seeing another side of Holly she didn't like. When Holly wanted, she could be as nice and jovial as any child. Just before Christmas in 2003, Holly had to move out of the Beckoms' home and live with her grandparents.

She wrote Carol Morgan's daughter a letter, thanking the family for their help.

Holly's letter, in part, read: "I am very thankful to have you in my life. You are like my second mom that I never had. Thank you for everything you did for me, I love you."

That was the good side of Holly, but there was also a bad side to Holly.

"If Holly can't have her way," Carol stated, "then she really gets angry. We've seen her, as a child, so many times abuse and disrespect her grandparents."

Carol and Anita were so puzzled by Holly's behavior that they referred to her as two different people: "the nice Holly" and "the mean Molly." After the pot incident, Anita's older daughter gave her an ultimatum. Either Holly went back home, or she would go and live with her father. Anita did not want to part with her daughter, so she informed Holly she could come and visit—even stay overnight—but she would have to live elsewhere.

When Carla was busted and arrested in 2003, she was housed in the Fayette County Jail awaiting her trial. She, no doubt, was going to be sentenced to a three-year term at the Metro State Prison, and that meant Holly had no place to live. Carla's few remaining friends and family met to decide what was best for her fourteen-year-old daughter, but no one wanted to take on this extra burden. It was a difficult decision to make, but there had been a lot of bad blood between Carla, her parents and her brother and her friends. She and Holly had simply worn out their welcome with all of these people, and they, literally, had nowhere to live.

Over the last couple of years before 2003, Carla and Holly had only stayed with the Colliers occasionally. They were also living intermittently with airline mechanic Scott Moore, the father of Carla's second child and Holly's now eight-year-old half sister, Samantha. Moore had his share of discipline problems with Holly as well.

"When her mother would go to work at night," he stated, "Holly would sneak out of the house and meet her friends. I'd follow her and I'd find the little aluminum wrappers she used for her marijuana. When I would confront Holly, she would say, 'There's nothing you can do about it; you're not my father.'"

After Carla Harvey went to prison in 2003, Moore said he told Holly she couldn't continue living at his house. Sandy Ketchum's offer for Holly to live with her never materialized, and by then, Carla had already talked with Connie Earwood, the mother of Holly's friend Haley Earwood. The two girls were the same age, and in the same grade. Connie worked at a school over in the Flat Rock area, and for convenience sake, Holly was enrolled in the same middle school as Haley.

"What happens if Holly doesn't want to stay with us and runs away?" Connie asked Carla.

Not to worry, Connie was told. *If Holly runs away, call the police and they will dispatch a unit to the house right away.*

Kevin Collier had met both Connie and Haley Earwood. He kept in touch with his niece and believed this was a good choice for her, that it would provide the much-needed stability in her life. While she was living with her mother, she had missed more days than allowed at Fayetteville Middle School and had to repeat the eighth grade. Thanks to Connie's efforts, she was now attending Flat Rock Middle School in nearby Conyers, and making A's and B's in most of her classes.

But when it came to Holly's personal life, she wasn't doing too well. She was so rebellious and disobedient that her relationship with the Earwoods, which had started out so very promising, had now turned and was going sour. For whatever reason, Holly just could not shake herself free of Sandy Ketchum.

In a letter written by Holly while she was on vacation in Tennessee with the Earwoods, she reassured Sandy of her love:

I really don't know whut 2 write, I need a blunt. I'm startin' 2 come off my med, so I'm in a bitchy-ass mood.

*Everything is getting on my nerves . . . I'm so happy
you called me! I thought I would never see u or hear ur
voice again! I missed u so much, no one could understand how much! Shit! I miss u rite now, I started
missin' u when we said "bye" on the phone! Everyday
I would find myself thinkin' 'bout u. I had to ignore the
fact that I missed u, because it made the whole thing
worse. I can't live without u in my life, so I'm happy that
you didn't forget me. O-ya! What if I get ur name tat-
tooed on my left titty? That will be my first one.*

Holly's letter also referenced several incidents where she
and certain members of the Earwoods were arguing:

*Connie's a fuckin' bitch, but I can play that game too!
(LOL) me and Haley have been fightin' since last night!
Man, fuck that hoe, she can go 2 Hell! Whutever—Haley
wuz talkin' shit and I wuz bout 2 kick her ass cuz she wuz
sayin' I wudn't get 2 see u and her daddy wud beat my
ass w/the belt if I tried 2 run away.*

It was the beginning of the end for Holly's stay with the
Earwoods. When she later ran away from them to be with
Sandy, the Earwoods decided it was time to wash their hands
of her. They realized Holly had more problems in her life than
they had bargained for.

Haley Earwood, Holly's best friend, tried to reason with
her. She knew Holly was no longer happy living with her and
her parents, so she wrote a letter to Holly and tried to express
how she felt about everything:

*I've been thinking, you're not happy here and you
sure as hell don't act like it. You always have this attitude when I try to talk to you, but yet you say it's me
with the attitude. I know it must be hard for you with*

everything that's been going on. I mean, your mom is in
jail, what worse could happen?!

Off and on, Holly had also been staying with Anita
Beckom and her family. Haley believed Holly might be better
off living there than with her. Holly was heavy into rap music
and was under the impression she could make a living as a
professional rapper. Haley told her if that was what she
wanted, then she should pursue her dreams:

Whenever I talk to you on the phone while you're at
Nita's, you seem so happy there. You seem way happier
there than you are here. Maybe it's cause you can be
"yourself" there and people don't shoot down your
dreams like you say my mom does. My mom does not
shoot down your dreams Holly, it's just that she's not
gonna go pay $200 for a demo when you never even
rapped in front of her before. All you can do is take a
chance and try it! Have you talked to Nita about what
you wanted to do???? I'm sure if you talked to her
about it and rapped for her, that she would help you
out. I mean, you always have so many good things to
say about her . . . why not try it?

Haley encouraged Holly to move in with the Beckoms:

Holly, what I'm about to say . . . don't take it the
wrong way or anything and get all mad at me. But if
Nita accepts you so much for who you are, how you are,
and what you do, then why aren't you living with her??
No, I'm not tryin to tell you to move in with her or that
I don't want you here . . . what I'm tryin to say is, it
just seems like you would be so much happier over
there and you could always come to my house and

*spend the night whenever you wanted to . . . Cause
Holly, your real family is what you need right now!*

   Carl and Sarah Collier were Holly Ann Harvey's grandparents. They were, after all, *real family,* and, according to their
friends and neighbors, exactly what Holly had always needed.
Though the Earwoods had been a stabilizing force for Holly,
she continued to run away and use drugs. After Holly finished
her last term of school at Flat Rock Middle School in May
2004, Connie Earwood informed Carla the arrangement with
Holly was no longer working out. After talking with Connie,
Carla then called her parents and asked if Holly could move
back into their Riverdale suburban home until she was released from prison, which she believed was just a couple of
months away.

   While living with the Earwoods, Holly had visited her grandparents and had spent several weekends with them. They knew
that she was doing drugs, that she was rebellious, and that she
resented any of their attempts to control her. Yet, she was still
their granddaughter—and they loved her.

   Betty Green, a close friend of Sarah's, said the Colliers had
a wonderful relationship with Holly when she was small.
Green pointed out that in those days, Holly had a bedroom
upstairs and across from her grandparents, and her whereabouts could be easily monitored and her behavior controlled.
But now, she'd heard rumors in the neighborhood that Holly
was sleeping in the downstairs bedroom and sneaking out at
night. She wasn't so sure how things were going to work out
with Holly.

   Holly continually complained about how strict her grandparents were. She said her grandmother was always on her
case and yelling at her, that she would never let her go anywhere or do anything with her friends

   Scott Moore, Carla Harvey's live-in boyfriend, said he
didn't see it that way.

"I never thought her grandparents were too strict. They would let her go out and socialize, but just not with some people. But anytime her grandfather told her she couldn't do something, she would say, 'You better let me do what I want, or I'll call the cops and tell them you hit me.'"

It was obvious to Carl and Sarah's friends that they were having great difficulty dealing with their granddaughter. Holly believed her grandparents were old-fashioned and behind the times. She had no intention of going to church, as her grandparents had hoped, or conforming to the rules imposed on her. She preferred MTV to church and would rather listen to the music of rap artists than hymn writers.

"The Colliers were salt-of-the-earth people," Frank Ellis, senior pastor at the Fayetteville Baptist Church, said. "They lived consistent, steady lives and were hardworking, wise people. They were always involved in the church, not in leadership positions, but quiet areas of ministry. The Colliers often took up money and greeted people at Wednesday-night church suppers. But they carried a quiet sadness. They often asked fellow churchgoers to pray for their situation and they started soliciting prayers for their granddaughter."

Holly had made it clear she was not going to be part of her grandparents' religious nonsense. But old-fashioned or not, Carl and Sarah Collier believed they were responsible for their granddaughter. And until her mother was released from prison, this fifteen-year-old would have no choice but to live under the auspices of her seventy-four-year-old grandfather and her seventy-three-year-old grandmother.

The Colliers had talked to their son, Kevin, about this situation. There were some things he should know. They each told him their own set of horror stories, but there was nothing, by now, he could not guess. The question was: what did they plan to do about it?

Carl said he felt as helpless at the age of seventy-four with Holly, as he did at the age of forty-four when he had tried to deal with her mother. Then it had been his daughter who had raged in desperation and drunkenness. Holly had not been as wild as her mother, or as dangerous, but there was a sameness, nonetheless, between the two. Like her mother, Holly was always sliding between hysteria and stupor. Even her loneliness was becoming dangerous.

In the past, Holly had been known to lie against her grandparents to dramatize reality. But whatever happened in the past was over, and they were willing to forgive.

Kevin Collier believed his parents were afraid of Holly in a way that he had never before seen his father frightened. And he was frightened for him.

Kevin thought his father was probably right about what to do with Holly. The best place for her was either with her mother or in an institution. Holly could be institutionalized once they proved she was a threat to them and herself. The courts would be on their side, and probably step in and take custody of Holly.

Kevin didn't think he understood the situation, nor did he need to be involved at this point. He advised his parents the best way to deal with Holly—and for Holly to change—was for them to continue to show their love. If she didn't respond to that, then they should think about getting her out of their house and into an institution. But that wasn't going to be easy.

"Don't worry, we'll be okay," Kevin's father assured him. "We're used to Holly's antics by now."

"I know you still love her, Dad," Kevin conceded.

"How can we not love her?" Carl admitted. "After all, she's still our granddaughter."

Although Holly resented it, she had come full circle, returning to the only home she had really ever known. She would be okay, everyone agreed. Once she got settled into her grandparents' routine and got a little structure in her life, she would be just fine.

But there was a hardness in Holly's face and in her voice

that hadn't been there before. It was as if she were at odds with the world and everyone in it. Suddenly, and without warning, she had become the thunder that could easily cut through a soft breeze, and the storm that could violently rage without any warning.

Part III

DOUBLE TROUBLE

Chapter 21

Kevin Collier had heard about Sandy Ketchum, but did not meet her until June 6, 2004. Holly had called him and asked if she and a friend could come over to his house. He assumed the friend she was referring to was Haley Earwood.

"No, it's not a problem," Kevin assured her. He was as forgiving as Holly was apologetic. "In fact, I've missed seeing you and it will be nice to be with you again."

Sometime midmorning, Holly arrived with her new friend Sandy. They were both smiling mischievously and staring at each other like lovesick puppies. As Kevin talked with Sandy, he couldn't help noticing there was something strange about this girl. She reminded him of a neighbor's child who was lost, found, and asked to stay for lunch; then she decided to stay forever. She was a quiet, mousy, brown-haired, brown-eyed girl who dressed and acted just like a boy. She kept fidgeting with her hands, avoiding his gaze as he avoided hers. Sandy was a year older than Holly, and she kept her hair cut short and stylish, not much longer than Kevin's.

Kevin had never been around a lot of gay people, but he assumed by the way Sandy acted and dressed that she was gay. The fact that his niece was hanging around her puzzled him. Holly had inherited her mother's good looks, petite build, and effortless poise. She could razzle and dazzle any teenage boy she wished to have. He couldn't understand why she was with this gay girl.

"I've got to run around for a while and take care of a few errands," Kevin told the girls. They stood there giggling and smiling at each other, the way men do over baseball and cars, but they assured him they would be fine and would be home when he got back.

When Kevin returned at 11:30 A.M., the girls were nowhere to be found. Kevin circled the neighborhood, thinking maybe they had just gone for a walk, but he saw no sign of them. He waited for a while at home, knowing surely they would call him, if for nothing else but to say they were okay. Finally Kevin grew worried and called his parents' house to see if they were there.

"What do you mean Holly is with Sandy Ketchum?" an outraged Sarah Collier screamed in the phone. "Don't you realize what you have done?"

Kevin was floored. Other than the times she and Carla had gone at it, he had never seen his mother so ballistic. He didn't know Sandy was not permitted to visit Holly over at her grandparents' home, and that they had told Connie Earwood over in Conyers the same applied there as well. Somehow his parents knew about Sandy's troubled childhood and were concerned that her father, Tim Ketchum, had been divorced three times. They believed this sixteen-year-old Ketchum girl was a bad influence on Holly.

"Under no circumstances is Sandy allowed to visit or be with Holly again," Sarah ordered. "Is that understood?"

"Understood," Kevin said, taking his marching orders. "Then I guess Holly's not going to like being told what to do and is going to give you some trouble over this. It's beginning to turn out 'like mother, like daughter' all over again."

Sarah Collier was still fuming over the incident.

"I don't care if Holly likes it or not, she and Sandy Ketchum will not be together. After I hang up, I am going to talk with your father about this and ask him to call the police."

"Do you really think it's a good idea to get the police involved, Mom? After all, they're just kids."

Sarah said what she had to say in a rough, outraged voice, then said no more. She would take care of Holly and her troublemaking friend.

When the girls were still missing the next day, Carl called the Fayette County Sheriff's Office and reported the incident. The call was transferred to Detective Phil McElwaney. Carl identified himself to McElwaney, then said softly, "I want to report my granddaughter has run away."

"All right, Mr. Collier, let me get some information from you." McElwaney reached across his desk and grabbed a missing person's report form. "Can you tell me how long she has been gone?"

"Well, she was staying at my son's house with a friend and they left sometime before noon yesterday." Carl paused, as if he were adding the number of hours in his head, before submitting, "I am guessing she's be gone close to twenty-four hours by now."

McElwaney knew it was still a little too early for an all-out missing person's alert, that in most cases the child ends up staying overnight at a friend's house. They got a lot of these calls, and—normally—everything was fine. But just to be on the safe side, he asked, "Do you have any idea where she might have been going?"

"No, but I can tell you that she's had a problem with drugs in the past and it's a possibility she may be using them again."

"Do you think she might hurt herself?" McElwaney had to ask. "In other words, is she suicidal?"

"I don't know at this point," Carl answered flatly. "All I know, she and her friend is missing and we would like your help in finding her."

"We'll do our best, sir, and it would help if we had her name and a description."

"Holly Harvey is her name. She's fifteen years old. And she weighs about one hundred ten pounds. She stands about five foot, six inches tall, and has brown hair and blue eyes."

McElwaney then asked for a list of Holly's friends and phone numbers. He assured Carl a team of detectives would make calls to her friends and they hopefully could shed some light on her disappearance.

For the next three days, McElwaney and his partner, Detective Bo Turner, made a number of calls, but all were dead ends. It wasn't until the following Wednesday, June 9, that they got a break in the case. This time the phone call was from Tim Ketchum

"I'd like to report my daughter Sandy Ketchum is missing," Tim said in a worried voice. "Me and my wife have been putting missing-person flyers all over town, but nobody has seen her since Saturday." He provided a description of Sandy and went through the normal line of questions asked when someone is missing. "One of the numbers she had called the day she disappeared was made to Holly Harvey's cell phone. I think my daughter and Holly could possibly be together."

Tim provided further information that the two teenagers might have headed for Sandy's natural mother's house in Griffin. He described Holly as a pretty little girl with a cherub face, who wore tasteful makeup and dressed in all the latest fashions. And when she had her hair pulled up and styled in a curly bun, she looked much older than her fifteen years.

"Has this Harvey girl ever given you any trouble before?" McElwaney probed.

"Never," Tim responded immediately. "Out of all of my daughter's friends, Holly Harvey is the one we like best. She has always been respectful and has never given us one reason not to like her. Up until now, she has never given us a problem."

On Friday, June 11, 2004, McElwaney and Turner followed

up on the lead Tim Ketchum had provided. Driving the short distance from Fayetteville to Griffin, they had found an address, they believed, where Sandra Ketchum was possibly living. As they pulled down the narrow road, they saw two girls sitting on the front porch of a ramshackle house. The girls fit the descriptions given to them of Holly Harvey and Sandy Ketchum. They stopped their car near the house and approached them.

"Hello, ladies," Bo Turner said politely. Built like six feet of concrete and with a head shaven clean, Turner was an intimidating force.

At five-ten and two hundred pounds of solid muscle, McElwaney and Turner stood like twin towers, only McElwaney had salt-and-pepper (more salt now than pepper) hair.

Turner and McElwaney walked toward the girls, with their hands held out by their sides, in the classic bodybuilder struts. They had no trouble talking the girls into surrendering.

Holly admitted immediately she was who the detectives were looking for, and a call was placed to the Fayetteville Police Department (FPD). As she stood in the yard and puffed away on her Newport cigarettes, McElwaney requested a female detective be dispatched to the scene for the purpose of transporting Holly back to her grandparents' home. Detective Debbie Chambers taxied to her home in Riverdale, while Sandy stayed with her mother in Griffin. Sandy's parents had also been phoned and they were on their way to Griffin as well.

Over the years, Holly had come to the Ketchums' home on numerous occasions and spent many nights over, staying with Sandy in her bedroom. Beth had even taken Sandy to Holly's house so they could spend the night together there. She had always made a point of speaking with Carla Harvey to make sure everything was all right. She didn't know everything about Carla, where she worked or how she made her living, and didn't ask, but she figured she must be pretty good at whatever it was she did. The Harveys lived in a nice apartment, Carla always had a new car, Holly had nice clothes, and her mother would buy her about anything she asked for.

The Ketchums were shocked when the police told them that Holly's mother was in jail for possession of drugs. They also learned from the police that Holly had been staying with Connie Earwood, and sometimes on weekends with her grandparents or her uncle Kevin Collier.

Carl and Sarah Collier were at Kevin's home when everyone had been searching for the missing pair that weekend. The Ketchums, however, did not know that they disapproved of Sandy and had ordered that the girls not see each other. They apologized to the Colliers, stating they didn't know until afterward that their Sandy had initiated communication with her biological mother, Sandra, behind their backs.

The Ketchums perceived Carl as a nice, quiet, and orderly man. Sarah, on the other hand, appeared to be very tight-fisted and critical. She was the type who said what she wanted to say and didn't care who heard it or how they took it. Their meeting with her had been cordial, but they anticipated they would hear more from Sarah.

As expected, Holly was not a happy camper when she got home, having been separated from Sandy. She silently blamed her grandmother and turned away from her.

You have no goddamned right to tell me what to do.

Holly ignored her grandmother's chilly response, but sat and listened as her grandfather admonished her about her attitude and her irresponsible actions of late.

"I'm very disappointed in you," Carl said sternly, but keeping his anger in check. "Do you realize how much your grandmother, your uncle Kevin, and I have worried about you?"

Holly looked down at the floor. She was fifteen. Didn't she have the right—no, didn't she deserve the right—to be happy? Her grandparents didn't have to act so high-and-mighty. How long would it be before they recognized she was growing weary of this shit?

Holly never looked up to answer her grandfather, until, at last, he told her to go to her room. Immediately, after skulking down to her basement room, she began plotting how she could sneak out and hitch a ride back to Griffin. She didn't care what happened to her anymore. All she wanted was to be with Sandy.

When the Ketchums returned to their Fayetteville home with Sandy, their phone was ringing. Beth walked over to the kitchen and answered it. It was Holly Harvey on the line.

"Can I speak with Sandy, please?" Holly asked nervously.

Beth didn't give in, telling her firmly, "I'm sorry, Holly, but that's not going to be possible."

"Why?" Holly asked in desperation. "Why won't you let me speak to her?"

Beth took a deep breath, then let it all out in one long bark over the phone. "I'm only going to be telling you this one time, 'Do not call my house again.'"

"No . . . oh, my God, please . . . ," Holly whined on the other end of the line.

"Look, Holly, this is my house and my phone, so do not call here again. You are not allowed to see Sandy, or talk to Sandy, ever again! Do you understand?"

"For how long?" Holly cried pitifully. "How long?"

"Forever, as I just said, it is over and done with."

That said, Beth slammed down the phone. She took a deep breath, feeling a wave of irritation, even real anger. Sandy had been told—and told bluntly—not to see Holly. She would talk to her sternly about that and she would be disciplined. There were plenty of parents who would disown her for less.

Sandy had been listening to the conversation from the next room. When she heard Beth slam down the phone, she walked into the room and confronted her stepmother. A cold knot was growing in her stomach, enough to demand from Beth, "Why in the hell were you so mean to Holly?"

"I wasn't mean to Holly. I was just being firm, and I meant every word of it. It's over between you two and you might as well accept that. We're moving on with our lives and Holly is not moving on with us."

Sandy's jaw was locked down like a vise. She didn't like what was going on one bit. Decisions were being made on her behalf, but no one was consulting her to see how she felt about it. She was growing tired of all this crap, having been told by everyone that there would be no more Holly in her life. She was almost an adult—so who in the hell had the right to tell her "just forget about Holly"?

Sandy thought about what had just happened, and turned to face Beth. She scrambled for something hard and mean— anything to strike back and make her hurt as much as she did would work. Every person has an Achilles' heel and Beth's was *You've got no right to tell me what to do. You're not my mother.*

Beth glared at Sandy, feeling a surge of real anger. She had been told and told, time and time again, by Sandy, "You're not my mother," and she was sick and tired of that. As long as she was married to Tim and worked to help keep a roof over Sandy's head, food in her stomach, and clothes on her back, then—damn it—she had the right to tell her what to do. Besides, this was not only her decision, it was something she and her father had talked about. They both had their minds set on it: no more Holly Harvey in Sandy's life.

"I don't give a damn what you think about me, Sandy," Beth wanted her to understand, "but as far as you and your little girlfriend are concerned, it's over. Do you hear me? It's over!"

Sandy burst into tears, turned on her heels, ran out of the living room and toward her bedroom. Halfway down the hall, she stopped abruptly, turned around, and yelled, "Just fuck you, Beth. Fuck you!"

Beth turned around in the kitchen and flew down the hall after Sandy before she could turn around. Sandy pulled her arms to her chest and covered her head. Beth's arms and fists seemed to fly out of nowhere, flailing like a pinwheel and stinging her body. Finally she was going to teach Sandy something she didn't have: respect for authority. It was time she learned who was in control and know what it felt like to hurt.

Sandy turned her face away, but Beth's fists rained solidly down on her back and head, again and again. Her flimsy defense was no match and she dropped quickly to the floor.

"No," she shrieked. "Stop it! Stop hitting me!"

Beth wrestled with Sandy on the floor and the two of them banged around the walls and on the floor to help keep themselves upright.

"Help, get her off me," Sandy screamed and yelled. "Somebody make her stop and get off me."

Sandy's muffled cries trailed from the hall through the living room and kitchen, then out the door to where her father was working outside. He heard all the melee and ran to where Beth and Sandy were rolling around on the floor.

"What the hell is going on here?" Tim screamed out.

He grabbed Beth by the arms and pulled her off Sandy. She fell against the wall, still spitting fire like a dragon. Sandy was crying and had peddled herself several feet down the hall, backing herself into a corner near her bedroom door.

"What's wrong with you two?" he said, looking first at one, then at the other. "Are you trying to kill each other or something?"

Sandy was the first to speak, telling her father how rude Beth had been to Holly.

"She was nasty, Daddy. I tried talking with her about my feelings, but she didn't want to hear anything about that.

Finally, out of frustration, I told her she wasn't my mama and couldn't tell me what to do."

Tim looked at Beth, who was still spitting and stewing like an angry cougar, and waited for her answer. He'd never seen his wife so angry.

Beth looked back at Tim, then at Sandy, and then back at Tim. "Oh, that's not all she told me," she said through her gritted teeth. She turned back toward Sandy, then shouted, "Go ahead. Why don't you tell him what else you told me!"

Sandy dropped her head, covered her eyes with her hands, and collapsed against the wall in tears. When Beth told her father all she had said, Sandy stood up and ran to her room, slamming the door behind her.

Doing his best to handle this crisis, Tim walked over to Beth, apologizing for his daughter's lack of respect. "I'm sorry, she had no right to say those things to you, especially that part about you're not her mother. I know how much you care about her. In fact, you've been the only real mother she's ever had."

"I know I'm not her mother," Beth cried, pacing around the kitchen like a wounded animal. "But I worry about her like she's my own child. I worry about her not going to school and getting kicked out of school. I worry about her taking drugs, cutting herself with knives, and having homosexual relationships."

Beth stopped square in the middle of the room and lifted her arms above her head, as if she were arguing her case before a judge.

"Damn it, Tim, what other person do you know who would love a child as much as I have loved Sandy?"

"No one," Tim said, then pointed out, "she's lucky to have somebody like you who cares about her." When he finished, his voice was soft and measured. "Nobody loves her as much as you do, honey."

"You're damn straight she is lucky," Beth yelled, turning her head toward Sandy's bedroom door. "You're damn straight she is!"

Beth scanned the room, as if she had suddenly remembered something she wanted to do. Seeing Sandy's PlayStation sitting on the shelf below the television, she bent down and duck-walked to the television stand and grabbed it from the lowest shelf. She had bought that for Sandy the first Christmas they had spent together. It was an expensive item and way beyond Beth's Christmas budget, but she had bought it anyway, remembering Tim's story about how Sandy had been slighted one Christmas by his ex-wife. She had wrapped the gift herself and put it under the tree, making certain Sandy had had a memorable Christmas. Beth treasured the Christmas picture she kept by her bed—the one where she and Tim were standing behind Santa Claus and Sandy was sitting on his lap, wearing a Santa hat.

Beth was still hurting, and had confused her desire to be loved with her desire to lash out. "It's been all for nothing," she said in a voice that was thick and hard. "All for nothing." She grabbed the PlayStation and jerked it off the shelf and away from the television, wrapping the cords around her hand as they came loose from their sockets. Clutching the box in her hands, she marched down to Sandy's room and kicked the door open.

Sandy flinched, then sat up in her bed. Beth was physically stronger than Sandy, so the teenager must have felt as helpless as a trapped animal. She had no idea what to expect next.

Beth held the PlayStation in her hands, then raised it above her head. In one quick motion, she threw the expensive computer down on the floor at the foot of the bed.

CRASH!

The PlayStation smashed on the floor and broke up into five or six different hunks. Shards of plastic slid under the bed and against the wall.

Sandy gasped, surprised that Beth would stoop to such

behavior. Beth knew how much Sandy's PlayStation meant to her. Sandy bit her tongue and took her medicine, but other plans were already formulating in her mind. And those plans included Holly Harvey.

At this point and time in her life, Beth didn't care what Sandy thought about her or Holly Harvey. She wanted to send her a message and let her know two can play those little games. And if Sandy wanted to be nasty, she could be even nastier.

Beth stood at the foot of Sandy's bed. Her face was blood-red and she was breathing hard. Her chest was heaving up and down. Just so Sandy got the message loud and clear, Beth screamed it out at the top of her lungs: "No, Sandy, it's not fuck me. It's fuck you!"

Sandy felt tears well in her eyes and covered her face with her hands to hide them. She wanted Beth to think she was hurt, humiliated by this incident; when, in fact, she was so angry, she could have ripped Beth's heart out with her bare hands.

The scene that Tim had walked in on that evening was a much more serious conflict than he had perceived at the time. Would the bond that existed between Beth and Sandy have a calming effect on the pressure building up inside, or would it become heated to a full boil?

Chapter 22

The day after Holly and Sandy were found by the sheriff's detectives at Sandra Ketchum's house in Griffin, and returned to their respective homes, Sarah Collier phoned Beth Ketchum. There was a hardness in Sarah's voice and she made it clear she wasn't pleased with the most recent turn of events.

"I don't think it is a good idea for the girls to hang out together or speak with one another," she said in a patronizing voice. "I am going to ask that you not allow Sandy to see Holly again."

Beth's feathers were a little ruffled. She had already made that decision, too, but she certainly didn't appreciate Sarah's tone.

"I understand what you are saying, Mrs. Collier," she said, keeping her temper in tow. "But you can't tell me what to do in my own home. That's a decision I am going to make with Sandy, and not with you because you've said so."

"Well, that's the decision we have made for Holly and we'd like for you to respect that," Sarah insisted.

"Sure, I can abide by that," Beth said, grinding her teeth. Obviously, Holly had told her grandmother nothing about their phone conversation. "I appreciate you calling."

When Sandy got home that afternoon, Beth told her about

the conversation she had had with Sarah Collier and informed
her she was not to see Holly again.

Sandy's eyes widened, then watered up. "Do you mean,
like 'forever'? Or is this just until this thing blows over?"

"Let me put it like this," Beth said, softening a bit. "It's not
forever, but it's until you two girls learn to behave like responsible people."

Sandy accepted her punishment and went about her business, fully believing the ban would be over soon. Two days
later, she received a letter from Holly, who had included her
new address at Plantation Drive, Riverdale, Georgia. She was
also grief-stricken and wanted Sandy to know how sorry she
was for getting her into trouble:

> *I called ur house yesterday to see if you made it
> home. Beth said we are not allowed to talk anymore. I'm
> so sorry that I got u in trouble. I hope you will forgive
> me. I love you so much! Please don't ever forget that.
> Maybe u will call me in a couple of months when u get
> off phone restriction. I'm gonna live w/my grandma
> now. So I'm a little bit closer to you, but I guess that
> doesn't matter. I know your parents <u>HATE</u> me now. Tell
> them I'm really sorry. I just wanted to be w/u forever,
> cuz it hurts so bad to say "bye" to you. I wuz so tired of
> havin to sneak around to see u & keep it a secret & then
> wonderin how long it would be before I see you again.
> It was worth the extra time we spent together. But its def-
> initely not worth never being able to see or speak to you
> again! Does that make any sense to you?*

Holly was worried that Sandy was dating someone else and
angry that she would keep something like that from her:

> *Maybe I can see u one more time before you turn 18.
> Are you gonna forget about me? Beth told my grandma*

that she didn't have to worry about us being gay, cuz u
had a boyfriend. I figured it was [Boy's name.] One of ur
friends called me today & I asked them if he wuz ur
boyfriend. They said ya'll started goin out like a week
before school was over. Sandy, that wuz almost a month
ago! U could have told me. Why would u keep some shit
like that from me. . . .

I know that we never broke up, but it's not really like
we go out. (or is it?) . . . U could have told me. Did you
not want me to kno? I should have known before now &
I wish I wouldn't have found out the way I did. Why wuz
u hidin it from me? Whut wuz u gonna do? Hide it from
me forever? That's not sumthin to keep a secret, when I
kno how much I love you & how I feel about u. I thought
u loved me? Do you?

Holly accused Sandy of lying to her about a secret relationship and was afraid she was going to hurt her:

U practically lied to me. What else have u been keep-
ing a secret from me? If I need to know, tell me now.
Please don't hurt me Sandy! Don't forget about me.
Write me back and let me know what's up. I LOVE YOU
BABY!

A week later, Sarah phoned Beth again, asking if she had
seen Holly.

"Why? Has she run off somewhere?" Beth asked with an
obvious bite to her words.

"Yes," Sarah answered, but never acknowledging she might
have been a bit hasty in judging Sandy the week before. "Do
you know if Sandy is with her?"

Beth's hands were clenched into fists and felt like two large
boulders dangling on the ends of her arms. Before responding

to Sarah, she mouthed the words to Sandy, "Do you know where Holly is?"

Sandy shook her head from side to side.

"Nope, Sandy's standing right here in the kitchen next to me," Beth responded, with a great deal of satisfaction. "She's not with Holly, this time."

But before Beth could land another punch, Sarah struck again. "I assume then you know the girls are gay and that they are romantically involved?"

"Do what?" Beth answered, reacting as if the chair had been pulled right out from underneath her. She remembered Sandy saying that she *loved* Holly, but surely that was a reference to their friendship. Beth couldn't believe it. Sure, Holly had stayed over, and the two girls had slept in the same bed, but didn't all teenage girls do that? As a teenager, Beth had slept with her girlfriends, but they hadn't been gay. It had never crossed her mind that anything was going on sexually between the two girls. She challenged that assumption, asking Mrs. Collier bluntly, "Why are you saying such things? Are you trying to deliberately hurt my child?"

"No, I'm telling you this because Holly told me," she replied. "Whenever I told her she was not to see Sandy anymore, she told me she was in love with her. I just think you should know the truth about them."

Beth needed more than Sarah's word for proof. "Well, tell me exactly what Holly told you?"

"Holly said she was in love with Sandy, and it was love in a romantic way," Sarah said flatly.

Beth was silent. A sensation suddenly came over her that people were watching Sandy with contempt. In her mind's eye, she saw them laughing at her. She could almost hear their muffled laugher as they held their hands to their mouths and pointed, their eyes glaring with cruel pinpoints of derision and their mouths mumbling derogatory words—all the slurs normally associated with someone who is gay.

Not long after Beth spoke with Sarah Collier, the mother of one of Sandy's other friends called her and asked if she knew Sandy was gay.

"God almighty, you're the second person today who has told me that," Beth confessed. After her phone conversation, she did some investigating, searching Sandy's room until she finally found notes and poems to and from the girl whose mother had called her. There were also some letters written to Sandy from Holly. After Beth read them, she knew then that Sarah Collier had been correct in her information. Sandy and Holly did love each other, they were lesbians, and they were having a sexual relationship.

When Sandy got home from school, Beth confronted her and asked her point-blank if she was gay. She was hoping for a short and lighthearted answer to this question, but Sandy just dropped her head. Her face was stained with tears and her lips quivered slightly, suggesting she might cry anytime.

"Yes, I like girls," Sandy readily admitted. Thinking Beth could probably handle it easier if she said she still liked boys, she threw in for good measure: "But I'm more bi-sexual than gay."

Beth's face reddened.

"You do know what that means, don't you?" Sandy said sarcastically. Her words came out in a cyclic jumble, as if she were in a hurry to spit it out and be free of it.

Beth knew what she meant; she just didn't know how to respond. Never in her wildest dreams, did she expect to be talking with Sandy about this subject. "Of course, I know what that means," she said, her voice rising hysterically.

Sandy's face was full of dread. She looked miserably at Beth, swallowed, and there was silence for a moment.

"Please don't make me do this," she mumbled from the couch. "Don't make me get mad again, for God's sake."

Sandy was shaking her head back and forth and seemed to mean it.

Beth attempted to recover. She was still holding the image

of her little girl, holding hands with another girl, and being ridiculed for it. "Don't you think you are a little young to know what that truly means. I know you're sixteen, but at that age you are going to have a lot of hormonal changes and that can all become very confusing. You are still in the process of becoming 'a little lady,' so you might better wait another year or two before you decide that."

Sandy was no longer afraid to admit she was gay.

"No, I'm not going to listen to all that anymore." She let it all out in a strangled sob. "My mind is all made up. I am all grown-up now and I know exactly who I am and what I want in life. And I've decided I want to be with Holly, forever."

Beth glanced over at Sandy and some of the flush had left her cheeks.

"Listen, I know you think you're all grown-up," she said, pumping a little parental muscle, "but that doesn't mean you are going to flaunt it here in my house. You're my child and I love you, but somewhere we gotta draw the line."

Sandy teared up again. "I don't understand what you are saying," she said, her voice breaking. "Are you referring to Holly?"

"I am," Beth confirmed. "As far as Holly is concerned, she is no longer allowed in our home and you're no longer permitted to speak or visit with her. Now, I've talked with Sarah Collier and that is the way she wants it. And that's the way your daddy and I want it, so that is the way it's going to be."

Sandy pursed her lips, turned, and walked back to her bedroom. It was obvious she was not happy at all with the turn of events in her life. She felt tears well into her eyes and covered her face with the back of her hands like a little child.

Tim Ketchum was stunned when his wife, Beth, showed him the love letters and informed him of what had been going on between his daughter and Holly Harvey.

"Is all this true, Sandy?" he asked, his face registering both hurt and surprise.

"Yes," she said in a low voice, rubbing at her temples. She didn't appreciate being confronted on this, especially in front of her father.

Tim looked at his daughter curiously, then rubbed a hand over his face. He looked ill.

"I'm obviously not happy with the choices you have made," he said in a strange and casual voice, "but I want you to know I'm resolved to live with it."

Sandy closed her eyes and continued rubbing at her temples.

For a moment, Tim didn't speak. He stood quietly looking down at his daughter until his mixed feelings dissolved in a wave of love. He saw Sandy as vulnerable and fragile, and his last words to her were whispered in a low, husky voice. "I know you've been through a lot of tough times, but nothing you ever do will change the love I have for you."

Sandy smiled, reached out, and gave her father a squeeze. Tim hugged his daughter.

"Nothing will ever change that," he said again, only this time he said it more calmly. "And that's the truth."

Sandy felt better about the situation. She was finally able to make a change that was essentially a change for her. Fate had been tempted and the boundary had been crossed. She had totally and completely accepted the fact she was gay. And the weird thing about it was that God had not struck her dead in her tracks and she felt no shame or torture for saying so. From now on, people would just have to accept her for what she was.

Chapter 23

After Beth and Sandy had quarreled over Holly Harvey, they spent the next four days, alone, and in the house together. Beth didn't trust Sandy and knew if she ever took her eyes off her, she would cut a path to wherever Holly was. She was thinking Sandy's relationship with Holly was maybe a phase thing and that given enough time she would eventually get over her. Time had worked in Beth's favor and had helped heal her heart from two bad relationships with her ex-husbands—so why wouldn't it work for Sandy? The two kept their conversation to just small talk, and Beth pointedly kept away from any mention of Holly, hoping to avoid angry recriminations.

At the end of the fourth day, Sandy surprised Beth by asking if she could talk to her biological mother. Beth talked with Tim, and although they were not pleased with involving Sandra again in their daughter's life, they reluctantly allowed Sandy to phone her. When given permission, Sandy rushed to her room with the phone and dialed the Griffin number.

The next day, when Tim returned home from work, Sandy approached him, alone, and away from Beth. She told him that she longed to have a relationship with her *real* mother. She believed that was part of her problem and thought it was time to get to know her—maybe develop a mother-daughter bond that she'd never had. And the only way she could truly know if that had been the missing ingredient in her life was to move in and live with her mother.

Tim told Beth about Sandy's request. Of course, she was hurt, since she had been the only person in Sandy's life besides Tim who had tried to help her.

"Damn it, Tim," Beth said in disgust, "I've been the one who has worked and helped feed her. I've clothed her and taken care of her the best I could. You and I both know that Sandra never game a damn about her poor, mixed-up daughter she gave birth to so long ago. She's never called Sandy—not once—she's never sent her a card, she's never remembered her birthday, or nothing that showed she loved her."

Tim agreed. Sandra was Sandy's mother, but, in effect, a virtual stranger to the sixteen-year-old, whom she had deserted fourteen years ago.

Beth also reminded Tim just what kind of woman Sandra was.

Tim needed no reminders of what kind of woman his ex-wife had become. By this time, she had six children, all by different men, and had custody of none of them. Presently she was living in a slummy, run-down, and drug-infested neighborhood in Griffin with another man of questionable character.

Beth thought it was not a good idea for Sandy to move in with Sandra, and made it clear to both father and daughter.

Tim and Beth tried to dissuade Sandy from seeing her birth mom, but she was adamant. Sandy brought up that Beth had never known her "birth daddy" until she was eighteen years old, and had to know something of the pain she was feeling.

Beth didn't argue the point. She knew the feelings of abandonment and hurt all too well, but she still didn't soften. As far as she was concerned, Sandra was not the best role model for Sandy.

The next day, Tim conferred with Sandy's probation officer and asked his opinion. The officer counseled that it might not be such a bad idea. As far as he could tell, Sandy was enduring some emotional tumult, and getting to know her birth mother just might have a soothing effect on the troubled teen. Tim reluctantly agreed that Sandy could move in with her mother for a while, but only until she could find out if that was what was good for her.

Beth Ketchum sat on the front porch as Sandy got her things ready. She was very angry at Tim for letting her go, but she was also angry at Sandy. When Sandy came outside and asked her stepmother for a suitcase to pack her things in, Beth told her, "You go and find one yourself. I'm not going to help you."

Sandy turned and walked back inside, but not before Beth added, "I don't approve in no way, shape, or form of you moving in with your mother, and in no way am I going to be a part of it."

Even after Sandy was all packed, Beth still fumed. She walked into her room and noticed Sandy had unplugged her TV set and stereo system and placed them alongside her packed bag.

"Just what are you planning to do with those?" Beth asked, pointing at her TV and stereo.

"I'm taking them with me to my mom's house," Sandy said sheepishly.

"Oh, no, no, no," Beth said, separating Sandy's TV and stereo from her things. "Anything you've accumulated under this roof, especially the things that me and your daddy bought for you while you were under our care, will stay here with us, young lady."

Sandy didn't like what Beth was doing, but accepted it as gospel.

Still stinging from Sandy's rejection, Beth gave her the final word. "From now on, if there is anything you need, then you best ask your *mama* for it. When you finally come to your senses and come back to your *real* home, then your stuff will be sitting here, where you left it."

Sandy bit her bottom lip to keep from crying, then picked up her one bag and walked to the front door.

Beth ignored Sandy, turned her back, and tried to remain a hard-ass, but when it came time for Sandy to leave, she broke down in tears. At the last moment, just as the car was pulling away, she ran outside and chased after them. Tim stopped the car and she climbed into the front seat beside Sandy.

Sandy was Beth's child, too, she had reasoned, and as her mother, she'd do the proper thing. She would see her off and make certain where she would be living was the right place for her. Beth knew that Sandy was not going into a good situation, but she had no idea just how right she really was.

Sandra Ketchum was standing on the front porch at her Griffin home, waiting for her daughter to arrive. It had been a while since Tim had seen his ex-wife and he could see that time had taken its toll on her body. Her creviced face and bloated body made her look so much older and harder than he had remembered.

As soon as the car stopped in the front yard and before Sandra could even say hello, Beth jumped out of the car, grabbed Sandra by the arm, and took her aside. Sandra knew she was facing a tigress in Beth. Beth told her, "Now you listen to me good. Sandy is my child *now* and she looks to me as her mother."

Sandra was a big woman, almost twice the size of Beth. If she had wanted, she could have opened up a can of whoop ass on her. But she knew Beth was as feisty and tough as a pit bull and she dared not cross her. She knew she would be the loser in the end.

Beth pointed her finger in Sandra's face, then warned her: "I'm telling you Sandra that nothing, and I mean nothing, better happen to Sandy. Her life is in your hands and you better not let anything happen to her. Is that clear?"

Sandra nodded. The message was loud and clear.

"Sandy is still on probation," Beth continued. She handed her a piece of paper with all the dates for when Sandy had to meet with her probation officer. "There are stipulations to her probation, and one of those is for Sandy not to see Holly Harvey. Is that also understood?"

"Yes," Sandra said under her breath.

Beth handed Sandra a large manila folder. "You'll also have to enroll Sandy in the Griffin High School for the fall semester of 2004. Here are copies of everything you're going to need, such as medical records and school transcripts."

While Beth and Sandra talked, Tim and Sandy walked inside, found her bedroom, and put her things on the bed. Sandra's home was nothing more than a dilapidated old tenant mill home. Someone had tried to make this rickety, paint-peeling-on-the-outside shotgun house attractive by adding some potted plants on the front porch and a few shrubs in the yard, but it still reeked of filth and poverty.

Inside the house, Sandra kept two large dogs and they moved about like they owned the house and paid the water bill. A second dog and a pen full of puppies were in the living room and it smelled to high heaven of dog crap and urine. Still, as if there were plenty enough food for everybody, two even larger dogs yakkety-yakked from another pen, outside and in the backyard.

"Food stamps must buy a lot of dog food these days," Tim joked when he knew Sandra wasn't listening.

Even though there was no air conditioner in the house, and the heat was so stifling one could barely breathe, Beth attempted to look through the rest of the home. Holding her breath so as not to vomit from the fetid smell of dog shit and putrid squalor, she attempted to move through the nickel tour, but retreated halfway before it was complete.

"Show me Sandy's bedroom," Beth said to Sandra, turning them around. Choking and trying not to gag, she figured Sandra had lived in this filth so long that she had become immune to it.

The room Sandy had put her belongings in was a little better than the rest of the house, but not by much. The walls were unpainted and the room was cluttered with junk. A mattress and box spring sat on the floor, covered by a nasty top sheet.

Beth couldn't take much more of this. She covered her mouth and turned her head, just as she was about to puke. She could see Tim's face and she knew he was thinking the same thoughts as she was.

Maybe Sandy is going to recognize this nauseating environment is nothing like the home she left and will become so disgusted that she will pick up her things, turn around, and get the hell out of here.

Away from Sandra, the Ketchums begged Sandy to think about what she was doing, look at what she was getting into, and reevaluate her situation. But, in all honesty, Sandy was just sick and tired of being told what to do by anybody. She had already lived with her mom and she knew she would let her do the things her daddy and Beth wouldn't. It was time for her to see what her mom was like without her daddy being around.

Sandy held firm.

"I'm sorry," she said, apologizing for the condition of the home. She considered this for a long moment, but finally said, "I really want to be with my natural mother."

Beth's mouth tightened. She ducked her head, threw up her hands, and swallowed uneasily.

"Well, I guess she's made her mind up," she said, then added by way of explanation, "Tim, what the hell are we standing around here for?"

Tim's eyes searched his daughter's face. He could see there was nothing more they could say or do.

Beth and Tim said good-bye to Sandra, hugged and kissed Sandy, then quietly left. They walked out of Sandra's home with their heads hanging down, knowing they had done their very best to try and talk their daughter out of this move and to convince her that her only home was with them.

On the way home, neither Tim nor Beth uttered a single word to each other. The only sounds that could be heard during the hour's drive back home was the sounds of sniffles and the two parents gently weeping.

Chapter 24

Carl Collier had long ago retired from Delta, but kept himself active with a house-painting business. Not only did Carl enjoy his work, but he supplemented his pension with his thriving business. At seventy-four, he showed no signs of slowing down and handled the workload as well as any man half his age.

Every weekday morning, his son, Kevin, worked with his father. This father-son team was always busy and there was a backlog of jobs to be done; so from 8:00 A.M. to 12:00 P.M., Kevin painted houses and then went home to get ready for his job at Delta.

Kevin and his father talked about this situation with Holly and how he should handle it. Carl said he felt as helpless with Holly as he did with Carla at her same age. When she was fifteen, Carla would bang her head against the wall or cause some other self-injury, then blame it on her parents. It was as if she would use lies to try and change reality. He wasn't sure if Holly was as wild as her mother, or as reckless, but there were similarities between the two.

At that point, Kevin was vaguely disturbed by what he was hearing about Holly from his father. Mentally he wrote it off as nothing more significant than Holly being a smart-ass, rebellious teenager. But the next day, after he had slept on it for a while, he felt he had good reason to question what was happening and wonder if there was a more sinister threat than he had imagined.

Kevin didn't want to push the panic button just yet, but he was frightened for his parents in a way that he had never been frightened before. In his heart of hearts, he wanted to believe his niece would do nothing threatening. But what concerned him most was that he was looking at his father—a man who had been through a lot of tough times—who greatly feared his fifteen-year-old granddaughter.

Even the Colliers' neighbors and friends had recognized that Carl and Sarah were involved in a troubled relationship with Holly. Since coming to live with her grandparents in April 2004, she had become very rebellious. The neighbors had witnessed several volatile incidents and heard frequent arguments between Sarah and Holly, which they believed had apparently led to Holly's repeated runaway attempts and trouble with the police. The scuttlebutt through the neighborhood was that Holly had threatened her grandparents and they had grown very fearful of her.

"It's so sad," said Hazel Thompson, a neighbor who lived two doors down from the Colliers. "The neighbors have been talking about how Sarah and Holly are always fighting. I don't understand it. The Colliers are a nice couple, you know. Sarah is very well-liked and always very pleasant. Everyone in the neighborhood affectionately calls her 'Granny.'"

Scott Moore had been living with Holly's mother before she was arrested and sent to jail. Holly had also lived with him for a short period.

"This doesn't surprise me," Scott said of Holly. "She started rebelling as soon as she entered adolescence. Her grandparents tried to bring discipline to her life. They had a whole bunch of rules set down for reasons. One rule was for their granddaughter to stay away from Sandy Ketchum, whom she had met at Fayetteville Middle School.

"Sandy is one of those friends they didn't want her hanging out with. They didn't like what she was doing. They didn't want her sneaking out of the house at night. They didn't want her playing her rap music or taking drugs. And they especially didn't want her carrying on her lesbian relationship with Sandy."

Holly was due to enroll as a freshman at Sandy Creek High School, while Sandy was last enrolled in the Coweta County school system. The Colliers had high hopes that since the two girls were no longer attending the same school, they would forget about each other.

But fat chance of that.

It was early, during midsummer on July 2, a common enough day in Georgia, with its dank, grouchy heat, when Kevin Collier got a call from Holly. She again asked if she and Sandy could spend the weekend of the Fourth of July at his house in Fayetteville. Kevin wasn't too keen on the idea, reminding her what had happened the last time they'd stayed over in early June. His mother was still giving him hell about that incident.

"Aren't you supposed to be spending the weekend with your grandparents?" Kevin asked curiously.

"Come on, Uncle Kevin," Holly pleaded. "You know how much I hate staying with them. They treat me like a prisoner and won't let me do anything."

Kevin had to agree. He knew how miserable Holly was there, and finally agreed to her staying at his place, but only after he got her assurances that there would be no trouble.

Holly assured him there would definitely be no trouble.

"Okay," Kevin finally consented. "As long as you give me your word."

Holly was elated. "I give you my word," she shouted.

"You know, I can't for the life of me see why my mom feels the way she does about Sandy," Kevin added. "She seems nice enough to me. Even if she comes from a broken home, as Mom says she does, then who hasn't? Hell, look at you, Holly. Your mom is a single mom, she's a stripper and a convicted felon, so I don't know why she's so worried about Sandy being a bad influence on you."

"Yeah, Mom's sitting in jail right now," Holly said as a matter of fact.

Kevin agreed. "You're right, so it's hardly an endorsement of our family's background. But you know your grandmother, backgrounds seem to matter so much to her. And with your mother being in jail and everything she's done—to me, it's just the pot calling the kettle black."

Holly thanked her uncle for being so understanding.

Kevin had cut Holly some slack, but he still wasn't about to let her off the hook. "Holly, I've got no intentions of mentioning this weekend stay-over to your grandmother. I figure what she doesn't know, won't hurt her. But you and Sandy better not screw this one up and get my ass in a sling again."

"I promise I won't," Holly reassured him a second, then a third and a fourth time.

The weather forecasters had called for overcast, hot, and lazy, with the humidity being so syrupy that it made the Georgia landscape look like an old snapshot that had lost most of its color. Most of the time during Sandy's visit over the weekend was spent inside and in the coolness of the air conditioner. Kevin got to know Sandy pretty well. He found she had not changed much. She was still very quiet. In fact, if she spoke at all, it was because he had pried it out of her. He still couldn't see how she and his niece had anything in common. Holly was a chatterbox, he couldn't shut her up half the time, and she always dressed feminine. Sandy was just the opposite. If they had an attachment, as his mother claimed they did, then it seemed a little over the top. He had written it off as kids being kids. As far as he was concerned, there wasn't anything much to it—just two teenage *girl* friends hanging out together.

Kevin was oblivious as to how close the teenagers really

were until his live-in girlfriend, Sandra Adams, spelled it out for him.

"It's true, Kevin. Holly pretty much opened up to me and told me that she and Sandy were lesbian lovers. I'd pretty much figured it out anyway from observing the way they looked at each other, but she just confirmed it."

After being told Holly and Sandy were lovers, Kevin was shocked and at a loss as what to do about it. Actually, as a thirty-nine-year-old bachelor who lived with his girlfriend, he didn't have much he could say to her. And, really, what could he do about it? He was not Holly's father. She still had a mother, albeit in jail, but Carla had given Connie Earwood and her husband, Russell, and not Kevin, legal guardianship over her daughter. And Holly also had her grandparents, who loved her and were concerned for her welfare. Kevin decided the best thing he could do for himself and Holly was to keep his opinions to himself and go about his own business.

The following week, on July 13, Holly wrote Sandy another letter. This time she was concerned over an incident where she had kissed another girl and wanted Sandy to forgive her. She again conveyed her love to Sandy, whom she called "Shawdy," and vowed she would love her—and only her—forever:

I got ur letter today. I started crying when we got off the phone last time. I'm sorry I said whatever I did. I love u baby! So much, it's sad. Why won't I Kiss u? I don't know. Just kiss me if u want to. I won't do you like I did [Girl's name]. LOL. That bitch forced her tongue in my mouf. She can't kiss, but u can. I just hope we don't get stuck together. LOL. "click click." Let me feel ur tongue ring.

Damn Sandy! I wanna fuck! I can NOT get drunk w/u. LOL. I will be bad! No, fer real, alcohol makes me mean as hell! I meant to put a hickey on ur leg! Ya Shawdy, we can make it happen. So, ur gonna be my wife? & we're gonna go to the bank to get you pregnant? . . . Ok, now do I want to be w/u for the rest of my life? I'm not sure how to explain it, but I'll try . . . I love u so much, I've never felt this way about no one. I mean I loved a lot of people, but never like this. There's no one thing that makes me happier than u do. I know I've told you this before, but I mean it. How do u really know u want to be w/me forever? I can't stand to be w/o you! It's fuckin drivin me crazy. . . .

Holly's letter also revealed her continual dependency on drugs. At the time, she was smoking large numbers of marijuana cigarettes, taking hits of LSD, and smoking crack. Her grandparents knew she was abusing drugs, but had no idea as to what extent:

I'm so fuckin high. I'm bout to get dat acid. If I came see u, r u gonna do some w/me. I am gettin' 3 or 4 hits of microdot . . . I love you Baby! I want to be w/you until I die. I miss you girl . . . LOL! I feel good Shawdy. I need [you] to come see me so we can fuck. Next time I see you, we are gonna fuck all night until I have to leave. I'll make it special and memorable for you, cuz I don't want it to be like any other time u fucked someone. Right?

Amanda is gonna let me borrow Alice in Wonderland. Let's trip on acid and watch that shit. I'm waitin on a phone call about it right now. It's 12:05 A.M. I think I'm getting $50. Calvin said he would give me $50 . . . Today is Friday. I'm waitin on you to get here. I'm so fucked up, Nigga, I feel so slow Sandy. I can't hold this pen . . . I have 3 oranges and one clomiton (whatever that shit is called) But u can't have it, cuz they don't last long enough & I'm gonna take it tonight, when u come to get me. I wuz gonna get us some "A" but now I gotta wait, cuz I'm givin someone—whoever is bringing u over here, *my $. But it's cool, I'm spost to be getting' $50 sometime soon and no one has that right now anyway. I'm FUCKED UP! I don't even know what I'm doin or talking about. It is 10:25 PM. Hurry up and call me! I'm listening to Lil' Wyte. He said, "if ur hoe get fucked, u can blame it on the bay . . ." I don't feel like writin dis letter! I'm too high! Fuck this I'm bout to play cards. I'll write more later. I love u nigga!*

Without realizing it, the two teenagers' infatuation for one another was becoming dangerous. It looked as if both Holly and Sandy were never going to stop using drugs. And until they stopped using drugs and broke this circle of destruction in their lives, neither would ever get better.

Chapter 25

Fifteen-year-old Sara Polk had known Sandy Ketchum since grade school. They had met when they were both eleven, when Sara and her parents lived with her grandmother in Fayetteville and where Sandy and her father had lived with her grandmother. Sara liked Sandy a lot and always thought she was a pretty cool girl. In no time, they were best buddies and started hanging out together. But when Sara's mother and stepfather bought a place of their own in Griffin and moved to the next county, she and Sandy kind of lost touch.

Over the years, Sara and Sandy wrote each other, but they did not see each other as often they would have liked. When Sara got word that Sandy was in Griffin or Sara was in Fayetteville, they tried to hook up, but over time they grew apart. Sara had heard that Sandy had been sent to the juvenile detention center and was on probation for using drugs and fighting at school. She thought maybe that was why she had stopped writing or trying to contact her, and was surprised to hear that someone had placed her on Sandy's probation officer's list of problem friends. Sara never did any drugs or skipped school, so she was angry to hear that her name was on that list.

In the summer of 2004, Sara learned from her friends that Sandy was in Griffin, visiting her mother. She knew Sandra

Ketchum and didn't think she was a moral person, and believed she was even worse as a mother. Sandy had told her years ago that her mother had deserted her when she was but fifteen months old. Sara never respected Sandra after hearing what she had done to Sandy.

Besides that, Sandra lived in one of the worst neighborhoods in Griffin and her house looked like and smelled like a pigpen. She found out later that Sandra was also letting Sandy do anything she wanted to do, including drinking, taking drugs, and hitchhiking. About every week, Sandy would start walking and then begin thumbing for a ride to Fayetteville. She said she was going to see her girlfriend, Holly Harvey.

Sara met Holly Harvey for the first time while visiting Sandy at her mother's house. She had just gotten back from a funeral and decided at the last moment to drop in and surprise Sandy. Sandy told her Holly was there, hanging out because she had run away from home. To Sara, it looked as if Sandy was embarrassed that Holly was at her mother's house with her.

Sara had always known Sandy was a lesbian and had girlfriends. She discovered it wasn't that Sandy didn't like guys, but girls just seemed to warm up to her quicker. They liked both her masculinity and her sensitivity. In the three years she had known her, Sandy had had a number of girlfriends, and as far as she knew, she had always been loyal and faithful to them.

In a moment away from Holly, Sara told Sandy, "I don't like your girlfriend too much. I think she's jealous of mine and your friendship, and the attention you are giving me."

Sandy admitted that was probably true. Sara was a cute and perky person. Holly was a jealous person and didn't like it when Sandy talked with other girls. Sandy told Sara that Holly probably thought she was her competition.

"I'm going to try and talk her into calling her grandmother and asking her to come pick her up at the Wal-Mart in Griffin,"

Sandy whispered to Sara. "Then we can be alone and spend some time together."

A half hour later, Sara and Sandy waited with Holly until Sarah Collier arrived.

Sara knew Sandy well and could see that she loved Holly a lot. She guessed because Holly probably paid a lot of attention to her and showered her with great affection. Holly was pretty and did have a nice body; Sara could see how Sandy had fallen for her.

Growing up, Sara remembered Sandy as shy, awkward, and tomboyish. The guys never chased after her, but for some reason, the girls did. Even though she was self-conscious about her own looks and always hiding her shapely figure with baggy clothing. And even though she said she suffered from some kind of skin disorder called eczema, that wasn't the real reason why. Sara knew that Sandy was cutting herself, particularly her arms and legs, with a knife, which she always kept in her possession.

Sara also knew that Sandy had been doing drugs for as long as she could remember. She had told her on several occasions she needed to straighten up and leave drugs alone. Sara assumed that was one of the reasons Sandy had moved into her mother's house. Sandra not only allowed her to use drugs, but was probably supplying them.

The other reason Sandy moved in with her mother was because of Holly. Ever since Sandy and Holly's little rendezvous, when they ran away together, they had been forbidden to see each other. Since Sandy was now living in Griffin, Sara continued to see and hear from Sandy on a regular basis. She knew Sandy was also spending a lot of time in Fayetteville seeing Holly. Even though Sandy, at times, denied how much she cared for Holly, Sara understood fully how much she truly loved her. She concluded that Holly Harvey must have seemed the sweetest addiction Sandy had ever been caught up in.

Chapter 26

In early July, Tim Ketchum had an opportunity to take a new job in western Georgia. It was definitely a step in the right direction and could mean a huge increase in his salary and retirement benefits. The plumbing company he was going to work for was one of the largest in Georgia and the owner had high hopes for him. There was only one catch: the Ketchums would have to move again.

"Beth and I have bought a house over in Franklin, a couple of hours from here, on the Georgia-Alabama border," Tim said, breaking the news to Sandy. She was sitting on the bed in her bedroom, staring out the window. "I'm sorry, I know this is a tough time for you, but we're going to move again."

At first, when the shock wore off, Sandy was okay with the move. Her parents had been telling her they didn't trust Holly any longer and they were worried that she might hurt her. Sandy was beginning to feel the same way about her pugnacious girlfriend, especially as their own arguments grew more frequent. But just as quick as that thought would appear, it would disappear, and leave her longing for Holly.

Later that weekend, Tim and Beth drove to Griffin, picked up Sandy, and took her with them to see their new home. Sandy seemed pleased with their selection of the home, which had large, roomy bedrooms and wide-open spaces. Believing Sandy was happy with their choices, they were hoping she would forget about Holly and all that had happened with her. They assured Sandy she would find new friends to replace her old ones.

Although Sandy pretended and was all smiles, she worried about it, staying up late nights thinking about it. Although she had not told anyone, she was not planning on moving anywhere. She still had not shaken her infatuation with Holly and had no intentions of ever being without her again.

Sandy felt a cold knot growing in her stomach.

It's not fair. They have no goddamn right to keep us apart. It's not fair.

Back at Sandra's house, Sandy paced back and forth in her room like a caged tiger. She believed things were never going to change in that people were always telling her what to do and bossing her around. No matter what she did, somebody was always there, assuming the worst. She knew she had made some mistakes, but what did it matter to them if she wanted to be with Holly?

There was just no way Sandy could move back in with Tim and Beth. Just as soon as she hit the door, Beth would be right on top of her, with that little twitch in her nostrils. She'd be giving her the third degree and wanting to know if she had been with Holly. Sandy knew she'd never have any privacy, for Beth was always rummaging through her things, prying, and nosing around in her room.

Sandy paced nervously in her bedroom.

Must have a plan. She began working it all out in her mind. *Holly and I could run away together. . . . We've talked about going to Florida . . . the beach. . . . There must be a plan for that. There's gotta be a way out of this.*

Sandy and Holly had talked before about running away to the beach. She had never seen the ocean, but Holly had fond memories of vacations to Hawaii, the tropics, and the Southeast's coast. The walls in her room were covered with pictures of her and her friends posing on the beach and lying in the surf. It looked so inviting. In Florida, she and Holly would be far away from the people who were always tossing them nasty looks, telling them to take their "gayness" to another town.

Let 'em talk, if that is how they get their jollies. We'll be able to laugh and say, Hell, let 'em take a fucking picture if they wanted to. It would last longer.

But there was no sense in the teenagers thinking about that trip to the beach now. Not anymore—since Holly's grandparents had put that plan on hiatus. They had snatched it away from them like candy from a baby. Now, hell, they weren't even going to let them see each other. An ugly grin worked its way up to Sandy's lips at the thought of Holly's grandparents and their attempts at keeping them apart.

Sandy suddenly had this emotional and physical craving to see Holly. It seemed to work itself up from her belly to her throat, to her mouth and her nose, making her cry out. She longed for her touch.

Sandy threw herself across her bed, having been forced to nurse her pain and momentarily postpone her plan to escape with Holly. She curled in the fetal position and tried to figure it all out. In the very center of her being, a certainty was forming, and the certainty was she was losing Holly. She felt the urge to cut, to mutilate herself, but instead she sat down with pen and paper and wrote Holly a note.

Sandy revealed to Holly how crushed she was at the thought of losing her. She was sixteen, old enough now to know what she wanted in life, and she wanted Holly. She felt like they deserved to be together. What gave anyone the right—her stepmother included—to be so goddamned high-handed that they could tell her what she could and could not do? She would come up with another plan. With God as her witness, she would be with Holly again, even if it killed her.

Staying up late at nights, Tim and Beth Ketchum were

seriously worried about Sandy living in Griffin and her infatuation with Holly. They knew that teenagers often lived on the edge, experimented with drugs, alcohol, and sex. By definition, they did things that seemed stupid or crazy to adults, but, for most teenagers, this type of behavior was a passing phase. They hoped Sandy was just seeking attention and mimicking her peers. They loved her dearly, but lately she had kept them off-balance. When things were good with her, they were awful good, but when things were bad, they were unbearable.

On July 11, Holly received a letter from Sandy. Sandy had her bandana and she wanted to know if she could keep it. She was also concerned about their relationship. Sandy wrote in her letter to Holly:

> *I had this dream that I went to your house, walked in your room, and found you fuckin' someone.*

Holly wrote her back the next day. She told Sandy she could keep her bandana and that she would keep Sandy's knife, although she had no idea why she would ever need a knife.

On Monday, July 12, Kevin Collier planned to drop Holly off at his parents' house, after she had spent the weekend with him. They knew and had okayed the weekend stay, but were unaware she had company—Sandy Ketchum—and Kevin wasn't about to enlighten them. He knew, of course, of their disapproval of the friendship, but thought his strict parents were overreacting. Besides, Kevin found it difficult to say no to Holly. She was, after all, still a little girl to him.

Kevin worked with his father from early morning and returned home around 12:30 P.M. After getting ready for work, he planned on driving Holly back up to his parents' house on his way to the airport. When he got ready to leave, he looked everywhere in his house, but Holly and Sandy had vanished.

He knew he was in hot water again and could already hear the blistering admonishment from his mom for permitting them to stay together at his house after especially being told not to.

Kevin called his mom and listened as she unloaded both barrels.

As soon as Sarah got off the phone with Kevin, she filed a child runaway complaint with the Fayette County Sheriff's Office and then drove down to the house in Griffin, where she believed she would find her granddaughter. She was right.

The Colliers were hoping an appearance on Monday, July 26, in front of a juvenile court judge at the Fayette County Courthouse would straighten Holly out. She was there in reference to the running-away incident in June. After hearing Holly's case, the judge ordered that she receive three months' probation and remain under her grandparents' custody. She would also have to submit to regular drug testing and not associate with anyone else on probation. That included Sandy Ketchum.

The judge also concluded that Holly would attend a three-week program called Breaking the Chain. This proven program was designed specifically for teens with low self-esteem and taught them such needed skills as problem solving and conflict resolution. In plain terms, it connected with teens on multiple levels and helped those like Holly confront their issues of fears and anxieties, self-sabotage, negative inner voices, and much more.

Holly was furious and stormed out of the courtroom with rage across her face.

As the Colliers walked across the parking lot of the courthouse, they could see the rage hanging across Holly's features like a dark cloud. In Holly's case, clouds didn't always mean rain, but it didn't rain without them. They braced themselves for the storm they knew was coming.

"Fuck you . . . fuck you . . . ," Holly mumbled on her way across the parking lot toward Carl's late-model Chevy truck.

She lit up a cigarette and took quick draws. Just as she approached the vehicle, she took one last drag, then crushed the cigarette out on the truck's hood.

Carl exploded. He leapt toward Holly and grabbed her by the arm. Shaking her by the arm, as if to shake some sense into her, he threatened to march her right back inside the courthouse.

"And I don't care if they lock you up and keep you there forever," he roared.

Sarah jumped in between them, begging Carl to calm down.

"Holly's been through enough already," she cried. "Let's all just get in the truck and go home."

If Holly's grandparents saw murder written all over her face, then that was fine with her, because that was certainly what Holly felt. And with a snarl, she let them know that, muttering venomously through a mouth that lately seemed to spew endless surprises, "I'm gonna kill y'all."

Looking at Holly standing directly in front of them, it was as if the Colliers were looking at a magic mirror and seeing their daughter fifteen years ago. Holly's eyes were spaced widely apart. The chin, the mouth, the pouting lips, were all her mother's. Her hair even hung in her face like her mother's. In their eyes, Holly's psyche was caught somewhere between her own self and her mother. She was a fusion, a ghost of both persons. The Colliers didn't know this person and they were afraid of her.

The next day at work, Carl mentioned nothing about Holly to Kevin. They were so busy working they didn't have time to talk about Holly's court appearance. However, on Wednesday morning, when the subject finally came up, Carl told Kevin about what had happened.

"She threatened to kill us," he said, with a heavy heart.

Kevin advised his dad that if he saw any little thing out of the ordinary, he should call 911. But he knew that his parents would not call the police until they absolutely couldn't take it anymore. He encouraged his father and assured him Holly was just being a disrespectful ass and mouthing off.

Things were very different at Kevin's parents' home. He knew his parents would not put up with any of Holly's shenanigans. Even though Holly was sneaky, her grandparents knew what she was doing. They knew about the dope and that she sneaked out of the house at night whenever she could. They were neither blind nor stupid, and were determined to domesticate this wild creature.

The Colliers had even talked to Kevin about sending Holly to the Georgia Baptist Children's Home. Perhaps, this would help tame her. Kevin suggested they not bring this up to Holly—at least not yet. They should investigate the situation, he advised, and find out all the facts before they said anything to her. This was the first step and he didn't want them to plunge everything into chaos before they got a good look at their options. Besides, Carla would be released from Metro State Prison in a few months and then Holly would be her problem again.

The Colliers knew Holly could be institutionalized—if for nothing but to protect them from her. They believed it was the best way to show their love and an opportunity for Holly to change. Maybe, it they got her out of their house and into a stricter environment, she would go straight. But that wasn't going to be easy. Carla would fight them every step of the way; then the courts would have to step in and take custody of Holly. And that would hurt them too much to have that happen.

The Colliers agreed Kevin was probably right. The best place for Holly was with her mother. But they shouldn't have to face this ranting and intimidation from anyone—least of all, their granddaughter. They knew it was hard for Holly, her mother being in prison, and being ripped and torn to pieces emotionally all the time. She never truly had a home. But, still, it wasn't right what she was doing to them. They were having to fight her off all the time.

There was something terribly wrong with grandparents arguing and fighting with their granddaughter all the time. It just didn't make any sense.

Part IV

DOUBLE MURDER

Chapter 27

After Holly's court incident, the Colliers found it impossible to communicate with her. All of a sudden, it was as if they had nothing to talk about and fewer and fewer reasons to talk at all. She had become increasingly rebellious and was continually existing in a drug stupor. The only explanation the Colliers had for such behavior was that Holly believed they no longer loved her.

Even though Carl and Sarah were deathly afraid of Holly, they really did love her. They didn't know what she was up to, but believed whatever it was, she was up to no good. On many occasions, Sarah would call Kevin, usually in a dither of some sort, positively rattled and carrying on about Holly.

"You know, she's threatened to kill us," Sarah told her son. "You just don't know what she could do to us if she really wanted to."

Kevin was silent. He had never told them about an incident at Wal-Mart, where Holly had been caught shoplifting. He and Holly were together, and she even had money in her pocket, but she chose to steal several items from the cosmetic department. Wal-Mart detained her, but agreed not to press charges, saying that Holly was banned from the store.

Afterward, Kevin talked with Holly, especially about Carla

and what a mess her mother had made of their lives. Holly told him she didn't want to make that same mistake. She begged Kevin not to tell her mother about the shoplifting incident, and he agreed. Carla later found out and got mad at Kevin for not telling her about it. But the way Kevin saw it, it was pretty much of a shell game with those two.

Kevin had always sympathized with his father when it came to Carla and Holly. The question he had never asked himself, he realized now was: How? How had his father put up with Carla in the first place? And now with Holly? And really, when it came right down to it, that was what he had done—he had put up with them. "And do you know she's still having this relationship with the Ketchum girl? They're doing drugs together, too."

Kevin admitted Holly was more than a French fry short of a Happy Meal. He understood why his parents wouldn't approve of her erratic behavior, they being the conservative Baptists they were. He also knew the two teenagers were doing drugs, 24/7, but he couldn't lay that blame on Sandy. Holly had been doing drugs for a long time. Carla even allowed it. So why didn't they just kick her out? Give her back to Carla and let her go back to where she came from? That's what he had done. Holly and her mother were high-maintenance problems and not worth all the grief they were giving them.

Because Kevin knew his parents would never turn their backs on Holly, he was as lost as a ghost in a snowstorm as to what advice he should give them. He was keenly aware that given his mom and sister's combative history, and since that situation had never been resolved, he didn't think he was the best person to help them deal with it. As far as his parents' relationship with his sister, it was as if all they were doing was playing defense. But it was hard to play that kind of game when his sister was always changing the rules. Hell, he didn't even know what the rules were.

It was just so awkward, so sad that no one knew what to do

or say to help Holly. All any of them could do was love her and go through the motions, until her mother got out of prison. Maybe then, she would listen to her mother. But Carla was such a flighty and irresponsible person, Holly was more of a mother than she was.

Carla had continually dragged Holly from pillar to post. She had not only imposed on her friends' and family's hospitality, but anybody else who would let her. Still, her parents had tried to do the right thing by her. They had brought her up to know right from wrong and taught her respect both for the laws of man and God. But she was rebellious and disrespectful. She had turned Holly against her own grandparents and taught her to be disrespectful to them, and now she was paying the price for it. Her daughter had turned out to be just like her, an ingrate, and there was little hope that she would recognize this before it was too late to do something about it.

On July 28, 2004, Carla wrote Holly a letter from the Metro State Prison. She began by expressing her sympathy about what a screwed-up deal she'd received being put on probation. But she also admonished Holly, advising her that she was headed down the wrong path.

"This ain't no joke," Carla warned her. "If you care anything about your freedom, young lady, you better fly right and straighten up."

Carla also queried her daughter, asking for details about the living conditions at her parents' home and how her mother was treating her. She knew how different the arrangement was at her parents' home versus what Holly was accustomed to when she was living with her. Holly had told her she felt like she had a ball and chain around her neck.

"I can't stand the thought of you being there and what you have to go through," Carla empathized. "You will never know how sorry I am for putting you through all this. I want you to have faith that this will all be over soon and believe that we are gonna be together and happy real soon."

Carla asked Holly for some of her jewelry and makeup. She could bring it to her the next time she visited her in jail.

When Holly saw her mother again, she told her all about what was going on at home. What upset her most was her grandparents' lack of trust in her and their failure to believe she knew what was best for her and how to achieve it.

Actually, if the truth were known, Holly's little hints and whining objections had been overturned by well-reasoned arguments, but Holly couldn't see that.

On July 31, Holly received another letter. This time it was from Sandy, who vented about what was bothering her. She was upset that Holly had accused her of still being infatuated with another love interest, and that she was about to dump Holly for this person. Sandy assured her that she didn't love Amanda Roberts anymore, that she was a relationship of the past:

> *Don't you realize everything I have sacrificed to be with you? Why can't you just forget the past and live in the present? I love you so fuckin' much that it drives [me] crazy not to be with U everyday. I mean damn! What do I have to do?*

Sandy then revealed it was 4:40 A.M. She had been taking drugs and drinking all night. Everything appeared in slow motion to her. She obscurely ended her letter with:

> *We're on fire! Anyways . . . damn! Can I put it in your mouf? Or can you put It in my mouf? Let me kno nigga! LOL! Damn! Sara's pregnant, Amanda's pregnant, who's next. Not you, I hope! LOL! Well, I glad 'cause I'm so fuckin' not. Blaze one.*

It would be a lie to say that Sandy was not concerned about her relationship with Holly. It seemed like the only thing they were doing now was taking drugs and having sex. What was once the exception now seemed to be the rule. Sandy worried about it, staying up late at night, thinking of what she could do to change that.

For reasons Sandy could not begin to articulate, she found herself passionately and dangerously in love with Holly. The two of them were constantly running away from home, trying to be together every minute of the day. They had, by a lot of measures, almost nothing in common. Sandy thought she could change Holly, and Holly thought she could change Sandy, and that caused a lot of friction and fighting in their relationship. They just kept at it—fighting, then reconciling— as if they had reached across a wide gulf and touched something deep inside of each other, but they didn't know how to get to the other side, and neither of them dared to let go. Their love was eternal, and they felt such a love had never been felt before in their lives.

Chapter 28

Most of Holly's problem stemmed from an unconscious need to be free from her grandparents. The freedom she wanted so badly had been stifled and her desire to be free of that was overwhelming and consuming.

Things were not going so well at Sandy's home in Griffin, either. The relationship Sandy had imagined as the unfolding of a beautiful flower had turned rotten inside. Her mother and her mother's boyfriend, Kenny, were always having nasty fights. She and Kenny used to literally have fistfights all the time. She had seen Sandra get beat to hell and back, and then Kenny get beat to hell and back. It was not a pretty situation.

That was part of the reason Sandy would go to Holly's house every weekend, so she wouldn't have to deal with Sandra and Kenny, their fighting and shit. But when she got to Holly's grandparents' house, she had to deal with arguments between Holly and her grandparents. This time she would tell Holly she couldn't take it anymore—going to her house every weekend, and hiding downstairs in the basement from her grandparents, was growing old.

It had been Holly and Sandy's dream to drive down to Jacksonville, Florida, and spend a week at the beach. But Holly's grandparents had told her no, for many reasons.

First of all, neither Holly nor Sandy had a vehicle or a driver's license. Secondly, school was just around the corner, and Holly needed to get her things in order. Third, they had no money. And four, Holly had already been told she couldn't see Sandy anymore.

When Holly's grandparents held steadfast in their decision, a rage rose across Holly's features like a dark cloud. Although she never raised her hands or threatened her grandparents in any way, she never agreed to it. A dark look would cross her face and suddenly she seemed somewhere else. Someplace far away. Someplace unpleasant. But then, just as suddenly as she had left mentally, she would return.

Holly's breath stopped in her throat with a little gasp.

"But what will I do without Sandy?" she asked in a soft, thin voice.

Sarah turned up her nose, as if there were a foul odor in the room. "I'm sorry, Sandy is not our problem."

Holly accepted the fact that Sandy was not her problem—but she was Holly's greatest concern. As soon as the conversation ended, she started working the phones, deliberately disobeying her grandparents, trying to drive them out of her grim, little world, ruled by her fury.

On Sunday, August 1, Holly phoned Sandy and assured her she was working on the plans for their beach trip.

"Don't worry, I'll take care of everything," she said with great confidence. "Just make sure you find a ride over to my house tonight."

"Okay," Sandy agreed, thinking all the time that might present a few problems for her.

I haven't been to the beach in like so many years, you know what I mean? I haven't gotten in a bathing suit in front of anybody. You know it was really hot last summer, I wore sweatshirts every day. It's like 100 degrees outside and I'm walking around in a sweatshirt and long pants, instead of shorts and a T-shirt.

Nevertheless, Sandy walked over to a neighbor's house and asked David Burnett if he would drive her to Fayetteville. Burnett truthfully admitted he didn't have any money for gas.

"Then Holly will give you ten dollars to take me," Sandy bargained.

Burnett asked Sandra Ketchum if she agreed that he could drive Sandy to Fayetteville. Sandra said it was fine with her, as long as Sandy was back home by Tuesday, so she could go out and find a job.

As soon as Holly's conversation ended with Sandy, she had started working on her new plan. At 8:45 P.M., she phoned her friend Brittany Anne Jensen, but Brittany told her she had to get off the phone. She promised to call Holly back soon, but didn't. Several minutes later, Holly called back and left a message on her answering machine. Because she sounded a little upset, Brittany called her right back. She apologized for not staying in touch, but said she would love to see her. It was just that neither she nor Holly could drive, and there was nobody to help them get Holly to Brittany's home in Lithia Springs.

Holly then blurted out that she hated her grandparents, especially her grandmother, and talked about how she didn't respect them. She said living with them was like being in hell.

Brittany chatted with her for a few moments, said she understood how miserable Holly could be living with her grandparents, and then said good-bye.

Despite Holly's grandparents' rules, Holly sneaked Sandy into the basement bedroom later that Sunday night, around 10:00 P.M. They had planned on spending the night together.

"I've called Calvin," Holly revealed heartily about a sudden change in plans. Instead of going to the beach, Calvin Lawson was coming to pick them up and take them to his apartment.

The corners of Sandy's mouth turned downward. She had never met this guy. All she knew about Calvin was that he was black, he worked for a construction company, and he had met Holly's mother at a strip club. What Sandy didn't know was that when Holly's mother got busted and went to jail, she had left her cell phone with Holly. One day Calvin called Carla's number and Holly answered. The two of them struck up a conversation and he quickly learned Holly, like her mother, had an insatiable appetite for marijuana and would do about anything to get it.

Sandy was certain Holly had cheated on her with Calvin in exchange for money and drugs. But—what the hell—he wasn't the only man with whom Holly had cheated. Holly's excuse was always because she was high or that the money she got from Calvin came to Sandy. According to Holly, that made it okay, so it shouldn't have been a problem to Sandy.

Sandy had lost her temper with Holly over Calvin before, but not enough to make her feel sick and tired or afraid to see Holly. A toke of marijuana would help blunt that feeling of rejection.

Oh, yes, it would blunt that feeling and more.

Shortly before midnight, Sandy slipped out of the Colliers' basement with Holly and followed her to the corner of Travis Street and Plantation Drive. They waited about fifteen minutes, until Calvin arrived.

Calvin stopped the car across the street and waved at the two girls. He looked at Sandy with interest, but only briefly, then quickly turned his eyes back to Holly. A quick assessment revealed Holly's shirt covered a nice summer tan. Her thick, wavy hair fell perfectly on her shoulders. The outline and shadows underneath her clothing revealed a nice, healthy bustline. No signs of a bra. Shapely legs moving graciously under a short skirt.

For Calvin, Holly was as fine as wine!

Holly and Sandy got in the backseat. As soon as Sandy sat down, she knew this guy was weird. Staring at them in the face, in the backseat, a porno tape was playing in the DVD player. Holly pointed at the couple in the film and giggled at their sexual Olympics, like a schoolgirl. Sandy turned her head and tried to ignore it, but it was pretty hard to ignore two people grunting and groaning every five seconds.

"Her name is Sandra Ketchum." Holly made the introductions over the heavy breathing from the tape. "But she likes to be called Sandy."

Calvin smiled and nodded, his eyes covered by dark sunglasses. He drove the teenagers to a convenience store, where he bought an ample supply of blunts and cigarettes. He then drove them to his apartment in nearby Union City.

Sandy was already a bit leery of Calvin's intentions, but became even more so when she walked into his apartment and saw another porno film playing on his big-screen television. *This man is a fucking pervert,* she kept turning over and over in her mind.

Calvin tossed his keys on the couch and walked over to the kitchen, where he kept a sack of weed and bags of cocaine. Sandy's eyes sparkled. She and Holly were very fond of "chronic," the street name for marijuana laced with cocaine. Throughout the night, he and the teenagers burned the candle at both ends.

While Calvin snorted the cocaine, Holly and Sandy smoked the weed laced with cocaine. Several times during the night, he and Holly would walk back to his bedroom and shut the door. Sandy was too wasted to even care, but the three of them kept at it all night, burning it up until both ends of the candle were gone, and partied until 5:00 A.M. They were really wired.

"I don't wanna go back to your grandparents' house," Sandy whined. "I'm afraid they will catch me."

Holly looked at Calvin, then back at Sandy. Pretending Calvin would not hear their conversation, she invited her to stay with Calvin.

"If you have sex with him, he'll give you eight hundred dollars and even let you drive his car the next day."

Sandy stared at Holly with self-pity, but it quickly turned to anger.

Holly grinned at Sandy, then at Calvin, as if they had some kind of dirty secret going on between them.

Sandy cut her eyes at Calvin and gave him a look that said: *I'm not your type, asshole. I'm not inflatable.* She then informed Holly she wasn't interested in selling her body for any amount of money, and she didn't plan on being around Calvin again unless she was in the same room.

Holly talked Calvin into taking them back to Fayetteville and he dropped them off at the Colliers' house somewhere around 5:30 A.M. In the darkness of the morning, the girls slipped back in the Colliers' home through the basement, unnoticed. They quickly undressed and got back in bed together.

It's been said by those who take hits of acid that it can make a person paranoid, but it also tends to sharpen perceptions. Holly sensed something was on Sandy's mind, but it was always so damn hard to drag it out of her.

After their little escapade with Calvin, Sandy argued with Holly. She had decided she no longer wanted to live this way. So eager to please Holly, she had not recognized what was developing between them. The risks she had taken for Holly weren't worth it anymore.

Why couldn't Holly understand the obvious?

Sandy saw Holly as having a very nasty attitude. It was the way she acted that unnerved her. She'd be nice at times, then cold and mean at other times. It was as if Holly would say things just to tick her off.

Sandy got up out of bed, put her clothes on, and walked away into the shadows. As she was leaving, Holly raised up in bed and pleaded, "No, wait, please stay." Her voice was nearly purring, and through her tears, she asked, "Why are you leaving? Have I done something to make you mad?"

In the darkness of Holly's bedroom, Sandy confronted her about the way she had been acting lately and the reality of what would happen if her grandparents caught them together again.

"Your grandparents have come so close to catching me so

many times," she said, trying to explain her paranoia. "And I don't want to risk going back to jail."

Holly lit a cigarette and smoked it down to short, little puffs. An ugly grin touched her lips at the thought. Suddenly another idea rose up from her naked body. She perked up like an old coffeepot, then swore, "I'd kill my grandparents before I'd ever let them do anything to hurt you."

Sandy laughed a little at the shallow statement. "Thanks, but I just need to leave," she insisted.

Another ugly grin touched Holly's lips. She crossed her arms, suddenly feeling cold, then handed Sandy her cell phone. "Go ahead," she said. "Call whoever you want to."

Sandy relaxed a bit, wondering from her relief whether she had been expecting something else. She started calling people she knew and asking them if they could come get her. Sandy tried several of her friends, but she couldn't find anyone willing to drive to Fayetteville. But since she had her stuff all packed and ready to go, she decided she was just going to walk home.

Holly came up on one elbow and looked directly at Sandy. "Please don't leave, I'll do anything to be with you. Anything you want!"

Holly's words picked up Sandy's heartbeat, increasing her metabolism a hundredfold.

Was Holly still thinking the best thing to do with her grandparents was kill them?

Sandy turned and faced her. "You're giving me goose bumps," she said thickly.

Holly was silent, looking pale and wan. She reached across the bed and grabbed a pen from the nightstand, as if to say she would put it in writing if that was what Sandy really wanted.

"You really don't mean that?" Sandy asked straightforwardly. "Tell me you don't mean that."

Holly quickly spat out her plan for killing her grandparents. They had tried to keep her and Sandy apart. Now they would catch them by surprise and they would pay dearly for doing that.

Sandy felt herself spinning out of control.

"Why don't we just wait until they are sleep tonight and steal their truck?" she suggested, thinking that was a better alternative. "We can just run away to the beach together."

"No, I just wanna kill 'em," Holly replied in a small voice, a bit hysterical. "I want you in my life forever."

Sandy had a small headache that throbbed dully. She swallowed hard. That was a very tall order.

Holly never caved in. She lit another cigarette and started talking again, sounding a little nervous.

"I swear I'll do it," she vowed.

In retrospect, Holly's declaration of her love for Sandy was more like an announcement of the reason why her grandparents were going to have to die. If something more needed to be said from Sandy—like a show of hands—then it never happened. But in their drug-induced haze, these brazen, confused teenagers were suddenly planning to murder two people.

And just so they wouldn't forget their plan, Holly took the pen and scribbled grimly across her arm—four printed words that read like a "things to do list."

Kill. Keys. Money. Jewelry.

Chapter 29

On Monday morning, August 2, Carl Collier got up early and drove to a house-painting job in Fayetteville. As was customary, Carl's son, Kevin, met him at the work site and helped him until noon. Kevin then cleaned up, bade his father good-bye, and drove off to his airport job in Atlanta. Kevin saw nothing out of the ordinary on this hot summer day other than his having to leave work early to attend orchestra practice at First Baptist Church in Dunwoody.

While Carl was working on the job, Sarah was at home packing. The following Monday, she was to fly to Hawaii and visit the islands with a dear friend. Carl would stay at home, in order to watch after Holly and keep her out of trouble. This particular morning, Sarah was busy trying on clothing she planned to take on the trip and suddenly needed her suitcases from downstairs. Unfortunately, the suitcases were inconveniently stored inside a closet in Holly's bedroom.

As Sarah opened the door leading downstairs and turning into Holly's bedroom, a wave of vulgar rap music blasted from behind Holly's closed door. She knew Holly was smoking marijuana because she could smell the pungent scent still lingering throughout the basement. She was chafed at the thought of Holly bringing drugs into her house again.

The Colliers' had already lost a daughter to drugs and crime. With Carla in prison on a drug conviction, the elderly couple had taken in their granddaughter, hoping they could rein her in, but they were losing the war. For days now, Holly had been moping around the house with a face long enough to step on. But Sarah knew she was silently planning and plotting somehow to drive her and Carl, once again, out of her grim world, where everything was ruled by her fury.

At first Sarah thought about waiting until she got back from Hawaii to deal with Holly, or letting Carl take care of it while she was gone. But deep down inside, she knew it couldn't wait until then. She and Carl had to face the rest of this nightmare together.

Sarah knew she and Carl wouldn't be able to reason with Holly, she could see that now. They had tried to reason with her before, and she had refused to listen. As far as she was concerned, Holly had destroyed her last and best chance for reconciliation.

Sarah phoned Carl. "I need you to come home now and take care of Holly," she said, her voice alarmed.

Carl was still trying to make peace with his granddaughter. The idea of going at it with her again wasn't exactly inviting. He had agonized over Holly in the same way he had agonized over his daughter's behavior fifteen years ago. *Like mother, like daughter,* he conceded.

"What is it this time, Sarah?" he asked in his small Southern drawl. "Can't it wait until I come home this evening?"

"No," Sarah said hysterically. Her anger rose like the mercury on a hot Georgia day. There would be no better time to take care of Holly than now. She couldn't say what the trouble was, not over the phone. "Just come home."

Around 3:30 P.M., Sarah phoned Chris Miller, a church friend, and asked her about some books she had loaned her. Chris suggested she would give them to her husband, Clarence, and he could pass them on to Carl at their 7:00 P.M. church meeting.

"I'm going to Hawaii on Monday to visit friends," Sarah said with a glee in her voice. "Carl says it would be good for me to get away."

"Is Carl and Kevin going to see after Holly?" Chris asked.

"Yes. They can handle her better than I can. They're more firm with her."

Chris was sympathetic.

Sarah sounded tired. "You know, Holly is killing us. She is sleeping all day, taking drugs, and leaving the house at night."

Chris was well aware Holly had been causing the Colliers a lot of problems. "I know you thought her mother was going to get out of jail this month, is that still going to happen?"

"We haven't heard anything yet, so we assume not." Sarah sighed. "It would be great if she did; then she could take care of Holly."

"I just wish you could get Holly in the Georgia Baptist Children's Home," Chris interjected. "Maybe it would help straighten her out."

"We don't have the authority to do that, as somebody else has power of attorney," Sarah explained. "But there is a lady in our church who works at the home and I plan on talking to her about it."

Sarah and Chris exchanged their good-byes and their I-love-you's, then hung up the phone.

As the afternoon wound down, Holly and Sandy were finishing off the rest of the chronic, which Calvin had given them. They discussed killing Holly's grandparents. At the same time Sarah Collier was upstairs and on the phone with a friend, Holly used her cell phone and called her friend Amanda Roberts.

"Can you come and pick me and Sandy up at my grandparents' house," she pleaded. "We just need to get away."

"Get real, Holly," Amanda snapped. "How do you expect me to come and pick you up, I don't even have a license."

Holly abruptly hung up the phone.

At 4:37 P.M., Sandy tried her luck. Using Holly's cell

phone, she called Samantha Colon and asked if Samantha knew where she could get a gun.

"No." Samantha was stunned. She asked Sandy, "Why do you need one?"

"So I can take care of business."

Samantha then turned to her boyfriend, Marc Aragon, and asked him sarcastically if he knew where to get a gun. Marc asked Sandy repeatedly why she needed a gun, but she wouldn't answer. Finally, after the seventh time of asking "Why do you need a gun?" he handed the phone back to Samantha.

"I-I-I-m scared, Samantha," Sandy said in a broken voice.

"Why?"

"I just am," Sandy said in a low voice. "I'm gonna go to jail for murder."

"Listen to me," Samantha admonished. "Don't you do anything stupid."

Sandy promised Samantha she wouldn't and that the next time she came to Fayetteville she would call her and come visit.

While Sarah paced nervously upstairs and waited for Carl to arrive, Holly and Sandy reviewed their plans and maliciously plotted the Colliers' death. The two teenagers were certainly not secretive about or ashamed of their evil intentions. They were even brazen enough to call their friends and ask how to obtain a gun to carry out their plans of murder. Although they did not succeed in finding a gun, they didn't let it hamper their plans for murder.

Shortly after 4:37 P.M., the girls finally decided to act out their murder plan. Realizing now a gun was out of the question, they suddenly had the urge to surprise Holly's grandmother, pounce upon her like a wildcat, and then stab her with a knife until she was dead.

"Let's do it right now," Holly insisted. "I'll call her on my cell phone and ask her to come downstairs."

"Oh, God. Oh, please," Sandy cried, cold sweat breaking out across her forehead. "At least wait until I hide in the closet."

Sandy hid in the closet and listened as Sarah walked downstairs and tapped on Holly's door. When she and Holly started arguing, Sandy was praying all the while: "Please, God, don't let nothing happen."

After Sarah turned on her heels and left the room, Holly sneaked out of the room, up the hall and stairwell behind her.

Sandy heard the bedroom door slam, then opened the closet door and poked her head through. She eased out of the closet and looked apprehensively at the closed door. Waiting until she was certain all was clear, she walked over to the bed, sat down, and covered her mouth with her hands.

Holly is really running things now.

Maybe at first, Sandy thought Holly wouldn't hurt anyone, but now she wasn't so sure.

Holly had slipped unnoticed into the kitchen. The room was cold and deserted. She went to the counter, where the carving knives were stored, and pulled three knives from the wooden block. She chose the three longest and scariest knives in the bunch. She grabbed a ham sandwich from off the counter, put it on a plate, and carried it, along with the knives, back downstairs.

"Want a bite of my sandwich?" she asked Sandy as she opened the door.

Sandy shook her head. She didn't have much of an appetite.

Holly showed Sandy the three knives. As they divvied the knives indiscriminately, there was both fear and confusion. They could live with either of those, but they couldn't go on living without each other. For three months, people had tried to keep them apart. Now they were finally going to be together, once and for all.

Sandy chose the smallest knife, one that fit perfectly in her jeans pocket.

Holly kept the other two knives. A big, fat butcher knife and a long, skinny boning knife. Holly never looked up. She was lost in her own grim, little world she was creating.

"I wonder if this knife is sharp enough to penetrate skin?" Holly asked, holding the biggest one that she had found in the kitchen. She held the butcher knife above her head and slammed it down into her mattress several times. The big knife sliced through the material easily until it was halfway buried into the mattress. *My grandmother will finally pay. Oh, yes, she will pay, just the way my mother and I had paid all these years when we had to listen to her. On and on, she nagged. Nag. Nag. Nag. An endless flow of put-downs. Yes, indeed. She would finally pay.*

A little timid about the whole situation, Sandy took the small knife out of her pocket and practiced stabbing it into the mattress. She punctured several holes into the mattress before she determined the knife was suitable.

Holly looked around the room at a color poster of three white poodles, hanging on the wall, adjacent to her bed and next to the closet. She pulled the picture off the wall and tossed it on the bed, glancing at it in wild and irrational hope. Slowly her hope gave way to anger.

"Let's kill them!" she blurted out, an ugly grin touching her lips at the thought.

Holly then held a large and slender boning knife above her head, whipping it straight down in front of her with great force. A dull thud sounded as the knife ripped through the picture and into the bed mattress, where she and Sandy had just slept together, hip to hip, and made love.

She raised the knife again and it whizzed by the side of Sandy's face, missing her only by a naked inch, striking the picture and a deep pile of bedsheets with a muffled thud.

Sandy massaged the pain at her temples.

This is gonna happen whether I like it or not.

Not certain if she was willing to stab anybody, Sandy pointed toward a glass seashell lamp resting on the nightstand and next to Holly's bed. She suggested, "Why don't we just knock them out with that lamp and leave?"

Holly must have thought that was a better idea. Before Sandy could make a move, her hands pawed wildly at the nightstand, jerking the lamp loose from the electrical socket. Sandy heard a thump as the lamp landed on the bed, followed by a hollow crash as Holly rolled over on the lamp and broke it apart. The lamp split open and the shells spilled on top of the bedsheets in every direction.

Sandy suddenly grabbed Holly by the arm.

"Listen," she said, looking and pointing upward.

There was a pounding noise upstairs.

Sandy's mouth was suddenly dry. She stiffened her tongue and felt it rising to the roof of her mouth. "I think your grandfather just came home."

The muscles in Holly's face sagged, pulling her jaws out wide until her mouth opened. At the same time, she began to shiver. These were all sounds she knew and recognized well. Several muffled thumps from upstairs. Hurried sounds. Hoarse shouts from upstairs.

Carl Collier was home!

Holly told Sandy she could not make out what they were saying, word for word, but she knew the script well enough by now. She had heard it all before and imagined her grandmother was ranting to her grandfather about her. She was probably telling him about the marijuana smell and how their heathen granddaughter was abusing drugs again. Holly jokingly referred to Carl as "the prison warden" and to Sarah as "the enforcer."

Holly assured Sandy, "They'll be coming down here and knocking on my door in about five minutes."

Sandy loosened her grip on Holly's arm. She seemed to shrink in her clothes. She, too, had felt this chill more than once in the past couple of months, when she had sneaked in and out of the Colliers' home to be with Holly. She had always been afraid of getting caught. As she struggled with what was about to happen, she listened to the muffled sounds, but could not determine if they were footsteps from upstairs or the horrible beat of her own heart.

"They're coming downstairs," Holly muttered in a panic, then grinned. It was like she had gotten a sudden glimpse of what she had accomplished. Her grandparents frowned on drinking and drugs, in any shape or form, and she had used that to lure them to the basement.

The two teenagers jumped up from the bed. Holly grabbed the picture and hung it back in its spot on the wall. Looking like wild characters from some late-night horror movie, they stood there in the middle of the bedroom, clenching knives in their hands, and looking at each other. Not yet out of high school, these two girls still had no idea they were about to decide what to do with the rest of their lives.

"You're not going to go chickenshit on me, are you?" Holly asked.

Sandy was still distracted by the noises she heard upstairs. "Of course not," she answered nervously, feeling a cold finger touch her heart.

"Good," Holly responded heartily, giving Sandy a lopsided smile. "Because it's about to go down."

Holly was out of control, Sandy could feel it. She had hoped there was a voice of reason somewhere in Holly's repertoire, but she only heard the voice of persistence. The stage was already set, and in Sandy's head, it was so real and frightening that it could have been her own thoughts. She was afraid the curtain was about to go up. She would try as hard as possible to prevent this nightmarish show from debuting. But sooner or later, she was convinced, the show would go on. With or without her, it was destined to happen. And once it started, Carl and Sarah were going to die like characters in their own version of a William Shakespeare tragedy.

Sandy waited until she heard Carl's heavy footsteps echoing in the stairwell before she panicked. Suddenly thoughts of her daddy and Beth slipped into her mind. She began to cry, and tears silently began to roll down her cheeks.

God help me!

Chapter 30

Never realizing they were being drawn to places they'd never been before, and would never have imagined going, Carl and Sarah Collier flipped the fluorescents off in the kitchen and descended downstairs. With the excuse of gathering several pieces of luggage stored in Holly's closet, the elderly couple turned left at the end of the stairs and walked toward Holly's bedroom. Loud, profane music still blared from behind the door.

Carl marched up to Holly's door, wearing a face more commonly seen in barroom brawls. He tried opening the door, but it was locked. He knocked hard on the door and shouted, "Open up, Holly."

Holly froze in place. No answer. She looked at Sandy, then reached around behind her and stuffed the boning knife in the back of her pants.

Carl knocked harder.

"I said open up." His voice was high, insisting. "There's a few pieces of luggage your grandmother needs from the closet and we need to get in."

"Just a minute," Holly droned.

Sandy shrieked, but the sounds never escaped her lips. She jumped over the bed and hid behind it. Since nothing had happened earlier in the day, when she hid in the closet, she didn't expect anything to happen then. But she didn't want to get caught where she shouldn't be.

Holly cracked the door open and a dim bit of light spilled out. Her way of looking at her grandfather must have sparked his own temper. He backed away from her and made one last effort to keep his anger in check.

"Okay, come on in," Holly said.

Carl stiffened, looking put out with the whole situation, and pushed the door open wide. Sarah followed him into the room when the door swung open. They turned toward Holly and saw an ugly grin across her face.

Carl's temper slipped another notch.

"We know you're doing drugs again," Sarah said, also flushed with anger. "We can smell it all over the house."

Holly stood beside her bed, breathing hard. Her face was the color of a rose linen tablecloth. Her eyes were shiny but flat, and her hair hung damply against her neck.

Sarah turned toward Holly's wicker dresser and began examining the contents on top.

"So where are you hiding the drugs?" She slipped past Holly without getting an answer, then said accusingly, "You know you're going to turn out just like your mother."

Holly's hands suddenly clamped into tight fists by her sides. The boning knife was hidden in her pants.

Sarah shifted in front of the wicker dresser, slamming the big part of her thigh into it, but barely feeling it.

"I want you to give me whatever it is you are smoking, do you understand?" she mumbled, all the while turning her back toward Holly.

Holly played dumb.

Sarah gave her a final and furious glance. Her lips were twisting and bucking as the words bottled up behind them and struggled to find their way out.

Holly stood there, shaking in the grip of anger and shame, until she finally came undone.

Oh, yes, I'll give it to you all right, she thought, clenching her teeth.

Holly reached around from behind her back and grabbed the boning knife out of her pants. She was about to make her move. One, maybe two steps more, and she could plant it square into her grandmother's back.

The shoe had suddenly switched to the other foot.

Before Holly could swing the knife over her head, Carl looked up and suddenly shouted, "What are you doing with that knife?"

Sarah turned around and saw Holly holding the knife out in front of herself. She and Carl were both staring at Holly carefully, as if she were a stranger that they had never seen before, and possibly a dangerous one.

Sandy saw the look of angry reproach on Sarah's face.

She then looked over at Carl and saw there was worry in his eyes now. Carl had raised questionable eyebrows at Holly.

For a moment, the encounter turned into an instant standstill, until Holly spoke up and said gravely, "I am going to kill myself."

"Then you go take it back into the kitchen where it belongs," Sarah snarled, ignoring Holly's antics. They always said every word she uttered was a lie, including the words "the" and "a."

Holly let go of a long, shuddering sigh. She switched the knife to her left hand and retreated out of the bedroom and toward the kitchen. As she left the room, Sandy could hear her grandparents mumbling about how much Holly and her mother were alike.

In a few seconds, Holly stepped back into the room. Her grandparents were in the closet, busily, pulling at the suitcases. Holly walked over to the closet and stood behind her grandmother. She looked at her reproachfully, then closed her eyes. Suddenly, and with all the fury she had ever known in her young life, she swung the knife over her head and down into Sarah's back.

Sandy could not see what was going on from behind the bed, but she heard Sarah Collier's bloodcurdling scream. She didn't realize she was clutching Holly's cell phone, but she was so startled she tossed it across the room.

Sarah's body was bent and doubled over in pain. She fell to her knees, clutching at the knife wound in her back.

Carl heard Sarah scream and stopped rummaging through the closet. With a sudden indrawn gasp, he turned his head around and shouted over his shoulder, "Oh, my God. What's wrong with you?"

Sarah screamed out in excruciating pain.

Carl turned around, eyes wide and staring at Holly. He saw her glaring and standing over Sarah, holding the knife that had been buried deep into her back, and knew then what was wrong.

"*What the . . . ,*" he shrieked, but the words never left his lips. Bursting from the closet, like he had been shot from a rocket, he lunged for his granddaughter, knocking her forward onto the bed, full length.

Sandy slumped farther behind the bed, afraid the Colliers would see her. She heard a bunch of rustling noises and somehow Carl and Holly had ended up at the foot of Holly's bed. He grabbed her by her elbows and shook her hard.

Holly's body grew tense. "Get off me!" she screamed.

Over the corner of the bed, Sandy saw Holly bring the knife down into Carl's back shoulder, expelling a bright splash of red blood onto his shirt. The knife had struck Carl between his shoulder blades, and for a moment, she saw only his desperate hands opening, then involuntarily clenching his shoulder.

Carl rolled off the bed and onto the floor. Holly jumped up and quickly stabbed Sarah in the back again. With a high moan, Sarah struggled to her feet, then fell backward against the wall with a *thump*. The blood from her back wound smeared the white Sheetrock like a splattered tomato.

Carl glanced at his wife sharply. It was a hell of a thing for him to see.

"No, Holly, please don't do this," Sarah shouted, trying to appease her granddaughter. Her face puffed and streaked with tears, she tried to appease with logic. "You're on drugs. You don't know what you're doing."

Sarah then sank to her knees again, her hair hanging in her face, and her words fell like a stone spiraling down into a deep well.

Carl jumped up from the floor and grabbed Holly from behind, locking his arms around hers. He pulled Holly backward and pinned her to the bed.

"Get the knife! Get the knife!" he kept shouting at Sarah.

Holly fought back in her fearful state. The combination of drugs and adrenaline was physically pushing her way beyond her normal capacities. She struggled, trying to break her grandfather's hold, and squirmed like a snake shedding itself of old skin.

Sarah caught the dresser, pulled herself up, and held herself against the door frame.

"Don't, Holly," she pleaded, her eyes circled with the white of shock. "Please don't do this." Her cries had ceased, but her fears had not subsided.

Carl and his granddaughter wrestled for what seemed like a long time, while Sarah stood helplessly by the dresser and watched. She was literally paralyzed by all that had transpired in the last few seconds.

Holly was captured and locked into her grandfather's arms like a straightjacket. Her eyes were fixed, and in the contorted twisting of her face, there was both fear and pain.

Sandy raised up a few inches from behind the bed. She looked around desperately, her eyes skating quickly over to Holly.

Suddenly Holly tilted her head toward her and shouted, "Aren't you gonna help me?"

Something inside Sandy snapped, and for a few moments, she was aware of what was happening, but only in a muted way. It was as if she were sitting behind the bed, watching, but seeing these things happen through an opaque wrapping of gauze. Her terror deepened. She had not believed that was possible, but it was a hundred times worse not being able to see anything clearly.

Holly screamed at Sandy again.

Vague, cowardly thoughts of curling up behind the bed and staying there passed through Sandy's mind, but something else tugged at her heart more strongly, and she let it go. Sandy turned and blinked at her. Her full consciousness now awaken, it all came back to her, and the terror and horror along with it. She took the knife from her back pocket and curled her fingers around the wooden handle.

Holly and Carl were still going at it. Sarah was shouting at Holly and trying to grab her hand. And Holly was slashing at her again.

Sandy hesitated again, still not wanting to get involved, but, at the same time, not wanting to back out of Holly's plan. She needed to reassure herself that Holly still loved her and that she was doing this for her—for them—to be together, forever.

"Please help me," Holly screamed a third time.

Sandy's teeth were chattering so hard, she had trouble speaking.

The Colliers had no earthly idea who Holly was shouting at and were surprised when they heard a crackle of the sheets and Sandy Ketchum jumped out from behind Holly's bed.

Sandy's muscles were strung as tight as wires on a baby grand. Maybe it was the drugs. Maybe it was the fear. Maybe it was the sound of Holly's voice in trouble that made her jump. But the deadly certainty in it urged her forward.

The knife swung in Sandy's hand and by her side, catching angles of light and throwing them against the closet door.

"Y'all need to stop!" she screamed at the top of her lungs. "Y'all need to stop right now before somebody gets killed!"

But it was as if everything were in slow motion, and the players were in a vacuum, unable to hear or comprehend what Sandy was saying.

Sandy ran into the fray and tried to break up the fight. She tried to climb under the shower of flailing fists, but she was knocked back against the wall.

Holly looked at Sandy flat against the wall, and started screaming at her grandparents, "I'll kill you for that." Her eyes were wild. She was the girl who had practiced with knives.

As the four-person melee reconvened, the Colliers turned toward each other in disbelief, realizing now they had been set up by their granddaughter and her lover. The marijuana was just a coy to lure them to the basement. Not having a chance to sift through their horrified thoughts, the stunned grandparents fought gallantly to defuse the crisis.

Sarah tried to get through to Holly again, begging her to stop. She could see the long boning knife in her hand, gleaming like a silver weapon. Her hands crossed in front of her face in a defensive posture.

Holly was still screaming, "I'll kill you."

Sarah froze, then yelled out, "No, Holly!" She cried out shrilly again, but Holly had already positioned the knife above her head and thrust it into her grandmother's left arm.

There was a grating, screeching sound as the metal met bone. The blow was hard enough to push her grandmother backward.

Sarah got her feet tangled and fell against the wall.

Sandy stared in horror at Holly. It was Holly—yet not Holly. Her eyes were lit with a murderous glow. Her familiar mouth now wore a quivering, joyless grin. She had the knife in her right hand. It whistled through the air and came down in the middle of Sarah's left arm with whistling velocity.

Suddenly, belatedly, it came to Sandy with a sudden numbing reality. Holly really was going to stab them to death. She screamed aloud, the sound of her cries insignificant against the blaze issuing from their brazen lungs.

Again Holly swung the knife down against Carl's back. He winced, shoved himself upward, then took a swing at Holly.

POW!

Carl's blow landed square on Holly's chin.

Holly grimaced, reacting as if her face were suddenly on fire. Blood began to trickle from her nose as she turned and stabbed at Carl again. He jerked his head away from her and his glasses flew across his face and smashed into the wall. Holly swung the tip of the bloodied knife by Carl's face, scraping away the flesh from his ear and guiding it in the hollow between his neck and shoulder, where she buried it deep into the fleshy crevice.

Sandy screamed and Holly jerked her hand back. The knife turned in her hand and dropped to the bed, cutting the mattress again. Sandy scooped it up.

Holly reached under the cover and grabbed the larger butcher knife. She waited a second before stabbing Carl again. He threw up an arm and tried to protect himself as she slashed away wildly. She saw his eyes widening and his other facial features drawing in.

Carl grimaced, then got control of himself. Well, at least a little anyway. He winced and jerked back hard. His teeth came together with a loud pop. His hands drew up involuntarily and then settled back down again.

Holly was still revved up, holding the knife in her hand like a poisonous rattler.

Chapter 31

Carl must have known by now that he was a target, too, and not without sufficient cause. The fear of being killed by his drug-fueled granddaughter must have been both terrible and real. Intense and unrelenting. The shoe had indeed switched to the other foot, and with such rapid speed that he didn't have to imagine what it was like to face death anymore. Death was right at hand and it was staring him in the face.

Sandy got caught up in the moment. She saw Holly's grandmother trying to stand, then went over to her and stabbed her in the arm and in the back of the head. When she realized what she had done, she went into some kind of shock.

Carl and Holly were in a fury by now. She was steadily pounding his back and arms with the big butcher knife. He brought his arms up to his chest in a protective shield, but it was no use. She was at him from all sides, poking and slashing.

Carl was still straddling Holly on the bed. He managed to trap Holly's right arm, but for a moment her left arm was up and swinging at him. She was trying to push him off her, while, at the same time, he was trying to block the pumping motions of her right arm, to keep the knife from jabbing and ripping his flesh again. With his right hand, Carl grabbed Holly's left hand and she was pinned.

Carl Collier and Sarah Jenkins met during high school in the 1940s, dated, and then married. They particularly enjoyed vacationing in the tropical islands with family and friends. *(Photo courtesy of Kevin Collier)*

The Colliers adopted two children, Kevin in 1965 and Carla in 1967. Their portraits hung above the Colliers' bed in the master bedroom of their Fayetteville home. *(Photo taken by Fayette County Sheriff's Office)*

The Colliers loved both of their children, but in the 1980s they began fighting behind closed doors with their adolescent daughter, Carla, who had begun challenging their authority. *(Photo courtesy of Carla Harvey)*

At the age of fifteen, Carla dropped out of school and ran away with boyfriend Gene Harvey. She and Harvey lived a gypsy's life, roaming from coast to coast. *(Photo taken by Carla Harvey)*

The Colliers were, however, elated when Carla gave birth to a little girl she named Holly. *(Photo taken by Carl Collier, courtesy of Carla Harvey)*

Although they were not happy with Carla's living arrangement with Harvey, the Colliers welcomed her back into their lives and doted on their new grandchild. *(Portrait photo)*

When Holly was 18 months old, the Harveys were in a horrible auto accident. Holly was thrown from the car and Gene Harvey was left paralyzed. Carla and Holly had no choice but to move back in with the Colliers. *(Photos by Kevin Collier)*

Even though the Colliers adored Holly (seen here in a portrait photo), their lifestyle clashed with Carla's and they asked her to move out.
(Photos by Carla Harvey)

Holly and Carla also lived with Kevin Collier, but their lifestyles clashed and they were again asked to move out. *(Photo taken by Carl Collier; courtesy of Kevin Collier)*

Holly loved her uncle and her grandfather. They became the father figures she never had. *(Photo taken by Kevin Collier)*

The older Holly got, the more unmanageable her behavior became. The Colliers wanted to travel and enjoy their leisure time. They were not interested in being surrogate parents to Holly. *(Photo taken by Kevin Collier)*

The Colliers were very proud of their son, Kevin, and rarely missed any of his musical performances. *(Photo taken by Henry Evans)*

At about the same time, Sandy Ketchum was developing some of the same insecurities as Holly. She had been abandoned by her natural mother and abused by a stepmother. In an effort to cope, Sandy began cutting herself and using drugs. *(Portrait and school photos)*

Tim Ketchum struggled to raise Sandy after a string of unsuccessful marriages. Finally, his marriage to Beth Ozley gave him hope. Sandy would later refer to Beth as the only real mother she ever had.
(Photo by Danette Hebert)

Sandy loved her father, but the real trauma in her life haunted her daily.
(Photo taken by Beth Ketchum)

Sandy and Holly Harvey met in middle school and discovered they had a lot in common. They bonded immediately, becoming friends and then inseparable lovers. (Photo taken by Tim Ketchum)

On August 2, 2004, the Fayette County Sheriff's Office received information that Carl and Sarah Collier had been murdered in their Fayetteville home. *(Photo taken by Fayette County Sheriff's Office)*

Upon arrival, Fayette County detectives discovered ample evidence implicating the Colliers' granddaughter.
(Photo taken by Fayette County Sheriff's Office)

The Colliers had been stabbed with knives from their own kitchen and left to die in pools of blood. *(Photos taken by Fayette County Sheriff's Office)*

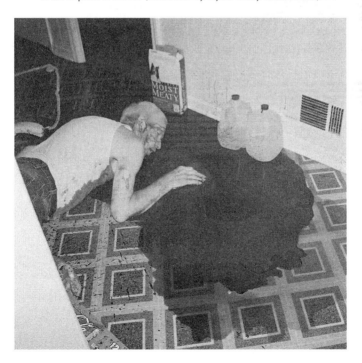

After noticing beach pictures of Holly posted in her bedroom, Lt. Colonel Bruce Jordan made a bold prediction that the teenagers were headed for the coast. *(Photos taken by Carla Harvey)*

Jordan led the cavalry charge that eventually led police to Tybee Island and the Colliers' 2002 Chevrolet Silverado. *(Photo taken by Fayette County Sheriff's Office)*

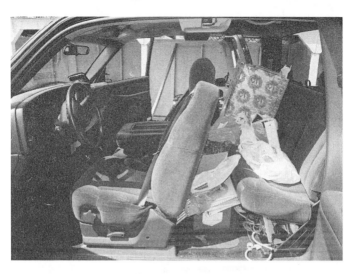

Crime scene investigators found evidence from the Colliers' murders still inside the Silverado. The blood-stained knives and bloodied clothing were among them. *(Photos taken by Fayette County Sheriff's Office)*

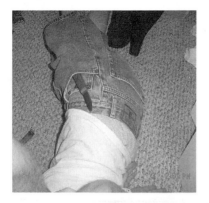

The teenagers were arrested inside the Tybee Island home. One of the murder weapons was found inside Sandy's front pocket. While Sandy was submissive and remorseful, Holly was feisty and defiant. *(Photos taken by Fayette County Sheriff's Office)*

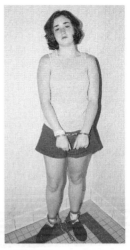

Sandy and Holly were arrested and later transferred back to Fayette County. The forensic evidence was overwhelming in their case and both girls faced a minimum of two counts of murder with malice and one count of armed robbery. If convicted on those charges, they could be imprisoned for a total of 42 years before being considered for parole. *(Photos taken by Fayette County Sheriff's Office)*

Newly elected District Attorney Scott Ballard spearheaded the state's case against the teenage killers. *(Photo by Robyn Cobb)*

Court scenes. *(Photos courtesy of the* Atlanta Journal-Constitution*)*

Court scenes. *(Photos courtesy of the Atlanta Journal-Constitution)*

It was difficult for the Colliers' family and friends to accept that their luaus had ended at the hands of their granddaughter and her lesbian lover. *(Photo by Kevin Collier)*

As part of a plea bargain, Sandy Ketchum (left) must serve a minimum of 14 years before she is eligible for parole. Holly Harvey has to serve a minimum of 20 years before she is eligible. *(Photo taken by Beth Ketchum and Carla Harvey)*

Sandy didn't see what happened then, but, for whatever reason, Holly broke away from Carl's clutches and he charged out of the room like a man-eating tigress was after him. Possibly, his heart was leaping into his mouth as he feared that each turn would bring him face-to-face with the tigress. If he could just get to a phone, or if he could make it outside, even if he could hold them off long enough for somebody to hear him screaming for help, he might be all right. But she had taken him by surprise and, in his terror, he had lost his orientation.

Severely slashed and bleeding profusely, Carl ran for the phone that sat on a table in the living-room area between the two downstairs bedrooms. The phone was there, next to the fireplace. He didn't think about what he had to do—just who was it that he had to call first.

The police? Kevin? A next-door neighbor?

But what would he say?

My fifteen-year-old granddaughter's stoned and gone berserk! Crazy! Homicidal! She's trying to murder me and my wife?

Any of those would work!

Carl maybe understood Holly's pain, but he no longer understood her rage. Her monstrous assault tonight was an incident he could no longer view as another sudden and destructive flare of temper. She was dangerous! He had had enough of her antics. She was getting out of his house tonight!

Holly bolted from the bedroom and chased after her grandfather.

Blood from Carl's wounds sprayed the hallway walls. Before he could dial for emergency help, she cut the phone line with the knife and proceeded to whack away at her grandfather again.

"I'll get you," she howled.

Carl turned and ran toward the stairway. The booming, the hoarse shouting, was right behind him now, the whistle the boning knife made cutting through the air. Panic squirted into his mouth like lemon juice.

"I'll get you, goddamn it," she howled again.

There was nothing of the real Holly in that howling, petulant voice. It ultimately whined in tones of rage and rose in lurid screams. Carl had to know that his granddaughter was no longer inside that body. It was the raving voice of a crazed face staring back at him.

Meanwhile, Sarah had reached for the corner of the room and pulled herself around it. She tried to get up, before Sandy pushed her down, making it impossible for her to do so. Getting slowly to her feet, dazed, her face was already puffed and swelling like an old tire with too much air in it. She was bleeding in four or five different places. With a high moan, she fell backward against the wall, near the door, leaving another big smear of blood on the Sheetrock.

Carl managed to escape the frenzied attack at the fireplace, then lurched toward the stairwell with Holly in pursuit.

Holly called back to Sandy. "Go ahead and finish her off," she yelled over her shoulder.

Sandy frowned, then nodded her affirmation. There was some strange urge overpowering her, pushing her to give in. Before she was completely aware of what she was doing, she drew the knife above her head, brought it down quickly and viciously, and stabbed Sarah in the middle of her left arm.

Sarah shrieked and jerked her arm away. Blood squirted out of her arm like a punctured balloon and shot all over the carpet.

"Why are y'all doing this to me?" she cried, her voice rising to a desperate pitch.

Clutching the knife tighter in her hand, Sandy's relieved breath escaped her in a long, hitching sigh. She had no choice now but to silence her. Drawing the knife above her head a second time, she brought it down even harder this time.

Sarah was caught so unaware of what was happening that her

hands were slow to come up in her defense. She loosened a gulp of air from her throat and slid down—all the way down—like a limp, unresisting rag doll.

"Stop," Sarah shouted now, finally finding the strength to move her arms. She struggled and tried to crawl away. "Oh, God, no. Oh, God, no," she kept screaming. She bent forward, attempting to dodge the blow, and when she did, Sandy slammed the knife into the back of her head.

Pop! The knife cracked through her skull and into the soft tissue of her brain.

Sarah fell clumsily to her knees, the blood pouring both from her left arm and the split in her head. The blood and goo from her brain smelled like rotten cantaloupes.

Sandy dimly saw the knife rebound in her hand, and what she had done came to her with sudden numbing reality. She blinked around stupidly, and there was the knife, still in her hand.

"Oh, my God," she exclaimed.

Backing away, Sandy dropped the knife with a dull thud and put both hands over her mouth. Above her splayed fingers, her eyes dropped terrified tears. Stunned at her own handiwork, she stood like a petrified tree, locked in place.

Sarah lay before Sandy half-cocked and in her pitiful state. Coughing and sputtering, she tried her best to keep from drowning in her own blood. Her face was drawn, her eyes dull and listless. She turned her head to one side and the blood drained from her mouth, spilling across her chest and shoulder.

Sandy watched the horrible scene play out in front of her. She had a vague idea she would see all of this again and it would haunt her later on in dreams. She was as right as rain, for this was a memory she'd have to live with for the rest of her life.

Chapter 32

There was darkness in the stairway, and even though Carl was severely wounded, it didn't stop him. Each step up the carpeted risers and toward the kitchen should have brought him great relief, knowing he had escaped the horror downstairs. But, instead, it only increased his dread, making him conscious that just ahead of him at the top of the stairs and in the short corridor was the door to the kitchen. And in the darkness behind that door, he somehow knew he would have to battle the thing that chased behind him. He reached out and grabbed onto the handrails and pulled himself upward. He held on—with no exaggeration—for dear life.

As Carl thumped through the stairwell, a shriek escaped from his lips each time the pain from his knife wounds shot through him like bolts of electricity. Leaning against the rail, he had made his way up the stairs and onto the short corridor. At the top of the stairs, he froze momentarily, then turned to see Holly coming up the stairs.

Before Carl crossed the short hallway into the kitchen, he stood there, wheezing, his eyes huge, affrighted. There were puffy bruises on his neck and just below his chin. Wet blood under his nose. The collar, back, and shoulder of his white undershirt were saturated with red blood. He must have tried to scream, but his closed throat probably would not allow a sound to pass.

At that moment, Carl was on his own and had to have felt a chill run through his shoulders. Holly was coming up the hall after him. Well, it wasn't the Holly he recognized, but someone else in her form.

Holly had shot into the hall, just as Carl made his way up the stairs, possibly as an attempt to call 911 again. She didn't look up at the top of the light green carpeted steps, but if she had, she would have seen her grandfather at the top of them, still silent, his unfocused eyes staring out.

Holly ran over to the phone lines near the fireplace and used her sharp knife to slice into them. With a huge burst of adrenaline, she half-climbed, half-vaulted the stairs. Still brandishing the knife and screaming hysterically, she shouldered her way up the stairs and into the kitchen, like a linebacker juiced on steroids.

Carl wiped away a trickle of blood from his mouth with the back of his hand. He reached inside the kitchen doorway and slapped on the fluorescent overheads. Just as he turned, he saw Holly racing up the stairs, and his heart again started racing, like a rabbit caught in a snare.

Holly caught up with Carl at the top of the stairs and they started fighting again. The struggle eventually made its way into the kitchen, where they wrestled until Carl's legs gave away and he stumbled against the cabinets. His hands splayed on the countertop, and he was able to straighten himself up.

The tigress was just inside the kitchen door, still crying out in that petulant rage. With a high moan, she lunged forward in her panicky state, with rubbery legs that seemed to push her way beyond their limits.

"I'm going to kill you," she screamed at her grandfather.

Carl twisted his body sideways and shifted behind the middle island. His arms, undershirt, and jeans were covered in blood. The fluorescents beamed overhead, but as he jockeyed for a better position, he struck his shins against the center island and fell backward with a look of anger and surprise. A groan escaped his clenched teeth.

Holly turned and stepped back in the foyer, looking for Sandy and calling back to her.

Sticky blood ran across Carl's forehead and into his eyes. His feet were moving as fast as they could go, but he was slipping and sliding in his own blood. He could taste the terror now, feeling it in the back of his throat. With what type of force had he come eyeball to eyeball?

He must have seen or heard Holly calling for her partner in crime.

Downstairs, Sandy was still standing over the bloodied body of Sarah Collier. Sandy was unable to move, speak, or feel. When she heard Holly's voice, she snapped out of her stupor and noticed that Holly and Carl were gone. She figured the only place they could have gone was upstairs. Panting, she heard a lot of noise coming from the kitchen, so she ran up the stairs and toward the sound of Holly's voice.

By the time Sandy got up the stairs and into the foyer, Holly and Carl were still going at it. Carl had braced himself and was standing his ground.

"For God's sake!" He finally forced the words out of his throat.

There was real fear in his voice—probably knowing, by now, if he was going to live, then he'd have to kill both teenagers. He reached out, grabbed the wall-mounted phone, and danced from one foot to the other, glancing between the two of them. With the receiver in one hand, he prepared to fight off the girls' attack and strike a blow with the other.

Both of Carl's arms gleamed in blood.

Holly stepped in the kitchen, grabbed the cord, and yanked it, tearing the phone off the wall. She brought the knife down again, and this time he stepped toward her.

Trying to avoid the flailing knife, Carl staggered around the kitchen island, leaving a trail of blood.

Holly was relentless, frantically stabbing at him from all angles. He finally succumbed to the ferocious onslaught and fell forward against the kitchen cabinets near the sink.

A groan escaped Carl's clenched teeth.

The Colliers' dishes were still in the sink. Carl's instinct took over and he fumbled loosely for a green glass cup. Sticky blood was running in his eyes. In a last-ditch effort, he grabbed the cup and fired a fastball at Sandy.

Sandy stumbled and almost fell. The cup passed by her face, just missing a hit, and exploded against the wall.

Carl ignored the pain in his body. He bared his teeth at Holly, jumping out at her, and, at the same time, possibly lunging for the open door.

Sandy turned just as she heard the knife whistle through the air and watched as Holly caught him perfectly as he lunged. She struck him in the neck with the big butcher knife and the agony exploded in his left side as the knife took him just above the shoulder.

"Oh, shit," he gasped, tumbling to the floor, the phone flying from his hand.

Holly must have pierced the carotid artery because blood shot out of Carl's neck like air from a hydraulic hose. The hole in his neck resembled a flesh wound that had been inflicted by a raging bull and one of his pointed horns.

Swoosh!

The bright crimson blood burst from the knife wound and exploded against Holly's face and chest. She cringed, her face taking on a surprised and grossed-out look.

Sandy watched as Carl stumbled and fell forward on the floor, three inches away from where she was standing. His eyes stared back at her in stunned disbelief. His face was pallid. He reached out and tried to catch her arm to brace himself.

Sandy screamed at the top of her lungs and leaned back against the wall.

Seconds passed.

Out came the knife from Carl's body, then in and out. In and out. It was the familiar sucking sound Sandy had heard from their morning exercise of stabbing the oil painting. Only, this sounded so scary, so surreal—the *slash, slash, slash,* of the knife into Carl's body.

Sandy was silent. Disbelieving.

Holly continued to slice at her grandfather, only this time it was with shallow cuts. The stabs were quick, but sharp and deep.

Sandy covered her face with both hands and cried out, "Oh, my God, no!"

Carl opened his mouth. There was a hissing, a spitting sound, and Sandy backed up a little to avoid getting covered in blood. He tried to scream, too, but his closed throat would not allow a word to pass.

Carl had fallen hard and heavy, just short of Sandy. His head and outstretched arm crashed at her feet.

Sandy knew agony struck Carl as he fell forward on his wounded side. Then he lay there on the tile floor, jerking and spewing blood, as if he were having a seizure. He crawled around in a sidestroke motion, like a snake that had just had its head smashed by a garden hoe, then shook spasmodically like a lethargic jumping bean.

Jesus Christ, Holly, you've killed him, after all!

For a brief moment, there was silence, broken only by the sound of Carl's blood gurgling in his throat. Literally paralyzed by the sheer horror of what had just happened, Holly and Sandy stood over Carl's body for what seemed like a long time. Staring at his body, they saw blood on his face from a scalp laceration, and blood also pumping out of his neck and shoulder like a faucet.

When Carl didn't get up, Sandy cringed. She watched the

blood gurgle out of his mouth and his body turn as stiff as cardboard.

Meanwhile, Sarah Collier had finally made it out of the downstairs bedroom and into the hallway. Determined to get away from this murderous attack, she had managed to stumble out of the bedroom, but only to fall back against the white Sheetrock wall in the hall. Her blood-soaked clothing painted the wall behind her a bright red and began dripping downward in long, thin lines. Braced against the wall, she pulled herself down the hall until she collided with a bookcase filled with books. The wall above the bookshelf and a number of hymnals, hardbacks, and paperbacks, and a spiral notebook entitled "300 Hymns of Inspiration," were left covered and completely saturated with her blood.

As Sarah's life forces slowly oozed out of her body, she struggled to walk, but made her way up the hall and around the corner of the short hallway at the stairs. When she reached the stairwell, she reached out and attempted to grab hold of the handrail, but stumbled and fell forward at the bottom of the stairs.

Sarah's nose was bleeding. Her shirt and shorts were covered in blood, and a horrible gob of blood had spilled out over her left arm. One side of her chest was a puffed, purple bruise.

She sat up, staring up at the stairs for a moment with shocked eyes. She had to have heard most, if not all, of the terror her husband was experiencing. Her face was ashy pale and set. She was breathing, but it was coming in long, harsh draws that shook her whole frame. Her eyelids opened a little, but then slipped back down again. She twitched a little, her consciousness seesawing lazily downward.

Sandy backed out of the kitchen and away from Carl Collier's bloody body. She turned around at the top of the stairs, took one step forward, then saw the worst nightmare she had ever seen in her young life. It was Sarah Collier, lying at the bottom of the stairs, against the wall. She was weeping in terror.

Sandy stood at the top of the stairs, looking down at her, and felt a pulse beating in her throat. The fright on Sarah's face was something one saw only in movies or bad dreams that surface late at night. Her body was like something that had been mauled by a wild animal.

Sandy felt her stomach churning, her feet retreating.

Holly stepped around the corner and frowned at her grandmother at the bottom of the stairs. Still covered from head to toe in her grandfather's blood, her face had changed to a dark and sinister look, and was growing darker by the moment.

Convinced that Sarah Collier was no longer an impediment, Sandy ran down the stairs and stood over the body and watched as lifeblood gushed from the numerous knife wounds. She eased down on her knees beside her, offering a prayer that she was not dead. Suddenly she saw the rise and fall of Sarah's chest. She was still breathing.

"Holly," Sandy called out. "Your grandmother is still alive. Let's get the hell out of here."

Sandy's own voice had taken on some of Holly's qualities. She sounded weaker now, slurred, as if she were drunk.

Holly ran downstairs to where her grandmother lay, spread-eagle, dying and unprotected, like a turtle without its shell. There was not a face, but rather a mask of blood through which Sarah's eyes under her glasses appeared. Holly was coming for her, hands out, fingers curled around the knife, and with hate in her heart.

"Why didn't you die, bitch?" Holly yelled—as if this confrontation had now changed somehow from a slaughter into a battle. As if she were some mercenary holding her foe responsible for initiating it, Holly stood over her grandmother and waited for her to beg for mercy.

"Oh, God," Sarah moaned, whispering like a child. "Oh, God, please. Oh, no."

Holly raised her arm above her head and brought the knife down, whistling with deadly velocity, and buried it in Sarah's soft stomach. Sarah's protective fingers fell away from her face and she dropped her hands, then grabbed at her waist. Holly brought the knife down and down again.

Sarah was suddenly submerged in an ocean of pain. She tried to cry out to Holly, to beg her to stop, but her breath had been knocked loose. As a means of defense, she could only force out a weak whimper. Barely any sound at all.

Holly—in her hoarse, petulant voice—roared above Sarah's moans and began stabbing her in the stomach again. There was a shift in Holly's body and Sandy couldn't really see what was happening, but she saw Holly bent over and jabbing the knife into her grandmother's stomach. Her right hand jerked back and forth like a mechanical arm in a Saturday-morning cartoon, beating out a steady and unrelenting rhythm against her grandmother's stomach. The blade end was covered with blood and skin.

"The bitch is too fat," Holly complained after each jab. All worked up and panting, she looked back at Sandy with a confused look. "It won't go in."

Sandy heard the knife whistle through the air again and watched as the agony in Sarah's face exploded. This time Sarah took the blow broadside as the knife plunged in just below the line of her breast and sliced open a large gash in her chest. Her lungs had to be on fire.

The next blow would have brought Sarah even more pain. Holly withdrew the knife and then came down again for a sudden, whistling downstroke. It was fully launched and landed in the same spot, further ripping her open like a rag doll as the knife struck on her wounded side, close to her nipple. Her murmurs were now replaced by a gagging sound.

Holly turned to Sandy, who was staring at her in horror. She then looked at her grandmother, staring her right in the eyes. She stood over her and swung the knife down again into her chest, hoping to close her eyes forever. Surely, she wanted that, more than anything.

Sarah lay on the floor. Her glasses were bloodied and still fixed on the bridge of her nose. Her mouth was open and suspended in final horror. Her eyes were staring upward, sightlessly at the ceiling.

After an unknowable time, there was stillness. Sandy forced herself to open her eyes, convinced Sarah would be dead by now. Finally she watched her grow stiff as the shallow breathing and expanding of the chest ceased.

Sandy winced, then risked another glance over her shoulder at Sarah. Bright red blood oozed slowly from her mouth and slipped through her teeth and out her jaw.

Holly and Sandy stood there, looking at each other with heaving chests, until their breathing finally slowed.

Are they dead?

They silently wondered.

It was a straightforward question, not the real test of loyalty between teenage lovers that it should have been—could have been. They looked at each other and mentally measured out which one of the them had actually, finally, finished the Colliers off? Who was responsible for removing the two people Holly thought had so dominated her and her mother's lives? Who had rid the couple of the persons who had stood between them and had defied their love?

The original mission of the teenagers' night, as still inked out across Holly's arm, was now lost in the messy efforts of consciousness. After executing Holly's grandparents, the teenagers—if they were to be together forever—would need to execute the rest of their plan.

Chapter 33

Sandy stood at the bottom of the stairs, staring at the butchered body of Sarah Collier. She then turned and looked down at her own hands. They were bloody and curled up into tight fists of tension. Her nails were digging into her palms like tiny barbs. Slowly she forced them open. They were bleeding.

Suddenly there were so many decisions for the killers to make:

What comes next? Should we leave her and drive away? Surely, we should call somebody and let them know they needed help. We just can't leave them lying here. Not that either one of the girls ever offered a reason why.

Several minutes had passed. The stabbing had stopped, but Sarah's blood was still oozing out, forming big pools, and staining the carpet.

Sandy half-stepped, half-fell up the stairs, as the blood pooled toward her.

"Oh, my God, no," she whimpered, hardly aware she had been reduced to this whimpering with her eyes shut, like a child. Her throat now only allowed her a whisper. "What did we do, Holly?"

Holly stood with her back against the stairway, looking at

Sandy. There was no mistake about the words describing what they had done. Each came out clear as a picture postcard: COLD-BLOODED MURDER.

"What are we going to do?" Sandy asked.

Holly shook her head. There was no time to wonder about that now.

"Well, we've got to do something," Sandy insisted in a panic. "What if we call the police? Let's say they attacked us?"

There was no help for that, either. When they found the bodies, they would surely know who killed the Colliers.

"We gotta go," Holly said, pulling Sandy along with her. "We gotta get our stuff and get the hell out of here."

Still drenched in blood, Holly and Sandy grabbed a few things from the back bedroom, then found Carl Collier's keys to his Silverado truck. They both glanced at the truck keys in wild and irrational hope.

Bouncing the keys off her hand and making them jingle, Holly led Sandy up the stairs, around the body of her grandfather in the kitchen, then out the carport door.

Sandy's heart swelled with fear, until she was sure it would burst like a balloon. Then, at last, as she plunged out into the carport, her hand curled around the kitchen door knob and she pulled it to her.

Holly opened the back of the truck and tossed a change of clothing, a few towels, and a couple of other things onto the backseat. The seat was crowded with boxed Christmas gifts and other items that her grandmother had planned on giving the church for the needy. She and Sandy then placed their bloodstained knives inside plastic bags and piled them high on top of the church gifts.

Suddenly Sandy stopped and pulled away from Holly. She thought she had heard something outside, in the yard and near the pool. She listened again. It sounded like a dog barking. The roar in her head was too loud to be able to tell, but she'd swear the barking was coming from inside the house.

Holly panted at Sandy in relief.

"Oh, that's just Sparky barking." She grinned.

Sparky, the dog, was Holly's grandparents' miniature collie. He was an inside dog, who normally was given the run of the house. During all the commotion, he had hidden upstairs. After Holly and Sandy left, he came out of his hiding place and had started barking.

Considering what the girls had just experienced, the neighborhood rested under a fragile kind of quiet. Their excited voices carried easily over the concrete driveway, down through the dense trees and up against the other brick homes in the neighborhood. The Colliers' house was in the middle of the neighborhood, intersecting with other streets in the community.

Holly knew about keeping the noise down at night from all the times she had sneaked in and out of the house. And from the many times her nosy neighbors saw her and snitched on her.

No matter, Sandy's heart was still whamming frightfully inside her chest. She was waiting any minute now for it to jump out of her body.

Holly suggested Sandy drive her grandfather's King Cab. Even though Sandy didn't have a license, she used to steal her parents' car at night and go joyriding. She knew how to drive a car, but, in her shaky condition, could she drive Carl's big truck and keep it between the lines?

Sandy jumped into the driver's side and Holly got in on the passenger side. Sandy's eyes flooded with tears as she fumbled with the ignition. It seemed sludgy, unwilling to turn in the lock.

Sandy screamed in the close confinements of the truck, then covered her face and her hands. She was sobbing again, choking on her own words. The confusion in her head was unbearable and it showed.

Holly reached over and attacked the ignition. She got the

key in the first time and twisted it clockwise. It fired up. The keys jingling merrily, Holly clutched at them victoriously. The big engine roared and a little groan of relief escaped her mouth.

Sandy composed herself and jerked the car out of park. The car growled into reverse and backed out of the carport without Sandy ever looking behind her. She slammed on the brake, causing them to bob, then put the car in drive and eased out of the driveway and onto Plantation Drive. It was almost dusk as the truck rumbled away in the fading light of the setting sun.

Sandy was still trembling. Her face and hands felt hot, massive, and swollen. She fell back against the seat, closed her eyes, and listened to the voices as they passed through her mind. It seemed there must have been hundreds of them, calling out, *Blood. Death. Murderer. What are you going to do now?*

Holly turned to Sandy, then stiff and sweating behind the wheel.

"Are you okay?"

Sandy looked at Holly and shook her head mechanically back and forth. No, she'd never done anything like this before. She was having a hard time knowing they had just squeezed the life out of two people, who didn't deserve to die. It was nothing less than lunacy to know that her frantic, uncontrollable rage had just helped Holly end her grandparents' lives.

The dank heat of early August coupled with the thought of what she had just done made Sandy sick to her stomach. There was something unfathomable about it, and right now, looking at the blood still on her body, how could she ever explain what they had done?

Maybe if Sandy closed her eyes and kept them shut, there would be a stillness and the nightmare would go away. And when she opened them, she and Holly would be sitting back in her bedroom before any of this happened. She would be telling jokes, Holly would be laughing, and they would be listening to her stereo.

As the nightmare replayed in Sandy's mind, below the tangle of her chaotic thoughts and below the trip-hammer beat of her heart, she heard the roar of the truck's big engine. And when the last little bit of white daylight around them changed as black as night, she knew they would be facing a new set of problems.

Part V

KILLER TEENAGERS
ON THE LAM

Chapter 34

The huge blue Silverado wove drunkenly from side to side, following Plantation Drive onto Highway 314. Slowly, painfully, Sandy pulled out into the hum of traffic, moving farther and farther away from the nightmarish scene and driving forward to safety and other options.

"You can't tell anybody what we've just done," Holly said, looking over at Sandy. In her mind, she had already begun clarifying the purpose of this process, the direction and the distance they were going. "We're going to be together forever and get as far away from here as we can."

Sandy was sweating hard. The dark, airless horror of the moment flashed inside her mind. As the skewed logic of fear caught on, she saw there were so few options for them. They had just murdered two innocent people in cold blood, her conscience cried out. For Christ's sake, they were teenagers, not hardened criminals. How long did Holly think they could avoid the police? Every time she said they were going to be together forever, it sounded wrong. It sounded improbable. It sounded downright impossible.

Whether or not it had come to Holly and Sandy's attention that Atlanta had long been known as one of the gayest areas in the South, and would be an excellent hideaway, was never known. It was old hat that underground Atlanta and the surrounding areas housed a lot of homosexual bars and hangouts where out-of-towners could go and party undetected. This would have been a good choice for the lesbian teenagers.

Only fifteen minutes away from Fayetteville, perhaps Atlanta might have been one of their options—yet the girls chose to ride around first and collect their thoughts. Holly immediately called Calvin and asked if they could come over, but when they went to his apartment, they didn't see his car, so they turned around and left.

At approximately 5:00 P.M., Holly called Amanda Roberts again and told her she and Sandy badly needed to find some drugs.

"Do you have our dealer friend's number?" she asked nervously.

"I don't have it," Amanda shot back. She could hear Sandy's voice in the background telling Holly what to ask. "Why should I have—"

Holly cut her off in midsentence. "Sorry, emergency, gotta go."

Sandy then called her friend Sara Polk.

Sara knew the call was coming from Holly's grandmother's cell phone because the number flashed across her caller ID. Sandy identified herself and told Sara she and Holly were coming to her house because they were covered in blood.

The cell phone began to break up and the rest of Sandy's call was gibberish. Sandy's older sister was in town, visiting from Indiana, and she didn't want her to freak out or anything. And she would, especially if they were covered in as much blood from being mugged as she imagined.

"That's not a good idea," Sara replied in a slightly strangled voice. But Sandy must have not heard her.

Around 6:00 P.M., just a few minutes after their phone call, Sandy and Holly drove the blue Silverado truck into Sara's yard. Still covered in blood, they got out of the car and limped stony-faced down the driveway. Sara was on the phone with her boyfriend, telling him about their phone call, and saw the truck pull up. She went out to meet them, but was determined no to let them come in to her house.

"Oh, my God," Sara exclaimed when she spotted them walking down the driveway. "What in the world happened?"

Sandy felt like she had slid down a rail made of razor blades. There was blood all over her, but she was so numb that she didn't feel a thing.

"We got jumped," she said, letting go of the breath she had been holding. "We just need a place to clean up."

The two girls fidgeted in the driveway and recited the events of their mugging like a story they had read in some magazine. Their bloody clothes had the distinct smell of iron and rotten meat mixed together. They stunk. Neither Holly nor Sandy wished to argue about that.

It probably took Sara a matter of seconds to respond, but if felt like longer. Her words hung in the air, beside the sour and undeniable smell.

"I'm sorry, but there's no way you're coming inside my house."

"What do you mean?" Holly asked defiantly.

"Please, Sara, we need your help," Sandy begged and pleaded. "We've been attacked and just need to clean up, that's all."

Sara looked into Sandy's eyes, hoping this was all a joke or something. They were covered in blood, but neither of them seemed injured. Sara waited for an easy explanation.

Sandy and Holly nervously puffed away on their Newport cigarettes and continued to beg Sara for assistance. They fumbled around for an explanation, but finally, after seeing Sara wasn't buying it, Holly blurted out, "Look, we've just killed my grandparents, okay?"

While Sandy seemed shocked, and looked as white as a ghost, Holly appeared excited and jacked up, like some kind of prancing and raging speed queen. She was holding up her hands and gesturing like there was something wonderful about what they had done—as if the blood on her body was something special. Holly looked like she'd be the one, later on, to keep her clothes and frame them so she could remember exactly how it had felt to murder someone.

Thinking Holly was genuinely marveling at what they had done, Sara asked incredulously, "Are you saying you killed your grandparents?"

With the wireless phone still to Sara's ear, she heard her boyfriend shout, "What?" He immediately hung up the phone and Sara then placed her phone down on the dashboard of the blue truck.

"Please just let us go inside and take a shower," Sandy continued begging.

Sara refused.

"Sandy, if you weren't covered in blood, then I'd drag you out of this truck and kick your ass," she told her.

Sara heard a door slam and saw her younger sister walking toward the truck. Maintaining her wits, she waved her sister back in.

"Y'all got to move away from my house," she said, trying to protect her family and making certain she in no way would be connected to their crimes.

Holly looked at Sandy and frowned.

"How about Holly's grandparents?" Sara asked curiously. "Are they okay? Did you really kill them? Do you think they might need an ambulance?"

Both girls shrugged, but didn't have answers to any of Sara's questions.

Sara ran back to the house, went inside the kitchen, and grabbed a large towel. She soaked it in water, then ran back outside and gave it to the girls. Tossing it to Sandy, she stood in amazement and watched as the girls stripped down to nothing, removing the clothes that seemed most badly stained by their victims' blood. Of course, this was basically everything they had on, including their underwear and socks.

Holly and Sandy scrubbed at the blood on their half-naked bodies. As Sara stood and watched them from underneath her front door's stoop, she then realized she had left her phone on their truck's dashboard. When she ran back down the driveway and reached for the phone inside the truck, she saw a bloody kitchen butcher knife lying on the front cab floor.

Sara's hand recoiled like a snake had bitten her. She wanted these girls to take their bloody clothing, along with their bloody knives, and get the hell off her property. Thinking like a cop, she suggested they dump their clothing and toss the knives off the bridge into the Flint River. Sara's plan was to later tell the police where to find them.

The girls quickly changed into the clean clothes they had brought with them and tossed the bloodied ones in the truck's rear cab. They'd have to get rid of that stuff later. The need for them to come to Sara's house had overwhelmed them, but—until now—there was never a plan. They had talked about running away to the beach, but only as one of their options.

This whole time, Sara was looking at Sandy, asking with her eyes: *How could you be a part of this? How could you go along with it? Why didn't you do something to stop it?* But her words came out in a mumble. "Why? Why, Sandy? Why?"

"I don't know why," Sandy said in a stupor. "We were just all cracked out."

Without even a word of gratitude, Holly and Sandy climbed back into the truck, backed up, and sped away down the dirt driveway.

Holly looked at Sandy, implying, *What a fine friend she turned out to be.*

Sandy didn't answer.

Sara's parents arrived just as the blue truck was pulling away. Sara ran over to her mother and blurted out the entire story. They went inside the house and immediately dialed 911.

Although a bit frayed at first, the next several minutes of conversation with the police went quickly. Sara understood something terrible had happened to her friend and Sandy was going to be arrested. But just maybe their brief encounter had helped postpone that or helped guarantee that it was done correctly without Sandy getting hurt. Perhaps it was that thought that energized Sara and filled her lungs with a fresh gust of air.

Holly and Sandy had left Sara Polk's home around 6:14 P.M. As Holly thought about their cold reception from Sara, her confusion slowly gave way to anger. They had been honest with Sara and she had treated them like shit.

"I don't give a damn what your fuckin' friend and her family thinks about us," Holly shouted. "Who are they anyway? Let them talk, I don't care. Let anybody talk who wants to. It's none of their fuckin' business what we do."

Sandy remained silent, while Holly continued to rant.

"How could anyone know what it was like living with my grandparents? It was a fuckin' prison. Who could expect me to live like that?"

Sandy was seeing a new side of Holly. It was as if she, being this close to the edge, had finally gotten her license to say whatever she wanted to say, do whatever she wanted to do, and be whatever she wanted to be. Holly was scaring her.

Sometime between 6:15 and 7:25 P.M., Holly and Sandy tracked down an East Griffin drug dealer. They desperately needed something to help them chill out, and with what little money Holly had stolen from her grandparents, they bought some weed. It was amazing what a little drugs will do to loosen your tongue.

On the way over to Sara Polk's house, the girls had danced around the idea of sharing their secret with somebody else. Until then, it had been an unspoken promise between them not to tell anybody what had happened. But now that Holly had let the cat out of the bag and told Sara, they decided to share it with a few other friends.

Holly and Sandy had left Sara's with heaving chests, but now after lighting up a joint and smoking it down, their breathing had finally slowed. Holly picked up her cell phone, then called and bragged to her friend Samantha Colon.

"Be sure and watch the ten o'clock news on TV."

"Why?" Samantha asked curiously. "What am I going to see?"

Holly's thoughts were as clear as a barroom haze. "You'll be surprised. . . ." Her voice then trailed off.

Samantha knew Holly was just talking big and thinking small. No doubt, she was having another of her famous sundown buzzes. If things were going her way, then there would be more bullshit to follow. She knew the ordeal and what it was like getting stoned and going wild, smoking grass and getting loud, like you're never gonna die.

A minute later, Holly made another phone call from her grandmother's cell phone. This time she challenged her friend Virginia Roberts to watch the evening news. When Virginia asked why, Holly hung up.

Sandy followed the back roads of Griffin and headed back to the main corridor of Highway 314. As the truck purred forward, the headlights cut a clear cone of light through the darkness and onto Interstate 16. As they rocketed along the highway faster and faster, Fayetteville disappeared with a final wave. It was the East Coast that seemed to beckon them now.

Sandy's face was strained and tense in the muted green dash glow of the truck's interior. The nauseating smell from the backseat was making her stomach churn, and the pot they were smoking only made her feel worse. She wished they had done as Sara had suggested and dumped the clothes and knives into the river, but it was clear now that was not a good idea.

Sandy had driven all the way from Fayetteville in a cold sweat, handling the big truck as delicately as if it were a vase from the Ming Dynasty. Although she had driven her parents' cars on many occasions, she didn't have that much experience, especially to be driving out on an interstate highway.

An eighteen-wheeler came speeding by Sandy and suddenly cut in on her. She cursed, hit the brake, and started fishtailing. If a cop had seen this, he might have nailed her for it. She hunched closer over the wheel and jockeyed for another position in the other lane. She was breathing in short, fast strokes, and her heart was thudding wildly in her chest. She didn't think she'd be this nervous, but she was.

"Guess you're kind of strung out," Holly said.

Holly was lying back in the seat and resting casually, as if she didn't have a care in the world.

Stiff and sweating behind the wheel, Sandy cut her eyes toward Holly, then replied curtly, "Yes, you could say that."

Holly reached in her bag behind the seat and pulled out a bottle of Adderall pills. She popped the top and shook out one for Sandy. "Here, take one of these and you'll be tripping in no time."

Sandy had watched the signs to Savannah and knew there were still many miles left to travel. She was getting tired—and God only knew what lay ahead and who was at the end of the "yellow brick road" waiting for them.

Holly placed the pill in Sandy's palm and then popped one into her mouth.

Sandy suddenly turned around and looked in back of the car, as if someone had stepped in dog shit and dragged it on the carpet.

"And what is that god-awful smell," she shouted, turning up her nose. "We've got to get rid of that shit in the back."

Holly shrugged. She didn't smell anything.

As the headlight searched the velvet sky for directions, Sandy cupped the pill in her hands and tossed it back against her throat. Hopefully, this would be all she would need to help her make it through the night.

Sandy wiped her lips with shaky hands. She took a deep

breath, then let it out. Ever since the killings, questions about love and duty had lain heavy on her heart. So much had happened these last two weeks. She'd never officially asked Holly to declare anything, but, tonight, that thought—that horrid thought—had come to her. Holly had chosen her. When she made up her mind to kill her grandparents, it was as if she had spelled it out for her: *You're the one, babe! You're the one I want to live the rest of my life with.*

There would be no betrayal, Sandy and Holly had said to each other. From the very beginning, they had been friends and lovers. During those times, trust had touched them deeply, causing each of them to swear their love and their lives. They had kept the faith with one another and remained true. Such friendships rarely cross the boundary of sexes, but this was more than a friendship. They had done something that very few people would ever do to protect their love. This was not about sex. This was a fusion of two souls.

Chapter 35

Tim and Beth Ketchum had arrived home from work late that evening, stopping to pick up a bite to eat. As soon as they walked in, Tim sat down on the couch and turned on the television, while Beth spread their dinner across the coffee table. They were going to relax and enjoy what little time they had left before they went to bed.

Tonight's Fox 5 weather, the television blared. *It was in the 90s, a muggy day. A lot of sunshine and a lot of heat, as the humidity continues to flow in the Fayetteville area.*

Beth looked up at the kitchen counter and noticed the light on their answering machine was blinking.

Fox 5's weatherman continued to drone out a weather assessment.

We have our first hurricane of the season, Alex, a Category I, and that means ocean temperatures were warmed. Cooler temperatures tonight, down to 81 degrees. But we can expect hotter conditions moving into Georgia and the Southeast by tomorrow.

Beth got up off the couch, walked back into the kitchen, and checked the machine. There was an urgent message from Tim's sister, Glenda.

"Tim, please call me at home as soon as possible. It is very important!"

Beth didn't wait for Tim. Thinking something bad had happened to Tim's mother or Sandy, she grabbed the phone and punched in Glenda's number.

"Hey, it's me," Beth announced. "What's the problem?"

"I need to speak with Tim," Glenda insisted. "Put him on the phone."

Tim got up from the couch and Beth handed him the phone. "What's up?" he asked in a solemn tone.

Glenda couldn't form the words on her lips, before she broke down and began sobbing. Finally it came out, little by little.

"A neighbor from across the street walked over to my house about fifteen minutes ago and told me he had been monitoring the police band radio."

Tim grasped at the receiver of the phone and waited in anticipation.

"And . . ."

"He asked me if Sandy was your daughter."

Tim's legs stiffened beneath him.

"And what about Sandy?" he shrieked.

Glenda took a deep breath; then she blurted it out through her sobs.

"He said the police are looking for her and Holly in connection with Carl and Sarah Collier's murder in Riverdale."

The news came hurling at him, through the phone line, knocking Tim backward like a jolt of 220 electricity.

"No," he cried out in grief. "Oh, my God, no."

Unable to grasp what he had just been told, Tim hung up the phone. He walked over to the couch, buried his face in his hands, and began to wail. He was crying so hard, Beth couldn't get a word out of him.

Beth had never heard such an awful sound in her whole life. It was as if their whole house screamed out. It came in great deep sobs and went on and on. While Tim stiffened underneath her weight, she grabbed the phone and redialed Glenda's number.

"What the hell is going on? Tim's on the floor crying like a baby and I want to know what you said to him."

Glenda was positively rattled and couldn't stop bawling.

"You need to ask Tim. He'll tell you."

"Tim can't tell me nothing," Beth screamed at Glenda. "He's so upset, he's about to have a heart attack." She demanded Glenda tell her what she had said.

"Okay, okay," Glenda snapped back in a terse tone. "Sandy has done gone and killed some damn body. Is that good enough for you?"

The phone line suddenly went dead.

Before Beth could hang up the phone, Channel 5's top news story was being broadcast live from Riverdale.

The hunt is on tonight for two teenagers, Holly Harvey and Sandy Ketchum. An APB has been issued for the girls and police believe they are traveling in a blue truck, license plate 177RC.

A color photo of Holly and Sandy taken on the front porch at Sandra Ketchum's house was plastered across the screen. Lieutenant Colonel Bruce Jordan's face followed their profiles.

The girls are on the run, Jordan said stoically. _They are in a panic. We think the murders of Holly's grandparents happened around seven-fifteen. We also think the girls still have the murder weapons with them._

The reporter cut in with his own commentary.

Police say Holly Harvey was no stranger to them. They had dealt with her before. There had been trouble with this teenager. But this is a very gruesome crime and the district has already been authorized the two teenagers would be tried as adults.

Tim doubled over. He tried to stand to walk, but his knees unhinged and he dropped to the carpet. His mouth hung open and his heart felt as hard as a fist. He was filled with intense pain, and all he could see were death images.

With Beth's help, Tim came to his senses, a little at a time. He told her he felt as if someone had stabbed him with a knife in his back, his legs and arms, and his chest. He didn't think he would be able to move. Even his feet hurt.

Somehow Tim was able to find his feet and staggered through the living room, out the kitchen, and to the back door. Beth pushed it open and he stumbled outside and they got into the car. They drove straight to Griffin and went to a friend's house, then contacted the police from there.

The police advised the Ketchums to remain put. Beth admitted she was a little nervous about her and Tim staying in their own home. They didn't know what Sandy was up to. It was possible that if she had bought some dope and some of her friends were mad at her, then they would take their anger out on them when they found out Sandy wasn't home. They never knew what kind of people Sandy had been hanging out with.

When the police asked Beth if Sandy had a driver's license, she told them no. Sandy and her best friend, Amanda Roberts, had stolen Tim's truck plenty of times in the middle of the night and had taken it out for a spin. There were even several occasions she remembered her car's gas tank being filled with gas, then getting up the next morning to find it on empty. At first she and Tim thought two teenage boys down the street were siphoning out her gas with a hose. But they learned later, it was Sandy and her friends driving around at night.

After an hour or so at their friend's house, the Ketchums began to feel like the walls were closing in on them. Tim had been recently diagnosed with Tourette's syndrome and he needed his medication. It would also give them an excuse to visit Sandra Ketchum. There were a few choice words they had saved for her.

Beth admittedly drove faster than she should have—and

than the law allowed—and she got to Sandra's house in record time. Sandra was sitting on her front porch, calmly smoking a cigarette when they drove up.

"Where the hell is Sandy?" Beth screamed as she and Tim jumped out of the car.

"I don't know," Sandra lied.

Beth pointed her finger in Sandra's face and screamed, "You know, goddamn it, and you best tell me or I'll beat the shit out of you until you do."

Sandra took a step backward and swallowed hard. When her boyfriend—the man she was living with—emerged from the back bedroom and around the side of the house, she suddenly regained her memory.

"Goddamn it, Sandra, you know good and well where that girl's at," her boyfriend shouted. "You bitch, why don't you go ahead and tell her *mother* the truth."

Sandra looked as if she had been slapped in the face. But she finally admitted her neighbor had actually driven Sandy to Holly's grandparents' house in Riverdale the day before. After hearing the news about the Colliers on TV, she called Sandy, but couldn't get through to her. She said she did leave her a voice mail and told her whatever she had done, then she had better get it undone.

That was all Tim and Beth had to hear. Their worst nightmare had just been confirmed, and a terror, which seemed even worse by Sandra's lies, was made more unbearable with her rat-infested accommodations.

Sandra's boyfriend offered the Ketchums his cell phone and they called the SCSO to find out what information they could. The police requested an interview with both Tim and Beth, then advised them to stay in Griffin, just in case the girls returned to Sandra's home for refuge. Tim assured the police of his and Beth's cooperation, but they would prefer staying at another friend's house in Griffin. Right now, he was very angry with Sandy's mother, and, without saying so, he was about ready to kill her with his own bare hands.

Rather than go home, Tim and Beth did drive over to a friend's house. They told them what had happened and there they sat for nearly all night, waiting for a phone call, like prisoners waiting for a death sentence.

Both Tim and Beth were consumed by the guilt of Sandy's crimes. Though neither would admit it, they were still shell-shocked. In a split second, Channel 5's news had altered not only their life, but that of their entire family. They wondered in silence if either of them would ever make it through the night.

Beth rested her cheeks against her palms, staring at Tim over her hands. She was so tired, her eyelids fluttered when she blinked. Five minutes more and she would be gone. She was almost relieved when the morning finally came.

Tim paced all night, chain-smoking and drinking beer the entire time. The ashtray on the porch was crammed with brown butts, which he had smoked down to the filters, and beer cans, which he had downed to the last drop. He stepped back into the kitchen, where Beth was trying to stay busy and take her mind off the situation. His jaw was set, his voice was as desperate as his mood.

"That's my little girl out there," he said, clenching his hands. "Goddamn it, that's my little girl the police are hunting down."

Beth avoided Tim's gaze, offering, "I know, Tim. She's my daughter, too."

Beth winced as she thought about what Tim must be going through. She could not imagine what these last hours had been like, but she truly loved Sandy and knew there would be a day when she, too, would feel his pain, sooner than she imagined.

Chapter 36

Bo Turner and Phil McElwaney, the two FCSO juvenile detectives, had already driven to Griffin and interviewed Sara Polk at the SCSO. Sara told them, at first, she thought her friends were pulling a prank, but when they admitted they had murdered Holly's grandparents, she knew she had to tell the police.

"It was really hard," Sara admitted. "I'm not a rat. I just hope Sandy understands why I contacted y'all. I hope they're not sitting there hating me."

The detectives assured Sara she had done the right thing and even coaxed her into calling Holly's grandmother's cell phone. No one answered. They drove Sara home and asked if she would call one more time. Before she called again, Sara wanted to know if she or her family was in any danger. She was assured that already in her neighborhood there were officers parked in unmarked cars, just in case the girls returned to her house.

It was way after nine now—and the sun had long set—but still no ring from Holly's cell phone. After Sara frantically dialed and redialed their number for an hour and a half, but got only her voice mail, Detectives Turner and McElwaney concluded the girls were not going to pick up or call back anytime soon. They thanked Sara and her family for their cooperation and drove back to the FCSO. Lieutenant Colonel Bruce Jordan had just begun a staff meeting when they walked in the door.

Like the majority of people at the sheriff's office, Jordan had been up since early morning. But he was wired now and fully awake. Encouraged by what his team had been able to piece together thus far, he was certain as to who had murdered Carl and Sarah Collier.

When it came to homicide investigations, a great deal of stock could be placed in Bruce Jordan's training. He had gone over everything in his mind with a fine-tooth comb. The biggest question was where had the teenage killers run to? As he stood there drinking from a bottle of water and scratching his head, suddenly he recalled the photographs found in the granddaughter's bedroom. Then it hit him square between the eyes.

The beach!

Jordan felt like he didn't have to think too far outside the box on this case to figure out where the teenagers were headed. The idea that young people are always impatient had suddenly struck him. And, after he reviewed those pictures, he had a hunch that they would find the girls somewhere on the East Coast, leaning toward the water, as if they might find some submerged truth there.

Old cops are entitled to their hunches. That's why they get to sit in the big chairs and wear their own clothes, rather than the standard-issue police uniform. The possibility weighed heavily on Jordan's mind, then hardened to a near certainty.

As Jordan thought about it again, it *was* so simple. The wide, expansive ocean, two girls frolicking in the surf and being free to do and be whatever they wanted. Until he saw those beach pictures, he had been working on a mystery without any clues. But those pictures explained it all.

Jordan quickly assembled his team of investigators around a conference table in the sheriff's office and asked to be brought up to speed on the case. He had appointed Ethon Harper as his lead detective, and because Jordan was still teaching and Harper was still learning, he would delegate tasks to his men and still run the show.

At the crime scene, a poem had been found with Holly's belongings that talked about her depression and that she cried herself to sleep at night. Detective Harper had met with Scott Moore at the sheriff's office, who advised them that Holly had recently cut her hair short to look more like Sandy. Moore also stated Holly was taking the prescription drug Adderall and provided Harper with her cellular phone number.

Not a lot was known about Sandy, other than she had been in trouble with the law before for drugs, truancy, and running away.

Young's Removal Services had already been to the Colliers' home, wrestled with the bodies, covered them from head to toe with a white sheet, and carried them out on a gurney. At approximately 11:55 P.M., the bodies of Carl and Sarah Collier were carted away to the state crime lab at the Georgia Bureau of Investigation (GBI), Division of Forensic Sciences, in Atlanta, Georgia. An autopsy was scheduled for the next day at 3:00 P.M.

An APB had been issued on the missing teenagers and the truck belonging to Carl Collier. Other jurisdictions were providing information that they may have sighted the blue pickup truck in their areas. With the help of ADA Dan Hiatt, drafts for the arrests of both Holly Harvey and Sandy Ketchum were written. Just before midnight, Detective Harper met with Chief Magistrate Charles Floyd and the warrants for their arrests were obtained. Just in case the renegade teenagers returned to the scene of the crime, the Uniform Patrol Division was providing continuous security at the Colliers' home until it could be released to the family.

Turner and McElwaney shared with Harper what they had garnered over in Griffin with Sara Polk. They related her story and how she had attempted to reach her friends via Holly's grandmother's cell phone number, but Holly never answered or called back.

It was a widely known fact among the FCSO that the U.S. Marshals' Southeast Regional Fugitive Task Force had the technological capabilities of tracking the two girls within a few feet via their cell phones, even if the phones were not turned on. Detective Harper had already met with them and provided all of the needed information, including Holly's cell phone number, Sarah Collier's cell phone number, and Carl Collier's vehicle description and license tag number.

Despite everything going on around Bruce Jordan, he never lost sight of what it would take to bring these fugitives to justice. He had everyone stop what they were doing and sit down around the sheriff's office conference table. Even though there were dozens of assignments going on around him, he took the time to meet with his officers and put all the pieces of the puzzle together.

"Okay, folks, what have we got here?" Jordan asked, running a hand through his short graying hair. One by one, he spelled out all the facts of the case. "Two kids. They kill their grandparents. They steal a truck. They cruise the neighborhood, looking for drugs. They call their friends and tell them to watch the news.

"Now, I know it is hard to imagine someone this young a murderer. Nothing personal with these two, but they made their decision long ago before tonight. Long ago before they were old enough to vote or buy their own cigarettes.

"But I don't believe for a minute what they did was not intentional. They chose to put this chain of events in motion and, like a storm, gained momentum and strength until two people were finally dead."

Jordan then lifted a stack of color photographs taken from Holly's bedroom at the Colliers' home off the table and passed those among the group.

"So, you tell me," he posed the question, "where do you think they are going?"

Most of those sitting in the room gave a half-shrug, then each offered Jordan their own hunch and opinion.

After several minutes, Jordan selected a handful of pictures from the stack and tossed them into the middle of the table. He gave his partners a confident look. They were all pictures of Holly and her friends at the beach.

Jordan's fellow officers looked skeptical.

"Do you think they are fleeing somewhere to the beach on the East Coast?" he asked.

A few investigators said they didn't. Jordan explained why he did, and after he finished, the detectives were polled again. The verdict had drastically shifted in Jordan's favor.

"Anything else you want to ask?" Jordan inquired of those sitting around him.

Everyone shook their heads no. He had answered all their questions.

Chapter 37

Holly and Sandy's excursion to the beaches of the East Coast had teamed up perfectly with the setting sun. Under cover of the night and heading east on I-16, they felt as if they were the only two people in the world. They rode in silence until Holly stirred and switched on a light inside the car. The interior brightened and she checked to see if everything was still there. It was all in the backseat, including the bloody knives and their bloody clothing.

The combination of adrenaline and drugs had begun to drain from the teenagers' bodies, leaving in its place headaches, cigarette breath, and one gigantic drug-induced thirst. The pill Holly had given Sandy hadn't calmed her down. She had wanted so badly to believe this nightmare was over, but it wasn't and she struggled to suppress her terror.

Sandy looked at Holly lying in the seat next to her.

"Holly?" Her voice was timid and hesitant. "What are we going to do when we get to the beach? We don't have any money."

Holly rose and turned to look at Sandy.

In the dim of the night, Holly's face looked more like a slick mannequin's head. It was not the normal face Sandy was accustomed to seeing: all lively, smiling and alert, with the eyes sparkling and open.

Rather, it was the catatonic face of a stranger. There was a hard, cold look about her now and her eyes had turned dull and opaque.

"Don't worry, we'll do what we have to do to get buy," Holly said flatly, without any emotion.

Sandy nodded, but never asked if "getting by" meant murdering someone else. The closer they came to Savannah, the need to hurry became more and more compulsive for her. She found herself continually looking at the clock in the dashboard. The hands seemed to be creeping along so slowly. She was scared all right, but—more than anything—the guilt was beginning to be more than she could handle. In the normal world, little girls don't go around murdering their grandparents with butcher knives.

Terror continued to sweep over Sandy. The pungent smell coming from the bloody clothes in the backseat was worse, and she was beginning to feel weak and light-headed. She whimpered, shivering at her vision of her frailty in the dim light.

What are we doing? We're acting like two murderers off the Lifetime Channel, plotting and trying to escape from the police. And all the while, there are two dead bodies back in Fayetteville, soaked and covered in blood.

Sandy closed her eyes. In her mind, she saw hundreds of unfamiliar faces, crowded together and lined up in a church. They were all crying and staring down as if they were looking into an open casket. She was looking over their shoulders, until one by one they cleared and let her pass. And when she reached the front and looked into the coffins, she saw the bloodied and butchered bodies of Carl and Sarah Collier.

Still driving Carl Collier's blue Silverado truck, Holly and Sandy arrived at the North Beach area of Tybee Island at about 10:00 P.M. As they traveled along the scenic road over gentle rises of water, which took them to a nice stretch of beach along the Atlantic Ocean, Holly became more animated. Almost like a child, she peered through the truck windows, marveling at the vast expansion of water on both sides of the long thoroughfare. The blacktop road leading into Tybee Island was curvy and to Holly's eyes reminiscent of all beaches with a repetitive pattern of indistinguishable cottages and beach homes and green clumps of mini forests on both sides of narrow dirt roads.

"Turn right," Holly barked, and pretty soon all the night had melted into a dark, densely wooded stretch of road.

Holly knew Tybee Island would appear quickly. And, as all beach towns do, it would come to them in the blur of neon lights and cheap T-shirt shops, with the smell of sand and salt water. And then, just like that, the long and dreaded distance would be over.

Sandy spotted a motel up ahead. She searched for Holly's eyes in the dark to see if it was time. The smell of blood was nauseating and she couldn't take it anymore. She was suffocating, and had to get out of the car and get out of there fast.

"Is this it, Holly?"

Holly was unaware of Sandy's pain. All she knew was that Fayetteville and Plantation Drive were far behind them now, and her spirit was uplifted by their journey ahead.

"I think this is it!" Holly squealed, jumping up and down in her seat. She was looking at Sandy now, unmoving and pointing. She told her to stop at a beach entrance, but as Sandy prepared to turn, she stopped her.

"No, that's not it. Keep going."

The next time Holly gave directions, however, it was with absolute certainty.

"Yes, turn, left here," she said. "That's it. This is where we want to go."

Sandy looked up just in time to catch a glimpse of a sign in the middle of town: WELCOME TO TYBEE ISLAND.

Chapter 38

Wasn't it strange what turns life puts a person through? One never knows what bends one is going to take, or where one is going.

The year 2004 was when Patricia Pellerien decided she had had enough of drugs and crime in her old neighborhood in Winder, Georgia. Patricia's boys, Brian Clayton, twenty-two, and Brett Shremshock, fifteen, were both at a vulnerable age and she believed they deserved a better environment. She was a registered nurse and had no trouble landing a second-shift position at a hospital in Savannah. This was hours away from Winder, a suburb of Atlanta, and as far east as she could go without a ship.

Early in the morning of August 3, Patricia, Brian, and Brett pulled into the driveway of a large A-frame house at the end of a lane along the marsh and the Atlantic Ocean. It was their first day in their newly rented home on Tybee Island and the beginning of a new chapter in their lives.

The family of three spent most of the day unpacking the hundreds of boxes strewn within the house and arranging furniture. When it came time for Patricia to leave for work at 8:00 P.M., the movers were still hauling in boxes and furniture. She had no reservations about leaving her oldest son, Brian, to finish unpacking with the movers and caring for his younger brother, Brett. Brian was very capable and responsible. In fact, as soon as they were unpacked and settled, he would be searching for his own job. Before going to work, Brian could help get Brett up and off to school each morning, while his mother would be up and waiting for him to return home after school. Things were going to work out just fine for them. She slipped into her work clothes, gave Brian and Brett her final instructions, and left for work in Savannah.

After the movers finally unloaded their last boxes at around 9:30 P.M., Brian and Brett decided they had done enough work for one day and deserved a little break. They made sure all the doors were locked in the house and started walking down toward the north end of the island, happy about checking out their new surroundings.

Just as Brian and Brett approached the hub of activity and nightlife at the North Beach area, they noticed a blue truck pass, stop, and then turn around. Although they were totally unaware, the two brothers had just seen Holly Harvey and Sandy Ketchum after they had fled the murderous scene in Fayetteville.

By now, it had occurred to both the girls that they had spent the last of their money on marijuana. They had no money left to rent a hotel room or buy food and cigarettes. But when they spotted two young boys walking toward the beach, Holly had an idea.

Whatever it takes, Sandy remembered Holly saying earlier.

"Stop and turn around," she suddenly shouted, thumbing at the two boys behind her. "Let's go back and ask those boys for a cigarette."

Sandy did as Holly suggested. She turned the truck around, pulled up beside Brian and Brett, and waited while Holly bummed a couple of cigarettes. She knew what this could easily lead into—another Calvin episode.

"Where you headed?" Holly directed her question at Brian.

"Me and my brother," he said, nodding at Brett, "we're going to walk on the beach."

"Mind if we go?" Holly was asking all the questions. "This is our first time here and we don't know our way around."

Brian smiled at the two dark-haired girls sitting in the truck. Only in his dreams was he accustomed to girls inviting themselves to tag along beside him. Nothing like this had ever happened back home in Winder, but it sure was a nice change of pace.

"Sure, we don't mind," he said, looking at his brother and nodding. "I guess." He wanted to kick himself for adding the last part.

As the girls drove around, looking for a parking space, Brian studied it and wondered who was the owner. The girls' faces were a little young to own such a nice and well-maintained four-door truck like the one they were driving. He was twenty-two, and knew neither he nor any of his friends could afford a truck like that.

Must belong to one of their dads, he thought.

The boys waited for the girls to park their truck across the street, in the Oceanside Nursing Home parking lot, then joined them on the sidewalk. At first the girls were shy and appeared reluctant to say anything, so Brian made a little small talk in an attempt to draw them into conversation.

"I'm Brian," he said, his confidence beginning to grow. "This is my brother, Brett."

Brett grinned and gave the two girls a little wave. He looked mature for his age.

"We just moved to the island ourselves," Brian said. "We used to live in the small town of Winder in Barrow County. You know where that's at?"

The girls looked confused and shook their heads sideways. Never heard of it.

"Winder is between Athens and Atlanta. My mother moved us here because she thought we lived in a bad neighborhood. She said she didn't want to raise her boys in such an atmosphere."

The prettier one looked at her friend. They both nodded their understanding.

When Brian asked the girls what their names were, they looked at each other again. The pretty one was the only one who seemed able to speak the King's English. Finally she blurted out, "Uh, I'm 'Casey' and she's 'Crystal.'"

The girls called themselves Casey and Crystal, although the brothers weren't so sure that was their real names. There was something about the way it seemed to stick in her throat the first time the pretty one said it. Plus, she was real nervous. Her eyes kept flicking around, as if she were afraid someone off the street might recognize them.

Brian wasn't naive enough to believe that teenagers told the truth about everything. Normally, they lied about their age so they could buy beer or cigarettes, or get into some club. They lied about their names when they met someone and didn't want to have a long-term relationship. He'd used that trick a couple of times himself.

This is common for the beach crowd, Brian old boy, so you better get used to it.

No doubt, Brian thought he'd be meeting a lot of other girls at the beach besides these two, so he guessed he might start thinking of his own pseudonym.

Around the corner, there was a big ocean filled with breaking and foaming waves. On the beach, young lovers lay together in the sand, waiting for the stars to work their magic and hoping for the feeling you only feel when love begins.

The girls and guys quickly paired up. Casey and Brian walked together, alongside Brett and Crystal. As they strolled onto the beach and in the sand, a cool wind blew off the water and across them. Brett's walking partner held her head up high and took a deep breath. "I've always wanted to see the beach," she said.

Brett laughed, but stopped when he saw she was not joking.

You gotta be kidding me? he thought before turning and looking at her with a lopsided smile.

Brett watched as the shadows of the moon danced across the girl's face and saw her looking out over the waves like a kid who was seeing Disney World for the first time. It was the first time he had seen her smile. He groaned.

This girl must really be whacked. She says she's twenty-one and ain't never seen the beach before?

There was a sad-looking moon shining down on these girls. They stopped and turned to face each other; then Casey pulled out a joint from her pocket.

"Want some grass?"

For forty-five minutes, the two couples strolled on the beach, smoking marijuana, then looped back and returned to where the truck had been parked carelessly at the nursing home. As they ambled toward the truck, the pretty girl—the one who said her name was Casey—turned to Brian and asked, "Could you do me a favor?"

He shrugged. It depended on what kind of favor she needed.

Casey smiled somewhat—the sly, shy routine. "Could you help us get rid of the truck?"

Brian looked away, then stammered, "Oh, geez, I don't know. Uh, I'm kind of new to the island, too. I got no idea how you could do that."

The same girl opened the back door of the truck, reached inside, and rummaged through her bags. Her friend ran toward the truck, offering to help find whatever it was she was looking for, but she shooed her away. Finally she pulled out a handful of gold jewelry and presented it to him.

"We want to pawn this," she said. "Know any places where we can do that?"

Brian scanned the jewelry resting in her palms. A couple of gold necklaces, a gold charm, and a pretty bracelet with diamonds. He was no expert, but it all looked expensive enough to him.

"Where did you get all this?" he curiously asked.

"It belonged to my grandmother. She died recently."

Brian handed the jewelry back to the girl.

"I don't know if there are any pawn shops on the island. At least I didn't see any on the way in. You'll probably have to drive into Savannah for that."

He stepped back and waited for her to put the jewelry back into the truck.

"Look, Brian, me and Crystal need a place to stay for the night. Can't you help us out this one time?"

Brian shot a mystified glance at Brett, who grimaced at the girl's proposal. The look across his younger brother's face conveyed everything he already knew. They hadn't even finished unpacking yet. His mom would hit the roof first; then she'd kill them. *Besides, isn't it kind of weird that someone would come to a beach resort without any money or a place to crash?* he thought.

The pretty girl smiled mischievously and moved closer to Brian. "Come on, guys, it'll be for just one night. We'll leave in the morning, and, I promise, after that, you'll never hear from us again."

"I . . . I . . . I just don't know if it's a good idea right now," Brian caught himself saying at the last minute, feeling his face blush crimson. He swallowed a few times before he spoke, giving himself time to think of a sure way out. "Don't you have any friends you can stay with, or family?" He still suspected the truck didn't belong to them, but didn't question them about it. He pulled away a few inches, before asking, "Why did y'all come to Tybee Island, knowing you didn't have a place to stay?"

The two girls moved closer to one another, as if they were putting up a defensive stance. "We just needed to get away." The pretty one was still doing all the talking. "It was kind of on a whim anyway that we came here. We had hoped to hook up with some of our friends who lived here, but when we went to their house, they were not home."

Brian didn't say anything for a few minutes. By now, all he could think about was that his mama sure as hell wasn't going to be pleased when she found out the first night on the island he had invited two strange teenage girls to spend the night with him and his little brother. This wasn't like he was bringing home a puppy or something. It was a little more serious than that. Finally he broke the silence.

"I just don't think it's a good idea for y'all to stay at my house."

Both girls were begging now. "Oh, come on, please. We won't be any trouble. We promise." They looked as if they were scared, on the verge of tears. If there was one thing Brian was, it was a softy for crying girls. But still suspicious of the two strangers, he pleaded his case.

"You don't understand. We just moved in and everything in our house is a mess."

The girls begged again, this time even harder.

"Okay, okay," Brian finally gave in. "But I'll have to ask Mom first to see if it is okay for you to stay."

The girls looked relieved. They thanked Brian and agreed they would abide by whatever decision his mother made. They got a few things from the truck and followed alongside the boys.

During the short walk home, Brian sensed a nervous restlessness about the girls, especially the second girl, the one named Crystal. She was continually looking over her shoulder and became very anxious whenever they passed someone on the street or a car passed by them. Finally he turned to her and asked, "Are you okay?"

Before she could answer, her friend Casey provided, "We just got a lot on our minds."

Crystal shrugged indifferently, then shook her head.

Yeah, we just got a lot on our minds.

Brian was beginning to draw some conclusions of his own. The look these two girls just tossed over their shoulders at each other convinced him they were lying. These two girls were probably runaways. It wasn't uncommon from where he came from for teenagers to get mad at their parents, steal their vehicles, and take off for a night of joyriding and fun. He guessed that was what had happened here. No big deal. But on the way to the beach house, he did remind them, "Remember, this is only for the night."

The girls nodded in unison.

Just past the stoplight, down from the middle of town, Brian pointed to a light at the corner of a big house.

"The one with the porch light on and the boxes in the carport is ours."

The girls could see through the lights in the big windows that nobody was home.

Brian fumbled around in his pockets, praying he hadn't lost the house key somewhere on the beach. He finally dug deeper in his pocket and came up with just the right key to unlock the front door. He offered the girls a brief house tour; then he showed them the space in his first-floor bedroom over the open carport area. He thought they would be more comfortable there and pulled the top mattress off his bed onto the floor for them to sleep on. If they wanted, he had some old gym shorts and shirts they could change into.

When the girls dressed and settled, they and Brian sat around and smoked some more pot and drank a few beers. Brett was the typical little kid and was busy showing off in front of the girls and bragging about his collectibles.

At some point, Brian went into his mother's bedroom and swiped some of her prescription medication, Ativan. He then traded it with the girls for some of their Adderall. Afterward, he could already feel the heat of his mother's stare boring into him like a hot laser, and he suggested everyone go to bed. But before he could even get a clean sheet on the mattress, the girls collapsed and quickly cuddled up in each other's arms.

Brian looked up and saw Brett, shocked and standing in the doorway. He grabbed his little brother by the arm and walked him into another room. He had already noticed the way the girls interacted with each other, like they were boyfriend and girlfriend. He had suspected they were lesbians, but didn't know if his brother would understand it all.

Brett pointed out the obvious, as if it were some sort of enticement.

"Oh, God, did you see that?" he whispered, laughing and looking back at the girls huddled together on the mattress, as if he couldn't believe what his eyes had just seen.

Not wanting to make a big deal of the two girls, Brian nodded, hoping he could leave it at that. He knew people who were gay and had learned the last thing these girls needed, if they were gay, was someone standing there gawking at them.

Brett raised an eyebrow, much as Brian had done a few minutes ago. "I believe these girls are 'funny,'" he said, turning to his brother when they got in the next room. "Not 'funny' like 'ha-ha,' but, you know, 'funny' as in 'queer.'"

"Yeah, they're lesbians," Brian said nonchalantly. "You can tell by the way they look at each other and the way they touch each other."

"And that girl I'm with," Brett went on to say. "Uh, what's her name, Crystal?"

Brian nodded.

"She looks real 'butchy' to me," Brett concluded. "So I guess she must be the man."

Brett was becoming fascinated with these two girls and their relationship.

Brian was not only amused with his little brother's curiosity, but amused with himself as well. He thought about all the other times in his life when he had "picked up" girls. And here it was, his first night at the beach, and he just happens to hook up with two girls who are gay. That was just his luck.

Brian walked to the kitchen and phoned his mom at work. He told her all about the two girls, Casey and Crystal, and asked if these two girls could spend just one night at their house.

The idea of two strange teenage girls spending the night with Patricia Pellereon's two sons didn't sit well with her at all. Her answer was a quick and resounding "Hell no!" Not waiting for her son's protest, she informed him, "I don't want those girls or anybody else spending the night at our house! Don't you understand? We've just moved in, the house is a total mess, and we know absolutely nothing about these girls!"

Brian apologized and assured his mother he would take control of the situation.

"You need to get those girls out of my house and quick," Patricia ordered him in no uncertain terms, and with no room for compromise.

Brian hung up the phone and lumbered from the kitchen to his bedroom above the open carport. When he looked in on the girls, they were still sacked out on the mattress and gone to the world. He just couldn't force himself to wake them up and ask them to leave.

God, they're not hurting anybody, they're just sleeping, he consoled himself. *I'll just wait until they wake up; then I can slip them out before Mom gets home. They'll be back in their blue Silverado by then, and long gone by then. Mom will never have to know.*

Chapter 39

At 1:15 A.M., Lieutenant Colonel Bruce Jordan was advised by U.S. Marshal Lieutenant Mahlon Donald that they had picked up a signal on the two teenage fugitives somewhere close to Pooler, Georgia, on or near I-16, and they were possibly headed to the southeastern coast.

Jordan's hunch had been right on the money, but he knew how quickly all that could change. While wearing a cocky, tough attitude, he was not one to take it too seriously, knowing that "one minute you're a hero and the next minute you're a zero." Some people might think cops are cousins to the "Man of Steel," and that they eat thunder for breakfast and crap lightning by lunch. But by the time a cop gets as far up the ladder as Jordan, things change.

For the most part, Jordan could hang with the best of them. He was one of the best investigators the FCSO had ever had. He was tough, brave, and fair-minded. Of course, he had to be, to get as far as he had. By the time a person reaches the higher ranks, politics kick in, and the calls start coming from people who think they know police business, but don't have a clue as to what's going on.

Jordan wore the rank of lieutenant colonel and stood tall enough to catch a lot of the bureaucratic bullshit. He had taken a lot of criticism and heat from people who didn't like his attitude or the way he conducted his job. But he didn't care. His men knew he'd probably be sheriff one day and have his image embossed on a plaque in the FCSO headquarters like the other sheriffs. And they didn't care, either, as long as he did his job.

But Jordan had learned a long time ago that if you're ever going to catch a draft, then you got to stick a tail feather out in the wind. When he asked for volunteers to fly down to Florida, Detectives Turner and McElwaney were the first to raise their hands. They believed they knew Holly and Sandy as well as anyone, and it would be easier for them to recognize the girls hiding out along the crowded beaches.

At 4:58 A.M., Jordan hopped on the Internet, found two available seats, and booked his detectives on a one-way flight to Jacksonville, Florida. Turner and McElwaney had barely enough time to rush home, take a shower, grab a bite to eat and a change of clothing, before their plane took off in Atlanta. They were scheduled to arrive in Jacksonville at 5:55 A.M., where they would rent a vehicle and immediately begin searching the beaches and cheap motels along the Atlantic strip for the stolen blue pickup truck and the two juveniles.

At the same time, other law enforcement agencies and U.S. Marshals' Fugitive Task Force (USMFTF) members were searching the beaches in the Savannah, Georgia, area. Where were these girls? They could be anywhere south of Jacksonville, east to Savannah, or further northeast to beaches along Hilton Head and the Carolina Grand Strand. The police just hoped they would find them before they got hurt or they hurt someone else.

As the Atlantic Ocean lapped against the protective seawall just beyond the beautiful harbor at Savannah, the police never thought that the teenage fugitives were not far from them at Tybee Island, smoking pot and drinking beer with two young boys, and having a pretty darn good time.

About the same time police were wondering where the girls were spending the night, Sandy Ketchum was feeling her own eyes getting heavy. It had been a very long day and she looked forward to a good night's rest. But sleep didn't come easy. If you could call it sleep, it was light and uneasy, populated by dreams that seemed too vivid to be mere dreams. At least they were certainly more vivid than any dreams she had ever had before.

Although Sandy had tried to forget, she could not erase the death images of Carl and Sarah Collier from her mind. And now, as she longed for rest more than anytime in her life, they came to her in bloodied clothing and torn bodies.

With outstretched hands, the double apparitions came for Sandy, their eyes rolling wildly in their sockets and blood dripping from their faces and hands. With an ugly grin on their faces, the blood-streaked phantoms screamed and howled for answers.

Why? Why? Why?

The words kept coming from the Colliers' mouths, over and over.

Suddenly reality and dreams had joined together, flawlessly, without the hint of a seam. In her dream, Sandy screamed and buried her head in her hands as one of the apparitions approached her with the butcher knife still in his neck, buried up to the handle. He had a kerchief of blood tied around his face and the smell of his rotting flesh was unbearable.

Oh, dear God, Sandy screamed, but no one was there to hear her. After all, it was still a dream.

I'll kill you, the haunting voice boomed.

The ghostly figure took several more steps, then reached out for Sandy, booming out, *I'll find you and I'll kill you.*

With the sound of that booming voice, the whole place seemed to be secretly and silently alive.

Sandy suddenly awoke, bolted up in bed, eyes staring wildly. The loud noise was still in her ears, but—thank God—

the voices she had heard were only in her head. And the booming—well, it was nothing more than the racing of her heart and the sounds of a faraway police siren.

Outside, the wind blew in the trees and the limbs rattled against the window like dead bones. There was a storm approaching from the east and the Atlantic Ocean, and it made the trees dance in the windows. Looking at the shadows, Sandy lay in her bed, motionless, waiting until the leaves quieted and the shadows stilled.

Still clad in Brian's shorts and shirt, Sandy got up and pressed her face against the cool windowpane. She looked outside and down the street, both ways, straining her eyes for whatever was out there to see, but there was nothing.

My God, it's four in the morning. What did you expect to find outside?

It was a faint and sorrowful voice Sandy heard and she thought she was probably the only one awake enough to hear it. In response, there was no way of knowing what else was out there in the dark of the night. Slipping around those trees. Sliding in and out of the parked cars. Slinking hungrily near this house.

I'll find you! Then I'll kill you!

The voice came to her again, but she quickly dismissed it. It was only the wind off the ocean speaking back to her, gusting more strongly this time against the trees and blowing the leaves across the large glass-plated windows.

With the sound of that voice still ringing in her ears, she looked out the window again. She thought she saw something this time, maybe a block down, no farther. There, she saw it again, a dark shadow by the end of the road and near the trash cans. Was it the real thing or just her imagination playing tricks on her?

Perhaps the police were on their way now, intent on getting to her and Holly. They would be determined now, more than ever, to break them up, regardless of what she and Holly said or did to try and convince them otherwise. Perhaps that was already happening.

Sandy stood by the window a second more. A minute. Maybe two, even longer. But, no more. At last, she blew it off again as the wind gusting in the trees. The shadow at the end of the block was gone now, if it had ever been there at all.

Sandy reached in her front pocket and found a pill Brian had given her earlier. She wasn't sure if it would help her sleep, but, this early in the morning, anything would help. It sure wouldn't hurt.

Sandy swallowed the pill, turned away from the window, and crept back to her bed. She lay there and thought about what she and Holly had talked about.

The teenagers had agreed there was to be no betrayal of each other.

Pulling the blanket up around her neck, Sandy snuggled in close beside Holly. She was unaware that unconsciously, insidiously, the notion of betrayal had already crept into her thinking.

Chapter 40

Carla Harvey was one of several handfuls of inmates at Metro State Prison in Atlanta who normally got up early in the morning to enjoy the quiet of the moment. The prison facility housed over nine hundred female inmates, and, counting the 308 staff members, that was a lot of noise. Carla had found the only way to find solitude was to arise before the sun popped up and get out in the lounge before anyone else.

Before daybreak on Wednesday morning, Carla and one of her suitemates were up and sitting in the lounge. Carla was smoking a cigarette and her suitemate was listening to the radio. When an emergency police bulletin interrupted the broadcast, the suitemate recognized one of the mentioned names. Uncertain that she had heard it correctly, she waited for a second newscast to confirm what she had heard.

Finally the suitemate asked Carla, "Don't you have a daughter named Holly Harvey?"

Carla felt her body grow tense. She looked up, her breath stopping in her throat with a little gasp.

"Well, yes, but why?"

The girl almost lost the impulse to tell Carla what she had just heard across the radio. Finally she pushed out, "I think you need to turn on the television. Your daughter seems to be in some kind of trouble."

There was only worry in Carla's eyes now. She shook her head faintly, her dark eyes swimming in her pinched face. She turned the television to Channel 11 and saw the reporter standing outside her parents' home:

> *Police are still searching for the two teenage suspects, Holly Harvey and Sandy Ketchum, for the murders of Carl and Sarah Collier. According to Lieutenant Colonel Bruce Jordan . . .*

Carla fell back in her chair. "Oh, my God," she responded hysterically.

"Is that her?" Carla's suitemate asked sympathetically. "Is that your Holly?"

Well-bred surprise was replaced with well-bred regret. The words never passed Carla's lips. She just nodded, affirming that the Holly Harvey police were searching for was her daughter.

Carla was miffed and thought about calling her brother, Kevin. Surely, he knew about all of this by now. But why hadn't he contacted her?

Ever since the murders of his parents, Kevin Collier, understandably, had not been in the best of moods. Something about all of this disturbed him deeply and he was struggling to make sense of it all. How could this have happened? His parents were killed at the hand of their own granddaughter, wielding knives that they had shared together at the dining-room table. It just didn't make any sense.

Kevin thought about the day he and his father had last talked. He remembered that day specifically because he and his father had talked about Holly and how she had threatened to kill them. His father thought he could handle it, that Holly was not strong enough to hurt them. But his father had no idea that Holly and Sandy would both be lying in wait for him.

Kevin could deal with the possibility of his own death; that didn't bother him. But not his father's death. Not his mother's death. And certainly not like this. Not ever.

Kevin would have liked to have talked with his sister, Carla, if nothing else but to share his pain and grief with her. But maybe, just maybe, she had something to do with why he hadn't contacted her. Maybe a few hateful thoughts had crossed his mind. Maybe he felt she had as much to do with all of this as Holly. After all, she was the one who encouraged Holly to be disrespectful to her grandparents. She was the one who was in prison and had passed Holly in her troubled state off to her parents to raise.

Surely, it had occurred to Kevin that if Carla had been the mother she should have been, then this might not have happened. And, surely, it had occurred to him, if not for Carla and her daughter, his parents would still be alive.

Late last night, after he had left his parents' house and gone home, Kevin got a call from Anita Beckom. She had gotten bits and pieces of what had happened, but believed not only had Kevin's parents been murdered, but Holly.

"Oh, my God, Kevin," Anita cried, sounding both scared and out of breath. "I just heard about what happened. I can't believe it. It's like a bad dream. I just can't believe it happened."

Anita insisted she come over to Kevin's house, that he not try to bear this burden alone, but she was so upset that her daughter insisted she drive her. It was going to be a restless, impossible night for the both of them, so they might as well draw strength from one another.

The drive seemed to take forever for Anita. Her mind was a blur and most of what she did think about was related to urgency and immediacy. When she got to Kevin's house, her body was still trembling.

"No . . . No-o-o-o," she screamed, rushing toward Kevin. Her words came in a thin shriek. Her arms waved wildly in the air. "I just can't believe it happened. Who could have done such a thing as this?"

Kevin's voice stopped in the middle of his throat. Looking at the two of them, he had a lingering thought. First he looked at Anita, then to her daughter, and back to Anita, before suddenly getting the picture of what had happened.

"You don't know about Holly, do you?" he asked.

Anita took a step back. When her eyes cleared and she saw Kevin staring at her in surprise, she swallowed hard and choked out, "What is it?"

"It's my parents that are dead," Kevin said calmly. "Not Holly. She's all right."

There was a harshness to Kevin's voice, and it had a quality about it that made Anita think of someone who had just found out that their spouse had been cheating on them.

Anita shook her head as if to clear out all other thoughts.

"What do you mean, 'Holly is all right'?"

Kevin looked past the shock and bewilderment on Anita's face, then felt it on his own face. It's how people often appear when they confront the deepest and darkest secrets of humanity, and then the truth is revealed to them. Kind of what Moses' face must have looked like after talking to God in the burning bush. A "theophany" is the word that came to his mind. It's the place where our humanity stops and the revelation begins.

It suddenly hit Anita like a locomotive.

"Oh, no . . . Kevin. Oh, no . . . ," she kept saying over and over. A low moaning sound mostly came through her mouth.

Kevin took a deep breath, then let it all out. He admitted he had wanted desperately to believe it wasn't true, that it wasn't Holly who had killed his parents. But after all he had learned from the police, he didn't dare take the chance.

Anita stopped crying. Kevin's revelation was shocking, but how could it not be?

"I'm so sorry. I didn't know." She wiped her eyes clean with the palms of her hands. "I just didn't know."

Anita looked up and stared at Kevin, wishing she could believe Holly hadn't done this. Not just to his parents, but to Kevin as well.

In one way, what Kevin felt was relief, as he had gotten this one awful thought off his chest. In another way, he was still angry and hurting, and another awful thought arose to take its place.

"I would have never thought Holly would have killed my father," he said, swallowing the big lump in his throat. "I thought it would have to be Sandy who killed him, because Holly loved her grandfather so much."

Anita didn't flinch. She looked at Kevin's eyes flaring out beneath his dark, furrowed brows and saw there was the expression of pity in them. She grabbed him by his arms and pulled him closer to her.

Once more, Kevin was the boy she had seen so often defending his sister, the one she had seen most clearly in the days of Holly's youth, with tears rolling down his cheeks, wanting to know like every person in history why someone he loved was being mistreated.

Why do bad things happen to good people?

Kevin had surely read about it, but now it had happened to him. Was there a reason for it? Or were we all just some puppets on a stage at the hands of some demented puppeteer? Or is this what people call fate, where you just step up and take a spin on some crazy roulette wheel of life? But if it meant something, as Anita believed it did, and there was a God in control, what could he do about it but grin and bear it?

"Only God knows why and I'm sure there's a reason for it all," Anita offered in consolation. "I just pray that God gives you the strength to survive it."

Chapter 41

Tim Ketchum was searching the depths of his heart, trying to figure out not only what had happened, but asking where he had gone wrong. He had always spanked Sandy when she was little, but he didn't spank her when she got older. Maybe that was where he went wrong, but he always thought restrictions and takeaways were the appropriate methods of discipline for older children.

When Tim and Beth were first married, they started attending church regularly and tried to get Sandy involved. Tim enjoyed church and being around Christian people. Some people might not consider him a religious man, but he believed in God and respected His laws. He was hoping Sandy would take an interest in church, but she never did. At the time, she had only two things on her mind: drugs and Holly.

Even though Tim and his family had stopped attending church, that had never stopped him from believing that God was always in control of his life. He was convinced nothing ever happened unless God allowed it, and certain if anything happened, then God always had a reason. Of course, one question kept popping through his mind: *why did God allow this to happen?*

Tim clenched his fists, raised them close to his face, and shouted to whomever he thought was listening, "Yes-s-s-s-s. That's what I'd like to know, God. Why?"

Beth was in the kitchen and heard Tim out on the back porch crying out to God. She opened the door and walked outside to check on him. He tried to hold his solemn face, but he couldn't. He was on the verge of tears again, and Beth could see it. She suggested they drive to the police department and talk with someone there about what had happened.

Understanding Beth's true concern, Tim hypothesized about their situation. They were both silent for a moment as they considered what was best for Sandy. Finally Tim said, "Talking with the police is not only the right thing to do, it's the best thing we can do."

Beth was silent. She put a steadying hand on Tim's shoulder and gave a brisk, little shake and his eyes cleared.

Tim paused for another second, then cried tearfully, "I just can't believe this is happening to my baby."

Beth could see his heart was being crushed under the weight of all this.

Tim then let out a huge sigh, as if a huge weight had just been lifted off his chest.

"I'm so sorry," he apologized, though he was not so sure what he was apologizing for.

The Ketchums and Tim's sister, Glenda, and her husband, Larry Harmon, drove to the FCSO together and met with Detective Ethon Harper and Lieutenant Belinda McCastle, the Public Information officer. The officers answered the family's questions and told them all they were allowed to repeat. Sandy's aunt asked if she could appear on the morning news and plead for Sandy to turn herself in.

Tim and Beth provided an insider's look into Sandy's behavior and life at home. They also told the officers about Sandy's other emotional problems they had experienced with her.

"Several times in the past," Beth revealed to the police officers, "I would go in to discipline her for something bad she had done and would find knives in her bedroom."

"What kind of knives?" Detective Harper inquired.

"You know, just the common kitchen knives," Beth answered.

"We are familiar with your daughter's drug abuse and problems with the police in the past," Harper continued. "Do you believe she was still abusing drugs as of yesterday?"

"Yes," each family member said, looking at each other and nodding in unison.

"As quick as I tore down Sandy's drug-related pictures off her wall," Tim added, "and got rid of her paraphernalia, they'd be back again the next day."

"Did you know she was with Holly Harvey last night?" Harper asked him.

Tim shook his head.

"No, she's been living with her biological mother, Sandra, and she told us a neighbor took her to Holly's house. Sandra knows who that person was."

Harper was quiet. He glanced at a few papers in front of him, which appeared to be notes he had written down, then stated, "I understand this is not the first time these two girls have run away together. Any idea where they might be headed?"

Tim took a deep breath, looked at Beth, and shrugged.

"The last time Sandy and Holly did this, she made the comment that if they had not been caught, they would have been in Florida the next day. Maybe that's where they are going this time."

After the Ketchums returned home, Tim, amazingly, got dressed and drove in to work. When he told his boss all about what had happened with Sandy last night, his boss was flabbergasted.

"Then, what in the hell are you doing here?" Tim's boss asked in great concern.

"I don't know," Tim said in a daze. "I didn't know what else to do."

When Tim admitted his stomach was still one big bruise of throbbing pain, his boss insisted he go home and even called Beth to come and get him. Tim's tears had stopped flowing, but his eyes were still red and swollen. And when he saw Beth's car pull up in front, a smile of relief surfaced for a moment.

Tim got in the car with Beth. She smiled; then it faded as she dug in her cigarette pack for a cigarette. There was still one thing Tim needed to do that would be the hardest thing he had to do in his lifetime. He had to break the news about Sandy to his mother. She had practically raised Sandy and loved her like a daughter. She would want to hear about Sandy from someone in the family.

Tim called his sister, Glenda, and she volunteered to tell her.

When Glenda and a friend of hers, Debbie Brown (pseudonym), arrived at Doris Ketchum's home, Doris knew something was wrong.

"What's wrong?" Doris asked when she answered the door and saw her daughter and Debbie. She still had her apron on and was putting away breakfast dishes. It was too early in the morning for them to be standing on her porch unless there was an emergency.

"Why aren't you both at work?"

Glenda opened her mouth, but nothing came out.

"What is it, Glenda?" Doris coached. She opened the door and invited them inside.

Glenda sat down heavily in one of the chairs at the dining-room table. Her head dropped and her hands dangled heavily between her legs.

Debbie parked herself in the doorway, stolid and silent.

"Are you okay, Glenda?" Doris asked. "You look ill."

Glenda shook her head, saying she was okay. But judging from her face, that was the lie of the decade, if not the lie of the century.

Debbie looked down at Glenda and gently placed a hand on her shoulder. Scared or not, she knew Glenda had to tell her what had happened with Sandy.

Glenda began slowly.

"It's Sandy, Mama. She's gone and killed somebody," she said, watching the color drain from her mother's face.

Doris's jaws tightened. She looked down at her apron and wiped her hands in several tight, controlled movements. In a low voice, she uttered, "Oh, my God," then sat down in a chair across the table from them.

Glenda lifted her shoulders and gave a huge sigh.

Doris straightened up in the chair, folded her hands neatly in her lap, and stared at Glenda and Debbie in shock. For a few seconds, she found herself torn between wanting to get up and run to the back bedroom and bawl, or stay where she sat and listen to what her daughter had to say.

"When did this happen?" Doris asked, clearing her throat.

"Last night," Glenda answered, looking up at her mother.

"Last night?" Doris echoed. She took a deep breath, her shoulders rising with the effort.

"Yes, ma'am, the police are searching for her now," Glenda said.

"Oh, my God," Doris repeated. Her shoulders sagging now, she suddenly grabbed at her stomach in pain. She got out of her seat, walked to the sink, then returned and sat back down. It was Glenda's turn to follow her.

Tears came into Doris's eyes again, but this time her heart was thumping from anger instead of shock. She pressed her lips together, trying to form just the right question. Since Sandy was a baby, and the day her mother had abandoned her, Doris had always worried. She knew Sandy had gone through some rough spots, but thought she was doing better. Now the full implications of what she had done hit her right between the eyes.

"Why would Sandy go and do something that crazy?" Doris shouted.

Glenda looked at Debbie. She swallowed, tying to speak past the tightness in her throat. A lump as big as an orange had settled there. "I don't know, Mama. I wish I did, but I just don't know."

"You don't know?" Doris confirmed what she said, but it came out more of a rhetorical question and she apologized. Of course, Glenda didn't know.

Glenda waited until Doris calmed down, then offered what little she knew about last night. When she finished, she stood up. She needed a cigarette and she needed to pace. And she needed this nightmare to go away.

"It's just that she was having . . ." Glenda couldn't find the words. She tried again, but her brain went dead and wouldn't work.

Debbie stepped in and took up the slack.

"I'm sure Sandy wasn't thinking right. She couldn't have been in her right mind. If she had been, she would have never done anything like this."

Doris gave Debbie a careful look.

"Of course, she wouldn't," she said, feeling not so much angry now as blindsided.

Taking a deep breath, Glenda revealed to her mother all the police had told her earlier about Sandy and the Collier murders. Each new section she revealed made her feel like her heart would explode from her mouth.

"Fugitive" was one of Glenda's last words. "Yes, she was one of those now."

"So what's going to happen to Sandy when they catch her?" Doris asked. "Is she going to . . ." But she covered her mouth

with her hands and shook her head before she could get the
word out.

It was 12:15 P.M. and nobody knew exactly what had happened to Holly and Sandy. But everything about it screamed
as if it was too much pain to shoulder.

Part VI

FUGITIVES CAPTURED

Chapter 42

At approximately 9:00 A.M., the U.S. Marshals advised Lieutenant Colonel Jordan that they had located Carl Collier's vehicle at Tybee Island, near Savannah. With the assistance of the E-911 tracking system, they had been able to pinpoint the teenagers' location to a certain section of the island. The blue Chevrolet Silverado extended cab truck had been found in the Oceanside Nursing Home Center parking lot. There were no signs of the suspects, but they were on the lookout for them.

For a moment, the pulse in Jordan's head sharpened and focused. Being somewhat of a history buff, Jordan was familiar with Tybee Island. Not only was the island famous for its strategic location and military excursions throughout history, but was probably best known outside of Georgia as the home of the *Tybee Bomb,* a nuclear weapon that was lost offshore near there in 1958.

Jordan alerted the department's chief pilot Bill Riley to prepare their emergency helicopter. The department's slick black OH58 *Hawk One* had been purchased and operated entirely with drug-seizure funds. The aviation unit performed daily patrols and was on constant standby for use in manhunts, car chases, drug interdiction, and was the quickest way of responding as the "eye in the sky" during emergency calls for service.

Jordan and Riley would be flying into Tybee Island. Via Nextel, Jordan then contacted his two deputies, still in Florida. With the Nextel wireless phones, Jordan could communicate with his mobile officers, thus reducing the dependence on radio communication with dispatchers and improving the efficiency of their hour-to-hour, minute-to-minute, operations. Through the use of secure instant-messaging and direct in-vehicle access to federal, state, and local computerized information files from a special law enforcement telecommunications system, he and his men had all the latest advantages of technology that would keep them updated and informed on the progress of the fugitive investigators working in the Savannah area.

"I need you to head north about eighty-five miles up the coast to Tybee Island," Jordan instructed Turner and McElwaney. "It'll take you less than an hour to get there. The barrier island is only three miles long and has only about thirty-five hundred people living there. The U.S. Marshal from Savannah assures me there should be no difficulty finding the girls. There is only one road leading into the island and there is only one road leading out of the island."

"You have got to be kidding me." Turner laughed. "What a stroke of luck."

"Yeah, can you believe it? The location couldn't have been better even if we'd have constructed it ourselves."

Jordan was very familiar with the site at Tybee Island where his helicopter would land. There was a lighthouse nearby, at the entrance of the Savannah River, constructed in 1736 by General James Oglethorpe and a handful of settlers who came to establish a new colony in honor of King George. The lighthouse towers over the eastern coastline at an amazing 154 feet and is considered Georgia's tallest lighthouse. The famous evangelist and father of Methodism, John Wesley, had said his first prayer on the American continent at Tybee. The island had also been the temporary home of infamous pirates like Black-beard. Treasure hunters still claim today there is buried treasure hidden somewhere on the island. Jordan thought it ironic the teenagers had sought a touch of safety in Tybee Island, where a pirate flag had once flown over its shores.

"Because the girls don't have any money," Jordan hypothesized with Turner, "my hunch is that they will try and hook up with some boys to gain shelter for the night. Since they don't have any cash and aren't old enough to use a credit card to get a hotel room, they'll have to con someone into helping them."

Jordan didn't think that would be too difficult for Holly. From what he had been told, she was very manipulative and used people to get what she wanted. Those who knew her and Sandy were already saying she had used Sandy to help her murder her grandparents.

Jordan knew the suspects had headed to Sara Polk's house immediately after the murders, where they cleaned up and changed clothes. They had also wrapped up the murder weapons in towels and put them on the backseat. They had said they would burn the backpack and its contents, but there was no way of knowing that for sure. There was a possibility they still had those knives with them and were planning to use them in order to get what they wanted. The speculation was they would kill a second time in an attempt to get a car or to get enough money for food and a night's lodging.

The weatherman promised there would be a storm coming in by the end of the week. In the department's helicopter, the two men would follow I-16 like a long black snake that had decided to snooze awhile, until they reached Savannah; then they would cut over to Tybee Island. A silent prayer was lifted. Jordan hoped he was not too late.

Meanwhile, the press had gotten its first taste of blood and the story was everywhere in the news. The talk was of Holly Harvey and Sandy Ketchum and nothing else. All the public

knew thus far was that Carl and Sarah Collier had been brutally murdered in their own Fayetteville home, and the police
were conducting a multi-state search for the victims' granddaughter and her friend. The two teenagers were supposedly
heading along the East Coast, as far south as Florida, and as
far north as South Carolina. They had stolen Carl Collier's
truck, and, as bad as it sounded, they possibly could have the
murder weapons still in their possession.

Television crews were set up in the Colliers' front yard—
complete with police cars and yellow ribbons everywhere—on
the night of and the morning after the murders. Reporters candidly told the story of the two teenagers who were responsible
for all this, and that they had committed a crime so brutal that
most Fayette County citizens were having a hard time believing it really happened.

It was a sensational story and some reporters saw it as their
golden moment. In an effort to make a splash, they emerged out
of freshly painted news vans and rushed over to Sheriff Randall
Johnson for an interview. Practicing their assertiveness, they
asked, "Sheriff, what can you tell us about these murders?"

Smiling as usual, as if these encounters happened all the
time in Fayette County, Johnson offered a few of the basic responses. Then, with his arms folded across his chest, his expression suddenly changed.

"The Colliers were real good people," he said sternly. "I've
been knowing them for forty years. They were churchgoing
and hardworking people. But I'll tell you this, I've never seen
a crime more cruel than this one."

On the night of the murder, Scott Moore had called the
FCSO and volunteered information on Holly Harvey. Holly
and her mother had lived with him and he knew quite a bit
about her.

"I knew Holly was staying with her grandparents because
she had been too difficult to handle," Moore told the press.
"I also knew they were prohibitive in letting her see this girl,

Sandy. They wouldn't let her see or be with her, in any way like that."

Not surprisingly, the story was broadcast every hour on the hour. It was, after all, becoming a huge and tantalizing case. And if talk about a hurricane could frighten people and keep them on edge, just imagine what a heinous crime such as this one could do?

Chapter 43

That same morning, Brett Shremshock was the first one up at the Bright Street home. The small-framed, dark-haired teenager still couldn't shake what he had witnessed last night. It was like something he had seen on TV, like an episode from *The Howard Stern Show*.

"Those girls who slept in your bedroom," Brett said to his brother, Brian. "Did you notice they were acting weird?"

Brian was still half-asleep, but managed to get out, "What do you mean?"

"Like, you'd ask them a question and they kind of looked down and they wouldn't answer you."

"So what's wrong with that?"

"I don't know, it's just weird, man." Brett lifted his hands above his head, palms facing outward, then exclaimed, "I heard them in your bedroom last night. All night long, they just kept whispering to each other. What do you suppose that was all about?"

Brian was still mad at himself for letting the girls spend the night. He knew his mom was going to be angry with him when she found out they were asleep and in his bedroom. Out of his own frustrations, he shouted at his brother, "I don't know what they were talking about, Brett. And what does it really matter anyway?"

"Well, I think it's going to matter plenty to Mom when she finds out you let them sleep over last night."

"It's too late for that now," Brian said, with a worried look on his face. "She already knows they're here."

Patricia Pellerien had arisen around ten o'clock after a well-deserved sleep, then walked from her bedroom to the kitchen. Closing her eyes, she took a deep breath and inhaled the warm salt air. But before she could drink her morning coffee, she saw two girls emerge from Brian's room. Surprised that there were guests in her home without her approval, she marched to Brian's room, searching for an answer.

Hadn't I unequivocally told him last night that they couldn't stay?

With an uncharacteristic scowl on her face, Patricia stood at the doorway, motioning her oldest son out of the bedroom and into the kitchen.

"Young man, what are those girls doing there?" she asked, pointing a finger back toward his bedroom.

Brian cleared his throat, feeling his tongue swell to twice its normal size. In a low voice, he defended himself.

"I didn't know what to do. When I showed them my room, they just fell asleep right there on the mattress."

Brian lifted his shoulders and gave a heavy sigh, then apologized to his mother.

Patricia crossed her arms over her chest. She bit her tongue, finally nodding her understanding of his predicament. She assumed some of the blame for that. It was in her nature to always try and help people who needed help. She guessed it was her own interest in taking care of others that had probably motivated her to choose a career as a nurse, and maybe she had instilled some of this into her boys.

Their hearts have always been bigger than their bodies, she admitted to herself.

Brian and Brett both told their mother that they had gotten bad vibes from the girls. "Something's just not right about those two," Brian admitted.

"How so?" Patricia asked bluntly. It had been her experience that boys always thought girls acted weird.

"They're always whispering to each other and looking around," Brian pointed out. "The dark-haired one—I think her name is Crystal—she makes me nervous. She's way too quiet. She even asked me to help her ditch the truck. Why would they want to do that, unless they stole it from someone?"

After hearing her boys' concerns, Patricia believed the girls were runaways. They were either looking for a place to stay or a place to hide. She thought it best to talk with the girls themselves. Walking in with a smile on her face, Patricia introduced herself to the two girls.

"Hi, I'm Brian and Brett's mother."

The two girls seemed to relax a bit, giving Patricia the feeling they had been expecting something else. They talked with her about the beach and the weather; then their conversation turned strange.

"You don't happen to know of a pawnshop where we can sell some jewelry, do you?" the talkative girl asked.

"Good gracious, no," Patricia answered. She had just arrived on the island herself and didn't know where anything was. Out of curiosity, she asked, "Why in the world would a young girl like yourself want to know where a pawnshop is?"

"It's just that my grandmother died a couple of months ago and she left me some jewelry," Casey clucked. "I'm a little short of cash right now and it would help tide me over until I caught up with my friends."

"Oh, I wouldn't want to get rid of anything if my grandmother had given it to me," Patricia said in dismay. "Both of my grandmothers are dead and I would never part with anything they had given me."

Patricia was expecting to see a nice brooch or some other

family heirloom mounted inside a black velvet box. She was
shocked when Casey handed her a wad of common jewelry
shoved into a plastic bag. Inside the Baggie was an expensive-
looking tennis bracelet, but also an inexpensive-looking gold
necklace, a gold nugget charm, and two or three other golden
necklaces.

Patricia inspected the jewelry and turned it over in her hand.
She saw nothing of any great value; yet in her mind, there was
something suspicious about it. Like it had been stolen.

"And why did you say you wanted to sell all this?" Patricia
asked a second time.

"Because I have no money and no place to stay," Casey
said honestly.

Patricia handed the jewelry back to the teenager. "I'm
sorry, I can't help you," she said, shaking her head.

Casey nodded and fumbled with the jewelry, looking a bit
defeated.

Patricia walked out of the room and searched for her oldest
son. She found him in his room.

"Brian, there's something not right about these girls. I want
you to get them the hell out of my house today."

Brian shook his head, as if to say *I told you so.*

"I smelled trouble the minute I saw that jewelry," Patricia
ranted. "I think they're runaways and they stole that jewelry
they are trying to pawn. I want them out, I tell you!"

Brian thought about telling his mother what he thought
about the truck, that it was probably stolen, too. But she had
been through enough for one day. Besides, it was his fault
they were in this mess with these girls.

After Patricia had dressed and cooled off, she went back
into the living room, where the girls were still talking with her
sons. She watched how they interacted with each other and
came to the conclusion that Casey, the talkative one, was the
stronger of the two girls. She seemed very secure and in control, where Crystal appeared to be insecure and clingy.

When Patricia realized both her cell phone and land phone had not been activated, she asked Casey if she could borrow hers to call her service provider.

She talked with a service tech for forty-five minutes and he finally arranged for connections of both her phones. Toward the end of their conversation, she began to hear the sounds of a helicopter. She went outside, looked up in the sky, and saw a big black helicopter hovering over her house. It was as if the helicopter had the eyes of an eagle and was on the horizon searching for its prey.

Inside, Brian and Brett heard the helicopter humming above the house. They noticed Casey and Crystal suddenly got real quiet, and when the boys left the room, they started whispering to each other again.

"I have to go out and take care of some house business," Patricia told Brian as she handed Casey her cell phone back. "My phone is working now, so if you need me, call me on my cell phone."

Brian assured his mother he would have Casey and Crystal out of the house by the time she got home. He guaranteed it.

Shortly before noon, Holly's grandmother's cell phone rang. Holly wasn't sure of the caller and waited before she was sure the call came from someone she wanted to talk to. She recognized the number. It was Anita Beckom's number, but when she answered, it was a man's voice on the line.

"Hello, Holly, are you okay?" James Beckom asked.

"Who is this?" Holly asked sharply, knowing very well it was Anita's husband.

James didn't think this was the time to play guessing games.

"You know very well who it is, Holly."

Holly hung up the phone, then thought about it and called James back.

"I'm okay." Holly's voice was cold and passionless. It was a voice that conveyed detachment and self-preservation.

"Holly, you need to turn yourself in," James advised.

"I can't talk right now," Holly feigned. "We'll have to discuss this later."

James didn't waffle. "Holly, turn yourself in. I promise you I'll always be there to support you and never let you go without—"

"I love you," Holly interrupted. "I have to go now."

The phone went dead and Holly's voice was silenced.

Chapter 44

All Tuesday night and throughout Wednesday morning, Detective Ethon Harper had received information from people who had heard of the incident and wished to tell about their recent contact with Holly Harvey and Sandy Ketchum. Harper knew about the girls buying a bag of marijuana from a dope dealer, then later on calling their friends and asking them to watch the ten o'clock news. The information about them attempting to locate a gun was passed on to the units at Tybee Island for safety reasons.

Detectives Turner and McElwaney had already arrived at Tybee Island and met with both the U.S. Marshal and the Tybee Island Police Department (TIPD). Working on little sleep, but pumped up by hoards of adrenaline, they would serve as the go-between with this group and their boss, Bruce Jordan. The Tybee Island police had a small seventeen-man force, and even though it was their jurisdiction, they had agreed to play second fiddle in this operation.

All attempts at any apprehension of the suspects would be suspended until Lieutenant Colonel Jordan arrived in his helicopter. At 11:45 A.M., Jordan's helicopter touched down near the Tybee Island lighthouse.

Like a shark in the ocean, Jordan smelled blood.

SERFTF had provided six U.S. Marshals. With the aid of another sophisticated tracking system, called the *Stingray,* they could home in on the exact position of the fugitives' cell phone signal. They had pinpointed the area down to a two-block area and a group of houses where they believed the girls were hiding.

The marshals told Jordan they were hot on the trail, but they could not tell him exactly what house the fugitives were in. In addition to the U.S. Marshals, Jordan had assembled six men from his department and another six men from the TIPD. Rather than send an army of storm troopers to canvass the neighborhood, a strategy was mapped out and agreed upon.

"We can't afford any more delay," Jordan said, ordering them to mount their raid. He tried not to show his frustration. Instead, he drew in a quick breath, blew it out again, and stepped forward determinedly. All eyes turned toward him.

"We need to move now and take our chances."

At 1:50 P.M., Jordan ordered the eclectic force of eighteen men to assemble themselves in front of the two beach homes they suspected the fugitives were holed up in. From the east, the men felt the heat and humidity wring the sweat out of them as soon as they stepped out of their air-conditioned vehicles.

If Jordan was popping a sweat, it didn't show. In a voice, even and normal, he directed the men into position as easily as a seasoned traffic cop directs preschoolers at a school crossing. Confident and determined, he stood there like the chiseled figure of some Roman centurion, leading the charge of his well-trained legion against yet another helpless enemy.

At Jordan's command, the team of men suddenly broke away and rushed toward their first target on Bright Street. As they climbed the wooden staircase on the side of the house to the raised living quarters, the faint sounds of thunder slid away south of them. Banging on the front door, they shouted enthusiastically, "Open up, this is the police."

A middle-aged lady wearing a baseball cap, T-shirt, and

shorts came to the door and peeked out the curtain. She was wet with sweat and carrying a bucket of soapy water. After several failed attempts to open the door with her slippery hands, she succeeded, only to find herself staring at four men dressed in black fatigues, pointing black guns at her, and thrusting Department of Justice shields in her face.

"Oh, my God," she squealed.

When the officers burst in her house, the woman immediately dropped the bucket beside her, thrust her arms above her head, and fell facedown on the living-room floor, as if she had practiced this same routine over a hundred times last night before she went to bed. Water splashed out of the bucket and across her hair and face.

"Who are you and what are you doing here?" one of the men shouted.

The men in black were all still pointing guns at the woman, which had to have made her more than a little uncomfortable.

"I'm Dodie Gay and I live here," she said, sounding both afraid and amused at the same time. "I'm just tidying up here and trying to get the place ready for a new tenant."

The officers looked at the lady sprawled on the floor, then glanced at each other. She was an attractive lady, short and thin, but not very intimidating. They cocked their heads and read the T-shirt she was wearing. I PUT KIDS FIRST was printed in bold letters across her backside.

Because the lady did not look anything like the persons they were looking for, the officer in charge asked in a gruff voice, "Is there anyone else in the house?"

"No, sir!"

The officers looked disappointed.

After a quick search of the house, Dodie was shown a picture of a young girl and asked, "Have you ever seen this girl before?"

"No, I haven't," she responded, lifting her head a few inches higher off the floor.

"I'm sorry," the officer then apologized. "We're in the wrong house."

"Oh-h-h, okay," Dodie said, still confused by it all.

The officers turned and, without further explanation, left Dodie stretched out facedown on her living-room floor. Ironically, she made her living as a juvenile probation officer and was working as the director of Savannah's Crime Stoppers program. Knowing this was the best show in town, she got to her feet and walked out on her screened porch overlooking the driveway. She stood back, waited, and watched for the drama to unfold.

Bruce Jordan stood out front in the driveway, shading his eyes and shaking his head determinedly.

"Don't worry about it," he said, still peering at the wrong house on Bright Street. Now his voice wasn't quite as steady. It trembled a little. Regardless, by the process of elimination, he knew he had to have the right house this time.

Jordan shifted his position and redirected his men next door. Instilled with great confidence, he ordered his men to advance this time on the neighboring house on Bright Street. For him, the apprehension and arrest of the two teenagers was unfolding like a moving, synchronized opera. And, as all great lovers of opera appreciated, the performance was never over until the fat lady sang her solo.

Jordan silently promised Holly Harvey and Sandy Ketchum there was a very large soprano waiting in the wings.

Chapter 45

Inside their Bright Street home, Brian and Brett noticed that the two teenage girls were squirming like two-year-olds who needed to make water. As they heard the commotion outside, the talkative one looked out the window and mumbled to the other one, "Uh-oh! Oh, no!"

The quiet one let out her breath in a long sigh and stepped back from the window, where she had been watching. *Trembling.* Suddenly they were joined at the hip.

When Brett saw the panic in the girls' faces, he quickly did the math.

The cops had raided the wrong house! They're looking for these girls! And my house is the next place they're coming!

Brett turned and looked at the girls. They were still doing their rain dance. He left the bedroom, sprinted through the living room and down the stairs to the carports underneath the first floor.

"Are you looking for two girls?" Brett shouted in the direction of the police.

Bruce Jordan heard the excited young boy and saw him yelling and waving. "Where are they?" he screamed back.

"They're here! We just met them on the beach last night!"

Jordan pointed toward the first-floor living room above the

carports. The officers hustled up the steps and blew through the front door like TNT.

Brett watched as a large helmeted officer carrying a gun and riot shield burst on the scene and yelled out, "Get to the floor! Get to the floor!" The officer pointed his gun at Brett and the red laser dot popped out on his forehead like he had suddenly renounced his faith and become a Hindu.

Brett fell to the carpeted floor and put his hands over his head, assuming the surrender position, just like he had seen all the bad guys do on *COPS*. About that same time, Brian walked into the room and the red laser dots suddenly got friendly with his forehead.

"Where are the girls?" the cops demanded to know.

Brian pointed toward the back bedroom door and got down on the floor beside Brett. The policemen jumped over the two brothers and raced back to the bedroom. They broke the door open and found the frightened girls. They were huddled together and wrapped in each other's arms like a human cocoon, sitting on a mattress on the floor of the small room.

The police snatched the two teenagers to their feet and took them down like demon cobras. As the girls lay facedown atop the mattress and on their stomachs, the officers pulled their hands behind their backs and handcuffed them. Holly was wearing Brian's blue gym shorts and one of his old gray muscle shirts. Sandy was wearing a pair of blue jean shorts and a white T-shirt. Her hair was tied up under a blue-and-white bandana. Both were wearing tennis shoes and white socks.

All over Sandy's body were small scars, as if she had been cut hundreds of times with a sharp knife. On her upper left arm was a crude homemade tattoo. The inked drawing depicted an obtuse eight ball perched on top of a skull, baring its vampire teeth, with a set of crossbones underneath. Both of Sandy's legs and ankles were covered in small scabs, as if she had been attacked and bitten repeatedly by some type of insects.

"You're both under arrest for the murders of Carl and

Sarah Collier," Bruce Jordan announced as he walked into the bedroom.

Sandy looked as if she were stunned. Her mouth and eyes were wide open, like she had been hit with an electrical shock. Jordan's words scared her like a numbing explosion. As the officers rolled her over on her back, they noticed she had a kitchen knife in one pocket and a folding knife in another.

Good God, that girl is lucky she hadn't stabbed herself, Jordan thought.

As Jordan checked the snapped cuffs on her, a sense of total helplessness swept over Sandy, and she began to panic. She wanted to do something, like run away, but what could she do?

Jordan heard a low, rustling sound coming from the mattress. The flesh on his neck suddenly tightened. His eyes darted toward Holly and saw her trying to squirm her tiny arms out of the handcuffs. One of the U.S. Marshals swooped in and tightened the handcuffs as Jordan dropped down on one knee in the middle of her back, with his full weight.

"Ugh-h-h-h," Holly tried to scream, but her mouth was buried in the mattress.

Jordan lowered his head next to her right ear and murmured through clenched teeth, "Look, bitch, this ain't your grandmother you're dealing with now."

The bedroom contained very little furnishings. Jordan did notice a set of car keys lying near Holly's feet. He picked up the keys and jingled them in his hand.

"Are these the keys to the truck?" he asked, looking at the girls.

The girls did not answer as if the details of the crime had been a blur.

On the floor near Holly's head, Jordan spotted a small glass bottle. On the outside of the orange vial was a printed label, indicating the medication contained inside was Adderall and had been prescribed for Holly Harvey. A bloody fingerprint across the front of the bottle was clearly visible. On the mattress beside Holly was a small bag of jewelry, which included a gold nugget necklace and a gold tennis bracelet.

Jordan shook his head in disgust at the two teenagers.

"Take 'em to the living room and have them searched," he said, waving them away.

The officers stood the two girls up and walked them out of the room. TIPD corporal Tiffany Wall searched them and found nothing of significant value. Sandy had two cigarette lighters and a blue wallet in her pockets. Holly had nothing.

Patricia Pellerin had visited the cable-TV office about 1:20 P.M. Since seeing the helicopter hovering over her house about an hour ago, she had finally made the connection. It had to be in relation to the runaway girls. She rushed home just in time to watch the police officers surrounding the house next door, then switch over to her house, arrest and haul the girls away.

But her concern was not the runaway girls. It was her two boys.

As Holly was being led down the cascading staircase that dropped down from the front porch and onto the sand, Holly was lost somewhere in her mystical world. The police half-expected her legs to collapse and give way when she saw how many policemen were outside and lined down the banisters. But it was as if the staircase had suddenly transformed into a lighted runway and she was a teenage model, flattered with all the attention and applause.

Jordan was taken aback by the teenager's demeanor. And when she let out a goofy little laugh, he thought he was looking at the devil incarnate.

Detective Bo Turner had the same eerie feeling as Jordan. He was standing on the staircase with the other officers, and as Holly was led down, she spotted him. He knew from the expression on her face that she recognized him. That, no doubt, she was still steaming from the time they had broken up her little affair at Sandy's house after they had run away.

Oh, wow, look at me now and all the attention I'm getting, Holly seemed to be smirking. It gave Turner a weird feeling.

After Holly's little moment in the spotlight, Jordan had the feeling she wasn't going to cooperate. Believing Sandy was truly remorseful for what she had done, he believed she would tell them what they wanted to know about the murders.

"Are you going to tell me the truth about what happened?" he asked.

Sandy trembled, looked at Jordan with her big, sad brown eyes, then shook her head.

"Yes, I'll tell you the truth."

Chapter 46

The Tybee Island police station was about two minutes away from where Holly and Sandy had been arrested. Like most buildings belonging to small police departments, the station was a small cinder block, cubed building, trimmed in black, and sparsely furnished.

Tybee police officers Fredrick Anderson and Kevin Coursey booked, fingerprinted, and photographed the two tousled teenagers. They had just finished the paperwork, when Holly asked them a question they would never forget.

"Were either of you involved in my case?"

"No," the officers told her.

"Well, do you know if they died all the way?"

The officers glanced at each other, then back at Holly.

Officer Anderson gave her a surprised look. "I'm not certain as to what you are referring to?"

Holly dismissed the officer, shrugging it off as: "Then you must not know anything about my case."

Shortly after the two girls had been arrested, Jordan called Sheriff Johnson back in Fayetteville.

"Okay, we got 'em!"

For an instant, the room exploded with the kind of electrifying joy that only derives from long weariness followed by sudden triumph. Jordan ran his words together like a pompous teenage boy after his first date. He was on his way now to the TIPD for the purpose of interviewing the suspects and would call back afterward.

Jordan's interview with Sandy Ketchum officially began at 3:00 P.M. Bo Turner and Tiffany Wall had agreed to witness it. The interview room was a small, crowded ten-by-ten square room and had only two desks.

Sandy was read her Miranda rights and asked if she understood them. Her eyes were red-rimmed and glistening. She nodded quickly, her eyes darting from side to side. She understood what they meant.

"Then do you agree to waive your rights and agree to talk to us without an attorney present?" Jordan asked, seeming truly warm.

Sandy bit down on her lower lip, shaking her head again. Her hands shifted nervously in her lap.

Jordan knew then that Sandy was going to tell him the whole story. Just so there would be no misunderstanding, he asked, "Before we start, are you under the influence of any drug or narcotic substance?"

Sandy's throat was as dry as a cow chip. In a voice just above a whisper, she said, "I took some kind of pill around four o'clock this morning, but I can't tell you what it was. Just something Holly gave me."

Jordan waited until Sandy was ready, then baited her with, "Can you tell me anything about what happened last night?"

"Holly and her grandparents had been arguing, they wouldn't allow us to see each other. Holly had been discussing killing her grandparents for days. I had even called some of my friends trying to get a gun."

Jordan watched her carefully now and listened as Sandy told him how her friend had ended the conversation and told her not to do anything crazy. She said later that afternoon she and Holly began smoking marijuana laced with cocaine.

"Sandy, do you feel coherent and sober now?"

"Yes," Sandy said softly. "I've had no drugs since yesterday."

Jordan waited. She had more to tell him.

"Holly and I took knives from the kitchen earlier that day. Her grandparents came into Holly's bedroom in the basement to retrieve suitcases from her closet. I hid beside the bed and listened while Holly's grandparents began to get on her about her drug use. They had smelled the marijuana in the room. Her grandparents were telling her she was going to turn out just like her mother if she did not stop using drugs."

Come on, Sandy, what else, Jordan mused.

"Her grandfather turned to go into the closet, and when he did, Holly stabbed her grandmother in the back while her attention was turned toward her husband. Her grandfather came out of the closet, and he and her grandmother pinned Holly on the bed. They started shouting, 'You're on drugs, you don't know what you're doing.'"

"What were you doing at this point?"

"I was still hiding beside the bed, holding the other knife. I heard Holly say, 'Why aren't you helping me?' After I heard this, I came from beside the bed and began stabbing her grandmother. Shortly afterward, her grandfather ran from the bedroom and she chased after him."

Sandy turned her eyes away from Jordan, as if she were ashamed of what she had done. Her eyes were fixed on the floor. There was plenty more to tell, but she needed to get past this part first.

"I was still stabbing Holly's grandmother after she and her grandfather left the room, and when I finished with her, I went upstairs to help Holly. It was when I reached the top of the stairs that I saw Holly and her grandfather fighting in the kitchen.

"Just as I reached the top of the stairs, her grandfather threw a coffee cup at me. I turned my head away to dodge the cup, and as I looked back, Holly stabbed her grandfather in the neck and he fell to the floor."

Jordan took a deep breath. This was always the part he didn't understand.

"Sandy, why were you both so compelled to kill Holly's grandparents?"

This time Sandy didn't say anything. She just looked up at Jordan like a little girl and started crying.

Jordan glanced at Sandy, then looked away, scrubbing his eyes with the tips of his fingers.

Sandy finally stated through her tears, "We just wanted to leave to be together forever, that's all. But those people didn't deserve to die."

Jordan was silent, hoping the moment would sink in.

As almost an afterthought, Sandy told him, "Holly wrote some notes on her arm to remind her what she wanted to do. The notes were: 'keys, kill, money, jewelry.' She didn't find any money, but she found the keys to her grandfather's pickup truck and I drove us to Sara Polk's house in Griffin."

"Do you remember what you did with the knives?"

Sandy nodded, wiping her nose with the back of her hand.

"We placed them and our bloody clothes in a blue bag. If you look in the backseat of her grandfather's truck, it's still there."

Jordan clasped his hands out front. Sandy drew in a trembling breath, then added nothing else. What had happened was frighteningly clear. Sandy's interview had lasted only twenty-three minutes, but, by far, it was one of the most disturbing confessions Jordan had ever heard in his entire law enforcement career.

After Sandy's interview ended, TIPD officer April Smith escorted Holly into the room. She still had that same cocky smirk on her face Jordan had seen earlier.

Jordan sat quietly and stared at Holly for a moment. He could barely comprehend the full extent of her manner. He no longer expected something entirely different from the curiously odd girl who sat before him, who at one time had appeared to him as not only temperamentally, but also physically, incapable of committing the crime for which she had been arrested.

Jordan sat on the edge of the desk, stared at her, then waited until her eyes met his. When she met his eyes, he saw nothing in them. They reminded him of the kind of eyes painted on the face of a china doll.

"Whoa, don't sit her in front of me," he snapped, holding his palms upward and out in front of his chest.

Holly looked bewildered. She halted directly in front of Jordan, her eyes widening at the coldness she heard in his voice. She was not exactly pleased, and she let him see it.

Jordan bore into her, then asked darkly, "Are you going to talk to me?"

Holly reacted without emotion, almost confidently, as if she had nothing to hide. She looked haggard, her hair hanging to her shoulders in dirty tangles. Dark circles showed underneath her eyes.

But at the moment, it was Holly's voice Jordan noticed most. It was as unbelievably cold and as hateful a voice as he'd ever heard.

"No!" she shouted, giving him a taste of his own medicine.

Jordan terminated the interrogation immediately.

"Good, you little bitch," he snarled. "I don't want to talk with you, either, because I am gonna send you down the river."

The lines were drawn in the sand.

Jordan unloaded every frustration he had and put special emphasis on the statement "I am gonna send you down the river." He thought it was more than fair, since he would never rid himself of the sight of the Colliers' bloody bodies. One day, he assured her, whether she liked it or not, she would regret her action.

Holly glared at Jordan as she walked out of the room. She was fuming. At that moment, she decided she would work diligently at hating him for the rest of her life, or his, whichever ended first.

Chapter 47

When FCSO detective Ethon Harper and Lieutenant Greg Craft arrived at the Tybee Island Police Department, they recognized Carl Collier's blue Chevrolet Silverado beside a secured fence adjacent to the police department. They met with Jordan and their fellow officers, then talked with the U.S. Marshals.

The decision was made to wait for additional members of the FCSO forensic team, before they inventoried the truck's contents. Jordan reminded everyone to keep their fingers off the truck so they could get some good prints.

It was 4:00 P.M. before Holly Harvey and Sandy Ketchum were escorted off the island and transported to the Chatham County Youth Detention Center. For most everyone left standing in the Tybee Island Police Department, the excitement was over for the day. And, someday, they knew it would be over for good.

"God, has it been twelve hours since I've last eaten?" Bo Turner faked a Fred Sanford heart attack. "I haven't slept, either. 'Oh, here I come, Elizabeth. . . .'"

Everyone laughed at Turner and his antics.

Jordan looked at the exhausted officers standing around him. Their eyes were red-rimmed and bloodshot, as if they had spent the whole day fighting a brush fire. There was something heroic about their dedication to their jobs.

"I guess it would be nice for all of us to get a bite to eat," he suggested. "As kind of a reward for a job well done."

Someone suggested dinner at the nearby Savannah Shrimp Company and everyone agreed. The tab would be picked up by Lieutenant Colonel Bruce Jordan and the Fayette County Sheriff's Office. It was the least the county could do.

The officers talked compulsively at dinner—at first about anything but the arrest of the two teenage girls. Sports. Movies. Cars. Finally the subject of Sandy's confession came up and the inevitable could no longer be avoided. Shoptalk, they called it.

"Face it, we had the advantage this time around," one of the detectives opined. "It was like shooting fish in a barrel. These girls were in someone else's turf, so there was no lawyer eager to bust it up. We were far away from both their lawyers and their parents, so we worked fast and got all that we could. It's nice for a change to talk to someone without a lawyer beating the door down."

The all-encompassing question then came up: "Do you think the girls were sorry for what they've done?"

Inquiring minds always want to know.

"I truly believe Sandy was remorseful," Jordan offered. "She cooperated with us and had a complete understanding of what effect the killings will have on the rest of her life. She admitted to stabbing Sarah Collier in the heart and the back of her head. But after my long conversation with Sandy, I think she was in it for the love."

"How about Holly?" Harper asked.

"She was heartless," Jordan explained. "Emotionless. I don't think I have ever met such a colder person in my career. At the crime scene, we found that poem where Holly talked about her depression and said she cried herself to sleep at night. In the poem, she had also written, "All I want to do is kill." And back at the house, when she was arrested, we found her bottle of prescription medication. Her depression might be responsible for some of the way she has acted, but not all of it. I just think she didn't want her grandparents telling her what to do and flat wanted them dead."

Through the course of their dinner, the police officers went on babbling about Jordan and his hunch that the girls were headed to the beach.

"To be honest with you, it was a lucky guess," Jordan stated. "I remembered they had argued with their grandparents about going to the beach, so I started putting two and two together. Then it all started adding up."

Jordan gave credit to the U.S. Marshals. Had it not been for the work of the *Stingray,* the teenagers could have possibly killed again.

"Do you really think that would have happened?" someone challenged from across the table.

"Absolutely," Jordan exclaimed. "Holly and Sandy were desperate for cash. I think they were waiting for the boys' mother to return from town so they could steal her cash and her car. Remember when we arrested them, Sandy still had that knife in her pockets, not to mention the two in the truck. I think had we not gotten to them when we did, they would have killed the entire family."

It was a sobering thought, but there's something wonderful when events start lining up like the planets of an astrologer's charts. Because the girls had fled to Tybee Island, rather than Florida, the police avoided a potentially lengthy extradition process. And because they had fled to a Georgia beach, they were now in custody of the authorities from jurisdiction where the crimes were committed.

It's always beautiful and harmonic when two events line up and come together to make such differences in people's lives.

Chapter 48

Bruce Jordan had arranged an overnight stay for Holly Harvey and Sandy Ketchum at the one-hundred-bed Savannah Regional Youth Detention Center (SRDCY). Nothing more than the standard assessment would be given to the girls, as was given to all juveniles admitted to the facility, but it would give them safe housing and a protected environment until they could be transported to Fayetteville the next morning. The SRDCY staff was informed this case was a highly publicized case due to the heinous nature of the crime, that there had been a manhunt on for the girls, and that they were found on nearby Tybee Island.

At 7:45 P.M., June Stewart, a master's level Social Service provider (SSP), conducted a brief mental-health assessment on Holly Harvey. Stewart's first question to Holly was: "Do you know why you have been admitted to this facility?"

"I killed my grandma and grandpa; at least I think they died."

"What's the last thing you remember?" Stewart asked somberly.

Holly looked pained.

"There being blood everywhere," she said, tears slipping out of her eyes. "I remember seeing the knife."

Holly explained how she came to live with her grandparents. She told Stewart all about her mom in prison for selling drugs to an undercover cop and her paraplegic father burning his home down while smoking crack.

Poor child, with these type of parents, she didn't have much of a chance at having a normal life, Stewart thought.

Holly also stated how she had been angry with her grandparents for some time, but would not elaborate as to the reasons. She did, however, say there was a reason she had stabbed her grandparents.

"They were hitting me," Holly said a little stiffly. "I was just defending myself when I stabbed them."

Stewart noted Holly's extensive history of substance abuse. Holly told her she had been treated for it about two years ago, but did not recall where. She stated she used marijuana daily and smoked at least fifteen to twenty blunts each day. She admitted to using crack last weekend, but was not aware she had done so because someone had laced it in a blunt.

"Do you like taking drugs?" Stewart asked.

"I do like the way I feel when I use it," Holly answered truthfully, then attempted to validate her feeling with, "but I don't consider this as abuse."

Holly further told Stewart she had attempted suicide in the past, the last time being about a year ago. She had cut her wrist, but it wasn't serious and no stitches were required. She had been taking the amphetamine Adderall for her depression.

"Do you want to commit suicide now?" Stewart asked.

"No."

"When was the last time you have talked with a counselor?"

Holly shrugged. "About a week ago. I guess she was trying to determine if I was bipolar or not."

"What do you think about her doing this?"

Holly grunted, then presented a lopsided grin. "I think it's all bullshit."

"Do you have any difficulty sleeping?"

"Yes, I have trouble falling asleep."

"Any nightmares?"

Holly frowned, but went on regardless. "Occasionally."

"Can you tell me about those?"

"Well, the last one was about three weeks ago," Holly said, closing her eyes as if that would prime the pump. "I dreamed I pushed an old woman and she fell and busted her head. The blood was all over her and a nurse gave her something to help her. I don't know why she did that, but she did."

"Holly, do you ever get into fights?"

"Yes, if I am provoked."

"Do you know when to stop?"

Holly paused. "Yes, but I don't always do."

Stewart slid back in her chair and took a good look at the teenager. She wondered how many times had she acted out like this. And what reason would she have had to plan and devise, then lash out and kill two people she loved.

"What do you think is going to happen to you now?" Stewart was curious to know.

"I know I am going to be locked up for the rest of my life." Holly straightened up in her chair. "I will probably die for what I have done."

Stewart completed the interview and wrote her assessment. As part of her summary, she noted that Holly was cooperative, reported no delusions or hallucinations, and suffered from substance disorder, conduct disorder, and oppositional defiant disorder.

At 9:21 P.M., Sandy Ketchum was interviewed by Carlitha Givens, another master's level SSP, working at the facility. Givens quickly established that Sandy didn't want to die, although she expressed wishes to be dead. Sandy told her about how she had overdosed on pills in June 2002 because she had wanted to die, and then had to be hospitalized in Riverdale. On other occasions, she had gotten sick abusing alcohol and methamphetamines and admitted to cutting herself about nine times with a knife.

"Do you remember if you were high when you committed this crime?" Givens asked, recalling Sandy's extensive substance abuse.

"No," Sandy said, wiping her runny nose with the back of her hand. "I'd been smoking marijuana laced with cocaine the night before, but I don't remember anything after that. It all happened so fast."

"How do you feel now, Sandy?"

"I wish I was dead so I wouldn't have to deal with this mess." She said she was having flashbacks of the murder and couldn't get what happened out of her head. "I have given up hope for my life and all I want to do is just kill myself."

"And how would you go about doing that?"

Sandy shook her head. "I don't know. Whatever way is the quickest." Tears streamed down her cheeks and fell onto her chin.

"When's the last time you have been to counseling?"

"About two years ago. That was when I got out of DYS and they gave me medication."

"Do you remember what it was for?"

Sandy rattled her medications off as if it were a laundry list. Depakote for bipolar disorders, Risperdal for sleep problems, and Paxil for depression.

"And how long have you been having problems sleeping?"

Sandy paused and thought for a moment.

"Umm, since about September 2003. My medications didn't help me at all, so my mom took me off them."

"Do you live with your mother now?"

"No, I live with my father and stepmother number three."

"How do you get along with them?"

"I have a good relationship with my father, but not with my stepmother."

"How so?"

"I get upset with them real easily when they say things to me. Like my stepmom called me a bitch and told me she'd knock my teeth down my throat. My parents also tell me that

I will never be anything, that I won't amount to a thing. They say I'm going to be trash just like my mother."

Sandy told all about how her mother had abandoned her and how she was abused by her father's second wife.

"I still have bad dreams about her beating me."

"Do you lose your temper often?"

"Yes, very easily, especially when people aggravate me." Sandy smiled a little. "One time, when I got mad," she said, becoming a little more animated, "I crushed my knuckles on a cement wall. I get frustrated, too, when I can't do something right. I have problems concentrating. It's easy for me to wander off."

"Do you hear voices or anything like that in your head?"

"No, but I do hear music in my head that other people can't hear."

"Any medical problems?"

"Yes. My chest always hurts and I always have bad headaches. I guess it's because I'm still stressed out about everything that is going on. I still have charges pending against me for running away, you know, like unruly and ungovernable conduct."

Givens completed her summary. Sandy had been cooperative with the interview and was assessed to have bipolar disorder NOS (not otherwise specified), but in partial remission. In addition, Givens listed a substance disorder, which included alcohol, amphetamine, cannabis, cocaine, and an inhalant substance. Just as disturbing, Sandy had admitted to sniffing air freshener and recently using a lot of methamphetamines to get high.

Since Sandy was a suicide risk, she was escorted to her room, then dressed in a suicide-proof vest, and issued a suicide-proof blanket, a mattress, and a pillow. She was not allowed to have any bed linens or wool blankets and was prohibited from wearing any type of T-shirt, underwear, or bra. Officers were instructed to search her anytime she left or entered her room.

Givens recommended Sandy receive further psychiatric evaluation and treatment.

As expected, Sandy had difficulty sleeping that night. In one particular nightmare, she kept on seeing Carl and Sarah Collier's dead bodies. Their arms, hands, and faces gleamed in red blood. They chased Sandy down a long hall, and when she fled around another corner, she saw them creeping in after her. Finally they pinned her up against a wall, moaning and groaning. At this point, all their blood had drained from their bodies and they had turned the color of cheese. The smell was so rank, it made her eyes water and her throat close. Weeping in terror, she frowned down at them in utter horror. Their faces were so real and alive, especially Sarah's, whose already large eyes grew larger and even glassier under her bloody glasses.

Sandy woke up crying—everything seemed so real—then she realized where she was. She gasped, shivered, and sat up in the bed. She was so cold, she got the blankets and pulled them around her, reminding herself that the dream was just a dream and nothing more.

The next day, Sandy was still crying and upset.

At 9:00 A.M., Sandy reported her nightmare to Stewart and told her it was a bad one. She told her the worst part was the stench.

"All I see and smell is blood," Sandy cried, her eyes red and swollen. "I'm afraid and feeling worthless."

Back in Fayetteville, Sheriff Randall Johnson announced to the press that the two teenage girls who had murdered one's grandparents had been caught. Johnson spoke candidly about the severity of their crime.

"I've never seen a crime in my twenty-eight years in being involved with the police that is of this magnitude on their kinfolks," he said, shaking his head. "Your own blood and kin . . . I've never seen one no crueler than this one."

Chapter 49

FCSO Crime Scene Unit investigators Manny Rojas and Josh Shelton arrived at the TIPD the next morning at ten o'clock. They were there to meet with Lieutenant Colonel Bruce Jordan and Investigator Ethon Harper. The Colliers' truck had been stored overnight and Jordan had patiently waited until his full crew was assembled before he photographed the vehicle and inventoried its contents.

When Rojas and Shelton arrived on the impound lot, Jordan was standing next to the truck, with his hands clasped behind his back and leaning into the window. Looking like the proverbial cat that had gotten his canary—but was now looking for his bowl of cream—he maintained that position for better than a minute or two. Back inclined. Perfectly straight. Hands clasped behind his back.

Jordan was careful not to touch anything, but his men knew he was probably bug shit with excitement by now, waiting to open the car door, and bursting at the seams with curiosity so deep it was about to spring a leak any moment.

"Good morning, sir," Rojas greeted his commander.

Jordan squeezed out a *right-back-at-ya,* sounding like his normal self. But to his men, they could detect the excitement throbbing in his voice.

"Are we ready to take inventory?" Rojas asked in anticipation.

"Waiting on you guys," Jordan said, not taking his eyes off the truck's interior.

Donning latex gloves, the investigators opened the back door of the blue Silverado and found a blue backpack on the floorboard. Inside the backpack was a multicolored towel, which the teenagers had used to wipe the blood off the knives. Two large bloodstained kitchen knives were found wrapped in the bloodstained towel. These were the same knives they had stolen from the Colliers' kitchen and they were the very same ones the girls had used for their slice-and-dice routine on the Colliers. There was also clothing in the backpack, which appeared to be stained with blood, and an empty Newport cigarette pack stained with blood. No doubt, again, it was the Colliers' blood.

Upon seeing the knives, Lieutenant Colonel Jordan's skin suddenly went cold. He knew evidence would take jurors either way on a verdict. Who could predict where they would stand between "sin" and "sympathy" after seeing something like this?

After all the dust had settled at the police station and the evidence packed up, Detective Ethon Harper, juvenile detectives Bo Turner and Phil McElwaney, and Lieutenant Greg Craft returned to the house on Bright Street and questioned Patricia, Brian, and Brett. The detectives met with each of them separately and then met with all of them together. Although the mother and sons were cooperative and willing to talk about the traumatic incident, they were all, understandably, a bit shaken. Almost overnight, their lives had been altered significantly and Patricia wondered if any of them would ever recover. She assured her sons this would be the last time they'd ever invite a stranger into their home.

In a separate meeting with the detectives, Brian told the detectives how he and his brother had met the two girls and what had transpired that night. He stated when they got back home, the two girls stayed in the first-floor bedroom with him, and the way they interacted was more like boyfriend and girlfriend. He also confessed they all had smoked marijuana together while walking on the beach. In addition, he had stolen some Ativan from his mother's room and traded it with the girls for Adderall.

"I think the Ativan knocked the girls out," Brian confessed. "I slept on one end of my bed and they slept on the other end, all cuddled up together."

The detectives then met with Brian, his mother, and his brother.

"The real names of the girls your sons brought home with them Tuesday night were Holly Harvey and Sandy Ketchum," Detective Harper informed the bewildered trio. "Holly is fifteen and Sandy is sixteen. Earlier that day, they attacked and stabbed Holly's grandparents to death with kitchen knives, stabbing each of them at least fifteen times."

Patricia looked first at Brian, then at Brett. This time her heart was thumping with fear rather than anger.

"The girls were very angry at their grandparents because they disapproved of their relationship and would not allow them to take their trip to the beach."

Patricia pressed her lips together, trying to ask the right questions.

"We had plenty reason to suspect all of you were in danger," Harper continued. "They needed money and were looking for a place to get rid of the stolen truck. They still had the murder weapons and could have easily killed you, taken your money, and stolen your vehicle."

"One of the girls told us that they and the boys had all smoked pot together," Bo Turner stated, staring at the boys as if he could will the truth out of them.

Patricia did not like the direction or the tone this conversation was taking. The cops were talking to them as if they were hardened criminals.

"We're also wondering why your boys would let these horrible girls into your house in the first place?" Turner asked bluntly.

Patricia was clenching her teeth so hard that her jaw ached. It sounded to her as if Brian and Brett were being accused of conspiring with the girls.

"I want you to know my sons had no idea of who these girls were and what these girls had done," she said in her sons' defense. "They just felt sorry for them and were only trying to do the right thing by giving shelter to what they thought were two apparent runaways."

The detectives listened, but implied there might be more to the boys' story than just giving the girls a place to sleep. Not many people would invite two total strangers into their home without some kind of hidden agenda. Maybe the boys had a little more in mind than a stroll on the beach.

Not knowing why she had to explain herself, and feeling more than a little resentful that she felt she had to, Patricia interrupted the police before she lost it.

"I don't know what you're trying to get them to say, but if you're saying that they were soliciting sexual favors from these two girls, then you're wrong. I can assure you that my sons were being perfect gentlemen and had no intention of doing anything like that with these girls."

"Just maybe their meeting was planned," Detective Harper said a little too smugly. "Maybe Brian knew these girls somehow and also knew that they had killed the Colliers."

Brian turned to his mom, watching all the color drain from her face. He took a deep breath, then hissed out a protest between his teeth.

"That's not true. I knew nothing about them, but what they told me. And if they would have told me they had killed somebody, then I would have called the cops immediately."

Patricia inhaled deeply. It was a humiliating experience for the detectives to accuse her and her boys of conspiring with these girls.

"Look, we're law-abiding citizens," she said angrily. "How can you sit here in my living room and try to turn this on us? How can you make me and my family out to be the bad guys, when these girls you have in custody are homicidal maniacs?"

The detectives sympathized with Patricia, but if she had seen what they had seen at the Colliers' home, she would understand where they were coming from.

Later that evening, Patricia Pellerien confessed to news reporters from the *Atlanta Journal-Constitution* that she and her boys felt lucky. In no way attempting to hide her relief, she told her side of it.

"We thought we were helping runaways. These girls were very young. They were dirty. I thought something was up, you know, maybe they were runaways. I just wanted to make sure they were okay."

Patricia swallowed trying to speak through the tightness in her throat.

"But now I feel that through"—she paused to catch her breath—"money and a car and my jewelry, I think they would have not hesitated to stab us and rob us. Who knows what else they were capable of?"

Patricia lowered her head. She sounded tired of the whole thing. She took a deep sigh, then made her last comment on the subject.

"You know," she said, her voice dropping a notch, "they could have been waiting around to kill us and take my money. We're lucky to be alive."

Chapter 50

The orange glow from the revolving light of the tow truck from Fayette Wrecker Company pulsed throughout the parking lot at the Tybee Island Police Department. There was a hydraulic whine from the tow truck and Carl Collier's blue Silverado was pulled onto the flatbed. The FCSO detectives—Shelton, Rojas, and Harper—would follow the tow truck the entire trip back to Fayetteville. They wanted to make certain the truck made it back to the sheriff's office without any glitches, where it would be processed for evidence.

Holly Harvey and Sandy Ketchum were being transported in two separate SUVs. Sergeant Tracey Carroll and Corporal Lennelle Coker, of the FCSO, had flown from Atlanta to Fayetteville to assist the U.S. Marshals in the transfer. Holly was silent during the entire drive back home, but Sandy was talkative and emotional.

"I keep smelling that god-awful blood," Sandy cried along the way. "I see it over and over in my dreams. Those people didn't deserve to die."

Lieutenant Maholn Donald, the Fayette County officer attached to SERFTF, sat in the front seat of the SUV that transported Sandy. He listened to Sandy talk about her tormenting dreams and express remorse for her crimes. When Sandy casually mentioned, "You know, I'd like to write a book," he assumed she meant a book about the killings.

"I hate to tell you this, but if you are a convicted felon," Donald pointed out, "you're not allowed to profit from the sales of your story."

"Oh, no," Sandy quickly corrected herself, "I just want to write a book of poetry, that's all."

They're just kids, Donald thought. *They have no earthly idea what they have gotten themselves into.*

Grieving county residents and sheriff's deputies anxiously awaited the return of the two teenage girls charged with the brutal murders of Carl and Sarah Collier. The community was shocked and disturbed by the senseless slaughter, and the case quickly surfaced in the national press. At first it appeared their motive for murder might have been money.

"I'm not sure if these teenagers took money from the Colliers' residence or not," Sheriff Randall Johnson responded when asked to comment on the robbery motive. He said he thought the crime was premeditated and that he was taken back at the nature of the killings, but he didn't know anything about robbery.

Lieutenant Colonel Bruce Jordan clarified that robbery was not the motive for the Collier murders and offered reporters his assessment of the situation.

"I believe Holly Harvey was emotionally distraught by the forced separation from her lover," he said.

As Jordan thought about the Colliers' bloodied bodies, his original dislike for Holly washed over him again. He promised her he would send her down the river, and now he was going to have his say, every last word of it.

"I believe she wished for everyone to suffer the way she suffered. Now, Sandy Ketchum's reason for going along with Harvey's demented violence is unclear. But I believe the evidence at trial will be that their motive was to gain freedom and to be able to stay together forever."

Fayette County newspapers and surrounding county newspapers, in and around Atlanta, had already gone to press and were out on the racks. The front-page headlines proclaimed: POLICE CAPTURE TEEN GIRLS WANTED IN DOUBLE SLAYING. The words could have been read from any sidewalk four football fields away from the courthouse. Under the headline was a huge picture of Holly Harvey and Sandy Ketchum. As expected, the photo caused a huge sensation, got lots of attention, and sold a lot of newspapers.

The media was going straight for shock. But, of course, they had no choice. It was a bloody, heinous crime, committed by two teenagers. Talk around the state was of this crime, and nothing else. It was a wonderfully sensational story and it deserved to be written as such. Not to mention, it was shaping up to be one of the biggest criminal cases in Georgia's history. For some upcoming, hotshot rookie reporter, it was a golden opportunity to advance a career.

At the time the teenagers had been captured, not much about their lesbian affair was known. Someone had mentioned Sandy was gay and had several girlfriends. Someone then said Holly was bisexual and had both girlfriends and boyfriends. Others who knew them said they didn't know if the two girls were having a sexual relationship or not. They knew they were very good friends, but as to whether they were lesbians, it might be just a rumor. Reporters went so far as to camp out around Metro State Prison, where Holly's mother, Carla, was an inmate, hoping for a chance to interview her about the crimes.

It didn't take long for the rumor mill around Fayetteville and Atlanta to get started. Once it did, everyone was happy to fuel the fire. A couple of loudmouths on the radio took turns holding court and ambushing the girls. It was surprising to hear how reckless these so-called talk show hosts were with their innuendos and thoughtless versions of the truth.

There were some journalists and reporters who maintained

their integrity, using a host of confirmed and reliable sources, and newspapers such as the *Fayette Daily News,* the *Atlanta Journal-Constitution,* and *The Citizen* worked diligently to capture what really went down. When they were sure of their facts, they printed it. When they weren't so sure, they waited until they had enough of the facts to offer a professional opinion.

Most disturbing were the photos that accompanied the articles. In many ways, the photos were more ominous than the articles themselves. The public was not only reeling over the brutal deaths of two elderly folks, but they were absolutely mortified to learn the accused killers were children. And to see these children who had plotted and stabbed the Colliers to death exit the police cars, chained at the wrists and at the ankles, was truly disturbing.

Veteran law officers were calling the teenagers' crime the most gruesome murder scene they had ever seen. During the attack, Sarah suffered more than twenty stab wounds to her chest and back before dying. Carl sustained no less than eighteen wounds to his chest and neck.

"The detectives are still following up to make sure the girls weren't involved in any other crimes that have been committed on the way to Savannah," Sheriff Randall Johnson told the press. "We don't know if they pulled anything else, but I can tell you this one is the worst I've ever seen. One stab is considered impulse, while stabbing fifteen times is considered rage."

A team of uniformed police officers were making the rounds of homes within several blocks of the Colliers' home. They wanted to make certain there were no other murders in the neighborhood and to see if any of the Colliers' neighbors had seen or heard anything in the last twenty-four hours. The media was not far behind, ringing those same doorbells.

"They caught them?" the Colliers' neighbor Randolph Epps responded from his porch to Channel 2's reporter Jo-Quitta Williams. "Great, God will have His vengeance. Sarah tried to do what she could for that child. I can't believe Holly did this. She took an angel; she really did.

"But as far as I understand, her granddaughter was a typical teenager. She wanted to go out and party and do what she wanted to do. But Ms. Sarah wanted to raise her right and they were catching some problems with that."

Epps was holding on to the leash of the Colliers' tan-and-white dog, Sparky.

"I often saw Holly sneak out of the house. I seen her once up in the street myself and I told Ms. Sarah. And she said, 'She's a teenager and she's giving me problems.'"

Sara Polk also talked to the media, but because it had been a very traumatic experience for her, she would not allow her face to be seen.

"I want everyone to know that turning in my friends was the single most difficult decision of my life. I didn't do it for the publicity, but I did it because it was the right thing to do. Killing two people, brutally, is morally wrong. And I turned in my friends because they were accused of murder.

"It's really, really hard, because I'm not a rat. I don't sit here and go tell on everybody for everything they've done, because people have done wrong things. But, it was to the extent of their wrongness. To do something like that and not have any regret whatsoever, that takes somebody without a heart."

When the reporter told Sara the police were calling her a hero, she said she didn't feel like one.

"I just pray that maybe Sandy regrets it and understands why I did it. I hope that she isn't sitting here, hating me right now, because it was for the better and not for the worst."

Another one of Sandy and Holly's former classmates, Jessica Fortner, said they, too, were trying to understand the horror police had described.

"It's really surprising and shocking, especially when I knew them. I didn't think people my age were capable of anything like that."

Chapter 51

Chief Medical Examiner Kris Sperry completed autopsies on the bodies of Carl and Sarah Collier at the GBI Division of Forensic Sciences, pursuant to the Georgia Death Investigation Act. Sperry's report was immediately forwarded to FCSO's Bruce Jordan.

In his report, Dr. Sperry concluded that Carl Collier bled to death from the result of multiple stab wounds. His body was heavily saturated with liquid and clotted blood. The blue denim trousers he had worn to work that day were soaked in urine and blood. And on the upper right front of his sleeveless undershirt, there was an oval hole that corresponded to a stab wound in his chest.

Upon closer examination, Sperry noted a superficial knife wound on Carl's brow. His ear was partially amputated, and on the right lateral side of his head, extending down to his neck, was a significant slashing wound. On the upper surface of his right shoulder and at the base of the neck, four more superficial incisions, varying from 2.15 to 6.5 centimeters in length, were found.

The most serious wound was on Carl's neck. It was here that Dr. Sperry observed a large gaping wound that began at his left midclavical and extended inward 5.7 centimeters, then across and down. When the knife punctured Carl's neck, it struck the first thoracic vertebra in the midspinal region, notching it. It also had ripped open his carotid artery, creating a gaping, massively hemorrhagic three-centimeter wound. The track of the knife sliced into the esophagus and the trachea and down into the upper region of the right lung, which was also extensively hemorrhagic. In a matter of seconds, blood seeped into Carl's right lung, filling it up like water filled a plastic bag.

Another stab wound was found in Carl's midsternal region, slightly to the right of his midline section. On his left shoulder, there was a slashing wound that stretched across his flesh, 9.7 centimeters in length. Several more superficial and nonthreatening wounds were found in this area. Worst of all, on the upper portion and back of Carl's right lung, just below the base of the neck, the knife had ripped a gaping teardrop-shaped incision. The cut extended toward the base of his neck for nearly three inches.

Four additional knife wounds were found on Carl Collier's left shoulder and back. There were even more on his left arm and hand. Carl must have attempted to defend himself with his left hand, as a defensive wound was noted in this same area.

Carl Collier suffered no less than eight superficial and deep stab wounds to his face, head, and neck, and nine more in his chest and back area. Sperry underscored that all of these wounds contributed to his death by exsanguination, but the wound into his left neck had done the most damage. The knife had penetrated his left neck, incised the aorta, and started a massive internal and external hemorrhaging.

Sarah Collier had fared no better than her husband—actually worse. Sperry stated that she had also sustained multiple stab wounds of the head, neck, chest, and abdomen, and right and left upper arms. Her most fatal blow was the wound that had entered the right shoulder, which transected the right axillary artery (below shoulder), led to massive hemorrhages—and ultimately her death.

Sarah's Hawaiian blue floral print shirt was saturated with blood, with one very large, gaping hole that corresponded to a stab wound. Her white brassiere exhibited "incised defects," which also corresponded to stab wound injuries. Her blue floral print shorts were also heavily bloodstained and had defects associated with stab wound injuries.

On the lateral left neck, below the angle of the jaw, was a horizontally oriented 3.3-centimeter stab wound incision. On the right parietal scalp (back of the head) was a stab wound that had perforated the right parietal bone into the cranial vault, slightly penetrating the brain.

On the right breast, above the nipple, was a 4.5-centimeter stab wound incision that extended deeply into the tissues of the breast. On the upper right breast was a large, gaping stab wound, which measured thirteen centimeters in length. The margins of the wound were focally irregular, reflecting removal of the blade and reinsertion, during the course of the infliction of this wound.

On the midanterior thorax (chest) was an inverted angulated gaping stab wound, measuring thirteen centimeters in length. The stab wound penetrated the fat into the peritoneal cavity (gut) resulting in mesenteric hemorrhaging (intestinal bleeding). Overlying the right lateral inguinal region (lower gut) was a 2.3-centimeter stab wound. In the lateral midright abdomen region were two more superficial punctures. Just above it was another knife wound.

On the right posterior midthoracic area (midback) was a deep stab wound that measured 5.5 centimeters in length. The knife had penetrated into the thoracic cavity, notching the right tenth rib. The attack incised the lower lobe of the right lung.

On Sarah Collier's upper left arm was a deep, gaping, 7.5-centimeter stab wound that pierced the arm. Another stab wound was found on the left forearm, as were two more superficial defensive wounds on the left hand.

At the juncture of the right arm, with the left shoulder, interiorly, was a large 6-centimeter stab wound that transected the axillary artery, causing massive hemorrhaging that had led to exsanguination. On the right posterior lateral (side) upper arm, three more stab wounds were found.

On the dorsal right forearm was an obliquely oriented deep slash wound, measuring 11.5 centimeters, which had penetrated deep into the musculature and severed numerous tendons. Two more stab wounds were located on the right hand.

On the posterior right upper arm, adjacent to the shoulder articulation, a large, gaping stab wound measuring 6. 2 centimeters was found. The wound extended deeply into the musculature and soft tissue of the posterior arm and shoulder. Another superficial stab wound measuring 4.4 centimeters in length was discovered on the posterior midright upper arm.

Chapter 52

The two teenagers arrived at the Fayette County Sheriff's Office and were transported to separate juvenile detention facilities. Holly was transferred to the smaller Clayton County Regional Detention Center (CCRDC) in nearby Lovejoy, where she would join about fifty other juveniles, 80 percent males, who had been charged with crimes or had been found guilty of crimes and were awaiting disposition of their cases by a juvenile court. Sandy Ketchum was taken to the state's largest youth jail for offenders between the ages of nine and seventeen, the Metro Regional Youth Detention Center in Atlanta (Metro RYDC).

After Sandy had settled in at Metro, she was escorted to a waiting room, where the public telephones were only four feet off the ground—about the right height for a child. Everything about Metro looked and felt like an adult prison—with razor wire outside the facility and electronic doors inside—except for the inmates. It was a sobering sight for Sandy to see little girls holding on to teddy bears and still sucking their thumbs, dressed in standard jailhouse garb—navy jumpsuits, orange T-shirts, orange socks, and orange plastic flip-flops—shuffling around with metal shackles fixed around their ankles.

Sandy placed a phone call to her parents' home in Franklin.

They had been staying with friends in Griffin, but there was nothing they could do but wait. Later that afternoon, after hearing on the radio that Sandy and Holly had been captured, they returned home.

Sandy's father answered the phone, but upon hearing his little girl's voice, he became racked with grief so powerful and consuming that he could not talk. Sobbing and breathless, he handed the phone to Beth.

"Mommy?" Sandy managed to squeeze out.

Beth's eyes moved reflexively toward Tim. She could not imagine herself doing this.

"How are you doing?" she asked weakly.

For a few seconds, Sandy was silent. Finally she blurted out, "I swear I didn't kill nobody."

Never one to beat around the bush, Beth confronted Sandy with a straightforward practical way of dealing with her problems. She was in a hell of a mess that no amount of money would buy her out of, and it was too late for pleading, *I don't know* and *I'm sorry*.

"I have fixed and gotten your ass out of every trouble you've ever been in," she told her in a voice of utter coldness and pragmatism, "but there ain't nothing I can do to fix this. I don't know what in the hell happened, but you're in this thing for the long haul."

Sandy again denied killing anyone. In fact, she was horrified at the thought of taking another person's life. It all had happened so fast, she said, and if she had done it, some separate entity outside of herself had been responsible. The fact was she had tried to stop Holly from killing her grandparents.

Beth could hardly believe what was happening. She looked at Tim and shook her head uncomprehendingly.

Sandy sensed Beth's rejection and asked despairingly, "Do you love me?"

"You know we do," Beth answered.

Sandy choked back her tears. "Will you be sticking by me?"

"Yes, but only under one condition," Beth stipulated. "You're gonna tell me what happened, because I can't support you until you do. I want to know what in the hell went wrong, since that is the only way I can help you."

Sandy listened carefully, first once, then again, as Beth re-stated the conditions. Slowly she told Beth her version of the story.

"I was over at Holly's house. We were doing drugs, and things just got out of hand. Holly's grandparents got killed and we stole Holly's grandfather's truck and ran. Then we got picked up."

Beth was relieved to know that Sandy at least had come to grips with what she had done. But, before they could go any further, she had to know the answer to one question.

"Sandy, tell me the truth. Did you kill anybody?"

"No," Sandy said without hesitation.

"Then explain to me in detail exactly what happened," Beth insisted.

Sandy let out a long sigh, then continued her story.

"Holly and her grandmother got into an argument. Her grandfather then come down to her bedroom and both of them got on top of Holly. Holly hollered for help.

"I then jumped up from behind the bed, where I had been hiding, and saw Holly stabbing her grandmother. I got into a wrestling match with them and tried to take the knife away from Holly. Holly was under her grandmother and began screaming, 'I can't breathe. Get my grandmother off me.' That was when I took my knife and stabbed Sarah Collier in the arm and in the back of the head, but I didn't kill her.

"Holly then chased her grandfather upstairs and I heard all this hollering and screaming going on. When Holly ran into the kitchen, I'd gone up to see what was happening and Mr. Collier seen me. He grabbed a coffee cup and threw it at me. I ducked and it missed, then smashed into pieces against a wall. Then Holly stabbed him one more time in the neck and he fell to the floor dead.

"When me and Holly went back down to the basement, we found Mrs. Collier at the front of the stairs. Since her grandmother was still breathing, she then started screaming at me, 'She's not dead! She's not dead!' I started crying, 'No, no, no,' and that she was dead. Holly just began stabbing her grandmother and screaming, 'This fat bitch won't die.'

"After Holly stabbed her a couple of times, we made sure she was dead and quickly packed up and left."

Sandy told Beth she didn't remember much after that. After they killed Holly's grandparents, it was all a blur.

Beth took a deep breath. Was it possible that Sandy was telling the truth? Maybe she hadn't killed anybody. Or was it possible that in her narcotic haze she didn't know what the truth was? That she couldn't see beyond what her drug-induced stupor allowed. Then again, maybe she had no particular need to see any further. Maybe this was her way of compartmentalizing information.

There were a lot of questions that needed answers. Sandy had told Beth what had happened. Sometimes Beth could hear her heading toward a horrifying detail and skating right past it, but she didn't worry about that now. In the end, the truth always came out. Sandy was in jail, charged with the murders of Carl and Sarah Collier. And that crisis was more than enough to keep her occupied.

Tim Ketchum was still suffering from the shock at the enormity of what his little girl had done. He was a hardworking man, but had little money and no assets to show for it. As far as he could see, barring a miracle, his little girl was up shit creek without a paddle. It was possible she could spend the rest of her life in jail.

Kevin Collier was interviewed that same day by Fox 5's Aungelique Proctor. Wearing a red shirt and a white baseball cap, his eyes swollen, Kevin stated, "My heart is broken.

I still can't fathom my niece would actually kill my parents over a beach trip."

Kevin said his mom and dad were perfect parents, and he didn't understand his niece's need to kill them.

"My niece's living arrangement with my parents was potentially more than volatile. Unfortunately, I couldn't foresee the tragic turn of events and my parents, who were such a loving couple, were struck down in some kind of 'pre-planned' murder."

Kevin stumbled over his words and fought hard to hold his tears back.

"I'm very angry with what happened. . . . There's mixed emotions. I'm just at a loss for words."

As Kevin planned his parents' funeral, he said he was angry and had unanswered questions for his defiant niece.

"I don't understand why she had to kill my parents to go to Florida. She had left the house plenty of times before. I don't understand why she thought she had to kill them before she left. But I see she made it to the beach. Hopefully, for the last time."

Kevin paused, then gathered his anger.

"These girls definitely need to be tried as adults and prosecuted to the full extent of the law. I want them tried as adults and I believe they should face life imprisonment. That's justice."

Holly and Sandy had been arrested on Tuesday, then brought back to Fayetteville and transferred to the juvenile facilities on Wednesday. It seemed as if everyone in Fayette County had an opinion as to what happened and why. Most blamed Holly and Sandy's guilt on what was wrong with society.

Kids today just don't have any values and appreciation of life anymore.

The media kept the debate hot, challenging their viewers, listeners, and subscribers to make the call. Was what happened to Holly and Sandy the result of the breakdown of the family unit, the removal of God and prayer from the school, TV violence, or any one of seemingly thousands of society's ills?

Scott Moore told the press Holly's troubles were a result of her not wanting to live by house rules.

"The Colliers were pretty strict grandparents, as most parents should be. She and Sandy had been in trouble before and they often spoke of running away to Florida; so, I guess, Holly didn't like living with her grandparents. She didn't like living with me, either, but I never thought something like this would happen. Hooking up and trying to sneak out is one thing, but sitting there and taking it out on her grandparents, who are seventy-something years old, now that is pure crazy."

Chapter 53

When FCSO detective Harper arrived back in Fayetteville, he was advised the photographs taken of Holly Harvey and Sandy Ketchum when they were fingerprinted at Tybee Island Police Department were out of focus and blurred. The photos were taken as proof that the slight bruising on the girls might have been caused during their struggle with the Colliers. Investigator Manny Rojas and Josh Shelton were asked to visit the juvenile facilities and retake the teenagers' photographs.

In addition, Harper was also meeting with those persons who had spoken with Sandy and/or Holly the night of the murders. It was confirmed the two teenagers had called around, looking for a gun to "take care of business."

David Burnett told Harper he had given Sandy Ketchum a ride from Griffin to Fayetteville the night of the murders. He said her mother, Sandra Ketchum, had approved it. Holly met Sandy outside by the bushes on Plantation Drive and gave her $10 to pay him for the trip.

The Colliers' home was still being secured by the FCSO uniformed patrol units. While discussing the arrest, the investigative unit remembered seeing the butcher block located on the kitchen counter. They were now convinced the two knives located in Carl Collier's truck and the knife located in Sandy

Ketchum's pocket may have originated from that same butcher block. Investigator Manny Rojas was sent back to the crime scene to collect the butcher block. Also, while Rojas was there, he was asked to collect the dog painting from Holly's bedroom with the cuts in it.

Harper had requested details for Holly Harvey's and Sarah Collier's cell phones and copies of the 911 tapes from the Spalding County and Fayette County Dispatch Centers. He and Lieutenant Colonel Jordan had also met with Kevin Collier. Kevin and Anita Beckom had visited his parents' home. Since they were having so many problems with Holly, his father had hidden his .38 revolver in the house. While Kevin was there, he was unable to locate the pistol, as well as a jewelry box. When shown the jewelry Holly had stolen the night of the murders—the jewelry she had wanted to pawn on Tybee Island—he identified it as belonging to his sister, Carla Harvey.

A very unflattering Metro prison picture of Carla Harvey was being circulated among the press and had been posted on TV channels and in the newspapers. For the first time, all of Fayette County knew the connection between mother and daughter.

There was nothing smooth and symmetrical and complete about this case. It all came out in rough edges, ragged parts, and a puzzle that didn't quite fit together. There was a circle of life and that circle had been broken. But, somehow, there was a story behind the murders that was vivid and powerful and poignant. Looking at the pictures of Holly and her mother, one couldn't help but wonder, *what went wrong?* How could such a young girl commit such a heinous crime against her own family? Those were the burning questions in the fire of the public's mind.

Kevin talked to the press about his niece's misguided life and the mother who was never there.

"I think my sister was always a friend to Holly, and never

a mom. She has always been defiant and always in control of her mother. Her mother would leave her alone at home.

"Carla loved her kids, but if somebody wanted to go out, she'd go out with them. She was either bartending or dancing. She was an exotic dancer at the Gold Rush, the Crazy Horse, and the Pink Pony.

"Carla and I were adopted and raised in a wholesome atmosphere. When she went to jail for three years on possession of drugs, that made my parents feel like failures. That's not the way they had taught us. That was probably why my parents were determined to discipline Holly. It was a struggle."

It was ironic how these two teenage lovers who were desperate for their freedom—and to be with each other forever—were now separated and having to follow the strict prison rules. No longer tethered at the hip, they were beginning to understand it was going to be a long, tough road ahead.

Fayetteville was one of the fastest-growing towns in the metro Atlanta area, but it still had maintained its small-town, conservative values. After all the information about these girls in the media, was it possible they could ever get a fair shake in a Fayette County courtroom?

Fayette County lawyer Lloyd Walker didn't think so. A graduate of Harvard University and the University of South Carolina School of Law, Walker was a soft-spoken transplant from the mountainous western regions of Idaho, who had forsaken corporate law and opted to defend a portion of our society that cannot afford to pay for legal counsel. Walker was an active member of the Indigent Defense Committee for the Griffin Judicial District and his task was to ensure legal representation for all the indigent persons from Fayette, Spalding, Pike, and Upson Counties. The majority of Walker's cases were in the juvenile division.

On the day after the Colliers' murders, Walker was in the juvenile court talking with other lawyers when he learned that one of the suspects, Sandy Ketchum, a former client of his from juvenile court, was involved in a murder. He recalled he was still representing her on a charge in juvenile court that had not been adjudicated. Officially, he was still her attorney in that case, and unless her family had hired another attorney, there was a possibility her rights had been violated if she, while in custody, had talked to the police without an attorney—namely him—present.

Sandy Ketchum's parents were not content with Walker being their lawyer. Tim and Beth had witnessed Walker in court and they were not very pleased with what they saw. Walker was a portly man and his clothes never seemed to fit quite right on his body. The times that they had seen him in court, his shirttail was either hanging out of his pants or he was stepping on his too long pants. On several occasions, he didn't even wear a tie or a belt in the courtroom.

The Ketchums thought Walker's sloppiness just didn't come off well with the jurors and they sought help from bleeding hearts on the Internet. With the help of a friend, they issued a plea on AOL Hometown for donations to Sandy's defense fund. The Ketchums admitted they had limited funds and lived from paycheck to paycheck, but they wanted the best representation for Sandy and asked for the public's help.

Another member of the Indigent Defense Committee, public defender Judy Chidester held the same core beliefs as Walker, and when it became apparent the two teens and their families did not have the resources to hire their own attorneys, she volunteered to represent Holly Harvey.

Chidester was a graduate of Georgia State University and the Emory University School of Law in Atlanta. In Fayette County, she had been active in local politics, serving as vice-chairman of the Fayette County Democratic Party and a member of a controversial group known as Women in Numbers (WIN). WIN encouraged pro-choice advocates to run for public office, and its members often carried the label of "feminist." Being labeled a feminist, liberal, pro-choice Democrat in a predominantly Republican constituency in the Deep South did not phase the fifty-two-year-old grandmother at all. Long ago, she made the decision to stand up and be counted and fight for what she believed in.

Immediately Walker and Chidester volunteered to carry the crosses for the teenagers.

"They're young, frightened children whose faces shouldn't ever be seen by the public," the legal duo cried out as their first two points of opposition to the press. "And they are minors who are going to be charged as adults for murder."

On Thursday morning, August 5, the FCSO called a press conference. Spokesman Lieutenant Colonel Bruce Jordan was dressed in lawyer's clothes—a black suit, white shirt, and black-and-white tie—and stood behind a wide lectern. The place was packed. Jordan offered some hellos, shook some hands, and exchanged a couple of nods. He had been around Fayette County a long time, and knew a lot of people. He nodded and smiled, and—like always—caught the odd looks of those who were suspicious of the police.

Jordan laid out their crime in disturbing detail and talked about why he thought the murders were premeditated and what he thought the teenagers did in the aftermath of the murders.

"I believe Holly Harvey masterminded all this. She is a cold, calculating killer. She even tried to slip out of custody after being arrested. Harvey is . . ." Jordan paused, took a deep breath, and searched for just the right words. "She is the coldest and probably the most heartless person I have ever interviewed, especially after killing someone from the immediate family. It almost made her giddy to know that we had brought so many people in to arrest her. Sandy showed more emotion and cried, knowing she faced murder charges, but not Holly. By looking at the alleged murder weapon, Holly's intent was clear.

"I'm telling you both those knives were wicked. And it turned my stomach when I opened the towel and saw them. I don't think any reasonable human being can look at these knives and not know the intent was clearly to kill these people.

"They are vicious killers who knew what they were doing and planned to get away with it. These girls are cold-blooded killers, but they are not smart killers. Even though they had the plan written on her arm, they had no money and they used their cell phone to call friends as they drove down I-16 toward Savannah. We had a lot of informants that night.

"Holly is manipulative. In my opinion, from what I know about her, she uses people to get what she wants. We found a poem in which she allegedly desires to have people suffer as she suffered and a desire to kill. All of that will be turned into evidence.

"And the motive for all of this," Jordan revealed further, "was the two girls wanted to be together forever in a romantic relationship. They were having a lesbian relationship that the Colliers discouraged, so they murdered them to seek freedom and so they could be together forever."

Jordan said Sandy Ketchum had been remorseful, was cooperative, and had a complete understanding of what effect the killings would have on the rest of her life.

"I've had a long conversation with Sandy," Jordan said. "I think Sandy was in it for the love, but Holly Harvey is emotionless. And there will be evidence presented at her trial that she had not cried all the way up to the point of her arrest. I spoke to her that day. She was callous and cocky."

Later that afternoon, the two teenagers were transported from the detention centers to the Fayette County Courthouse in Fayetteville. Their scheduled appointment with the Magistrate Court judge Charles Floyd Jr. was at 2:00 P.M. They were both bound by wrist chains and ankle handcuffs and were wearing tan bulletproof vests. There were family members waiting to support them, the press to publicize them, and others just wanting to see if their heads would rotate 360 degrees and they'd vomit pea soup all over the courtroom.

Before the girls were brought in the filled courtroom, their appointed attorneys asked Judge Floyd to remove media cameras from the courtroom.

"Our clients are juveniles, children," Lloyd Walker argued. "We have to start now focusing a little bit on the rights of my client. I understand the seriousness of the crime. But we don't need to add in this courtroom the media that is brought on by people in this state."

Walker said the case had already received a tremendous amount of attention in the national news media and that TV and still cameras should be kept out of the courtroom.

"This case has already drawn a media circus, and my client has the right to prevent any further pretrial publicity. Reporters should be allowed to observe the proceedings, but the cameras should be banned from the courtroom. Allowing the cameras to record my client's face would do further harm to her right to an impartial jury trial."

Floyd allowed media attorneys and reporters their say-so. He listened as they argued that the teenagers had been charged as adults, and insisted that the public had a right to see how the judicial system handled murder cases. This wasn't an ordinary case and few people in Fayette County and the surrounding areas wanted to miss it. Most folks would not be able to attend the proceedings, so they would rely on the press for coverage. And the press was determined to give them the details.

The judge denied Walker's motion, allowed the cameras to stay, and ordered the proceedings to begin.

"Bring the defendants in," Floyd boomed from the bench.

The cameras rolled on, and the nation got its first view of what many were already calling a modern-day version of *Thelma and Louise*.

Holly Harvey walked in first with her attorney, wearing all her prison jewelry and the tanned vest. Underneath the vest, she wore a blue cotton T-shirt and jeans. Her hair was parted in the middle and turned up on the ends. She wore no makeup and her face was bland.

Holly's facial expression was partially hidden by a large amount of thick, dark hair with red highlights that fell in front of her face. But as she sat her small frame behind the defense table, she appeared to be smirking as she eyed the courtroom, packed with family, strangers, and the media. Her uncle Kevin Collier and friend Anita Beckom sat in the front row behind District Attorney Bill McBroom's table, but she never looked at them.

Holly's accomplice, Sandy Ketchum, walked in next with a solemn expression on her face, and was led to the attorneys' table, where Lloyd Walker was seated. She, too, was dressed in the same prison-issue tan protective vest, blue T-shirt, and blue jeans. Her reddish, dark brown hair hung over her forehead. She sat down and leaned back into her seat, never conversing with her attorney, as if she was in such great remorse that she could not bear it.

Both girls were a little over five feet tall, but looked like confused children.

On the state's side of the courtroom, Lieutenant Colonel Bruce Jordan, who had spent the better part of three days with little sleep, glanced up at the suspects as they walked into the courtroom.

Tim and Beth Ketchum sat in the front row, totally distraught. There was sweat on Tim's forehead. His stomach felt worse than ever. He wished he could believe it was the flu, but he knew better.

Other family members struggled with their emotions during the hearing as Holly and Sandy were being tried as adults and could face a maximum of life in prison.

Judge Floyd advised the girls of their Miranda rights and said he could not consider setting a bond amount for either suspect because they were charged with murder. The decision would be up to a superior court judge at a later date.

Floyd then asked Holly if she wanted the charges filed against her read aloud in court. Her attorney asked to hear the two charges of malice murder and felony murder. The charges against Sandy were also read aloud.

As the judge read each teen's charge against her, and by the time he had reached ". . . to which you did unlawfully and with malicious forethought cause the deaths of Carl and Sarah Collier, a human being, by stabbing them with a knife," fear had already fallen over their faces.

Holly put her head down on the table and her body started shaking. "I can't believe they're dead," she said at one point during the hearing. Chidester attempted to comfort her, placing her right hand on her shoulder.

Clearly upset at the predicament she faced, Sandy sat beside her attorney, quivering in her chair. Her heart was sore and afflicted, full of a hurt that seemed to double its weight. When the judge read the charges, she recoiled a bit, as if her heart had been touched by a red-hot poker. Overwhelmed by guilt, she put her head in her hands and wept, contracted with pain.

There was no testimony during the arraignment hearing.

Holly left the courtroom first, her hair hanging over her eyes. She turned her head and looked at Sandy, then dropped her head and walked out of the courtroom.

Sandy's family broke down when Sandy stood and walked away from them. When she turned and looked back at them, her face crumpled and she started weeping again. She walked out of the courtroom, having not been granted bond, and in worse shape than when she had walked in. She was hoping to get out and be with her family while she awaited trial. But after her bond was denied, Sandy was worse off than ever. In her heart, she knew she would never return home again, and this one flash of hope that had been made available to her, then snatched away at the last moment, made walking away unbearable.

The media had determined the difference between the two

accused killers might have been revealed when they left the courtroom. Holly turned around for a quick peer at Sandy with nothing but a cold stare on her face. Sandy's face, however, was red from sobbing. She wept openly throughout the whole hearing, and as she left the courtroom, she glanced into the crowd, looking for a comforting face.

It was an emotional day for both families, and after the girls were escorted outside the courtroom, several family members left in tears, sobbing uncontrollably. Some were unable to see because of the tears as they fled the courthouse interior, followed by news cameras in hot pursuit. One family member reached out as she passed and put her hand in front of a television camera.

Beth Ketchum was probably the most distraught of those, as she had already told the press that the teenagers had often written love poems to one another, and from reading those, she felt Sandy had been pressured into murdering the grandparents by Holly. As she fled outside to the hot Georgia pavement in the parking lot, she refused to speak to the news media.

Melissa Shepherd, one of Sandy's closest friends at Newnan High School, spoke to the reporters about her: "Sandy and I were friends during a three-month period earlier this year. We spent the night at each other's homes, talked on the phone a lot, and spent time together every day at some point. I knew about Holly and Sandy's relationship, and saw there was no chance of this relationship folding. But Holly had to have talked her into this, saying, 'Let's do this, because this is the only way we can be together, or whatever.'"

Lloyd Walker was not particularly eloquent with the press.

"She is upset and she's remorseful," he said to a reporter from Fox 5. "That's all I can tell you about that. All I can tell you is that both the family and my client are very sorry about this situation."

Holly's attorney, Judy Chidester, was more articulate.

"They are remorseful. She's fifteen. She's terrified. She's

very distraught. During the entire hearing, she was crying. I think she understands the seriousness of the charges against her, but as to the reality as to what it means to her life, no. I don't think she understands that."

"Do you know why [she killed her grandparents]?" the reporter asked candidly. "That is the question everyone seems to be asking."

"Not at this point," Chidester responded. "I anticipate having a long meeting with her. I will spend a lot of time with her and I will be discussing some of those issues with her."

Norma Camblee, an elderly lady and a close friend of Sarah Collier's, told the reporters she came to the court to see the two teens for herself, especially to see the granddaughter the Colliers had tried so hard to straighten out.

"And if she was in such remorse," Camblee pondered, referring to Holly's attorney's comments, "why did she do it? She had plenty of time to think about it. I kept asking, why? Why kill them? I feel sorry for 'em, I really do."

Alan Wang, of News Channel 2, spoke to Kevin Collier about Lieutenant Colonel Jordan's comments.

"No doubt, they planned the murder," Kevin said with grave disappointment. "Holly had allegedly written notes on her arm. I honestly didn't think she was capable of that. Not little, innocent, sweet Holly, who I knew. I just didn't think she was capable of that. I don't understand how she could have turned on them like that. But she was nice at some points and then a monster at other points.

"Sandy was bad news. They didn't want Holly around her. They wanted to go to the beach, but my parents refused. That is when they hatched this plan."

News Channel 11 broadcast an investigative piece on the Collier murder case. The segment began with the blurb:

Fayette County lead investigator Lieutenant Colonel Bruce Jordan described Holly Harvey as "cocky, callous,

stone cold, and without remorse." We spoke to Dr. Sherry
Blake, child psychologist, about the gruesome list on Holly
Harvey's arm and the poem she had written.

"The fact that she had enough foresight to write down
things to remember, she was organized," Dr. Blake opined.
"And with psychotic behavior, you don't get organized behavior. You wouldn't get a check list of things to do. About the
poem—I've dissected the poem, and the reality is she is hurting so bad that she wanted someone else to hurt as she hurt,
which again reveals serious, serious problems."

"How can Holly kill her grandparents?" the reporter asked
Dr. Blake.

"Drugs are likely to be involved, but a psychological profile would provide answers. The teenager's complete lack of
remorse is a front. That's a facade, and that facade masks a lot
of emotional stuff. It may be years before anyone can peel
back, or may never be able to peel back, the layers of that
facade to get to the real person, because we have no idea at
what age she was really hurt or damaged. The fact that Sandy
is remorseful shows that she is mentally healthier than Holly.
Nonetheless, she was under her influence at the time of the
murders."

Holly and Sandy's arrest suddenly thrust Fayette County
into the spotlight. As everyone described the girls, it began to
sound like a movie script. Sandy was the sweet and naive accomplice, who was talked into committing this crime by
Holly, the cold and calculating killer. But the way investigators described how the Colliers had been slaughtered, it
would leave anyone shaking in their boots.

On Thursday evening, the producers of ABC's *Good Morning America* contacted Kevin Collier from New York and invited him to appear the next day on their show. Lieutenant
Colonel Bruce Jordan was also contacted and he agreed to
appear on the program with Kevin. Diane Sawyer would con-

duct the interview from her anchor position in New York, and discuss the preliminary facts on the case with the two men via satellite feed from Atlanta.

Jordan was all set to go, until he got a phone call from the show's producer saying Kevin Collier would not be appearing with him. When he arrived at the studio in Atlanta on Friday morning, he noticed two chairs set up in front of the cameras.

"Then who is going to occupy this second chair?" Jordan asked the producers.

"We'll be interviewing Sara Polk, the young girl who phoned the police about the girls' visit."

Jordan raised his hands in protest. He had not had a chance to interview Polk and was sure she hadn't told his detectives all of what had happened that night.

"Oh, no, that will never do," he exclaimed. "You will not interview her sitting next to me. The smoke hasn't even cleared yet and it would be unethical for me to sit here with one of the key witnesses on nationwide TV before any trial."

There was pandemonium in the studio. Jordan was put on the phone and a conference call made to New York. They needed him to tell the story, but he didn't budge.

"No, sir, it won't happen this way," he assured them.

Finally Sara Polk was put in a car and driven to another studio in Atlanta, and the interview went on as scheduled. For those who watched the broadcast of Diane Sawyer interviewing Jordan and Polk, they were never aware the two were miles apart and sitting in different studios.

"Colonel Jordan," Sawyer began, "you have said this is an absolutely cold-blooded act. One of the most hardened people you have ever arrested is a girl named Holly?"

"Yes," Jordan said firmly.

"And this is premeditated—no doubt in your mind?"

"Yes, we'll be able to show the premeditation began several days before the actual killing," Jordan said assuredly.

"And you said that something was inscribed on her arm to remind her of the four things that were important to her during the crime. What were they?"

Jordan remained firm, then blurted out, "The word 'kill,' the word 'keys,' the word 'money,' and the word 'jewelry.'"

Sawyer's face tensed suddenly. "So she had her list of things to do, in effect?"

"Yes," Jordan answered.

"Motive? Again, we have heard that they were allegedly romantically involved and that the grandparents rejected that. Is that the best motive you have? What do you think?" Sawyer asked, looking at Jordan dubiously.

"The motive I think that will be presented at trial will be that they wanted their freedom and their opportunity to be together forever."

Sawyer grimaced, then turned to Sara Polk.

"Sara, you were the key evidence in calling the police, [and it] made a big difference in this case. The two girls drive up in your yard, covered in blood, did you know both of them?"

Sara explained the connection between her and the two teenagers. She told Sawyer she was astonished by the nature of the crime and that Sandy Ketchum was ever involved.

"It never hit me that Sandy would have done something like this," she said. "Especially not premeditated. Holly, I could have expected it from her, but not Sandy."

Sawyer was curious. "When you say you could have expected it from Holly, what about her?"

When Sara revealed Holly's cold and callous nature, Sawyer asked Jordan to confirm that assessment.

"Colonel Jordan, is this a correct report? When Holly was arrested, [I understand] she laughed?"

"Yes. In the room where Holly was initially arrested, there were only about four of us in the room. When she walked out of the room, there were several people from the Southeast Fugitive Task Force. She saw about nine people, and when she saw how many people were there to arrest her, she openly laughed at the officers as she walked by."

Sawyer was astonished by now. She thanked her guests, then concluded, "This is a story that has the police stunned by what they say is the cold-bloodedness of it."

That same afternoon, Superior Court judge Paschal A. English Jr. granted a bond hearing for the girls. Despite the fact that both teenagers were being held under a suicide watch in separate juvenile detention centers, English ruled they should have a chance to present their case for bond on August 19.

Chapter 54

Anita Beckom was on the brink of physical exhaustion. Since the night of the murders, she had been helping Kevin—whom she had grown to love like a brother—through this difficult ordeal and assisting him with the funeral arrangements. In her absence, her husband, James, had picked up the slack at home, but she still had two daughters who needed her.

The day after the Collier murders, Anita had invited Carla Harvey's eight-year-old daughter, Samantha, to stay with her and her family. She thought Samantha, or "Sam," as she liked to be called, would enjoy visiting with her youngest daughter, Tabitha, and find comfort staying with her family.

But the whole time Sam was with the Beckoms, she kept making comments about her grandmother Sarah Collier.

"I'm glad they're dead," Sam would say to anyone who would listen. "My grandmother was mean and she had no right to tell us what to do. I'm glad she's gone; she can't hurt us anymore."

Anita talked with Sam's father, Scott Moore, about his daughter's behavior, but he said he didn't see anything wrong with what she was saying. That was the way she felt, and there was nothing he could do about it. When Anita asked if Sam planned on attending her grandparents' funeral, he replied,

"She doesn't need to go to the funeral. She'd just be standing there and shaking old people's hands."

For as long as she could remember, Anita had babysat Samantha when Carla was working or on one of her little business excursions. She could not recall Sam ever acting this way. Anita was seeing a different side of this young girl, and it frightened her. It made her think she was headed down the same road as her sister.

On the Saturday night before the Monday funeral, Anita arrived home at 2:00 A.M. She and Kevin had been busy making all the last-minute arrangements for the funeral and accommodations for his relatives. When she walked into her home, Sam was still awake, sitting on the couch and watching TV. She had not changed into her pajamas, washed her face, or brushed her teeth.

"Okay, Sam," Anita admonished her, "it's time for you to go to bed now."

Sam refused to obey, insisting her mother always let her stay up late and watch television.

Anita was stunned. She sat there silently, her lips pursed. Her tired eyes were still as she tried to work it out in her head. Finally she said, "Well, that is something that is not allowed at my home. Besides, school is just a few days away and you need to start preparing for getting up early."

Anita switched off the TV remote. Sam challenged her, switching the remote back on. After several attempts to deny her the remote control, Anita took Sam to the bathroom and handed her a toothbrush. Carla never sent over any toothbrushes with Sam, so Anita always kept an extra supply on hand. She placed one on the sink and told Sam to brush her teeth.

Sam grabbed the toothbrush and threw it on the floor. When Anita told her to pick it up, she refused and began shouting at Anita. "You're not my mommy, so I don't have to do anything you tell me to do."

All this made Anita feel slightly childish and she began to cry.

James Beckom heard all the commotion in the bathroom and rushed to his wife's aid. He suggested they call Sam's father and have him come pick her up.

"Are you crazy?" James whispered to Anita after they had gotten Sam settled in the living room. "Have you forgotten that this girl's sister just butchered her grandparents? Did you ever once think that Sam would do the same thing to you?"

When Scott Moore arrived, Anita suggested they talk in private about Sam's inappropriate behavior. She didn't want to say anything bad about the child in front of her. But it was as if Moore had dropped in without a parachute. He refused, saying whatever was said would be said in his daughter's presence.

"You need to teach your daughter respect for her elders," Anita shot back. "She's been here with us now for three days. Why is she still here? You knew I was going to be with Kevin for his parents' funeral. It's time for you to take your daughter home and raise her."

Kevin later apologized to Anita for his niece's behavior. Scott and Carla had an entirely different perspective when it came to child rearing. Kevin knew that Anita had done more for Carla and her family than she would ever admit in her waking hours.

Anita prayed that Carla would learn something from this tragedy. Whenever something like this happened to children, she believed there was always a part in it that the parent had to consider. She wondered if Carla had taken stock of all that had happened. Maybe through this chance collision with fate, she would recognize the damage she had done to her children.

On Friday, the Metro Prison's warden had called Sheriff Randall Johnson and asked permission for Carla to attend her parents' funeral. Kevin and Anita had even gone to the sheriff's office and attempted to intervene for his sister with Lieutenant Colonel Jordan, but he declined, stating it was too much of a risk for his department to provide transportation and assume responsibility for her safety. Jordan openly blamed Carla and her daughter, Holly, for the Colliers' funeral and wanted nothing to do with the likes of her.

"My family has suffered a great loss," Carla eventually released her own private statement from prison. "I've lost three people whom I love. I am thankful for all the people who are praying for us."

The community was stunned by the Collier murder case, as the details were both chilling and graphic. The following Sunday morning at Fayetteville Baptist Church, the choir sang, but it wasn't easy. The Colliers attended church there, and Sarah was one of their most faithful choir members.

"The church had been devastated by the murders," music minister Steve Hester told the press. "The thing that bothers me the most, personally, when I think about this, is what had to be going through their minds when it was happening, because I know how much Sarah and Carl loved their granddaughter."

While the community and church dealt with this tragedy, family and friends of Carl and Sarah Collier's prepared themselves for the final farewell. On Monday, way before the eleven o'clock hour, nearly one thousand still-shocked mourners made their way to the Fayetteville First Baptist Church, one of the oldest churches in Fayetteville, to say good-bye to the Colliers and try to find closure. It was clear that this couple had touched so many lives. With the late-summer sun shining brightly, Kevin Collier and his friend Anita Beckom walked, arm in arm, leading a processional of relatives and friends into the church. The large stream of people had come to comfort him, share his pain, and pay tribute to his parents. They wanted him to know that if anybody ever deserved a ticket to the other side, it was his parents.

As the crowd silently filed into the church, each mourner was handed a copy of the funeral program, which featured a picture of the Colliers on the front and a special message from Kevin on the back.

On the back of the program it noted that "Due to circumstances beyond our control, Carla Collier was not able to
attend today's celebration."

Side by side in death, as they had been in life for fifty-five
years, the Colliers' caskets sat beside each other at the front
of the church. Carl's casket was draped in the American flag
and was to the left of Sarah's gray coffin, which was covered
in a brilliant display of red roses and baby's breath. A poster-
sized picture of the couple and sprays of flowers stood on
easels between the two coffins. Double rows of Delta workers sat on the far left side of the church in their work uniforms
as a tribute to Carl. On the right side of the congregation,
Sheriff Johnson and members of his staff sat among the
crowd. Their group of mourners included Lieutenant Colonel
Bruce Jordan, who had walked over with Johnson from their
county offices. It was Jordan's first for attending a victim's
funeral of a crime he was investigating.

In tribute to the slain couple, and as a gesture of love to
Kevin, a large number of church members from the Atlanta
First Baptist Church were in attendance. The renown Dr.
Charles Stanley served as their pastor, and their famed orchestra and choir were legendary. The group assembled on-
stage with the Fayetteville First Baptist Church choir, filling
the eighty-seat choir loft to its capacity.

Despite the circumstances of the gathering, Kevin had
wanted his parents' funeral service to be a celebration of their
life on earth and in heaven. After all they had been through,
he believed they deserved more than a few prayers, a eulogy,
and a slow ride in a hearse.

John Glover, the director of special events at First Baptist
Church of Atlanta, was the first of three ministers Kevin had
asked to speak.

"We've all read about Carl and Sarah in the newspaper
about them being dead, but don't believe it," Glover said, over
the crowd of people softly weeping. "They are not dead. Carl

and Sarah knew Jesus Christ and their spirits are in glory today. They are not dead. They are more alive than they have ever been.

"Secondly, they are happy. We are sad, but they are happy, because they died in the Lord and are with Jesus. They're in the heavenly choir now and are just singing up a storm."

Glover tried to make some sense of the tragedy.

"People are often confused about death and dying and the will of God," he said knowingly. "Is it God's will that a vicious murder take place and a teen kill her grandparents? Did God do it? Can we blame God?"

Glover paused, then asked the media not to take his words out of context.

"Many people are confused about this. It was not God's will, not his timing and place in the manner of death for Carl and Sarah Collier. Two girls were not acting as agents of God's will. They stepped out of God's will and they used their moral freedom to defy God. Things like this are not in the will of God, they are not in his realm of intention. God allowed it to happen because of our free will. But people suffer because of wrong, immoral, and evil choices."

In one of the most moving parts of the ceremony, Glover invited Kevin to come and take his seat in the orchestra, saying, "Kevin wanted to play in the orchestra. He knew his parents would be proud."

The Colliers were once members of the First Baptist Church in Atlanta and had gotten Kevin involved early taking brass classes. Glover had just started his ministry at the church and followed Kevin's progress as a student until he eventually joined the church's orchestra.

With the strings and percussion sections of the orchestra playing in perfect tune, Kevin played his trombone and poured his heart into every note as they performed several musical numbers his family loved the most. The congregation joined in singing Andraé Crouch's "My Tribute" as the lyrics to the gospel classic were flashed on two giant screens in the church.

Pastor Glenn Stringham, Fayetteville First Baptist's senior adult pastor, followed the musical interlude. Stringham had known the Colliers for fifty years. The very night of their murders, he had been called by a neighbor of the Colliers and alerted as to what was going on. When he arrived at the Colliers' home, Sheriff Randall Johnson told him that Carl was dead on the kitchen floor and Sarah had been found dead in a pool of blood at the bottom of the basement steps. Johnson also related that there had been a horrific struggle and that there was blood everywhere. The police had no doubt as to the person responsible for their deaths—none other than their granddaughter Holly Harvey.

Stringham was well aware of the problems the Colliers had been having with their granddaughter. They had requested support and prayers from not only him, but other members in the congregation. He also knew about Holly's juvenile court appearance and that she had been sentenced to probation after running away with Sandy Ketchum. The Colliers told him they were afraid Holly was headed down the same road as her mother.

The benevolent pastor stayed and ministered to Kevin that night at his parents' house. That was the least he could do for the bereaved son. Two days later, Kevin had called him and asked if he would go inside the home and get clothes for his parents to be buried in.

Before Stringham became a minister, he had served in Vietnam as a military policeman. He was accustomed to crime scenes and a lot of bloodshed, but he never forgot what he saw inside the Colliers' home. Blood had soaked through the carpet and to the bare floors. Blood had splattered on the walls and cabinets downstairs and in the kitchen. It was a thousand times worse, knowing that the blood he saw was once the life force of two people he loved. The sight had left Stringham with an empty feeling of death, but now, for everyone's sake, he had to put all that behind him and concentrate on the Colliers' lives.

Stringham seemed to express a lot of the sentiments in the congregation, when he smiled and said, "Kevin, this is just a small gathering of your parents' friends." He then related Carl and Sarah's devotion and recalled certain mission trips they had been on together. He stated that the Colliers were always faithful to the church and their family and friends, and were always ready to help whenever they were called. In a bold declaration, he brought the crowd to a silence when he speculated what might have been going on inside the Colliers' minds the night of the crime.

"In my heart," Stringham said sincerely, "because of what I know about Carl and Sarah Collier to be true, even on Monday night, as the blood streamed out from their bodies, they cried out to their Father, 'Father, forgive them for they know not what they do.' . . . One day [the teenagers] will, one day they will know. And I pray they will come to know Him."

Stringham concluded his inspirational message with the thought "Life is measured by what is left behind, but treasured by what is sent ahead. I thank God for the lives of Carl and Sarah Collier."

Fayetteville First Baptist senior pastor Frank Ellis talked about how Carl and Sarah Collier had faced death because of a wicked plot to execute them.

"They could have made some simple decisions that no one in this church would have second-guessed," he added. "We could have said to them, 'You went way past the second mile a long time ago,' that they could have had another ten or twenty years of retirement, but Carl and Sarah had learned to live a life of sacrifice."

The next song of celebration was one of the Colliers' favorite hymns, "It Is Well with My Soul."

"Kevin, your mother was singing that song this morning," Minister John Glover exclaimed, addressing the crowd a second time. "She loved the choir, she loved the orchestra, and she loved seeing you play."

Glover told the congregation that Kevin had been Carl and Sarah's pride and joy. He recalled when Kevin made all-state band and toured Europe, his parents flew over to London just to hear their son play.

As expected, Glover did not even mention the Colliers' daughter's name.

There were a lot of smiles and laughs in the assembly of mourners as Glover eulogized the Colliers.

"Carl was a hard worker and always got up at the crack of dawn," Glover said. "He just loved to work. In fact, there is someone out there now who has a ladder still at their house. Carl was painting your house, but wasn't able to finish the job. I promise you, a few days from now, Kevin will come over and retrieve the ladder."

Glover also talked about how Carl was always consistent in his discipline with his children.

Bringing the service to a close, Glover alluded to the Colliers' love for their children.

The final song of celebration before the caskets left the church was a stirring rendition of "How Great Thou Art," with Kevin playing a small portion of it as a trombone solo. It was the hardest thing Kevin ever had to do in his life, to play at the funeral of his mother and father, but it was the most rewarding.

Then as the pallbearers moved to the front of the church to escort the caskets outside, Widor's "Toccata" played. The song had special meaning to Kevin.

"Widor's 'Toccata' will remind you of the wedding recessional when two are united in marriage," Kevin wrote in the funeral program. "Today, may this melody remind you that Mom and Dad are celebrating their new union with Christ together."

With the music swelling, the pallbearers rolled the coffins of Carl and Sarah down the middle aisle. As each coffin passed by Kevin, he reached out and patted it as it went by.

Once outside, Kevin and Anita stood together and greeted his parents' family and friends, who wept and expressed their grief over their loss. As they waited for the coffins to be loaded in the hearse and readied themselves for their graveside ceremony, Kevin, wearing sunglasses and dressed in a dark suit, white shirt, and red tie, read a statement to the press.

"Because of their love and faith in Jesus Christ, I did not lose my parents last week. They just beat me to heaven, where I will see them again. My hope and prayer is that while justice is being served, God's infinite love and forgiveness be recognized by all, making an ugly situation become one that is precious and life changing."

TV crews filmed Kevin and Anita as he read his statement, and newspaper reporters stood crowded around them. Besides the local and Atlanta daily newspapers, there was talk of reporters in attendance from *USA Today* and *People* magazine.

The graveside processional started with two police vehicles, followed by two hearses, and then the family car. Many years ago, the Colliers had purchased burial plots at the Westview Cemetery in Atlanta and this would be their final resting place. As the string of mourners passed, law enforcement officers stood at attention with their hats over their hearts and waited until the string of cars had cleared.

Before joining the processional, a reporter spoke with one of Sarah's longtime friends from Florida.

"I spoke with Sarah on Sunday night," Rachel Henderson said. "She told me she was looking forward to going to a biblical theme park in Orlando. She said, 'I want to see that Holy Land.' Little did I know, she'd be visiting the *real* Holy Land the next day."

Chapter 55

Judy Chidester sent word to the press that she had talked with her client in the detention center on the day of the funeral and she was very distraught.

"Upon learning that the funerals were taking place, Holly broke down sobbing. She asked me, 'Does the whole world hate me?'"

Two days after the funeral, on Wednesday, Detective Ethon Harper rceived a call from someone who wanted to pass on some mail that was received at Plantation Drive, addressed to Holly Harvey. The mail had already been opened. One item was a letter from Sandy Ketchum written to Holly after the murders. A second item was a letter to Holly from Carla. The letter contained a cartoon clipped from a magazine Carla had read in her jail cell. It depicted two fish swimming in an ocean and pondering a baited hook. The bubble above one of the fish reads, KEEP YOUR MOUTH SHUT AND YOU WON'T GET CAUGHT.

Harper also met with Sara Polk and she related in detail her visit with Sandy and Holly on the night of the murders. Polk remembered the girls saying, "Look at all this blood," as they sported dried blood on their face, arms, and hands.

"Holly also showed me a large knife with blood on it," Sara

said, still shaking from the incident. "I asked her about being upset and she told me she had tried to cry, but could not."

Polk added that the girls had made the comment they were going to burn their clothes and destroy the knives. And when they changed clothes, they were both wearing black tank tops. Holly had on gray fuzzy pants and black-and-pink shoes, while Holly wore cameo pants and white tennis shoes.

Only a girl would remember anything like that. Polk chuckled at the thought.

Polk also recalled when Sandy called her back the last time and told her there would be something on the news about the murders, she asked her Holly's grandparents' names. She said when Sandy told her their names, she could hear Holly laughing out loud in the background.

Since the girls' capture, media outlets were having a field day. Expert witnesses were talking about the case on television and in the newspapers as often as Pez dispensers were popping up on eBay.

Rodney McDaniel, one of the Colliers' neighbors who lived on the other side of the street, said the killings caught him by surprise because the neighborhood was quiet and peaceful.

"Who would have ever expected something like this to happen in the neighborhood?" McDaniel said. "It's a sign of the times, I guess."

On August 19, at 10:00 A.M., two of Fayette County's youngest suspected killers on record entered the packed courtroom. Wearing prison-issue blue jeans, gray T-shirts, and tennis shoes, shackled at the hands and feet, Sandy came in first, a huge leather belt around her waist that joined to her cuffs. After the cuffs were undone, she was led to one end of the tables in the front of the courtroom.

Holly then came in, dressed in a blue T-shirt, jeans, and tennis shoes. After her prison garb was collected, she was directed to a second table on the other end. Their court-appointed attorneys sat between them.

Once Tim Ketchum stepped into the courtroom, he realized his life had become a George Jones song. All red in the face, looking both sorry to be there and reluctant to leave, he took a front-row seat in the gallery beside his wife and niece. When he saw his child being led into the courtroom, outfitted with chains, he turned all red in the face. He offered her a crooked smile, then waited until she sat down before he leaned forward and rubbed the center of his forehead with two fingers. He looked like a man who was suddenly overcome with a full-blown migraine headache. He told his wife it felt like an ice pick had been planted in the center of his forehead—the kind of pain he normally got when he swallowed ice cream too quickly and had to wait for it to melt.

Beth Ketchum fell back in the pew beside her husband and wept. As she cried, her shoulders came up in a kind of defensive hunch and her head bobbed up and down like a cork on the end of a bream line in water.

Although the teenagers' lawyers still protested the cameras in the courtroom, they had turned their attention to meeting with their clients and preparing for this bond hearing. It was still a leap for the county's narrower minds to match the evil of the crime with the mysterious homosexual love story that was being told. Some Fayetteville teenagers were talking about what had happened, and although they disapproved of the murder, they thought the love story was kind of cool and sexy. The lesbian twist was interesting, but out of this had emerged a one-of-a-kind bigger picture at what teenagers would be willing to do for love.

Holly showed no emotion as she sat down in her seat at the table beside her attorney. She looked straight ahead for most of the hearing, glancing over at Sandy occasionally.

When Sandy first came to her seat, she turned and looked with red-rimmed eyes at her family seated less than ten feet away from her. She then sat in a seat behind her attorney, who scribbled on a yellow pad and appeared to ignore her. Sandy kept her head down and wept. She mumbled to herself as tears began to fall from her eyes, across her cheeks, and form on the tip of her chin.

The stern-faced Superior Court judge Paschal English sat on the red oak bench before the girls and waited to proceed. Four TV news cameras were positioned at the back of the courtroom, taping the entire proceeding and capturing the reactions of the suspects' friends and family, who sat on opposite sides of the courtroom.

As the bond hearing proceeded, both girls wept. Holly sat with her head down on the desk and wiped her eyes as she listened to Chief ADA Dan Hiatt describe the horrific nature of the murders. Sandy cried and her body shook as she wiped at her eyes with a tissue.

When given the nod, Lloyd Walker quickly called his first witness, Tim Ketchum, to the stand. Tim wore a gold-and-black open-collar knit shirt and black pants. Sandy wiped her eyes with a tissue and nearly lost her composure when her father took the stand and was asked, "Is Sandy Ketchum your daughter?"

Tim acknowledged Sandy was his daughter and testified about her childhood. He talked about the mother that didn't want her and how she had deserted Sandy when she was just a baby. He then recalled Sandy's sad saga and the succession of three stepmothers, of whom the second had physically abused her. As a result, he surmised, Sandy was always running away, on drugs, and repeatedly in and out of trouble with the state.

"My present wife has a good relationship with Sandy," Tim testified. "She's done her best in raising her for the past four years."

Tim admitted further that Sandy had failed court-ordered drug tests while on probation in Coweta County for running away and obstruction of justice.

The past month had not been kind to Tim Ketchum. He

looked weary, tired, and exhausted. Choking back his tears, Tim regrettably told the court that he and Beth had agreed to Sandy's wishes for her to get to know her real mother, Sandra Ketchum. After talking with her probation officer, they agreed for her to move in with Sandra at her Griffin home. The stipulation was that Sandy not associate with Holly in any way. He revealed Sandra did not live up to her part of the bargain. Not only did she allow Sandy to see Holly, she even made it easy for her.

Assistant District Attorney Dan Hiatt took the floor to cross-examine Tim. He asked him about Sandy's temper and got him to admit that his little girl would hide knives in her bedroom when she got upset.

Tim explained that his wife knew more about that than he did.

Lloyd Walker then called Beth Ketchum to the stand. Under questioning, Beth revealed she had no major problems with her stepdaughter and that they had always gotten along. Sandy had been placed on one-day community service for her drug test violation, but, other than that, she had no major problems with her stepdaughter.

On behalf of the state, ADA Hiatt called his first and only witness, Lieutenant Colonel Bruce Jordan. Dressed in a blue blazer with his badge pinned on the outside, a white shirt, a red-and-white tie, and dark slacks, Jordan was the state's best and strongest witness. He had seen the gruesome crime scene in the Colliers' kitchen and basement and described how the bodies of Carl and Sarah Collier had been found. He said the evidence indicated they had tried to fight off their granddaughter and her friend during the brutal knife attack. The bloodied knives and the girls' bloodstained clothing had been found in Carl Collier's stolen vehicle when the girls were arrested on Tybee Island.

Jordan's testimony was graphic, but he assured the hushed audience in the crowded courtroom that his facts were straight out of Sandy's mouth, and from what he swore was a voluntary confession. As he related what Sandy had told him, Holly dropped her head and tears began streaming across her face.

"Carl Collier was stabbed about fifteen times," Jordan said calmly. "And Sarah Collier closer to twenty times."

Jordan then recalled how Holly had tried to escape upon capture and how giddy it made her feel to see all the attention she had drawn.

"In my opinion," Jordan concluded, "Holly Harvey and Sandy Ketchum are cold-blooded killers and would be an extreme flight risk."

During cross-examination, Sandy's attorney asked Jordan if he had tried to contact the girls' parents, since they were juveniles.

"We did," Jordan responded. "But that one talk with Sandy at the Tybee Island Police Department was the only conversation I had with her. She did talk a little bit to one of our female officers who helped her back to Fayette County."

"What did she say?" Walker queried, knowing full well what the implications of Jordan's answer would have on the judge's decision.

"She told her that she couldn't get rid of the smell of blood and that those people didn't deserve to die," Jordan answered.

Jordan also said that Holly had refused to talk to the police, and after asking her once, he did not ask her again. He noted that with Sandy, however, it was very apparent that she wanted to talk with him.

The teens' attorneys pleaded passionately for the judge to release their clients on bond.

"Sandy needs and wants to be home with her father now more than ever," Walker avowed. "We cannot forget they are children. Up until now, everybody has failed her."

Kevin Collier, Holly's uncle, and Anita Beckom, her godmother, attended the hearing, but they did not testify on Holly's behalf. In fact, nobody testified on her behalf. As she sat and pressed her forehead to the defense table during most of the thirty-minute hearing, she wept. She felt so alone. Leaning into her attorney, she asked in a whisper, "Is there anybody going to testify for me?"

Attorney Chidester had to tell the judge and acknowledge that she had no one to testify for her client.

"Your Honor, she has no home anymore, except where she is in juvenile detention. She had nowhere to go and she's never really had that."

Judge English wasted no time and quickly denied the girls' request for bond, agreeing with the prosecution that the girls were an extreme flight risk. In addition to the murder charges, he added armed robbery to both girls' rap sheet and set a preliminary hearing on all charges for August 31.

The two girls sat a dozen feet away on opposite sides of their attorney, but they never spoke or interacted with each other. When they found out they were not going to be granted bond, they both wept.

Sandy's father, stepmother, and several other relatives were in the courtroom, sitting in the first pew, not more than ten feet behind her. They sobbed during most of the court hearing.

As the girls were led from the courtroom, a spectator on the Ketchum side yelled out, "We love you, Sandy."

No one yelled out to Holly.

Tim Ketchum hustled out of the courtroom as fast as he could and snatched a breath of cleaner air in the courtroom foyer. He wiped his brow with his hand and composed himself, then stepped forward and hunted out Kevin Collier in the crowd.

When Tim and Kevin met, they embraced and wept.

"I'm so sorry," Tim mumbled through his tears. "I'm just so sorry."

Kevin nodded, then patted Tim on the back as if to say he knew Tim was hurting, too.

The Ketchums then regrouped and rushed out of the courtroom. As they emerged from the courthouse, disappointed and angry that bond had been denied, TV news crews rained down upon them. They locked arms and walked mechanically toward the parking lot, ignoring one reporter's repeated attempts at a response. When his TV cameraman rushed in to capture their grief, Tim's brother-in-law, Larry Harmon, spat on the camera lens.

"It's a shame y'all can't find nothing else better to do," Beth Ketchum hollered over her shoulder.

Carol Morgan, Anita Beckom's mother, said she felt sorry for Holly, but everyone had tried to help her along the way, and now she must pay.

"She's like a granddaughter to me," Morgan told a news reporter. "She's the loving, vivacious and beach-loving Holly we've always known. We've always made her a part of our family since she was born, but this other Holly accused with her girlfriend of murder is unrecognizable. Something has happened to her. It's like the light has gone out of her eyes."

The girls had been charged as adults, but their attorneys were not optimistic about their chances of moving the case to juvenile court.

"I hope the district attorney will reconsider and try these girls in juvenile court," Lloyd Walker told *11 Alive*'s John Shirek. "A preliminary hearing scheduled for August thirty-one will be a help to us as the state lays out its case against them. The public does not know the whole story behind the case. And there's a lot we can do to address the underlying problems my client might have and help her get a real handle on what's going on in her life."

Judy Chidester said her client had a lot of problems, too.

"Regardless of what you think of my client, these were her grandparents. During the hearing, she was crying. I think she's pretty much acting like a scared fifteen-year-old, which is exactly what she is.

"I hated to tell the judge that she had nowhere to go, but I couldn't put people up there who would say, 'Holly can come stay with us, we'll watch her twenty-four/seven.' Holly's mother is in prison on drug charges. Her father has been absent from her life. He is an ex-con, who became a paraplegic about twelve years ago, after a car wreck—a wreck that may have left Holly Harvey with a brain injury. He has said, 'Give her my best. I love her, and she's in my prayers, but I'm not coming up there.'"

Chidester was brutally honest.

"This case against them is going to be tough to fight. There's no getting around that, and it would be ingenuous for me to act like that wasn't the case, that this was a weak case, and I don't believe it is."

Norma Chamblee and Jeannette Abernathy, longtime friends of the Collier family, attended the hearing and spoke to reporters afterward. Chamblee said she was familiar with some of the trouble the Colliers were having with their rebellious granddaughter and said her heart went out to her.

"They need a hug and someone to say, 'I love you no matter what you've done,'" Chamblee said. "I pray for them every day, both of them. I just wanted to go up and hug 'em. I know Holly has led a troubled life, and from what I heard in court, Sandy has been faced with a difficult life as well."

Abernathy agreed. Her heart also went out to the troubled teens. "Just spare them when they are incarcerated," she said. "They didn't have a chance with their background. They needed to be rehabilitated."

When reporter John Munford, of the *Citizens News Reporter,* asked the two ladies what they thought the teenage killers needed, they responded:

"They needed more love."

Chapter 56

What we are about to show you is a rare look at evidence from one of the most disturbing cases in Fayette County. The voice-over began the Channel 2 broadcast segment, which depicted the evidence police had against the teenage killers. Channel 2's cameraman panned to the cutlery set with the missing knives taken from the Colliers' kitchen. *The apparent missing ones, now found, being logged in as evidence. They laid this canvas oil painting on the bed and practiced stabbing it. First with the scissors that did not penetrate, then with the knives that cut clean through.*

The cameraman then focused on the knives used in the murder.

Police say cuts match the puncture marks found on the bed.

A camera shot was shown of the overnight bag that contained the evidence.

Inside the bag, two pairs of jeans with suspected blood on it were found; a beach towel, a white bra with blood, and a pair of red rings with crimson blood on it.

Lloyd Walker watched the episode on Channel 2, and spoke against such charades as this.

"I think it is unfortunate that the sheriff's department has put the spin on it that they have. The sheriff's department's public display is tainting a potential jury. I am going to ask to move the trial to another county. It sure is difficult accepting that the people of Fayette County haven't been completely and thoroughly prejudiced about this case."

During the thirty-five-minute bond hearing, there was no testimony presented about the relationship between the girls. Holly and Sandy remained in separate juvenile detention centers and—as far as authorities knew—they had had no contact with each other since their arrest.

When asked about Holly's relationship with Sandy after the bond hearing, Judy Chidester maintained it was inconsequential to the tragedy.

"I think it's inappropriate for the police to have released such information," she said. "This didn't have anything to do with what happened. I think [the relationship] is a misdirection."

When Ketchum's attorney, Lloyd Walker, was asked about the girls' alleged lesbian relationship, he said bluntly, "I'm not going to discuss that."

What Walker really thought about "this lesbian thing" was of no significance to his client's case. He could see there was a genuine emotional attachment between the two girls, but he viewed it as nothing more than teenage infatuation. It wasn't a big deal for him, but he believed the media had dramatized the lesbian issue because of the appeal and interest that the issue would have on its TV audience and newspaper readership.

Dr. Barbara Rubin, a gay Atlanta psychologist, said the teens were clearly troubled with serious mental-health issues, none of which had to do with whether or not they were lesbians.

"This is not a gay story," she said. "They didn't do this because they are gay."

Asked if there was a chance of the girls getting a fair trial in Fayette County, Chidester and Walker both agreed that it was highly unlikely their clients could receive a fair trial in Fayette County, or anywhere in the state for that matter.

"I don't know where we could move the trial to," Chidester

said. "And I'm upset with the amount of information released by the sheriff's department. They've released evidence that may not be allowed in a trial."

The media blitz had everyone in Fayette County talking about the bizarre events of this case, but attorney Lloyd Walker had difficulties with the manner in which the FCSO's office seemed to be passing it out like candy.

"[Bruce Jordan] has been way too forthcoming with evidence and information on this case," Walker complained to anyone who would listen. "It makes it practically impossible to obtain a jury that would be untainted by it. It is way over and far above what is necessary for the public to know."

When asked about the macabre "to-do list" found written in ink on Holly's arm when the police arrested her, the three bloody knives, and the bloodstained clothes police found when the teens were arrested, Walker could only shrug his shoulders and admit, "Yes, they do have a very strong case."

However, it was just that same notion that bothered Walker the most about this case. The public had already been saturated in too many details of the case and to find a fair and unbiased jury in Fayette County would be impossible.

"I'll take the first twelve people off the street and try this case," he avowed. "As long as they have not been prejudiced by the media and those in the Fayette County law enforcement community, and they have no preconceived notions of my client's guilt. But I don't think that is going to happen and that is why I'm going to ask that the trial location be moved elsewhere in the state."

Another distressing problem Walker was having with the media was that they released statements as facts, based on information released by Bruce Jordan. He cited an article written by Rochelle Carter in the major Atlanta daily, the *Atlanta Journal-Constitution*.

"Carter's article is based on ambiguous statements released to the press by Bruce Jordan. She states as fact that Sandy

Ketchum alone had killed Sarah Collier, saying, 'Ketchum then came out of her hiding place, knife in hand, to help the girl she loved.' But the testimony in court does not support those factual assertions made by this reporter.

"In addition, the newspaper printed a statement Carter attributed to Sandy, declaring she told Jordan, 'I finished with Mrs. Collier and went to join Holly,' and this simply is untrue. Sandy has never admitted to killing anyone, nor has she said she emerged from her hiding place with knife in hand."

Walker demanded Carter and the *Atlanta Journal-Constitution* print a retraction, but he never got a response. An effort was already under way to try and convict his client before she had a chance to defend herself, and he thought a gag order would not be improper.

But as Walker ranted and raved for a few minutes about the leaks from Bruce Jordan, the prosecution believed what he was really doing was performing for the press. There was no way a court could tell the media not to print something. According to the First Amendment, they had a right to print what they had heard. The prosecution saw Walker's act as a smoke screen. He had lost his attempt to get his client bail, so he needed to impress them with his zealousness. If this was Walker's purpose and intent in accusing Rochelle Carter of being underhanded, then it had worked.

Chapter 57

The legal battle between the state and the defense attorneys really began in earnest on Tuesday, August 31. The teenagers' attorneys quickly raised objections to Chief Magistrate Charles R. Floyd, who ultimately ruled there was enough evidence to bind both girls' cases over to a Fayette County grand jury.

Lieutenant Colonel Bruce Jordan was the only witness to testify. He told how Sandy Ketchum confessed to the crimes during an interview with him after her arrest. She had told him that she and Holly had smoked marijuana laced with cocaine before stabbing the Colliers in the back with three kitchen knives. Sarah Collier had suffered the brunt of their most vicious attack—twenty-two stab wounds, with the most severe around her heart. Carl Collier had been stabbed anywhere from twelve to fifteen times, and had severe gashes to his throat.

Indicating a possible defense strategy, Sandy's attorney, Lloyd Walker, asked Jordan if he tried to contact the girl's parent before interviewing her.

"I did not speak with either of Ketchum's parents before the interview," Jordan responded. "The other detectives were trying to track down both girls' families, but after I learned from District Attorney Bill McBroom that they would be tried as adults, it wasn't necessary to get their parents' permission."

When asked about Sandy's reaction to the slayings, Jordan said, "She couldn't get rid of the smell of blood, and every five minutes she was smelling blood. She said those people didn't deserve to die."

"Was Sandy Ketchum ever read her rights?" Walker asked.

"Yes"—Jordan nodded—"but she did not sign a waiver of her right to remain silent. She verbally waived it."

"Was the interview taped?"

"No," Jordan answered, as if it were no big deal. "The Tybee Island police station didn't have taping equipment."

Walker also probed how the U.S. Marshal Service tracked the girls as they sped toward Tybee Island after the killings. That drew a quick objection from ADA Dan Hiatt, who said revealing that information might jeopardize current U.S. Marshal investigations. Hiatt argued that the details of how the girls were tracked were irrelevant to the proceedings. Walker countered that if the U.S. government had a supersecret technology that allowed them to track the movement of the private citizens in their personal vehicles, "I'm sure the rest of the country would be interested in that."

Floyd ruled that the question could be asked of Jordan in special testimony behind closed doors in the judge's chambers.

The teens' attorneys reasoned that any confessions their clients made after their arrests should not be admissible because they did not have lawyers or guardians present. And that even though the girls were being tried as adults, they still deserved some of the protections entitled to children.

"They're still juveniles, and there are still rules and regulations that have to be followed," Chidester said, attempting to make her case. "My client is very scared. She's very remorseful."

Lloyd Walker was of the same opinion as Chidester.

"The law gives juveniles added protections over and above

those given to adults," Walker debated. "The fact that they are juveniles is not forgotten, even if they're tried as adults."

After hearing nearly an hour of gripping testimony from Jordan, Judge Floyd was not swayed by the defense's arguments and ordered the case against the girls be sent to the county grand jury for consideration of an indictment.

Inside the hearing, the defense attorneys had taken issue with how their clients had been handled by the sheriff's department when arrested, but outside the hearing, they conceded they were facing an uphill battle. There were, after all, a large amount of evidence: bloody clothes, the murder weapons, the Colliers' stolen truck and jewelry, plus the testimony of their friends, like Sara Polk. Polk had heard Holly's chilling confession when she held up a knife and said, "I just killed my grandparents."

"They do have a very strong case," Walker admitted glumly.

The Fayette County District Attorney's Office would present the case to the grand jury on September 15 and ask that the two teenagers accused of violently stabbing Carl and Sarah Collier to death on August 2 be indicted on murder charges.

The court cases were expected to draw much attention to Fayette County, particularly due to the dramatic nature of the crime. The media posturing began with the defense lawyers for the teenagers arguing before Superior Court judge Paschal English that bad publicity generated by graphic police reports had prevented them from getting a fair trial.

Holly and Sandy were being tried as adults. They faced two counts of felony murder and two counts of malice murder for the deaths of Carl and Sarah Collier, plus armed robbery. Unless they struck a plea bargain, they would be facing a maximum sentence of life in prison without parole.

While they were united during the murder spree and the following escape to Tybee Island, Holly and Sandy had taken different paths since their arrests, which came less than twenty-four hours after the killings. Rumors about the case were that Sandy had been cooperating with the police, leading to the possibility that she could face a somewhat lighter sentence than Holly. The police still believed Holly had been the instigator behind the killing and actually masterminded the whole thing.

Holly's attorney's description contrasted with the picture of a cold-blooded killer as painted by Lieutenant Colonel Bruce Jordan.

"During interviews and whenever the conversation steers to Holly's grandparents, or Holly's mom, who currently is in prison on felony drug charges," Chidester maintained, "she has been very emotional. She is very frightened, very upset, very scared, and very emotional. She seems to be genuinely distraught and remorseful. She appears to me to be a terrified fifteen-year-old."

Chidester stated several people had contacted her to express concern for Holly, including a person claiming to be a chaplain at Metro State Prison, where her mom was incarcerated.

"He wanted to know how Carla Harvey could get in contact with her daughter," Chidester said. "I asked for a letter so I could authenticate his story before proceeding. I don't expect there to be a lot of cheerleaders at Holly's side. She has had a difficult family life. Anytime I try to talk about her mom or her grandparents, she starts to weep and break down. Holly seems to understand most of our conversations, but she sometimes gives me that look of a typical fifteen-year-old, and I think to myself, 'Does she really understand?'"

Because Sandy had already given a statement and said things that were damaging against Holly's case, the two girls would be tried separately.

Lloyd Walker blamed the system for what had happened to his client. He believed it was time for the community to do something other than wag their tongues and point their fingers at these teenagers.

"The evidence shows that a lot of people have failed Sandy,"

Walker said. "Up until now, everybody, including the state, has failed these children. District Attorney Bill McBroom could try them as juveniles, but the Colliers were such long time Fayette County residents, I don't expect that to happen."

Walker noted that regardless of whether they were tried as juveniles or adults, state law required the trial to be conducted in Georgia Superior Court. What he didn't appreciate was the media's incessant use of so-called "experts" to analyze this case who were quick to offer a motive for the murders.

"Such so-called professionals do not have access to all the facts of the case upon which to make a solid decision," Walker contended. "I understand that everybody wants to know why this happened, but such uniform speculation on behalf of experts is counterproductive."

The media disregarded Walker's comments. It was Walker's job to defend his client, but it was their job to keep the public informed. *News 11 Alive* interviewed noted child psychologist Sherry Blake, who said the motives that allegedly compelled the two teenager girls to murder were likely somewhere in the past.

"You've got to wonder where [Holly] got such rage at the age of fifteen," Blake said. "I think the grandparents probably represented something that she resented, that she really was enraged with, and that may have been stability and structure."

In reference to Jordan's comments about Holly being giddy when she walked out of the beach house and saw all the police officers who came to arrest her, Blake told *News 11 Alive,* "The fact that she could laugh and smile, that's a cover. That's a facade, one that with this child is very thick."

And to Jordan's revelation of a poem written by Holly that referred to her depression, the fact that she cried herself to sleep at night, that she wished for everyone to suffer, and that all she wanted was to kill, Blake opined, "The control and manipulation that comes in from her anger, and emotional problems, she has outlined in her poem, so her idea she could control is not surprising to me at all."

Blake added further that Holly had psychological problems, that she was disturbed and there was a difference between a bad child and a disturbed one.

"A bad kid may not listen, gets into trouble, gives the teacher a hard time, but a bad kid doesn't kill," Blake said. "A disturbed child will kill."

Holly's attorney was livid after seeing the broadcast.

"I've been practicing law for a long time and I've never seen the degree of evidence being released," Chidester chimed in. "It's made it virtually impossible. . . . There's obviously no way we can have a fair trial in Fayette County. And I don't know where we can have one. It's virtually become an open book and I am very upset about that."

Lieutenant Colonel Bruce Jordan responded to Chidester's accusations.

"She's asked for this public hearing today, and then we have it. Then she's on the news complaining that so much information is getting out. She was told she could have a change of venue two weeks ago and much of the information released has come out during this hearing. If she doesn't want it out there, then she needs to quit having these hearings that are not necessary.

"The legal community cannot understand why Chidester would ask for bond and a preliminary hearing in a case she knows, based on the amount of evidence, will be bound over to a grand jury. So the only way to stop it is to get the lawyers off TV, and stop having these public hearings, and it will quit."

When Lloyd Walker was asked by the press if there was a chance of a plea bargain, he answered, "It is too early to speculate on that. But don't rule anything out."

Before the girls' case could be sent to the grand jury, the next procedure was the mental assessments of the suspects. Lieutenant Colonel Jordan had painted quite a shocking picture of Holly, and her mental status could alter the trial significantly if she decided to cop an insanity plea.

Channel 11 televised an interview with Kevin Collier and Anita Beckom. Standing inside his parents' house, Kevin told reporter John Shirek that he was praying for the girls and for justice.

"It's still soaking in," Kevin admitted. "It will take time for wounds to heal. I believe I am still angry."

Kevin and Anita walked Shirek through the garage and into the kitchen, where the Colliers' appointment book was still stuck on the refrigerator door. Just inside the door, his father had been found lying in a pool of blood, stabbed fifteen times. Eight steps away from the kitchen door was the stairway to the basement, where his mother had been found in a pool of blood, stabbed twenty-two times. Framed photos of his beloved parents and troubled sister and niece were still hanging on the walls. And by the stairway was the small basement bedroom of their granddaughter, where she had lured them into the room with the smell of marijuana. Holly's bedroom was a mess, clothes scattered everywhere, the cutouts of bloodstained carpet taken by the investigators clearly visible in the camera's eye.

Kevin grimaced and shook his head. "It doesn't seem like it took long at all, but I'm sure it seemed like it took hours when it happened. I'm sure of that."

Those familiar with the murder case thought they had heard it all, until they heard Kevin say, "I love Holly, no doubt, but justice has to be served in this case. She did something wrong and she can't get away from it. I pray for the girls every day."

Anita Beckom wanted Holly to know she prayed for her to get help and for justice to be served.

"I hope Holly understands that my family and I still love her very deeply," Anita told Shirek. "But she did wrong and she's going to have to pay."

On September 17, a Fayette County grand jury was presented with the evidence against the two teenage girls accused of killing Carl and Sarah Collier. The indictments remained under seal at the courthouse until they were opened by Judge Paschal English, at which time the results became public record. The word was that the two girls were being kept in two different juvenile detention facilities so that they could not have any contact with each other. Sandy Ketchum had been cooperating with the police, and they needed her to testify against Holly, who was being touted as the mastermind of the crime.

Chapter 58

Scott Ballard was a hometown boy. For the last six generations, a Ballard had registered to vote in political elections
at the Fayette County Courthouse. His grandfather William
Ballard was a former sheriff of Fayette County, and his father,
Charles, was, and continues to be, a practicing attorney there.

Ballard graduated from Fayetteville High School in 1977,
then went on to the University of Georgia and got his law
degree from Florida State University in 1984. After law school,
he decided to move back home and join his father's private
practice. In March 2004, the forty-four-year-old believed he
could make a difference and filed as a candidate for district attorney of the Griffin Judicial Circuit, which included Fayette,
Spalding, Pike, and Upson Counties. District Attorney Bill
McBroom had been in office for twenty-four years, but when
the tallies were counted in November, Ballard garnered 64 percent and was elected.

"I have practiced law in the Griffin Judicial Circuit for
almost twenty years," Ballard told the voters. "When I
started, the prosecutors had earned an aura of invincibility
and all were outstanding trial lawyers. They were confident
negotiators who recognized which cases to dismiss or plead
and which to try. When they announced, 'Ready for trial,'

they meant it, and the citizens of this circuit deserve no less today."

Scott Ballard noted his predecessor had over three hundred cases backed up on the court trial calendar, and that many of them would be dismissed before the defendants ever walked into the courtroom and stood before a judge. He was determined to change that.

"I want to hire the most skilled trial attorneys that I can persuade to join me and accept the call to public service as prosecutors," Ballard promised. "I also want to personally prosecute as many trials in Superior Court as an assistant district attorney and implement a system so cases are analyzed and prepared as soon they are received in office."

One of the first cases handed to Ballard when he took office in January 2005 was the Collier murder case. As the outgoing DA McBroom and FCSO's Bruce Jordan brought him up to speed on the case, he saw nothing but tragedy written all over it.

Scott Ballard had three children of his own. His daughter was a senior in high school, almost the same age as the suspects.

"The defendants are just kids," he empathized as he reviewed the case. "It was bad enough the victims' granddaughter was a suspect, but the manner in which the grandparents were killed is horrifying. It's a scary thing to think about. All of us have been told no by an authority figure, and we know the resentment when that takes place. But few of us, or almost none of us, would take it to the lengths these girls did."

Ballard agreed with McBroom that the two teenagers should be tried as adults. Because of the severity of the case, he believed the juvenile court would never handle such a horrific case. And even though there were some mitigating factors in both teenagers' lives—such as the fractured family life, drug and alcohol abuse, and neglect—this was still not nearly enough to overcome the enormity of their behavior.

Ballard said he was chomping at the bit to try this case and he would personally prosecute it. Though there was talk about a change of venue, he knew this murder case would receive nationwide attention in the press, regardless of where it was tried. He had never prosecuted a case, but was excited and looking forward to trying this one personally.

"Oh, sure, we're going to want to try this case," Ballard told the press, standing outside his office. "I do believe, though, I can find Fayette County jurors willing to set aside their knowledge of this case and be fair. I think they've certainly heard about the case, and you've always got to make sure you give a fair trial to the accused. And we'll do that whether it's right here or anywhere else. It doesn't matter to me where we try the case."

The trials had originally been scheduled for late March, but likely wouldn't begin until spring 2005. Certainly newly elected DA Scott Ballard added a new wrinkle to the Collier murder case, but attorneys for the defense expected the same stance from him as from his predecessor.

"I don't think it will be delayed much longer," Chidester said. "It will be tried in the late spring or earlier."

The extensive pretrial coverage had given the defense attorneys no choice but to ask for a change of venue. Incoming Griffin Judicial Circuit DA Scott Ballard said he would not contest the change of venue.

"I'm concerned about what was provided to the news media from the sheriff's department," Chidester said, adding that she had received calls from New York, Utah, Los Angeles, Britain, and abroad about this case. "I think information released by the sheriff's department tainted the jury pool. The sheriff's department will probably disagree."

Lieutenant Colonel Bruce Jordan said that gag orders were used to shut up litigants and the lawyers. He understood the First Amendment to guarantee there's no way a court can tell a newspaper not to print anything.

There was no doubt the defense had some problems if the

cases were adjudicated in Fayette County. Largely, it was decidedly conservative Republican territory, and would, in all likelihood, not play out well for the defense. They could, however, appeal to the Georgia Legislature and ask them to intervene on the girls' behalf. After all, they were just children and deserved some constitutional protection and consideration. That was a strategy that could have some merit in the court trial, but it would only lay the groundwork for the appeal, which would come after the trial. This case was also very unique in that there were mitigating factors in both the girls' lives that should affect the outcome of the trial, especially the sentencing phase.

But, above all, the witnesses, evidence, and facts of this case pointed directly at the girls' guilt. There was no question about that. Just the idea of two zapped-out and troubled adolescents butchering two senior citizens would not sit well with most jurors. It didn't matter what defense strategy they employed—sooner or later, somebody had to pay the piper. The girls probably stood a better chance of being acquitted if the attorneys challenged the DA in a match of "rock, paper, scissors."

However, the best defense was always a good offense. Even though the teenagers' lawyers were well aware of the reality of their cases, they would make the state prove the evidence they had was overwhelming and admissible. Before they would negotiate any plea bargains with the DA, all these issues would have to be laid out on the table for them to see. There was little benefit in the defense giving away the farm until they knew exactly what the state had to offer.

Chapter 59

Sandy Ketchum was having great difficulty adjusting to prison life. It seemed like her turbulent nightmares would never end. Just as she felt herself healing from the troubles of last year, the bitter smell of blood would hit her nostrils and it would start all over again. The image of that dark, bloody night even invaded her thoughts while she was awake. At night, while she was asleep, the ghostlike forms came to her in her dreams, swinging the knives from side to side, gouging their bodies, sending out puffs of blood and red spray against the wall.

Sandy never imagined that there could be so much pain in a life where there was nothing physically wrong. She hurt all the time. Of all the visitations, the one that pained her the most was that dull whacking sound of the knife. How much of the Colliers' death was her fault, she didn't know. But she felt like she needed to know the truth—if not for her sake, but for her father and mother's sake.

By this time, the locked doors and prison bars had begun to frown back at Sandy, as they had done in juvenile jail. However, now she was in the world of real criminals—not just children—where the game was played for keeps. There would be no walking out of this facility and going home.

Sandy turned over in her bed and stared at the hall, her

heart thudding heavily in her chest. Her ankles were cold. She sank down against the wall, trying desperately to think, but it was so hard. Depression was trying to get into her head and she could not rid herself of it.

There was a time when Beth and Tim were going to church. They had attempted to get her to go, to clean up her act, and give her life to God, but she had wanted no part of it. Now, after having rejected God all this time, she wondered if her prayers would make it to the ceiling.

"Help me, God," she muttered under her breath. "Please help me!"

Sandy was suddenly aware that she felt closed in and extremely nervous in this tight ring of cement. The Colliers' ghosts were coming for her again. She could hear their breathing—it sounded quick and hollow. She rolled against the wall and closed her eyes, hoping it would all go away.

When Sandy was a little girl, she would pretend that the bad people were not here and they would all go away. Of all the memories that were part of her life before the murders, this had helped to calm her; this had helped her not to be afraid. But it didn't work this time.

At this precise instant, Sandy thought she had never felt so miserable in her entire life. Her head ached terribly, and she loathed the sick throb of smelling stale, musty prison air. Her mouth tasted like day-old cat food. Her ears rang and her heart thudded like it had an extra heavy beat, like a tom-tom.

In the worst of Sandy's dreams, her consciousness seemed to flicker in and out, offering her snippets of home movies, but never the whole picture. In one of those, she heard a dreadful noise, a bloodcurdling scream, and then someone started chasing her. She was at the bottom of a stairway, and as she turned and moved up the stairway, the steps on the riser got smaller and longer. She was scared and kept seeing a bloody figure behind her, an old gray-haired man wielding a knife, mocking her. He seemed to be saying, *"Kill, kill, kill, kill."*

For the moment, Sandy's brain froze in panic and she could not think. Then, as if from far off, she heard another voice, a woman's voice, moaning and crying. Suddenly a door closed behind Sandy and she was in the dark, closed in, and it was as cold as a refrigerator. Her breath stopped in terror. An almost drowsy gasp stole through her veins.

The woman would cry even harder as the door swung shut behind Sandy. In the faint light, Sandy could see the face of the woman. It was old, ghastly, and bloody, and she was mesmerized by a small silver key on the wall. Somehow, Sandy knew this silver key unlocked the closed door behind her, stopped all the insanity, and made the hungry shadows, not resting easy, disappear.

Sandy then shrieked in terror as both the bloody bodies started coming at her again. They were reaching out, crying, and moaning. Sandy breathed hard and trembled. She pedaled backward and stepped back from the bodies. She remembered thinking, *Christ, I need a joint . . . just one joint, just a little one, to end the nightmare.* At this point, it would only be for medicinal purposes, but she had no joint. She had to grin and bear it.

Just as the ghostly figures were closing in and touching Sandy, she saw all the blood and guts from the walls swimming around her, and that broke her paralysis.

What in God's name are you doing? she screamed.

Sandy then awoke from the nightmare with a muffled gasp. She felt her throat tightening with fear and her hands clutching at the blanket from her bunk. In the very center of her being, a certainty formed, and the certainty was that she was losing her mind. She screamed and suddenly remembered her mommy and her daddy. More than anything in the world, she wanted to be out in the sunlight.

After the dream, Sandy lay on her side, pulling the blankets on her bed up to her chin. A sheath of brown hair fell across her cheek. She heard conversations from down the hall, drifting up to her as lazy as smoke in the air.

"Isn't that Sandy Ketchum screaming down there?" a juvenile officer asked another.

"Yeah, I think it is. She's the young girl who killed those two old people."

Hardly any light filtered in Sandy's cell, so the juvenile officer never saw her face.

"Are you okay, Sandy?"

Through her tears, Sandy smiled and said, "I'm okay."

But Sandy knew the strain was showing and that it had been one hell of a hard time since the murders. Sandy reached up and felt her throat. Her skin was raw. In a moment of quiet desperation, she had cut her throat with a razor blade.

After Sandy was arrested, she had not been able to remember. The night before the murder, she lay awake, thinking, coming to her decisions. This was necessary, she told herself. Holly's grandparents didn't belong in their lives, as her mother and father didn't belong. Neither did her feelings of guilt over her mother. It was necessary for Holly's sake and for herself, if she was to save anything. The handwriting on the wall was brutal, but clear. Her grandparents had to die.

Was it a spur-of-the-moment thing or a grandiose plan? She wasn't sure. These were the thoughts and questions that filled her every evening. But now, she was haunted by the faces of Holly's grandfather and grandmother, who said to Holly, "You're nothing but a whore and a drug addict, just like your mother."

Chapter 60

The first legal movement in the murders that shocked Fayette County was early that year in 2005. On January 25, Judy Chidester filed the necessary paperwork that would ultimately waive Holly Harvey's arraignment on February 2. At the same time, she told the court that her client was not guilty of the multiple felonies against her.

Lloyd Walker waited to file a waiver for Sandy Ketchum, who was expected to appear before Fayette County Superior Court judge Johnnie Caldwell Jr. to answer the same charges as the younger murder suspect. Walker entered a not guilty plea for his client as well.

Each girl would be tried separately, tried as an adult, and face two counts of malice murder, two counts of felony murder, and one count of armed robbery. Their trials were on docket for March 21 and March 28. It was predicted by most Fayette County court officials that the lurid murder trial would never see the inside of their courtroom, that the trials would most likely be conducted outside Fayette County, possibly somewhere in South Georgia.

On Thursday, March 24, 2005, at the Fayette County Courthouse, Griffin Judicial judges Paschal English Jr. and Johnnie Caldwell met with DA Scott Ballard and attorneys Judy

Chidester and Lloyd Walker for the purpose of discussing trial motion dates, trial dates, and trial locations. The clerk of court and a court reporter were present as well.

At the beginning of the meeting, DA Ballard suggested several possible trial locations, but the teenagers' lawyers did not like any of the locations, stating that these areas were still in range of television media. The defense was looking for a venue that got most of its TV news outside the Georgia area. They reminded Ballard that the case had gotten a lot of attention in the media, especially since the FCSO had been so quick to supply information and any of the aforementioned areas were believed to be prejudicial to a potential jury. Finally a small remote town in southern Georgia, Thomasville, in Thomas County, was suggested, discussed, and agreed upon.

However, Ballard still had several concerns about their choice of location. First of all, he feared once the trial location was announced, the media would swarm on the small town like a bed of fire ants and it would be impossible to avoid all the sensational, tabloid news coverage. This being the case, the defense still could use the tactic of pretrial publicity in defense of their clients.

Secondly, the planning, implementation, and control of the trials in Thomasville worried Ballard. It would be difficult to conduct both trials at the same time in the smaller courthouse. Even if the trials were held successively, one after the other, how would coverage of the first trial not prejudice the second? And how could the court officials in Thomasville conduct their own business and put the town's daily operations on hold for a minimum of at least two weeks, while they played host to one of Georgia's most sensational murder cases?

Last of all, even the mundane details worried Ballard. What if the witnesses were sequestered? And for how long? Would they be able to find accommodations near the courthouse? Extended stays in distant Thomasville could be very inconvenient, not to mention the extra cost that taxpayers would have to bear.

Ballard knew the strength of his case. The evidence police

had compiled against the teenagers was very compelling and his witnesses were solid. The forensic evidence was as damning as any case he could have ever hoped for. The GBI Division of Forensic Sciences in Atlanta had tested the contents of sealed packages received from the Fayette County Sheriff's Office. Inside the packages was everything that had been found in Carl Collier's truck on Tybee Island, including the kitchen knives and two pairs of blue jeans. In accordance with an approved search warrant, three tubes of blood taken from Holly and three from Sandy had been collected and shipped to GBI, along with blood samples from Carl and Sarah Collier. Forensic biologist Diana Williams would testify that the DNA obtained from one knife and one of the pairs of jeans belonging to Sandy matched with reasonable certainty the blood sample belonging to Sarah Collier. And that the DNA profiles from the second knife matched Sarah and Carl Collier.

Since the FCSO had played by all the rules in that all the crime scene items and blood samples had been legally obtained, Ballard was very confident the DNA results would stick. He was eager to prove himself as a prosecutor, but, as a former defense attorney, he knew there were no guarantees once a jury had been chosen. Human nature played a huge role in the outcome of trials, and all it took was for one quirky juror to go the opposite way and the tide would be turned.

The newly elected DA considered his options, said his prayers, then decided to offer the defense a plea deal. What he proposed would be fair to the defendants and, in the long run, in the best interests of the citizens who voted him into office. Because Sandy had made statements to the police that implicated Holly, they would be tried separately, in back-to-back trials. The change of venue and the need for extra security and travel and accommodations for personnel and witnesses could cost the county about $400,000.

After talking with Bruce Jordan and Kevin Collier, and receiving their approvals, Ballard offered Sandy Ketchum one life sentence on the condition that she would testify against

Holly. He offered two consecutive life sentences to Holly. In doing so, he would save the expense of the trial and the trauma to the victims' family that a trial would bring. What he really expected was that Sandy would accept her plea, but Holly would refuse her plea and take her chances in the trial. He would be surprised if both accepted the deal.

Chidester and Walker had not received the discovery evidence from the DA's office, but they had a pretty good idea of what they would see when it came across their desks. Evidence pertinent to the prosecution's case—such as the crime scene photos, murder weapon photos, taped interviews with suspects, and other physical evidence—would be hard for them to refute. The prosecution had a gem of a witness in Sara Polk, and there was no way they could suppress her testimony about Holly and Sandy's visit to her house, covered in blood, brandishing knives, and boasting about the murders. They could challenge the legality of some of the evidence, such as the statements Sandy Ketchum made after her Tybee Island arrest, but it would be hard to exclude the other evidence from being seen and heard by a jury.

Judge English turned to the defense and asked, "Have any plea offers been discussed?"

Chidester and Walker had not seen the prosecution's discovery evidence, so they had not felt inclined to solicit any offers from the DA.

But it was March, and the premature warmth brought hope for the spring.

"Judge, I am prepared to offer a plea," Ballard announced in his surprising statement. "My office is offering pleas to two murders with malice that would carry two life sentences to run consecutively for Holly Harvey, and two felony murder charges carrying two life sentences to run concurrently for Sandy Ketchum."

Georgia law defines murder with malice as killing someone intentionally, with malice aforethought. Felony murder is a less serious charge and gives leniency to those who killed unintentionally. Based on conversations with Lieutenant Colonel

Bruce Jordan, Ballard was assuming Holly had planned the murders and manipulated Sandy into helping her kill the Colliers. Both girls were guilty, but the DA was assigning Holly the greater responsibility for the crimes.

Lloyd Walker's client was facing two counts of murder with malice and one count of armed robbery. Under the statutory mandated sentencing rules, Sandy could, if convicted on all charges, be sentenced to a total of forty-two years behind bars before ever being considered for parole. If she accepted Ballard's offer of felony murder with two concurrent life sentences, it was a possibility the Georgia State Board of Pardons and Paroles could parole her after having served only fourteen years.

If Judy Chidester's client accepted her deal, she would have to serve a minimum of ten years for each charge. Holly would be required to serve a total minimum of twenty years before she became eligible for parole.

Neither Judge English nor Judge Caldwell had any comments about Ballard's deal. He had spelled it out clear enough to the defense attorneys, and if they wanted it, then they had better jump on it. The conference ended, lasting just a half hour, and sent the defense lawyers scurrying back to their clients for a decision.

Later, Lloyd Walker spoke to Ballard in private. Walker wanted to know, since his client had cooperated fully with police and had given them a full confession, and was willing to testify against Holly at trial, would the prosecution still honor the deal if Holly accepted her plea bargain before Sandy? Ballard assured Walker the plea arrangement was good for eight days. As long as Sandy accepted the deal before Friday, April 1, he would honor it—no matter what Holly Harvey decided to do.

That afternoon, Walker turned the plea arrangement over and over in his mind. He knew both judges were strict and any chances of softening the plea bargain were nil. He had also learned that Ballard had discussed the plea bargains with Kevin Collier and he had approved of them. The following Tuesday, he discussed the deal with Sandy's parents, then arranged a visit with Sandy at the Metro RYDC. Prior to his visit, he had received word that Sandy was depressed and not adjusting well to life behind bars. He had called Dr. Nancy Aldridge, the prison psychiatrist, and asked whether Sandy was competent to make a rational decision in regard to the plea.

"She is depressed," Aldridge reported, "but otherwise okay. I think she is competent to make that decision."

On Tuesday afternoon, Walker met with Sandy and her parents at Metro. He explained the plea bargain and what it would mean to her. She could take her chances with a trial, and the outcome could be as much as forty years in prison if she lost.

"I've not seen the discovery evidence," Walker told Sandy, "but I have a good idea of what I will see and it's not going to be in your favor."

Sandy turned and looked at her parents with a frightened little-girl face.

"If you accept this deal and Holly does not accept hers," Walker explained further, "then you must fully cooperate with the prosecution case and testify against her. There will be questions in court about your role in the murders, which you will have to answer. You will have to truthfully tell in open court who stabbed whom, and when, and with what knife, all in open court."

Sandy took a deep breath and let it out again. She and her lover had once made a vow not to roll over on each other. Now she had to make the decision to go against what she had promised. Could she live the rest of her life, knowing she had turned on Holly? Would it be one she would regret every minute, every day, for the rest of her life?

"Listen to me, Sandy," Walker advised. "You're in this ugly situation because of Holly. Despite any feelings you might have for her at this point, it is time for you to take care of Sandy."

Sandy thought a few moments. She did not have a problem owning up to what she had done and accepting the consequences for her actions. What she had done the night of August 2, 2004, was horrible and unforgivable, but she didn't want to spend forty-two years of her life in prison for it. She had already made one bad decision—would she make another one?

"All things considered," Walker encouraged, "I think it is a good deal for you. You'll be eligible for parole in fourteen years and this gives you a chance to salvage something of your life."

Sandy quickly did the math. She would be thirty-one years old in fourteen years. If she was released from prison then, she would still have some of her life left to do the things she wanted to do. For her sake, and for her family's sake, she wanted to make the right decision. She looked at her parents, then back at Walker, and nodded. From a voice that spoke of self-preservation, she told him she was interested in taking the deal.

Walker gave Sandy a day to think it over. The next day she informed him of her decision and he drafted the letter, then faxed a copy to DA Ballard, along with a follow-up note asking for assurances from Judge Johnnie Caldwell for approval. He also advised Judy Chidester that Sandy had accepted the DA's offer.

On Thursday, Walker received an extremely large and prolific file from the DA's office. Inside the file was all the discovery evidence—i.e., crime scene photos, police reports, medical examiner reports, and the DNA evidence. It was pretty much what he had expected and there was nothing in there that would cause him to ask his client to reconsider her decision.

There was no mistake about the words describing what these teenagers had done. Each of their acts came out clear as a bell. They would be fooling themselves if they ever believed they could find twelve people who wouldn't convict these girls. After reviewing the gruesome pictures of the Colliers—these photos of pure blood and gore—they had a snowball's chance in hell of getting acquitted.

Chapter 61

Since her capture on August 3, 2004, Holly had not fared well in prison and had spent most of that time distraught, depressed, and under suicide watch. In the beginning, it had taken Judy Chidester several visits before Holly could even speak comfortably to her and assist in her defense.

"Do my mother and Uncle Kevin hate me?" Holly had asked, as if she had always been saccharine sweet. "And how is Sandy? Is she all right?"

During Chidester's visits, Holly would get visibly upset and cry, often to the point where she cried hysterically. Holly had said little to the police. It was as if she were holding on to something, hiding something deep down within herself, something so deeply submerged that it was impossible to get to it. But, some issues had to be resolved for the purposes of a defense strategy.

Chidester became so concerned about Holly's emotional state that she alerted prison authorities and asked them to keep a close eye on her.

"Of course, she's looking at two counts of malice murder and armed robbery, and who wouldn't be upset about that?" Chichester stated.

Holly was having significant problems understanding the legal trouble she had gotten herself into.

"Do you think I will be home before school starts the next term?" she would ask Chidester at times.

Holly had been in prison for seven months now, and that was plenty enough time to consider how severe the consequences would be for the atrocious acts she had committed if she was found guilty. Chidester had assured her time and time again that she would not be facing the death penalty because of her age. Likewise, she could not be sentenced to life without the chance of parole. But Holly was facing forty-two years in prison, and Chidester was concerned that if she refused the plea bargain and opted for a trial, then she might be experiencing menopause in jail.

One of the things Holly didn't understand was why the DA offered Sandy a more lenient deal than hers. Chidester told her that based on what Lieutenant Colonel Bruce Jordan told Ballard, Sandy had cooperated with the police in their investigation and she had not. Suddenly the words Bruce Jordan had told her came true.

"*This ain't your grandmother you're dealing with now,*" Jordan had chastised her the day she was arrested and handcuffed. Then, after the arrest, when she would not talk with him, he had told her, *"I am gonna send you down the river."*

Jordan had lived up to his promises.

Chidester believed Holly had been treated unfairly by Jordan in the media. He had described her as coldhearted, without remorse, a stone-cold killer, and evil. She didn't find that to be the case at all. Holly was remorseful and she had been torn apart by her murderous actions. But people react differently in situations like this. Holly's emotional system had simply shut down and she was in denial when captured at Tybee Island. That was why she kept asking the Tybee Island police officer, "Are my grandparents all the way dead?"

Because Holly could not explain why she had done the things

she had done, she did not cooperate immediately and was labeled as not remorseful and uncooperative.

"Sandy is just as guilty as me," Holly had reminded her lawyer. She said, at first she had resisted going upstairs after her grandfather, but it was Sandy told her to do so.

"She said, 'Go get him,' and I was, like, 'Nope. Then I changed my mind when I realized he was going upstairs into the kitchen and trying to use the phone."

Chidester was of the opinion that neither girl would have been capable of committing the murders without each other. Few people would argue that these teenagers' lives had been anything but normal. She was never sure if Holly had been the ringleader or not, but believed both girls had been impaired by the drugs. Not that their drug use would ever be a mitigating factor at the trial, as Holly and Sandy were both on prescribed drugs for depression. The information that she had showed that in the weeks prior to the murders, they had stopped taking their medications. Nevertheless, they had admitted to smoking marijuana laced with crack the day of the murders, but Georgia law made no concessions for legal or illegal drugs, voluntarily or nonvoluntarily. Anyone under the influence of drugs had no excuse for murder, and certainly had no hopes of that being a legally viable defense. At best, defense attorneys hope the drug issues would help get their clients a lighter sentence after a conviction at trial, but it often worked against them.

Chidester was hoping to avoid a trial and believed once Holly grasped the seriousness of the charges against her, she would agree. When the DA's discovery package arrived at her office, she quickly opened it. Inside the file, among all the other evidence, was four hundred of the most disturbing crime scene photos she had ever seen in her long career as a defense attorney. She recognized immediately that Holly needed to see these photos, in order to come to grips with what she had done.

Chidester selected several of the most graphic photos and took them with her when she visited Holly at the Clayton

County juvenile jail in Lovejoy. One of the close-up photos captured her grandfather's body lying facedown in a pool of blood. His grotesque, wide-eyed death face stared horribly at the floor. Another photo illustrated the hideous, ghastly scene at the bottom of the stairs, where her grandmother lay faceup, saturated in blood, and with a horrified look on her face.

Chidester felt compelled to show Holly these photos. These would be the same photos the jurors and family members would see at trial. She was convinced Holly did not want these carnage photos displayed at trial.

In Chidester's conversation with Holly, she explained the **plea** bargain and the risks she faced in going to trial. When she was certain Holly understood everything she had told her, she laid the gruesome crime scene photos out in front of her like a deck of playing cards.

"What would you think if you were a jury member and you saw these?" she asked her.

Holly stared at the photos on the table in front of her and all the color drained from her face. She became extremely distraught and started shaking in uncontrollable fits.

"No, no, no," she muttered under her breath.

Chidester breathed deeply.

"I want you to think about all that I have told you before making your decision," she advised. "Can I also have your permission to speak with your mom about the plea bargain?"

Holly agreed. She would think about everything her lawyer had told her, but she didn't want to speak with her mother about this decision. The next day in a phone conversation, she told her lawyer to accept the plea deal.

"The only thing," Holly requested, "is that no jury, the public, and, most of all, my family will never see those pictures."

"I assure you that will not happen," Chidester replied.

On Wednesday afternoon, the defense lawyers' decision to accept the plea deal was communicated by the DA's office to Judge English and Judge Caldwell.

English's response was "Hell, let's do this tomorrow then."

That same Wednesday morning, Judy Chidester received a call from Judge English's office. English asked if she and her client could meet him at the Fayette County Courthouse the next day and consummate the plea bargains. He was hoping to avoid turning his courtroom into a media circus.

When Chidester arrived the next day at a little before 11:00 A.M., the courthouse was buzzing with reporters and TV crews. When she inquired of several reporters as to how they had learned of the rushed hearing, they replied, "Bruce Jordan."

The Collier murders had not only shattered the peace of the town, but the defense lawyers took strong exception to the way the case was being handled with the media. They believed the conduct of the investigators involved in this case shed serious doubt at their willingness and ability to conduct themselves fairly and impartially.

Furthermore, the defense argued, it would have been difficult to impanel a jury, a good jury that would be representative of their clients' peers, given the climate of the opinion in Fayette County, but even more difficult to find a jury in this county completely free from prejudice, contempt, or hatred toward their clients.

Chapter 62

The media was calling the Collier murders one of the most heinous crimes in Fayetteville County's history, and the pressure was so thick for justice, one could almost feel it in the air. Because of the critical issues of the plea bargains, the judges wanted a seamless transition to the trial and had scheduled the two girls to appear separately at the Fayette County Courthouse on Thursday, April 14. Holly Harvey's trial would begin at 10:30 A.M. and Sandy Ketchum's at 11:00 A.M.

"This is a nonsensical crime," Superior Court judge Paschal English would concur before the day was over. "One of the most brutal I have seen in my thirty years of judicial work."

Judge English had graduated from the University of Georgia in Athens and received his doctorate degree in jurisprudence from there as well. He had served as a chief assistant district attorney in the Griffin Judicial Circuit for twelve years. The Fayette County Courthouse was his domain and the legendary old warrior ruled his courtroom with an iron fist. Because he believed criminals should suffer and serve long sentences, he received 100 percent of the vote in his last election from the conservative counties he served.

English was also familiar to a lot of people outside of the state as one of the contestants stranded on a remote island, competing for a $1 million prize on the highly rated 2002 CBS-TV show *Survivor: Marquesas*. Producers of the show considered English, a retired U.S. Air Force colonel and Vietnam vet, one of their most popular competitors on the show. Nicknamed "Pappy" by his fellow contestants, he finished fourth in the reality show, but only after drawing the "purple rock."

"All rise," a bailiff announced as Judge English crept through the door and shuffled to his seat, his black robe trailing behind him. Once situated, he surveyed the crowd and said, "Good morning," then explained the purpose of the proceeding.

English then nodded at another bailiff and the door on the right of the courtroom opened wide. Holly Harvey had been waiting in the foyer, where a certificate of appreciation for her artwork from the Fayette County Board of Education had once hung on the panel walls. She was ten years old then.

This time Holly Harvey was led manacled through the courthouse and took her seat at the defense table to the right of the bench. The now-stoic sixteen-year-old appeared to have gained about twenty pounds since being incarcerated. She was neatly dressed in a pink-trimmed black dress suit her mother (who had recently been discharged from prison and was seated in the gallery) had provided to deputies while her daughter was still in a holding cell.

Holly froze. Nothing seemed to be working for her. Any attempt at smiling came across as nothing but a smirk. Any attempt at confidence came across as just short of cockiness. And any attempt at humor came across as psychopathic and cold-blooded.

If Holly's style of dress was chosen to make her look younger and sweeter, it hadn't worked. Her hair was slicked down and turned in at her shoulders. Her face was a waste of good makeup, as the red blush that covered it added ten years and turned her into a girl much older than her years. And, of course, her pink outfit was marred by the leather belt around her waist, where her hands were bound by stainless-steel handcuffs. It was totally impossible to make her look warm and cuddly.

As Holly settled in her seat, a hush settled over the courtroom. The air suddenly felt crisp and cold, as if the temperature inside the courtroom had dropped a full 10 degrees. A camera set up at the back and in the corner of the courtroom filmed the proceedings. A thick row of spectators crowded the courtroom and included Kevin Collier, Carla Harvey, and Tim and Beth Ketchum, in the front row in the gallery.

Sandy Ketchum's lawyer, Lloyd Walker, sat apprehensively on the end of the front row, focused on the impending drama. The fate of his client was inescapably linked to how Holly handled herself in court. Holly's testimony was the last missing piece of the puzzle in this well-publicized case and Walker wanted to make certain it fit into place. That was his skill, his profession, making big problems go away.

A story had started going around in Fayetteville and other areas. Talk was that since the night of the murders, Holly had grown inward, contemplative, as if she were finally trying to make some sense of her life. Pretty soon, it was being taken as gospel. Even those who knew better started talking about it.

Judge English asked for Holly and her lawyer to step forward. At the same time, DA Scott Ballard rose from his seat at the prosecution table and walked to a lectern at the front of the bench. In a series of questions, Ballard asked Holly if she understood the charges against her, and was she satisfied with her defense? When she answered "Yes, sir" to all his prepared questions, he then read a synopsis of her crime and asked if she understood the nature of the offenses she had been charged with, and was she freely and voluntarily entering her plea today?

Holly let out a long, soundless exhale. Her forehead wrinkled and her mouth drew down in a grimace of pain before she again answered, "Yes, sir."

"Do you also understand that by entering a plea of guilty,

you waive the right to a trial by jury and the right to counsel at that trial?" Ballard rumbled.

"Yes, sir."

A string of other legal questions followed, none of which Holly probably fully understood, but her attorney had gone over the questions and she knew enough to respond with "Yes, sir." The most important questions asked of Holly were in regard to the negotiated plea, the maximum possible sentences on the charges, and the fact that the plea could be accepted or rejected by the court.

Holly's face was calm, her voice chillingly indifferent. She assured the court she understood all the implications of those questions. In her acknowledgments, she confirmed she should be punished and that she freely and voluntarily had accepted the plea deal.

The judge's nostrils flared a little. He looked at Holly's lawyer and inquired, "Mrs. Chidester, anything you're wanting to say, or Miss Harvey?"

Spectators in the gallery straightened up in their seats. The role of a cooperative, remorseful young adult was not a natural for Holly. It had never been one of her strong points. That was one of the reasons why many of the spectators were there. Holly Harvey was as mismatched with Judge English as a Little Leaguer would have been with Barry Bonds in a home run derby.

"Your Honor, Miss Harvey asked me to make a few comments on her behalf," Chidester said with a little uneasiness in her voice. Like all lawyers at this point, she was feeling a trifle bit guilty over what she had or hadn't done as a defense attorney. The truth was, she had done a superb job defending Holly and the judge recognized that.

Dressed in a blue business suit Chidester stood by her client. The sandy-haired lawyer had her glasses on—without them her features seemed so much softer—but through them her eyes assured Holly everything was going to be all right. She looked at the judge, smiled, and nodded.

"First I'd like to say that this case for me has been personally and professionally very difficult because of the nature of the crime and because of the fact that my client was fifteen years old. That's made it difficult. There have been a good number of people that have come forward, people that knew her from church, people that knew her from school, that have come through me to offer their support and prayers for Miss Harvey. And I've given her all those messages, and she wants to express gratitude for the people who have offered to keep her in their thoughts and prayers. She has asked me to express her deep remorse over her actions. It's something that she says she can only hope that one day she will forgive herself so that she might ask others to attempt to forgive her. We would ask that the court accept this plea that's been negotiated with the state and enter it accordingly."

English turned to Holly. He spoke calmly, his eyes never leaving hers. He mixed no words and his questions came fast and steady. In a climactic flourish, Holly took a deep breath and tried to confirm all the judge had to say.

"Miss Harvey, how old are you right now?"

"Sixteen," Holly answered, in an almost soft, toneless reply, which was so unlike her. It was almost as if she had been replaced by someone she didn't know.

"Speak up," the judge exhorted.

Judy Chidester stood by her client. She kept a hand around her to steady her.

"Sixteen," Holly answered again, this time louder.

"Sixteen?" The judge echoed her response with a befuddled tone to his voice. He covered his face with his broad hand, then continued.

"First of all, I want to make a finding for the record that, based on the questions that were asked to you, I find that you are freely and voluntarily entering your plea of guilty to the charges of malice murder—two counts of malice murder."

"Yes, sir."

"I'll also accept the factual basis that Mr. Ballard presented in support of these pleas." The judge paused, then shifted gears. "Now, the person or people you killed were who?"

Holly's mouth drew down in a quivering bow. "My grandparents," she said, her voice breaking.

"And what were their names?"

"Carl and Sarah Collier."

"How old were they?"

"Their seventies. I'm not sure."

"In their seventies?"

"Yes, sir."

Judge English was doing what the Colliers had attempted to do. He was going to chastise her harshly, and it was going to be a slow, painful ordeal.

"Were you living with them at the time?" the judge asked, continuing with the unpleasantness.

"Yes, sir."

"Why were you living with them at the time?"

"My mother was incarcerated."

"For what?"

"Possession of marijuana."

English rolled his jaw. He covered his nose as if a stagnant odor had suddenly drifted out. He was silent for a moment, then started asking a series of questions about Holly and her relationship with her grandparents.

Holly answered the judge's questions in a low, talking-to-herself voice. She answered one question, answered a second question, and then, on the third question, her cheek, neck, and forehead turned bright red and she got the shakes.

"Was Sandy related to these people that you killed?"

"No, sir."

"Then how was it that she became part of this criminal enterprise—endeavor?"

"Well, we had got high on some crack. Then—"

"Crack, meaning cocaine?" English interrupted her in a harsh, haunting voice.

"Yes, sir."

"Where'd you get it?"

Holly wore an utterly blank expression. She simply replied, "A friend."

"A friend?" English responded in a low murmur.

Spectators and family members in the gallery fell into a grim silence.

A sudden tidal wave of emotion came crashing over Carla Harvey's face. It was as if she had been caught in a nightmare and ominous clouds were rolling in over the sound of Holly's voice. With every word about "a" friend, the sky grew darker.

Holly revealed to the court that Calvin Lawson had supplied her and Sandy with crack cocaine the night of the murders. In detail, she told how Calvin had driven from Union City early in the morning and picked them up outside the Colliers' home. He then drove them back to his apartment, where they took the drugs.

"And how old was he?" English asked.

"Thirty."

English shook his head. "Thirty?" he said offhandedly. "How did you meet him?"

"Friend of the family."

"A friend of whose family?"

Now Carla had her second nightmare. Her heart was racing. Her forehead was wet with perspiration. The wicked storm was blowing in.

Holly paused; then in a voice almost too low to hear, she said, "My mother's side."

English glared down at Holly from the bench.

"A drug friend of the family?" he demanded to know.

Holly averted her eyes, then nodded her head.

"Is that right?" English shot back, crowding her thoughts.

"Yes, sir," Holly said, looking up at him through watery eyes.

"And who introduced you to Calvin?"

"My mother," Holly responded guardedly.

English did not let her comment go by. He did not like her answer. He did not like it at all. After a moment's hesitation, he added, "Your mother?"

Carla Harvey was sitting in the front row in the gallery, next to her brother, Kevin Collier. When Holly revealed Calvin as her drug supplier, Carla slipped down in her seat.

"Uh-oh," she muttered several times. "I'm dead, I'm dead."

The judge's comment had left Holly off-balance and exposed. All she could manage was a nod.

"How long had you known Calvin?"

"Just a few months."

"A few months?"

Holly nodded.

"Did you get your drugs from Calvin?"

"Yes, sir."

"This was crack cocaine?"

"Yes, sir."

"Any other drugs?"

"Marijuana."

English looked disgusted in his demand for answers. It was as if Carla Harvey had orchestrated her daughter's life into a crescendo of drug abuse. Note by note. Bar by bar. In a singsong voice, he commented, "It's the same as your mother, isn't that right?"

Holly nodded. "Yes, sir."

English responded with acrid disapproval. He then solicited the rest of the story and asked Holly about her relationship with Sandy Ketchum.

Holly repeated most of what she had already told the judge

about her relationship with Sandy, not knowing exactly where all this was going.

English listened until she finished, then leaned on the bench and crossed his arms.

"Now this is where I want you to explain to me fully how it was that you decided to stab your grandfather and grandmother," he said, staring at her as if he could will the truth out of her.

Holly gave a half-shrug, as if she hadn't given it much thought before now. At last, her sobs and sniffles began to change themselves into words, most of them incoherent at first, but they became clearer as the tears dried up.

"Well, Sandy was, like, 'We should take their truck and we can get something to calm us down.' I said—I didn't mean anything by it—but I was, like, 'We'd have to kill them to do that.' But I didn't mean anything. Then she was, like, 'Well, we can hit them in the head with a lamp.' And I was, like, 'Well, that might just make them pass out. Then they will wake up.' She was, like, 'Go get a knife.' So I had went and got a knife. And she was like—she had stabbed the bed to see if it was going to be sharp enough. She said it was sharp enough."

All at once, Holly felt dull and sad. Suddenly she didn't want to talk about it. She didn't feel up for it. She felt her heart wasn't up to the prospect of it, kind of like the way a heart has grown heavy in the process of grief.

The judge sensed Holly's hesitancy to continue. He didn't know exactly why, nor did he say.

"All right, let me stop you there," he interjected. "You practiced stabbing."

Holly went back to nodding her head.

"Is that right?" the judge clarified.

"Sandy did."

"Did you stab anything other than the bed?"

"The wall."

"Was anything on the wall?"

"A picture frame."

"Was anything in the picture frame?"

"It was a painted picture of some puppies."

"A painted picture of some puppies?"

"Yes, sir."

"And you practiced and Sandy practiced stabbing the puppies?"

"She did."

"Is that right?"

"Yes, sir."

"Why?"

It was a fair question. All the color had gradually drained from Holly's face. The judge looked at her, then at her lawyer. The same look to both of them. Half-bewildered. Half-accusing.

Fascinated, English repeated his question. It was as if the concept of murder had taken on a new dimension for him, particularly this one. He nodded at Holly and she answered the question.

"To see—she was seeing if the knife was sharp."

"Well, then, why was it necessary to stab the bed also?"

"I don't know."

"How many knives were there?"

"One at first. Then after it started, then I called her to help me."

Holly's face was as round and bland as the face of the moon. Then the judge, as if he might have realized his questions sounded impolite, insensitive, and crass, interrupted her in midsentence.

"All right"—English held up his hand—"wait a second. We're not there yet. I want to draw everything out about this. Do you understand me?"

"Yes, sir," Holly said, feeling Chidester's gentle hand on her shoulder.

The judge explained to Holly that he had not yet accepted her plea, that all he had done was make a determination that her plea was free and voluntary. He told her he had accepted the factual basis to accept the plea, but he wanted to satisfy himself that this was the correct thing to do.

"And what I'm hearing so far," English uttered with dead finality, "gives me a lot of concern about you. Now, you tell me about this knife. Who went and got the knife?"

Holly's demeanor suddenly changed. Her hands were joined tightly in front of her, sweating, seemingly working against each other. Her face was pale and pinched, her eyes were dark and fathomless. She looked up at the judge and answered solemnly, "I did."

English responded quickly and prickly, asking all about the knives.

Holly flexed a little, floundering for an answer, before being jolted out of her reverie. She said she had chosen the biggest knife from the kitchen and took it back to her basement bedroom. Then Sandy had told her that when her grandparents came down there, she should start stabbing them.

English spread his hands and looked at Holly self-righteously.

"Had they ever done anything to you, other than raise you?"

Holly shook her head. She looked pained.

"What?" English asked curiously. Looking at her and the confusion on her face, he was probably forming his own ideas about that.

Holly hesitated. She blinked her eyes savagely, driving her tears all the way back. No question of evasion now. It was down to telling the truth or risk being seen a liar.

"Only the family knows," she said. "My grandmother used to scream at me and tell me all kind of things."

English leaned forward. "What kind of things?"

The question brought Holly close to tears again. While she fought them off, she told the judge, "She used to tell me that the only reason that I lived there was because—so I didn't go to DEFACS. And when I was, like, ten, she used to call me a slut. And my grandfather, he hit me."

Holly stopped, out of words, and waited for the deluge of questions.

English stared at Holly, knowing there were experiences in children's lives that varied from evasion to the plain truth with no varnish on them.

"Was this why you decided to kill them?" he asked.

"No, sir."

"Well, why'd you decide to kill them?"

A slow red cloud seemed to eclipse Holly's reasoning. Like a single sick chord on an out-of-tune piano, she completed the final note of her rage.

"For Sandy," she answered.

"I'm sorry?" English asked, his already large eyes growing wider.

No two words were meant to hang in the courtroom the way these two did.

"For Sandy," Holly repeated.

English's eyes met Holly's and theirs had the same dazed look. He sat there looking stumped and trying to understand how a thing like that could happen. Staggered by the thought, he asked again, "For Sandy?"

Holly shook her head.

"You decided to kill your grandparents because of Sandy?" English asked.

Holly nodded again. "Yes, sir."

The judge probed further for a reason and asked objectively, "Why?"

"I don't know," Holly said, shrugging.

"You do know," English said, with an unpleasing foreboding rising in his throat. He looked down at her with his wrinkled brow and narrow eyes. Free to slaughter the witness, causing the walls to seemingly shake when he bellowed, "Tell me the truth."

For a moment, Holly was unable to breathe. The shock of the judge's demand had knocked the wind from her. He didn't look like the type that would forgive many mistakes. Finally she found her breath and her voice again.

"So that we could be together."

"What do you mean, you could be together?" English asked, his eyes searching her face. He interpreted her answer to be beyond the reign of reason.

Holly's eyes had the blank look of someone on the verge of fainting. She winced, then offered, "So we could leave."

"Where would you go?"

Chidester put a steadying hand on Holly's shoulder.

Holly blinked at him, as if she were far away. "Anywhere."

English rubbed at his temples generously. It was a bitter pill to try and swallow. Hs face burning now and his face tightening, he said nothing for a few moments, then questioned her about Sandy's background.

Holly could feel her eyes getting heavy and her thoughts beginning to drift. Chidester was still standing beside her. She gave Holly a brisk, little shake and her eyes cleared. She then was able to answer the judge's questions.

English cocked his head at Holly curiously. He swallowed uneasily and considered for a long moment what he knew about the killings. He stared at her silently, then asked for her to explain exactly what happened in detail.

As Holly recalled that dreadful day, her eyes flooded with tears and she managed simultaneously to look both self-righteous and truthful. The courtroom was stunned by what they heard her saying. Even those with bleeding hearts winced when she talked about how she had closed her eyes and stabbed her grandparents, even after they had scrambled away from her, until they were dead. Those who were already familiar with the case thought it bizarre enough when police reported the to-do list scribbled on Holly's arm—that is, until Holly finished recounting the gruesome details of the crime.

It was hard for anyone to understand how she could have committed such an atrocious act on her own kin.

After hearing all of Holly's gruesome details, the judge was still unmoved. He was tired of young people—killing and supposedly getting away with it. He looked at her smugly, then asked in an oily voice: "So it's like you had gutted a deer?"

Holly nodded.

Spectators in the courtroom were surprised. She had sworn to tell the truth, but no one expected to hear it. Her confession had literally sucked the air out of the courtroom, and for a long minute, everyone held their breath and waited for the next surprise.

The judge correctly gauged the temperament in the courtroom and moved on to the aftermath and their escape to Tybee Island.

For those who knew Holly, they could see her pain was real. Her emotions were difficult to watch and sit through. She looked at the judge and swallowed hard. Her face was troubled.

"Anything else you're wanting to say?" English probed again.

"No, sir," Holly said, studying her hands.

"You understand, if I accept this plea, what you're pleading guilty to?"

Holly shrugged, looked down at her hands again, then whispered, "Yes, sir."

"And you understand the sentence that has been recommended to you, which is the only sentence a juvenile can get in the state of Georgia for something like this?"

"Yes, sir."

"Do you understand that?" English asked again. His face was sober and dignified, as befitting his position.

Of course, Holly did, and she forced herself to say so.

"Yes, sir."

"You're getting two life sentences, consecutive. That's the recommendation."

Holly gasped as if he had slapped her. "Yes, sir."

"Do you understand what that is?"

Holly shrugged because she really had no idea. "My lawyer tried to make it clear as she can," she responded, glaring up at the judge through a wavy sheen of tears. "I know that I have to serve at least twenty years."

"Twenty years?" His words rang through the courtroom like a cold, clacking, boney finger.

Holly nodded, fat tears spilling down her cheek.

"That you have to serve at least twenty years?"

"Yes, sir."

"At which time, do you realize that you will become eligible for parole?" English asked unconvincingly.

"No, sir."

"Well, I don't know that anybody knows how the Pardon and Parole Board works. But, in any event, if it is twenty years, ten years for each life sentence—and I wasn't being derogatory about Pardon and Parole, I just don't understand how they work, how they compute sentences. But in the event you are eligible for parole in twenty years, that doesn't mean necessarily that you will be out in twenty years. You understand that?"

"Yes, sir."

"But I guess there is a possibility that you could be out in twenty years, and you do understand that?"

"Yes, sir."

"So you think twenty years is a pretty good exchange for killing your grandparents?"

Holly considered this for a while and stared blankly back at the judge.

What Judge English gave Holly next was a stern and lengthy admonishment. It was a tongue-lashing so severe—a withering assault so scalding, so compelling—that a rabid street preacher heaping such upon sin would have paled in comparison.

"I've tried to think, in the thirty years I've been doing this, twelve of which was where Mr. Ballard is right now, eighteen of which has been as a judge, I've tried to think of another case that I have been involved with, connected with, or heard about that was, number one, as brutally savage as this was—and I've seen some hardened criminals come through this court.

"And yet a fifteen-year-old little girl comes in front of me and admits to savagely killing the people she lives with. And I can tell you this, I can't—I can't think of another case in the thirty years that has been as nonsensical or as brutal as this.

"I can tell you this and you won't remember this. You probably won't remember any of this once you get off into the prison system. If there was another alternative, a harsher alternative, for sentencing you, I'm sure Mr. Ballard would be requesting that. You are fortunate in that you were just a little too young for the full force of the law to be invoked. I say you're lucky. It may be worse that you spend the rest of your life or a lot of your life in prison; I don't know."

Holly raised her head to look at the judge. Her body throbbed dully. She was getting a headache.

"So what would you have chosen to be your punishment?"

Holly stopped staring at the judge, looked downward, and breathed deeply. "I think I should be dead."

"Well, we both agree on that," English muttered.

Holly was silent.

"Have you and Sandy talked since that day?"

"No, sir."

"Not at all?"

"No, sir."

"So you don't know what's going to happen to her?"

"No, sir."

English frowned a little, then added, "Don't care?"

"I care about her."

The judge sat looking at her, the frown on his face very deep now. He almost expected her to say she cared about Sandy, but he wondered if she had feelings for anybody else.

"You care about your grandparents?"

"Yes, sir."

"Have you talked to your mother?"

"Yes, sir," Holly answered, her face puffed and streaked with tears.

English leaned in toward Holly and asked condescendingly, "Have you talked with Calvin?"

"No, sir. I don't want to."

"Well, Miss Harvey, I will advise you, ma'am, that I will accept your plea, because that's the only thing we can give you."

"Yes, sir."

In a few short sentences, the judge epitomized what the law was all about:

On count number one of indictment number 04R-342—that is the indictment charging you with malice murder—I will sentence you to life imprisonment. On count number two of indictment 04R-342—that charges you with malice murder—I will sentence you to a consecutive life sentence.

English then turned to Holly and asked, "So that you don't misunderstand this, you do understand that these life sentences are one after the other, consecutive?"

"Yes, sir," Holly answered, feeling a knot form in her stomach.

The judge's voice registered well-bred surprise.

"Now, I've never understood this, either," he admitted, "but I am obligated to advise you of a sentence review. I don't know that there's anything a sentence review panel could do on a life sentence, which is the minimum sentence and the maximum sentence. But for purposes of the record, I will advise you that you do have the right to have this sentence reviewed, and Mrs. Chidester is familiar with the sentence review process.

"Now, let me ask Mr. Ballard, because I already know the

answer to this, because he briefed me full on what was getting ready to take place this morning. And one of his immediate observations, and one of his immediate concerns, were whatever family members are left, family members to the grandparents, and he advised me that they had been educated on what was going to take place, the sentence. And they, I think, were in agreement with the sentence. Is that correct, Mr. Ballard?"

Ballard stood up from behind his table and addressed the judge. "That is correct, Your Honor. They are."

English turned and stared at Holly. Her heart had been weighed against a feather of truth, but he wanted to know if there was anything else she wanted to say before she left the courtroom.

Holly felt everyone was looking at her with such hate and disgust, she wanted to shatter like a piece of glass. Finally she blurted out, "I just hope that everybody can forgive me."

Holly's lawyer, Judy Chidester, had lived to fight another day. As they led Holly out of the courtroom, Chidester uttered a long sigh. When the judge asked her if she had anything to say, she replied in her soft Southern voice, not quite as steady as she had wished, "No, Your Honor."

English had nothing but respect for the defense attorney.

"Well, I know it's been a very difficult case for you to become involved with, Mrs. Chidester," English said apologetically. "Let me thank you for the work you've done—and people don't realize what goes into these things to get to this point—but you've done quite a bit of preparation. You've been in my office a number of times requesting different things, and you were prepared, I think, to go to this trial on this, should it have to take place. And I thank you for your efforts in this regard."

"Yes, sir." Chidester smiled. "You're welcome, Your Honor."

"And, Mr. Ballard," English continued, "I thank you, too, for the expedient manner in which this thing was put together.

It was a complex, complex case from the standpoint of just gathering the evidence, waiting for certain things to be returned to you from an evidentiary standpoint."

Ballard smiled back at English, ten years dropping from his face as he did so.

"Well, thank you, Judge," Ballard said brightly. "But really, the credit really goes to the Fayette County Sheriff's Office. Within seventeen hours, despite the fact that this—these girls were at the coast of Georgia, they had them under arrest."

"Well, lucky for me," English said—the words rushing out of him, but not fast enough to keep up with the memories and the surge of emotions they brought on—"my entire career has been spent in the Fayette or the Griffin Judicial Circuit, and I've been involved in traveling to Fayette County for thirty years. My office has been in Fayette County for eighteen years and I concur with what you say. Fayette County, from my perspective—and I've done a lot of traveling—has the most professional and best law enforcement in this country of ours. And I'm not just talking about this case. But since you are giving credit to the Fayette County Sheriff's Office, the residents of Fayette County are indeed fortunate to have a sheriff like Randall Johnson and a staff like the Fayette County sheriff's department to protect them, because they are, again, some of the most professional people I have ever been around—professional people. And I've been involved in the military all my adult life, so I've been around a lot of military/law enforcement–type of individuals. And thank you for your comments, Mr. Ballard."

"Yes, sir, Judge." Ballard nodded. "Several of them didn't go to sleep until they had them in custody."

A smiling, satisfied thought came into English's mind.

"Well, I'm glad they were the ones that were involved in the investigation, because, as you said, it was brought together in a very quick fashion, very professional fashion, and I think you're ready to go to trial if you had to right now."

Chapter 63

For almost forty-five minutes, Judge Paschal English had grilled Holly Harvey with unceasing questions about her life and her role in her grandparents' murders. Although many of Holly's answers to English's questions were disjointed, their oral sparring was as good as anything seen on television. But, at any time, had Holly gotten to the point in her story where she lied or refused to answer English's questions, he had the right to toss out the plea bargain. Judge Johnnie Caldwell could have easily followed suit in Sandy Ketchum's case.

The evidence was overwhelming in the Collier murder case. Sandy had confessed earlier and agreed to testify. For the first time, Holly had confessed to killing her grandparents and explained in detail how they had been murdered. She had said she and Sandy were in love and the reason she had killed her grandparents was "for Sandy." The incredible account of the brutal, nonsensical murder wrapped up shortly before noon and ended with Holly being sentenced to two life terms in prison.

The FCSO had one of their busiest days arranging the transport of the teenage prisoners to the courthouse. There was another case being adjudicated at the courthouse that day and the sheriff's deputies were a bit overwhelmed. Judge

Johnnie Caldwell had arrived at the courthouse well before his scheduled 11:00 A.M. hearing, but no one had informed him of the delays and he was obviously very annoyed.

Lloyd Walker had listened to Holly's response to Judge English's questions. Because she had held up well, Walker believed his client was almost out of the woods. Her fate rested now in the hands of Judge Caldwell, who was very popular among conservative voters. He had a well-deserved reputation as an unsympathetic jurist when presiding over violent criminal cases. In his last election, 60 percent of the people spoke in favor of his conventional law-and-order credentials and he won by an imposing margin.

Johnnie Caldwell started out as an attorney in Thomaston, Georgia, in Upson County, in the late 1960s. He took a job as an assistant district attorney in the Griffin Judicial Circuit, then ran for the district attorney and won. Caldwell's father was a politician and deeply engrained in the old Democratic Party, when a party known as the Dixiecrats called the shots in the Deep South and nominated South Carolina senator Strom Thurmond as their party's presidential candidate. The elder Caldwell's political connections would help get his son appointed to a judgeship in 1997.

Caldwell had earned a reputation as a tough, prosecutorial, tyrannical judge. The courtroom was his arena and he ran it as such. Prosecutors and defense attorneys alike feared Caldwell and dreaded litigation in his courtroom. Immediately, at the conclusion of Holly's proceedings, Lloyd Walker jumped up and hustled over to the courtroom.

"Are we going to have a plea or not?" Caldwell asked Walker sternly.

Walker apologized. "The DA is still in Judge English's courtroom, Your Honor, explaining the defendant's plea. I anticipate that should conclude any minute now and he will join us."

Walker did his best one-man dog and pony show, stalled, and nervously glanced at the door, anxiously awaiting the arrival of Scott Ballard. As soon as Ballard arrived, he, Caldwell, and the DA entered the judge's chamber and discussed the plea arrangement. Caldwell was still hot under the collar for having been kept waiting, for which both Walker and Ballard profusely apologized.

The three men walked back into the courtroom and the hearing began. Ballard took his position at the front of the courtroom, while the judge coldly announced for the bailiff to bring in the suspect. Stroking his chin and looking at his gold wristwatch, Caldwell eyed Sandy impatiently as she was led to her seat at the defense table, just to the right of the bench. The hearing was already an hour late, and he saw no reason why Sandy's case couldn't be handled judiciously and briefly.

Sandy's attorney was taking no chances with Caldwell. He had cautioned her earlier not to get on the judge's bad side. Walker had asked Sandy's parents to bring some nice clothes for her to wear at the hearing, not wanting her to appear in front of the judge and the unavoidable cameras in prison togs. But when a side door opened at the front of the room and Sandy was escorted in by a female court officer, a silence fell over the courtroom like a heavy blanket. Still the master of the grunge look, Sandy was dressed in blue jeans and an oversized yellow prison smock, with a wrinkled long-sleeved olive shirt underneath.

Sandy appeared to have just emerged from a shower. She wore no makeup, no eyeliner or lipstick to make herself attractive. Her short hair was wet, parted in the middle and pulled back, then glued against her head. Her dark brown hair framed her sad, round face, and those who knew her could tell she had put on some weight while languishing in jail.

Of course, "languishing" was perhaps too strong a word for what the judge would have thought Sandy had been doing in jail the past six months. If languishing was what one called it, she had been free to write all the poems and letters she wanted and practice her artwork. The juvenile facility she was staying in was as comfortable as many bed-and-breakfasts, the food as palatable, and the service much better. The only problem was that Sandy couldn't open the door and go for a walk when she felt like it. Still, all in all, the accommodations and treatment were a hell of a lot better than Sandy and her codefendant had afforded Carl and Sarah Collier.

Because this was the attitude that permeated the courtroom, Sandy's hearing would be much briefer than anyone anticipated. But each second seemed to last a minute, and each minute seemed to last an hour—all frozen in one horrible snapshot of disbelief.

Tim and Beth Ketchum sat in the front row behind the defense table. On the way over to the courtroom from Holly's hearing, Tim told his wife he felt like something had gored him in the stomach. He didn't realize his legs had gone rubbery, though, until Sandy walked in and took her seat. He then felt his legs trembling. Beth saw his body trembling, reached over and took Tim's hand, and he let it be taken.

Scott Ballard stood just to the left of the bench facing the defense table. The judge nodded benignly at Ballard and scribbled on a paper in front of him. Ballard then called for Sandy Ketchum and her attorney to come forward.

Sandy and her attorney both got to their feet and walked to the front of the courtroom. Her body shook, as if she were freezing. She appeared too traumatized to speak and managed only a low, moaning sound.

Ballard held on to the same ream of paper he had used in Holly's hearing. From these pages, he would ask Sandy the same thread of questions as he had asked Holly. Ballard began with the easy questions, so she could learn to follow the bouncing ball.

"Your correct name is Sandra Ketchum?"

"Yes, sir."

Sandy's eyes were red and swollen from crying. She was

nervous and spoke in a soft, haunted voice. She answered all of the questions Ballard asked and assured the DA she had been satisfied with her attorney's services.

Caldwell furrowed his brow at her, perplexed. He watched her closely, mused aloud, then made a mental note to check some papers relating to a last-minute detail.

Sandy got a sudden glimpse of what she was there for when Ballard asked her if she understood the three charges brought against her and the three consecutive life sentences she could have gotten for those offenses. Her Adam's apple seemed to double in size. She frowned, and answered "Yes, sir" to all the questions, and went on regardless.

Ballard continued, asking Sandy if she understood she was waiving her right to trial, the presumption of innocence, and everything else that went along with that.

"Yes, sir," Sandy responded to all Ballard's questions.

"Do you further understand the terms of the negotiating plea?"

Sandy glanced over her shoulder at her family, who were staring back at her like nightmare survivors from a hospital bombing. Suddenly her eyes stung and her chest was tight. She felt tongue-tied and awkward, but somehow was able to squeeze out another "Yes, sir."

"Do you understand the recommendation made by the state may be accepted or rejected by the court?"

Another "Yes, sir" from Sandy.

"Do you understand the maximum possible sentence on the charge, including the possible and consecutive sentences and enhanced sentences provided by the law?"

"Yes, sir."

"Do you understand the mandatory minimum sentences depending on the charge?"

"Yes, sir."

Judge Caldwell looked down at Sandy, then took over the questioning.

"Miss Ketchum, did anybody promise you anything to plead guilty to something you say that you are not guilty of?"

Sandy's heart took a frightened leap into her chest, but she managed to speak neutrally.

"Excuse me?"

"Did anybody promise you anything to get you to plead guilty to something that you say you are not guilty of here today?"

"No, sir."

Caldwell raised his eyebrows.

"Did anyone force or coerce you in any way to plead guilty to something that you say you are not guilty of here today?"

Sandy felt herself reddening again. Hoping the judge wouldn't notice, she quickly answered, "No, sir."

This time the judge let the silence stretch.

"All right," Caldwell finally concluded, "let me say, based on questions and answers that I've heard, based on the voluntaries of your plea, I do find that you have freely and voluntarily entered a plea of guilty to these offenses without any threat or coercion or the benefit of reward, by the factual allegations concerning these pleas."

Scott Ballard took the floor once again. Sandy went back to staring at the floor.

"Now if we were to proceed to trial," Ballard summarized, "we would have shown on August 2, 2004, that Sandra Ketchum and Holly Harvey basically lured Holly's grandparents, Carl Collier and Sarah Collier, into Holly's bedroom and, using knives, stabbed them to death and then stole the truck, took their keys and drove to, first, a friend's house, and, later, Tybee Island, where within seventeen hours, they were apprehended by Fayette County sheriff's department and placed under arrest."

It was Judge Caldwell's turn to look puzzled. He resumed questioning of Sandy, asking, "Is that true, ma'am?"

Sandy nodded. "Yes, sir."

"Is that what you're pleading guilty to?"

Another nod, then another "Yes, sir."

The judge averted his eyes from Sandy and looked out over the courtroom.

"All right, then, let me also say that, based upon the allegations stated in the record, as well as your admission to guilt to these offenses, I do find that you're guilty of these. Is there anything anyone would like to say before I set the sentence in this?"

An odd, twisted smile rose from the corner of the DA's mouth.

"Yes, on behalf of the state," Ballard offered, "I want to explain our recommendations to her. Our recommendations, of course, are one life sentence is—there are several reasons— one is that Miss Ketchum immediately cooperated with the police. Secondly, she entered this plea, and had agreed that she would give testimony against Holly Harvey, had there been a trial for her. And, third, she, from the beginning, unlike Holly Harvey, showed significant remorse for her actions.

"Based on those factors—and it's my belief that her willingness to enter this plea and to testify against Holly induced Holly to accept the offer of consecutive life sentences. Based on that, we recommend the sentence be accepted."

"How about the law enforcement and victims' family?" Caldwell inquired.

"Yes, Your Honor," Ballard said, glancing toward Kevin Collier seated in the front row behind the prosecution's table. "We have consulted with the victims' family, and they are in accord with this recommendation and similarly we have consulted with law enforcement and they are in accord with it as well."

For the past few months, Lloyd Walker had talked softly and soothingly to his client, quieting her fears bit by bit. He had gone over enough of this with Sandy that she was able to surmise what would happen if they went to court. He seemed to have succeeded in curing the worst of her hysterics. Walker redirected the judge's attention to his client, who stood quietly next to him at the lectern and waited to speak.

The judge looked up at Sandy and nodded.

Sandy took a deep breath. She had rehearsed this speech in her mind thousands of times and promised herself she would not break down and bawl. She would try as hard as possible to keep that from happening. Not just for herself, but for her mama and daddy. She would try very hard.

"I'd just like to say that if everything were right," Sandy began, relieved at the sound of empathy in her voice. For the first time in a long time, she felt as if she were speaking with her voice and not a recording from a narcotic slumber. "And if I could take their places and give them them my life, I wouldn't think twice, and I'm real sorry that this happened."

Caldwell looked calmly at Sandy and licked his lips. His gaze at her was a lot cooler than it had been when she first arrived. Even his words were icy, almost bitter, and spectators in the courtroom wondered how many times before this had he tangled with situations like this.

"Let me say, ma'am, that I've done this for a long period of time in some capacity for some thirty-three years," Caldwell said at the end of a long sigh. "And it behooves me that I don't understand the violence that people commit one to another. Particularly that young people, such as yourself and the other young woman, did on certainly two innocent individuals, but also two elderly individuals, who certainly were not, probably, able to defend themselves, had they wanted to in this instance.

"Having been the district attorney here for fifteen years and on the bench ten, and having tried twenty-two death penalty cases in my tenure, I would have no problem, had the law allowed us to do so, to have tried you for the death penalty in this case. However, that cannot be done because of your age, likewise because of state laws, as well as the recommendations.

Let me also say to you that if it were not for the recommendation of the district attorney, law enforcement, as well as the victims in this case, I would not accept this. I would give you five consecutive life sentences, I would tell you this right now."

Sandy nodded. She hadn't expected the judge's harsh admonishment, as she believed he was beginning to see that she possessed real sympathy for Holly's grandparents.

"On this count two of malice murder," Judge Caldwell announced gravely. "I will sentence you to life in prison. On count three, which is the other felony murder, I will sentence you to life in prison and that will run concurrent. On this armed robbery, which carries ten to twenty up to life, I am going to sentence you to serve life to that as well, and that will also run concurrent with these other offenses."

Life sentences. The judge's words echoed down a long and silent corridor in Sandy's mind. *What did he mean? Twenty years or thirty years?*

Before Sandy could grasp those thoughts, Caldwell informed her, "Now you have the right to have this sentence reviewed by a sentence review panel. That is a panel of Superior Court judges who meet periodically in Atlanta to see if I've been too harsh on you. Of course, life is all you can get on the murder offense; you could get from ten to twenty on the armed robbery. They can reduce that sentence if they wanted to. If you want to avail yourself to that, I will ask your attorney to help you with that. You also have certain rights concerning your right of habeas corpus. You can discuss that with your attorney, things of that nature, and any other type you feel that you may have."

Unlike her cohort, Sandy had not been forced to go into excruciating detail about the killings of Carl and Sarah Collier. And since her prison terms ran concurrently, she had been given just the one life sentence in prison. The leniency was due to her initially cooperating with the police, her expression of remorse for the crime, and her willingness to testify against Holly.

But Caldwell didn't see it that way. Instead of letting in sunlight, Sandy's dark cloud had let in shame and remorse. The judge smiled at her, but it was perfunctory. There was a crime, there were two victims, and here was the punishment.

It was as simple as that.

"You can take her out now," Caldwell said, nodding to the bailiff.

Sandy Ketchum, the picture of woe, looked at her family and a rush of grief and disappointment rushed through her like floodwater. She looked down at her hands, made into tight, clenched fists of tension, and watched as the court officers handcuffed her wrists. There was no mistake about what she had done. Absolutely. But what she heard the judge say made her feel sick and afraid.

Sandy left the courtroom, escorted by the county deputies, without saying another word. The moment those double doors closed behind her, muffling her footsteps, she felt more lonely than at any time in her life. The jackhammers in her head returned with a fury. Her face felt as if it had been warped, all alive and riveted on the outside, but all cold and dead on the inside. She shook her head violently as the judge's contemptuous sneer flipped over and over in her mind. The tears that had threatened all day now came in a cloudburst. She dropped her head and wept in grief and loss for her past, and in terror for her future.

Chapter 64

The sad saga was finally over. Immediately after Sandy had been led shamefully out of the courtroom, the proceedings concluded and the spectators in the gallery stood in silence. Beth Ketchum covered her face with her hands and collapsed against her husband. Tim patted her shoulder and steadied her.

From the moment Sandy was led into the courtroom to the time she exited as a sentenced murderer, only 12½ minutes had elapsed. The whole ordeal seemed slow, subjectively, but it hardly seemed slow in the way that dreams happened. Especially, the bad ones. They play out, slowly, painfully, over and over again in your head, and seem to last forever.

Twenty years! Tim pondered while on his way out of the courtroom. It was as if the concept of time had gained a new dimension for him. Maybe it was the thought of Sandy's approaching seventeenth birthday, two days later, that started fresh tears running down his cheeks. But he knew they wouldn't be celebrating it this year, and for God only knows how many more years. He'd heard it said that *time heals all wounds,* and he longed for some truth in that maxim.

Tim felt a flulike weakness in the joints of his knees and the muscles of his thighs. It moved upward into his stomach and then landed in his heart, speeding it up. There was an alarming moment when he thought he was going to drop to the floor and faint. He leaned heavily against Beth's shoulders, his stomach continuing to drop and making him feel on the verge of vomiting.

Concentrating on taking smaller, even steps, a part of Tim wanted to lie down on the floor and die, while another part of him wanted to break into a run, and still another part of him knew that if he tried that, he really might faint.

Tim and Beth were invited to speak at a press conference. In the beginning, they had tried it a couple of times. On the day after the murders, they had received sixty-seven phone calls from the press. At the courthouse, news reporters mobbed them and shoved cameras into their faces.

Are you afraid of your daughter? Total strangers would shout at them. *What do you think about her now?*

Tim wouldn't have minded it so much if it was just him and his feelings they were asking about. That was okay, he could handle that. But when they started saying things about Sandy, that was when he really got heated. Sandy was depending on them. They were all she had, and they were all the help she could ever expect.

Tim Ketchum turned with his wife by his side and walked out of the courtroom, like a defeated soldier who was finally going home after a long and bitter war.

The television cameras turned away from the Ketchums and focused on Kevin Collier and Carla Harvey. Kevin was dressed in a brown suit, a white shirt, and a brown tie. Carla was in a fashionable white two-piece suit. There was no sign of emotion from either of them as they stood together in the courthouse foyer, still in the grip of their anger and shame. The brother and sister acknowledged they were stunned by all of what had been said by the teenagers in the courthouse today. They never thought it could be possible, but after they had agonized over it the way they had, they knew it had to be true.

Kevin told the press he had not spoken with Holly since the murders, but he knew he eventually would.

"After all, she is still in the family," he assured them.

Kevin said he felt fine, it was his stomach that was still a bit queasy. His anger at Holly had evaporated over the long months, and a sudden sound of irritation and relief escaped his closed lips like a very small explosive.

At the press conference several of Kevin's closest friends asked him, if his niece was released from prison the next day, would he take her in?

Kevin stared at them, wondering, *Which of the five thousand answers should I give to that one? The way I felt the day I learned my parents were butchered in their own home? The way I felt the day I buried them in the grave? Or this morning, as I listened to my niece tell how she unmercifully snuffed out their lives?*

Kevin's thoughts and feelings toward his niece were all different. They crossed the spectrum from the rosy pink outfit she wore in court to her dead black heart he had seen in court. It was a difficult question for him, but, after all was said and done, he had given it a lot of thought and didn't believe she had really meant to kill his parents.

"I don't think she was in her right mind," he felt comfortable saying. "I do believe they were on drugs."

Pausing for a moment, Kevin considered his words very carefully, before adding, "And, I still love her."

Kevin was standing beside his sister in the courtroom foyer when Sheriff Randall Johnson ambled over and offered Kevin his hand.

"I want to say I'm sorry for the loss of your parents, Kevin," Johnson said, shaking Kevin's hand, but never looking in Carla's direction or speaking to her.

As Johnson walked away, Carla felt her face burning. She said nothing to Johnson, but leaned into Kevin and shot back briskly, "What's wrong with him? They were my parents, too!"

The lawyers, Bruce Jordan, Kevin Collier, and Carla Harvey gathered together for a press conference in the sheriff's office a few blocks away from the courthouse.

Carla swaggered down the hallway and into the courtroom, looked at all the cops lined along the back wall, and offered them a smirk. Bruce Jordan looked over at her with a hint of wariness. She glared at Jordan and he scowled at her.

By tomorrow morning, anyone who read the paper would know them all like family—as the reporters quickly discerned the police's distaste for Holly Harvey's mother. All other issues seemed trivial in comparison.

Scott Ballard said he wasn't sure if Holly had told the truth and was very surprised to hear some of her statements. He hadn't known about Calvin supplying them with the drugs, and felt she had placed a lot more blame on Sandy than probably she deserved.

"But I am still wondering how these girls could commit such brutal, heinous murders," Ballard said. "Especially when the victims were Holly's elderly grandparents. I did, however, take great satisfaction in how quickly the case was solved by the sheriff's department, and how quickly the girls were apprehended. I am right proud of them. I also thought the judges did an excellent job, since they had had to set aside their usual schedules to handle these high-profile cases that had snowballed rapidly into the events of the last two weeks."

Judy Chidester didn't see anything new in Holly's responses for the state to holler about. Granted, the revelation of this supposed thirty-year-old man supplying them with marijuana laced with cocaine on the day of the murders had set off some fireworks, but she saw more than that would have been a deal breaker.

Whether or not Chidester believed Holly had told the truth, the whole truth, and nothing but the truth about what happened the night of August 2 was insignificant. She knew when it got right down to it, and a person had her neck out on the chopping block, who of us wouldn't try to redirect some of the blame? Self-preservation is, after all, a basic instinct of human nature. But at this point, it really didn't matter. Two elderly people were dead and buried in their graves, and the two young people who were responsible for them being there had been convicted and were going to pay for it with a substantial part of their lives. No matter how one shuffled the cards, it always came out a dead man's hand.

"Holly is very remorseful," Chidester told the press. "She hopes one day she can forgive herself so others can forgive her. A number of family members and friends who previously knew her have contacted her and offered her their support, and she appreciates that tremendously.

"I do find it interesting that Bruce Jordan has remarked that certain things Holly said were 'inconsistent with the evidence,' such as her saying Sandy had a part in the murder. There was nothing that proved, as Jordan suggested, that Holly was the ringleader and that the 'love-struck' Sandy was simply following her orders. I think it wouldn't have mattered anyway in the scheme of things, since both girls' conduct was egregious, and there was more than enough guilt to go around."

Before the hearing, Chidester considered Judge Paschal English an old friend, but found his conduct and remarks to Holly very inappropriate.

"It was the way the judge drew out every sordid detail of the murders that upset me," Chidester said. "The whole time he was talking with her, he was glaring at her, as if he was obviously disgusted by her. When asked what she thought should happen to her, she replied, 'I should be dead.' He then agreed with her."

There was another issue that upset Chidester during the trial.

"Another thing that has haunted me. I had thought I had seen it all, but here comes Carla Harvey after the hearing. She's out of jail and in the courtroom watching all this take place. Afterward, she approaches me now and says she had never been able to impart any meaningful life lessons to her daughter in the short and often interrupted time they spent together. But now she could. Carla then turns to me and says, 'I can teach her how to get along in prison.' Can you believe that?"

During the press conference, Kevin described his parents' relationship with Holly as "unconditional love."

"They loved her to death," he said, choking back his tears. "This, today, is part of the closure. It was difficult to listen to Holly in the courtroom. It always sends chills up your spine to hear something like this—especially about your parents."

The press asked Bruce Jordan, if the pair had gone to trial, what kind of problems would have been prevented? Jordan explained the difficulties of holding a trial out of county, but assured the news reporters it would not have had any bearing on the outcome of the case.

"One of the most convincing was the DNA on the knives," Jordan revealed. "Carl's blood was on both knives. Sarah's blood was on one knife."

Carla Harvey was asked about her daughter and she quickly defended her. "She said she was on drugs. The daughter I raised would not have done this. I always tried to love her."

"Carla, do you feel responsible in any way for what your daughter Holly has done?" a news reporter immediately fired back at her.

Carla looked surprised that someone would have the audacity to ask her that question. She believed that was a loaded question and suspected there were other motives for having been asked that. Eyeing the cameras warily, her eyes flicked wildly at the officers around them. She cocked her head at the reporter curiously and swallowed uneasily. She could see Jordan's face creased into a smile.

"I don't feel sorry for anything," Carla said defiantly, her face red with anger. "I take no responsibility for what has happened. This was all Holly's doing. She's old enough to make her own decisions."

Jordan stared at her for a moment. He bit his lip and silently cursed her refusal to accept responsibility. A raw force of emotion rushed up and blunted some of his thoughts toward her. It was humid in the room, under the blaring lights, but he knew it was more than the humidity that brought the slick and slimy sweat to his stomach and legs. He shook his head sourly, then turned toward the newshounds.

As Holly was being grilled in open court, she had told the judge—to the surprise of law enforcement officials—about Calvin, a friend of her mother's, who allegedly supplied her and Sandy with crack cocaine and marijuana the day before they embarked on their murder spree. Holly told the judge that her mother had introduced her to Calvin, and it was the scent of his marijuana cigarettes that she and Sandy used to lure her grandparents to the basement before attacking them with a large knife.

During the press conference, the reporter asked DA Scott Ballard whether Calvin would be charged for his alleged involvement in the case.

"The reason Sandy Ketchum received only one life sentence is because she had immediately cooperated and talked with us and helped and was willing to testify in the trial against Holly Harvey," Ballard said. "This was the first time any of us have heard Holly's story and I was not aware of Calvin."

Lieutenant Colonel Bruce Jordan also indicated he was not aware of Calvin and added that he would be following up on that information.

Carla Harvey was asked if Calvin was a friend of hers.

"He's not exactly a friend," Harvey said. "I knew him from my work." She didn't mention she had met Calvin at the strip club, where she was employed as a stripper. She declined to identify for the press where she worked or Calvin's last name.

The reporters continued to hound her for the last name of Calvin—the mysterious drug dealer—but she refused. In response to the press, Carla Harvey would only speculate as to how Calvin knew her daughter.

"He might have encountered Holly after he called my home to speak with me. Holly must have answered the phone and talked with him then."

Jordan gave Carla a little puzzled smile. He frowned a little, then leaned over to Kevin and whispered into his ear, "She's not leaving this building until she gives us that last name."

It then dawned upon Kevin how his sister had reacted when Holly told Judge English about Calvin. He knew if she wanted to save her ass, then she best cooperate with the police and give them Calvin's full name.

The thirty-seven-year-old Carla knew she would be facing more jail time if she didn't roll over on her friend Calvin Lawson. Her smirk and swagger had left her long before she left the conference room; and under questioning by Detective Ethon Harper, she finally gave up Calvin's last name.

"I'm glad it has come to a closure for the families on both sides," Sheriff Randall Johnson said after the press conference. "It's real hard to see people you've been knowing all your life—maybe forty years—and to see them just slaughtered."

However, it still wasn't over. There was one more grotesque situation in this debacle that needed to be taken care of. A few hours after the press conference, thirty-seven-year-old Calvin Roland Lawson, the man accused of giving marijuana laced with cocaine to Holly Harvey and Sandy Ketchum the night before the Collier murders, was arrested. Authorities informed Calvin that the two girls had stayed with him at his apartment the night before the killings and that he was being booked on suspicion for felony murder. Because the girls used drugs that he had supplied them to lure the Colliers to the basement, that made him an alleged accomplice in their murders.

Lawson was charged with one count of felony murder in

the stabbing deaths of Carl and Sarah Collier. Felony murder is defined as anyone who commits, or is found to be involved in, a serious crime during which any person dies.

Lieutenant Colonel Bruce Jordan said he knew that someone had sold the drugs to the teenagers, but Holly Harvey had not been talking to the police, so today was the first time she had talked about Calvin. Supposedly, she had met Calvin through her mother, and those two had met at a strip club, The Gold Rush, on Metropolitan Parkway in Atlanta. The police were able to tie him into the girls by his telephone records.

By now, the people in Fayette County had a real thirst for blood. Calvin got out of the car, wearing an orange jacket, a black-and-yellow hat with CAT on it, blue jeans, and work boots.

Lawson was not a large man—he wasn't fat, either—but he was definitely soft around the edges. When he turned to look up at the reporters, there was something about his eyes that the reporters noticed immediately—drug abuser. As the television cameras rolled, he suddenly started squirming and became seemingly more interested in his feet than with what the reporters had to ask him.

Lawson did not seem to have a criminal past. Although he wasn't an Eagle Scout, he apparently had managed to keep his nose clean. He was employed as an excavator for a construction company, but just happened to have a penchant for teenage girls. He was expected to make his first court appearance at 2:00 P.M., Friday, in front of the Fayette County Magistrate Court officials, but that appearance was postponed until Saturday. Lawson remained in jail on Friday, until about 4:00 P.M., when the hearing was postponed indefinitely and the sheriff's officials dropped the felony murder charges.

"We dropped the murder charges against Lawson," Lieutenant Belinda McCastle announced to the press. "The weight of the testimony was going to be on Holly Harvey and Sandy Ketchum and we want to find more evidence to corroborate the girls' stories. There really wasn't enough to make our case stick, but we are going to continue our investigation and revisit that charge when the grand jury goes in session in July."

Instead, Lawson was charged with two counts of contributing to the delinquency of a minor and one count of distributing obscene material to a minor, all misdemeanors. The maximum penalty for each charge was a year in prison.

Lawson's attorney, Maurice Bennett, said in an issued statement that he was pleased with the reduced charges. A $3,600 property bond or $1,950 cash bond was set for Lawson on Friday, who opted for the cash bond.

Chapter 65

In an article "Why Teens Kill," journalist Gayle White, of the *Atlanta Journal-Constitution,* wrote that Holly Harvey and Sandy Ketchum now belonged to a small but shocking sorority of teenage girls who kill. White added that some of the criminologists, forensic psychologists, and psychiatrists who had analyzed their case agreed that details of the girls' lives and descriptions of their crime fit the patterns of teenage girls who commit horrendous acts of violence. She interviewed a number of those and offered their comments to her readers.

Kathleen Heide, professor of criminology at the University of Florida, and author of *Why Kids Kill Parents* and *Young Killers,* said girls who kill are, in fact, very rare.

"When girls do kill, they often have accomplices or act in groups, and they are more likely than boys to kill a family member or intimate associate. Dangerously antisocial teenagers slay not because they are mentally ill or want to escape an abusive parent, but simply in order to remove an obstacle."

Geoffrey McKee, a clinical professor in the department of neuropsychiatry at the University of South Carolina School of Medicine, believed kids who grew up outside a stable environment were more likely to find their identity in relationships outside the family.

Lauren Woodhouse, a forensic psychologist in Toronto, and author of *Shooter in the Sky: The Inner World of Children Who Kill,* said, "For girls, the search for a new sense of belonging often begins as their sexuality kicks in—usually from age twelve to sixteen—when they are no longer the little dumpling. They may feel vulnerable and displaced. A girl who doesn't have a boyfriend may bond with other girls—disenfranchised girls, not yearbook girls."

Dr. Gregory Moffatt, a nationally board-certified trauma specialist, professor of psychology at Atlanta Christian College, and the author of three books on homicide and violent behavior, wrote a regular column for the *Citizen* newspaper. Moffatt had followed the girls' cases from the beginning to their last court appearances.

"This is the very type of murder that drew me into the field of homicide to begin with," Moffatt wrote in his column. "I couldn't believe that people could be 'normal' one day and with no warning become brutal killers the next. In fact, they don't.

"Holly Harvey is alleged to be the leader of the two. Authorities say she manipulated Ketchum, who was in love with her. All homicide duos included a dominant and a subordinate. Ketchum followed Harvey's orders because of her infatuation with Harvey.

"Lesbianism, while it may add to the sensationalism of the story, is a peripheral issue, not a cause of the murder, this very easily could have been two boys or a boy and a girl."

"What does any sixteen-year-old know about love, homo- or heterosexual? The immature romantic tie served only to increase the likelihood that Ketchum would follow the lead of her more dominant partner."

Oddly enough, one of the last teen-style publication magazines, *Seventeen,* featured the recurring story about real-life murderers Holly Harvey and Sandy Ketchum. It was an interesting take on the story for teenage girls in many ways. There was the angle of the teenagers' tomboyish ways, making them outsiders; the girls' lesbian relationship and how it was received by the Colliers; the issue of having a parent in jail and/or being raised by your grandparents or stepparents; then the issues of body cutting, school truancy, drugs, sex, and, of course, the unfathomable murders.

It was interesting that *Seventeen* chose as the title of the article, "Lesbian Killers," as possibly no other title had quite the sensationalism as this one did. The deck teased: "Holly, now 17, was so angry that her grandparents forbade her to see her girlfriend, she decided to make them pay." The article appeared with a 17 WARNING sticker, but even more tantalizing, the caption read: "Faithful Relationship," under a full-page color photo of the two girls, entitled "The Murderers." More grisly color photos of the killers and their bloody knives adorned the next two pages. One of the subheads enticed readers with the topic "Forbidden Love."

In a sister column for the *Citizen,* Dr. Moffatt wrote, "I cannot know what is in [Holly's] heart, but I can see what her behaviors have communicated. In my opinion, she was demonstrating in court what she has always been, a selfish and manipulative girl."

Dr. Moffatt placed the lion's share of blame for the murders squarely on Holly Harvey's shoulders.

Kevin Collier hoped the sentencing had put an end to the nightmare.

"This was the last part of the closure that I need and the family needs," Kevin said, referring to Holly's confession. "Time will heal certain things. There's nothing we can do to bring my parents back, but time will heal the tensions and feelings I have for Holly."

Kevin and his friend Anita Beckom had cleaned his parents' home, sold some things, and given a lot of things away.

"I think the best word for my mom would be 'shopaholic,'" Kevin wrote to this author. "I think her shopping got her mind off her problems. Carla and Mom's problems stemmed from Carla's lifestyle."

Kevin never saw the crime scene photos, but had a good

idea of what the inside of the house looked like after the murder. The Colliers' last will and testament named Kevin as the benefactor of the house and the two insurance policies, but there still was not enough money to pay all their bills.

"I was left with enough money from the life insurance to pay all my parents' bills and funeral expense, except for the house," Kevin wrote. "Mowell Funeral Home was gracious enough to let me pay after I received the insurance money. I have been paying two house payments for the last two years. I did sink thousands into the house, remodeling the bathrooms and kitchen. I also put new carpet throughout the house and painted inside and out. The house is still on the market right now, but I have had a few offers so far

"I couldn't have done it without my beautiful fiancée, Rena. She had the ideas for the remodeling and also helped me with the painting. She did a fantastic job with the kitchen cabinets. The house just needed to be updated. Let's hope it sells fast, because I am close to being out of money.

"As far as the burial, my parents already had plots, but I had to pay the two thousand dollars to dig the holes. At the time, I couldn't afford it, so First Baptist Fayetteville got donations from their congregation and paid for it. They loved my parents so much and they said it was the least they could do. My parents had a lot of good friends at the church."

Although Anita Beckom and Carla Harvey have had a falling-out, Anita tried to keep in touch with Holly. Her daughter Tabitha went with her last Christmas to visit Holly in prison. On the way home, she asked her, "Mommy, how long does Holly have to stay there?"

When Anita told Tabitha, "Twenty-plus years," her daughter started crying.

"That's a very long time," Tabitha said through her tears. "I'll be a mommy by then."

Anita said she thinks about Holly every day.

"I'm not sure what I was able to do different than everyone else when it came to Holly," she said, "but somehow, some way,

I could always get Holly to do whatever I asked of her, and her not hate me or be mad with me. Holly is very smart. She used to say she was going to be a lawyer when she grew up. It's weird now, but everyone used to say to other kids, 'Why can't y'all be good like Holly.'

"Life sure has some funny turns."

According to Carla Harvey, Holly Harvey has been doing well at Pulaski State Prison.

"She has gotten a haircut. She's lost some weight and has taken up reading."

Carla Harvey seemed to be doing well. As a single parent, she worked two jobs as a waitress at the Huddle House, trying to make it work. She not only sends Holly care packages and money, but sends some of the same to Sandy. Carla said she didn't know how much longer she could keep that up, because she didn't have a lot of money.

Carla also said her daughter was full of regret.

"Every day for the next twenty years, she'll have to deal with that, the guilt. The pain. You know, making a mistake that we know put her where's she's at."

Carla said she's forgiven her daughter for what she had done, and they kept in touch through letters. The way she saw it, this was not a woman—not her daughter—but a fifteen-year-old girl who had faced major defeat at every step of her life. Maybe behaving this way was the only way she knew how to ask for a way to help her cope with life.

"Being a parent is the hardest thing I ever had to do," Carla said. "Holly never had a father around and I might should have been a little more strict on her."

Carla's boyfriend Scott Moore said he always saw a different picture of Carla.

"She never cared about Holly," Moore said candidly. "She never saw her. I tried to get in her life a couple of times, but she never cared. Holly did the right thing by pleading guilty."

Tim Ketchum ultimately broke his silence about his daughter and spoke to the press, for what he promised was the last time.

"It's been traumatizing," Tim said to a reporter standing outside his home. "It's killing us. I just can't explain it. I'm not that type of person to do something like this, and I raised Sandy not to be that type of person. I found it hard to believe they were capable of murder. I don't know. I just can't explain it."

Tears welled in Tim's eyes.

"I don't know what it was that drove her to commit murder. I've visited her in jail and I've urged her to turn her life around. I told her to go to church and to make something out of herself while she is in prison. 'I will, Daddy,' she promised me.

"I'm just very sorry this happened. And I have great remorse."

Until recently, Sandy lived out her prison term at the Pulaski State in Hawkinsville, Georgia. In November 2006, she was transferred from Pulaski to Metro State Prison in southeastern Atlanta. She was told the transfer was necessary because her mother, Sandra Ketchum, was being transferred there for a drug charge.

Sandy said she still has her share of nightmares, but was sleeping better these days. In a recent letter she wrote to this author, she sounded upbeat and positive about her future.

"Yes! Art and poetry are the two things that I live for. Yet, I can't decipher which is my favorite. But if I had to pick, I would pick poetry. Well, really, I don't know because my life without those two would be hard to fathom.

"I love doing tattoos. I've yet to do one with a tattoo gun so basically all my work has been done with one single needle, by hand. I'm hoping that one day I'll be able to get my poetry published and also become a professional tattoo artist."

Epilogue

The drama of the American justice system is the staple of American life. American justice has become a pitching ground for opposing ideas and different points of view and resembles athletic competition played under the rules of law, refereed under the scrutiny of a judge. Courtroom dramas are fascinating in that they reveal personalities, character, and motivation, but unlike courtroom scenes in television or cinema, true-to-life crime stories feature real players whose behavior and actions play out in weaknesses and strengths, brilliant analysis or bumbling stupidity, and conjure a wide range of human emotions. The investigation and enforcement of justice is played out on a stage whereby the drama brings into focus society's stresses and tensions, and reveals the political, social, and cultural conflicts America is embracing at the time.

No doubt, the Holly Harvey and Sandra Ketchum crime is one of the most fascinating crimes of Georgia, because it reflected many of the social issues of the new century. Just the crime itself, and especially the personalities of the accused, has a significant impact on our society, and its legal proceedings a dramatic effect on America's institutions and the law. The substance of their hearings reflected not only the character of the two teens, but the character of America. It explored the conflict at a time of increasing gay and lesbian rights, during a period of intellectual and emotional turmoil caused by America's confrontation with many new and unsettling ideas. The way a nation judges its accused reveals much about its character and aspirations. The confrontation would underline the sharpness of divergent views about homosexuality and pose clearly the still-unresolved question of who should determine what our children are being taught about it.

Grandparents are struggling with raising kids today. This crime would become a major focus not only on the mental state of two young killers—which was at the center of the defense in their trial for the brutal murders of the Colliers—but a conflict of age-old values and morals inflicted upon a New Age society.

Reverend Frank Ellis, senior pastor of Fayetteville Baptist Church, summed up the conflict between the three generations of women: Sarah, Carla, and Holly.

"I don't think that anyone could have ever imagined this would have happened to Carl and Sarah Collier, but it did. The Colliers were strong foot soldiers for the Lord. They were folks who were willing to get in the trenches and work and get the work done. They were just deeply loved across the board at our church. Loyal members. Here every time the doors were open at the church. They were here to serve.

"Although the granddaughter hadn't been a member here, they had asked the church to pray for her on numerous occasions. They've had a lot of heartbreak in their family with particularly this mother and her daughter. It was not of their making, but they had been very wise and very consistent in trying to be firm. And they were trying to take up some slack that grandparents shouldn't have to do anyway. But they were trying to step in that gap, with wisdom and love and patience. It's just a real modern-day tragedy."

Holly Harvey and Sandy Ketchum got the best deal they

could have possibly gotten. Both girls saved themselves at least an additional ten years and as much as eighteen years added on to the minimum they got. Even though they'll be in their thirties, before they can even start thinking about getting out of prison, at least they are alive and young enough to have some semblance of an adult life. There are rehabilitation programs in prison and the girls can educate themselves, prepare for a better future, and learn a skill or trade. Best of all, they are not going anywhere and can now honestly deal with their drug dependencies and psychological issues. With the help of a good therapist and lots of support from their families, these girls might still have a chance—like the writer Anne Perry—and become a worthwhile and productive citizen.

As the story closes, Holly Harvey and Sandy Ketchum are no longer tethered for life. Holly Harvey must serve at least twenty years of two consecutive life sentences, while Sandy Ketchum was sentenced to three concurrent life sentences and could be eligible for parole in fourteen years. And there are no guarantees, no written assurances, for all they are promised in prison is that all their yesterdays ended last night—and all their tomorrows started today.